The Pa

The Pacific Northwest

Growth of a Regional Identity

RAYMOND D. GASTIL *and*
BARNETT SINGER

McFarland & Company, Inc., Publishers
Jefferson, North Carolina, and London

LIBRARY OF CONGRESS CATALOGUING-IN-PUBLICATION DATA

Gastil, Raymond D.
The Pacific Northwest : growth of a regional identity / Raymond D. Gastil and Barnett Singer.
p. cm.
Includes bibliographical references and index.

ISBN 978-0-7864-4540-0
softcover : 50# alkaline paper ♾

1. Northwest, Pacific—Intellectual life. 2. Northwest, Pacific—Social conditions. 3. Regionalism—Northwest, Pacific—History. 4. Group identity—Northwest, Pacific—History. 5. Authors, American—Northwest, Pacific—History. 6. Artists—Northwest, Pacific—History. 7. American literature—Northwest, Pacific—History and criticism. 8. Arts, American—Northwest, Pacific—History. 9. Arts—Political aspects—Northwest, Pacific—History. 10. Political culture—Northwest, Pacific—History.
I. Singer, Barnett. II. Title.
F851.G37 2010
979.5—dc22 2010008150

British Library cataloguing data are available

Manufactured in the United States of America

McFarland & Company, Inc., Publishers
Box 611, Jefferson, North Carolina 28640
www.mcfarlandpub.com

Contents

Preface and Acknowledgments
by Barnett Singer

RAYMOND D. GASTIL ORIGINALLY conceived this project at Battelle Seattle Research Center, partly as an attempt to understand America in more defined, regional terms. Focusing on the Pacific Northwest, he built on his previously published and well-regarded book, *Cultural Regions of the United States*.[1] The ensuing project was also an attempt at crossing a variety of disciplinary fields. Finally, he hoped that such a book would add to the self-awareness of regional readers, particularly in the Northwest.

In other words, Dr. Gastil had already given much thought to the nature of American regions and their evolution. He then wished to assess contributions which had helped create a kind of Northwest civilization—shades perhaps of "Cascadia," well before that term became a buzzword![2] He also wanted to evaluate how regional reflections, influences, or connections helped figures like V. L. Parrington or William Stafford, dealt with below, to reach a wider world with their work.

But what impelled me, a European, French, and in certain courses, world and cultural historian to embrace such a project as its co-author? The answers include some background in American history and literature, love of the country both in a regional and non-regional sense, and a penchant for diving into projects subsequently requiring huge effort!

What of my belated, more recent decision to upgrade this work extensively throughout? An iconic Northwest institution, Microsoft, which became huge worldwide, partly through upgrades, perhaps offers justification for this careful refurbishing and refining of a manuscript we had first worked on in the 1970s and early '80s. The result? I have taken great account here of much which is new and exciting that appeared in Pacific Northwest scholarship of the '80s, '90s, and early 2000s—historiographical shifts and divisions, and informative work of high quality.

Looking back to the project's etiology, I was still a young scholar armed with a Ph.D. in history from the University of Washington, when I met and worked with Raymond Gastil at Battelle Institute, the Seattle branch of that think tank near the Washington campus. My research specialty at "U Dub," as Northwesterners call the University of Washington, was in French history. I had worked with a prestigious historian there, David Pinkney, himself the owner of good books in the field, and editor through the '70s of *French Historical Studies*. After gaining the doctorate, I was teaching courses at the university; but despite being a French history scholar, and in courses I gave, mainly a Europeanist, I embraced what was for me a new regional subject hook, line, and sinker. And that regional feeling is part of what led to the manuscript you are now reading.

In addition to the Northwest's stunning geography, I had from the outset enjoyed the company of other graduate students at U.W., with whom I'd chat on the terrace of the Student Union overlooking Lake Washington. I also revered my U.W. field professors, including one, Lewis Saum, in American intellectual history—an understated scholar of high quality, himself possessing a specialty in western history. Once graduated, and to supplement my income as an adjunct instructor at the university, I contacted Battelle, right at the base of hilly Laurelhurst. I then went to work as an assistant to Dr. Gastil, who impressed upon me that even though I worked in French history, I *did* live in this region, and that it was worthwhile getting to know it in a scholarly way, too. This is where we *were*; why not dig deeply, and really learn about it? So I went to work on the project, doing my own research, and my own article writing (primarily, on Northwest writers and history). And I then became a full-fledged co-author of this work on a lovely part of the country.

The Pacific Northwest, like the even larger entity we call (with geographical disputes), the American West, has an unlimited, overwhelming, rugged, massive quality about it, with none of the limited fragility of an April spring in, say, Connecticut, or even in a more effulgent North Carolina. This large region has more repetitive climates, more repetitive series of gray fronts or blue summer skies, more repetitive swaths of coniferous greenery on the coast stunned by what it greatly requires, rain; and more repetitive vistas in, say, the Palouse of Eastern Washington or in Central Oregon. When I was fifteen or so, I went with a group of fellows to a western movie in order to celebrate the New Year—*The Big Country*, a good one, as I recall. Well, the Northwest is "big country," supremely outdoors country, where ideas in the old days had to fight against outdoor necessities for survival; and more recently, against the many possibilities for espresso-oiled pleasure and recreation.

Thus there is a personal dialectic here. Yes, the West remains inside us but the East does so as well. Just as Thomas Wolfe wrote in *Look Homeward, Angel* about his Asheville, North Carolina, hometown from the distancing vantage point of New York, my moving back east has provided a necessary perspective. But it was my decision to resuscitate this project, finally believing that it needed to be significantly enhanced, "modernized" and (after much additional work) published.

I hope this book constitutes an informative, stimulating bridge between monograph and college text, especially for students in or of the American West. It should also interest general readers. And I am glad that we ended our story in the 1970s, for there are entirely new books on a much-changed Northwest since then that ought to be done. When we first began work on this in the Me Decade, Karen Carpenter and brother had a nostalgic hit song about how much had changed. The Carpenters, it turns out, didn't know the half of it! It's not only the Northwest's Microsoft and Amazon and Starbucks that became prominent, and not only the great emigration up from California and over from the East, not to mention (post–1990), from a more liberated China and elsewhere; and not only the efflorescence of movements of personal liberation right down to grunge bands. It isn't only all *that*, but on an even more global scale, it's America in its entirety that is reflected in more recent changes to the Northwest region.

Different, earlier versions of certain parts here (written by me) appeared in Washington State *Research Studies*, the *South Dakota Review*, *Studies in the Humanities*, and in a book edited by Edwin Bingham and Glen Love, *Northwest Perspectives*, published jointly by the University of Washington Press and University of Oregon Press in 1979. I thank those who granted permission to use this material in altered form. I also thank personnel at a variety of libraries where I worked on this project, including, in the Northwest, the University of Washington in Seattle, Reed College in Portland, and Oregon State University in Corvallis; in the Bay Area, the University of California at Berkeley and the University of San Francisco; and closer to home, libraries at Cornell University, the State University of New York at Buffalo, and Brock University, in St. Catharines, Ontario. The latter provided exemplary help via interlibrary loans. Professor Michael Allen of the University of Washington, Tacoma, read the entire updated manuscript, offering useful suggestions and encouragement. To him we owe special thanks. I also acknowledge for their support of this project Professors Richard Etulain, Edwin Bingham, Henry Grosshans (former editor of Washington State *Research Studies*), John Langdon, William Hoisington, Jr., and the late Professor Dorothy Johansen, who aided me with work at Reed College Library. In addition, I want to thank June Belton Bull and Andrew Gaiero for indispensable assistance; and finally, Kristi (in the initial stages) and Katherine, along with my daughter, Alexandra. Both of us also thank Battelle Institute in Seattle for first providing pleasant surroundings in which to work on this.

Introduction

WE LIVE IN A WORLD of mass institutions, mass populations, and instant communications. There remain differences among peoples, and it still makes sense to travel, but we increasingly inhabit McLuhan's well-intuited "global village," with ever more unity of culture and civilization. International standards, the instant impact of television, and the effects of multinational corporations too often cut the heart out of local efforts. And when international civilization, the great, post-industrial village of the future, declines and even falls, as many civilizations have in the past, there may be no alternatives, not even barbarian cultures, to replace it.

All that notwithstanding, we're convinced of the importance of regional culture—hence this study of the Pacific Northwest of the United States. It is true that regional study can easily become a specious romanticization of the second-rate, but that danger does not legitimate inactivity or neglect. Here we offer a selective evocation and evaluation of the Northwest's record and contributions through to the 1970s, hoping that by it, more historians, sociologists, or literary critics may focus on such regional distinctiveness in their own work.[1]

The Pacific Northwest of Oregon, Washington, Western Idaho, and Northwestern Montana was by the 1970s a region of roughly six million Americans, occupied as others were, in earning a living, raising families, and searching for amusement.[2] Yet this land is also one of memories, images, hopes, setbacks, and achievements, specifically its own, and which live beyond the births and deaths, or continual moving in and out, of its inhabitants. What this record leaves behind is a specific coloration embodying a regional version of the American experience in the twentieth century.

There are many ways to evaluate the Northwest experience, or to record creatively what has happened in the region. Sober historians have discussed both the pinnacles and plains of its human record. Less sober historians and novelists, poets and journalists, have rewarded the perhaps emotionally-starved children of the region with uncritical accounts of its achievements, and especially, environmental beauties. Yet there has always been a worm in the apple of self-approbation—the shattering consciousness that the best often departed the area, that the mainstream was generally thousands of miles away, that this is indeed, a "Far Corner"; and that the world "out there" has often scoffed at its regional claims to civilization. Examples abound. The heroine of Wallace Stegner's fine novel *Angle of Repose* fully enjoys the beauty and romance of Western Idaho, but still sends her boy East to school; for as she puts it, "from the local school he would emerge a barbarian, prepared for nothing and untouched by culture...."[3] In *Mariella of Out West*, the Northwest writer Ella Higginson had her heroine excoriate the comments of a haughty visitor who put down local sources of enlightenment. Yet Higginson later sent her heroine off to live in England with a refined man, in order to lead a more civilized life.[4]

The theme of spiritual impoverishment in a region bereft of a useable past has taken many forms in the region. A typically wan view was the one New York-Jewish novelist Bernard Malamud—who spent a number of years at Oregon State University—put in the mouth of a faculty wife in Corvallis:

> We miss a lot through nobody's fault in particular. It's the communal sin of omission. People here are satisfied. I blame it on nature, prosperity, and some sort of laziness, mine too.... Otherwise it's a lovely town, good will abounds, and there are many advantages for family living.[5]

To Thomas Griffith, growing up in Seattle and attending the University of Washington, the region could not give him all he wanted. When Griffith came to write *Waist-High Culture* in 1958, he tried to think back on his Northwest experience. The people at home, he thought, were mainly generous, indiscriminately praised everything, and for that reason, got the second-rate. On the whole, they seemed to prefer life to work. Feeling cramped, Griffith left Seattle, even though over and over he had said that no one would *ever* want to leave such idyllic surroundings. But life there simply did not engage him fully. To Griffith, it was characteristic of the West that the deeper people were scattered and in hiding, leaving visitors to mutter imprecations on its intellectual state.[6]

In a similar way, H. L. Davis, Oregon's Pulitzer Prize-winning novelist of the 1930s, could not return to his regional home once he had achieved national fame. The world was elsewhere, or as he remarked in passing:

> It was Oregon all right; the place where stories began that end somewhere else. It

has no history of its own, only endings of histories from other places; it has no complete lives, only beginnings. There are worse things.[7]

Comparatively speaking, one significant problem for the Northwest has always been its relationship to California. If Northwesterners have generally not seen themselves as an extension of California, then they have long been bound to see themselves in *comparison* to that huge state and area, a comparison in civilizational terms that has often come off badly. Indeed, this book was initially inspired by comparing two books, one on California and one on the Northwest. It is a comparison that painfully sharpens issues we wish to address here. In the first, *Americans and the California Dream, 1850–1915*, Kevin Starr presented a well-organized, exciting discussion of intellectual life centering on San Francisco during the period 1850–1914.[8] Starr detailed the vision here as one of a true promised land. Almost immediately at its birth as a state, people had come out to California in order to build a new world. The 1860s there were the days of writers like Mark Twain, Bret Harte, Ambrose Bierce, reformists such as Henry George, and of H. H. Bancroft's remarkable series of histories of the West, begun in the 1870s. In the 1880s, a native Californian who was to become one of Harvard's leading philosophers published a study of the state. It was a critical intellectual and social history meant to mobilize westerners, and by extension, all Americans, to make a greater effort to achieve the promise many had felt out there. Around the turn of the century, California entered another period of intellectual and artistic ferment, featuring authors such as Frank Norris, Jack London, Mary Austin, and Gertrude Atherton, not to mention John Muir, the naturalist; Isadora Duncan, the dancer; Luther Burbank, the scientist; Thorstein Veblen, the idiosyncratic economist; and so on. This was the period when the railroad millions of Leland Stanford were put at the disposal of David Starr Jordan in a noble experiment to build a great private university in the Bay Area, catering both to the poor and well-off, the practical and the theoretical.

California may never have quite measured up, but it still went on to more great achievements, charted by Kevin Starr in his subsequent volumes on Southern California; and then into the depression era and the '40s, before very real ailments began to surface and snowball, especially from 1990 or so. However before that decline, and the onset of discord and discontents, Hollywood had provided America its dreams, California's beaches had spawned lifestyles and music, and the University of California became one of the outstanding universities in the country.[9]

Let us look at the second of the two books alluded to previously. In 1972, Robert Cantwell published a rambling, but significant review of the Northwest experience entitled *The Hidden Northwest*.[10] In essence, Cantwell wondered why, with such a marvelous environment, and such promising people at the beginning, the region's civilization had remained comparatively sparse and indistinct. He did not perhaps go deeply enough, but by wrestling with the problem, at least displayed a sensitivity and sense of the issues a cut above most who discussed the region. Cantwell was a true Northwesterner derived from pioneer stock, growing up near the site of the Centralia massacre (of IWW workers or Wobblies) after World War I, and himself a worker for several years in a Northwest plywood factory. He then embodied a theme we see many times below—he left the region for brighter lights and a cluster of fine minds of, in his case, literary New York. There he became a proletarian novelist admired and encouraged by the likes of Hemingway, Edmund Wilson, Malcolm Cowley, Maxwell Perkins, Meyer Schapiro. And though he then spent most of his life as a fine journalist-book-reviewer-editor for *Time*, *Newsweek*, and *Sports Illustrated* in the East, Cantwell never gave up on the Northwest inside him, not least in fine fiction he published on it (or, owing to his many other projects, did *not* publish). A cosmopolitan and sophisticate, yet attracted to the outdoors, including on numerous vacations to western wilderness, he was very ready to find intellectual value in this beautiful region he had left behind; but by and large, he couldn't. Since the scenery did not actually exist on an intellectual plane, the attempt to explain its message too often (he felt) trailed off in a kind of foolish rhapsody.

Like many writers treating the region, Cantwell seemed somewhat on the defensive, implying by his very title that the book's purpose was to correct the image of the Northwest as a dark, gloomy, wild, and desolate area. His major protagonist is Theodore Winthrop, a young man of the mid-nineteenth century who wrote about his wanderings in the region and in his youthful enthusiasm, prophesied that a great civilization would rise amidst all this beauty. Testing Winthrop's proposition by examining the state of the area one century later, Cantwell largely found its promise unfulfilled in the cities and towns, and in thousands of miles of slash left behind by lumbermen. In addition, he considered the art, music, literature, and architecture of the Northwest too often commonplace. Strangely, he found the *chance* for an emerging civilization to be about where Winthrop had left it, in what still remained a massive wilderness.

Cantwell believed that the best Northwest intellectual creations were to be found not in history, fiction, thought or art, but in personal reminiscences (he himself always wanted to do a memoir of his working background south of Seattle, his Communist and anti–Communist struggles during the '30s, his dialectical ambivalence between America's East and West). His wan conclusion on his home region's cultural products?

> If they do not add up to a distinct regional character, they may imply something more valuable. It may be that the deepest wisdom of the Northwest consisted in *not* developing a unique regional society to set it apart from the rest of the country.... No other part of the country has so little to live down.[11]

Mainly, the quest (for Cantwell) had come to a dead end, but flickers of hope remained in his narrative that he had started to fan, yet ignored, or hadn't time to investigate further (given his death several years after the book was published). First, Winthrop's vision had sketched a civilization a "thousand years hence"—not only a wilderness, but *also* a well-tended garden. A century, in other words, was too short a measure. Secondly, Cantwell saw in reforestation and in restocking of the salmon a re-creation of the wilderness that had begun taking place since the 1950s, progress backward accelerated by vigorous environmentalism. Thus, despite population pressures, the region's most substantial heritage was being rebuilt. Finally, there remained for Cantwell a sense of promise yet greater than recorded fulfillment. The Northwest had always attracted idealists of high quality, hoping that a new world might be created there. That they might not have done as much as they had hoped to do was discouraging; but some of their spirit lived on, scattered over the land, and built into its institutions.[12]

In these pages, we memorialize without false plaudits the efforts of those who at least *struggled* to give meaning to the Northwest experience, for their lives and works are in themselves worthy of attention as part of the human record. The Northwest we evaluate is above all the story of particular individuals who contributed to the growth of civilization, though our treatment is skewed by emphasis on traditional humanistic values that interest us most. (We do not mean thereby to slight the success of institutions such as Boeing, Weyerhaeuser, Boise Cascade, or Tektronics.)

How does our present work fit within a true historiographical flood on the Northwest that followed our early efforts in the field? This is a complicated question to answer, and some readers connected to that field will doubtless form answers of their own, as they read through our substantive chapters; but let us here survey some trends of the past several decades. First, we have had clear, well-wrought texts for both students and general readers, preeminently, Gordon B. Dodds' *The American Northwest: A History of Oregon and Washington* and Carlos Schwantes' *The Pacific Northwest: An Interpretive History*, both readable accounts, with Schwante confessing, as others do, that it isn't easy even to define Northwest boundaries. (For our purposes we stick largely here to Oregon and Washington.)[13] Schwantes' fine work concentrates on social and economic, as well as political history, and we have found quite little duplication in our own, which as will be seen, contains much more biographical and cultural history and analysis to explain the formation of a Northwest consciousness. Dodds' book, too, is a clear account mainly of political, social, and economic history, and the hot new addition of ethnic history as well. But it is more synoptic than ours on the ideas and influence of key cultural figures, newspaper editors and other notables, literary people, and the like. To differentiate more fundamentally, our book is not a text, though it may certainly be used as such in classes. Instead, we hope to contribute to this field with what one might call perhaps a "semi-text"—in parts scholarly and monographic, in others more general, and again, with much more than the two estimable books mentioned on the influence of Northwest notables, mainly in the nineteenth century, and especially, on cultural-literary-intellectual trends in the region in both the nineteenth *and* twentieth centuries.

There has also been much fine, sometimes exciting recent Northwest history in more specialized works like William Dietrich, *Northwest Passage: The Great Columbia River*[14] and Robert Clark, *River of the West: Stories from the Columbia.*[15] And in easy-to-read, popular form, in Dale L. Walker, *Pacific Destiny: The Three-Century Journey to the Oregon Country*[16] and Michael Golay, *The Tide of Empire: America's March to the Pacific*, with parts on some of the nineteenth-century figures we discuss below. Golay reminds us that initial exploration, leading to conquest of the Northwest, was somewhat akin to the British Empire being acquired in a celebrated fit of absent-mindedness, by increasing serendipity, or by what business people now call adjacent opportunities. (One of the present authors has also argued much the same for the ad hoc creation of France's colonial empire.)[17]

In terms of historical genres related to the Northwest, military history may make something of a comeback, as it has done in history more generally. One good, recent example is Kurt R. Nelson's aptly-titled *Fighting for Paradise: A History of the Pacific Northwest.*[18] There are also quite recent books on the "Pig War," when Great Britain and the U.S. neared conflict in the idyllic San Juan Islands over the Northwest maritime boundary.[19] As for us, we certainly touch on some military history below, in conjunction with conflict associated with the fur trade, and especially, with the tragic displacement of Northwest Indians.

On the making of Oregon particularly, there is again a spate of fine, recent publications, including David Braly, *Crooked River Country: Wranglers, Rogues, and Barons*,[20] a strong, interesting, popular account on a rough and ready Central Oregon from 1825 to the mid–20th century; and David Peterson del Mar, *Oregon's Promise: An Interpretive History*,[21] an engaging book by someone who grew up amidst "Oregon chauvinism" and after leaving a number of times, returned a half-dozen more![22] There is also William G. Robbins, *Oregon: This Storied Land*,[23] by someone who came out to Oregon from the East in 1963, and wished to show both the region's strengths historically, including its reformist currents (which we treat quite fully below), but also its prejudices toward outsiders. Which of course shows how "subtexts"—i.e., autobiographical inclinations—have so impacted the making of Northwest historiography, not least in the present two interpreters intruding on this ever thriving, thronged field!

For Washington alone there is Robert E. Ficken's and Charles P. LeWarne's commissioned *Washington: A Centennial History*,[24] which takes the story from 1889 statehood. Ficken went backward with his 2002 publication, *Washington Territory*,[25] running from the 1853 creation of Washington Territory until statehood (1889), and differentiating a Washington ethos from a more general "Oregon ethos." He followed that with *Washington State: The Inaugural Decade 1889–1899*[26]—both on economic boom years, and years of populism and progressivism in the state that again receives more biographical-cultural and specific analysis from us below.

There is a plethora of monographic literature, some alluded to in our subsequent chapters, supplementing these more general works; again, for Washington alone one could point to (simply as examples) William L. Lang, *Confederacy of Ambition: William Winlock Miller and the Making of Washington Territory*[27] and Marilyn P. Watkins, *Rural Democracy: Family Farmers and Politics in Western Washington, 1890–1925*.[28] And on Portland and Seattle there are many more.[29]

Mention of urban history leads us to the vogue of other kinds of Northwest history by subject matter that fairly exploded since we began work on this project. Some have come, and some have mostly gone, but they have significantly altered the field. One that hadn't quite arrived in the '70s, when the Northwest environmental movement first got into high gear, was ecological history; but it now must be taken seriously as a genre, especially in this still environmentally-conscious region. Robert Bunting's *The Pacific Raincoast: Environment and Culture in an American Eden, 1778–1900*[30] is probably the best, most finished example in this field, showing both natural and human impacts on the physical Northwest, and thereby, on its history and vision. Bunting's scope is 1778 to 1900, ending in the year "when Frederick Weyerhaeuser purchased 900,000 acres of Washington forest land, completing one of the largest land deals in American history and symbolizing the forces of industrial capitalism...."[31] For anyone who has lived in the region this calls to mind the many disturbing swaths of clear-cut mountain country that are such tragic (or depending on one's point of view, not so tragic?) visual signposts of the region's consciousness—and guilt. Bunting reminds us early in his book, and poignantly, that western Oregon and Washington once featured the most important temperate rain forest on the planet. Equally poignant are superb, more localized monographs, like William G. Robbins' on the Coos Bay region of Southern Oregon, where "a mild, marine climate ... provides abundant moisture for one of the fastest-growing forest environments in the world," an area where "most believed that those massive timber stands would last forever." The savage impact of ever more efficient logging practices here is Robbins' grisly subject, as it is in William Dietrich's *The Final Forest*, on the fight for the last ancient, irreplaceable trees of the Olympic Peninsula, accompanied by a squabble over the spotted owl extending into the early 1990s, when he published this book. No one better describes the impact and tragedy of clearcutting, and the scrum of loggers, forestry bureaucrats, environmentalists, tourists, urban and rural aficionados, all vying for their own regional version—and vision. Also indispensable is Sallie Tisdale's personal, well-researched, lyrical take on a series of historical losses in the region—primordially, of trees, but also fragile wild flowers, beaver, salmon, wolves, elk et al. We *also* discuss at length the impact of environment in the Northwest, including with its many wounds, on the region's poets, novelists, and the like; but unfortunately, can't match this brand of ecological history, which owes so much to brilliant pioneering works in a still new field of American history, including William Cronon's masterly *Changes in the Land: Indians, Colonists, and the Ecology of New England*.[32]

Oral history has shown no signs of abating either, as in books like Ron Strickland's *River Pigs and Cayuses: Oral Histories from the Pacific Northwest*.[33] Perhaps some of this is now getting old; but in any event, aside from small amounts of interview material, for example, used in our chapter on Vernon Louis Parrington, we simply haven't embraced this genre here.

Probably the two kinds of Northwest history that made it most after we had begun this effort have been gender and racial/ethnic history—the latter especially prominent for the region. Some have, however, savaged these aspects of the "New Western History"—none more so than (excuse the pun) William Savage, a professor at the University of Oklahoma, who called people in such fields "presentist whores" wishing to negate much traditional historiography, and often implying "that there was nothing grand or heroic about white people conquering the technologically inferior." They frequently discount the importance of cowboys and the rest who once figured so prominently not only in Western consciousness, but in how the Western idea appealed to the rest of the country. However, the most stimulating discussion of these new vogues came from a New Mexico professor, Gene M. Gressley, who in the 1990s found recent western history "a boiling, roiling pot, as pungent as any chili issuing from 'Maria's' restaurant ... [and issuing] "from the template of the 1960s." Gressley delineated a huge, searing conflict in the profession between traditionalists and multiculturalists; but he saw the latter as inevitable winners, for "like it or not, America's future will be multicultural. The world is shrinking, the population of America is darkening." Tracing this surge to landmark babyboomer books, such as Patricia Nelson Limerick's *The Legacy of Conquest: The Unbroken Past of the American West*, he found gender or ethnic labeling, and general victimhood sweeping the field. Scintillating, engaged, quotable, Gressley held that "for the multiculturalist the cultural wars are not only necessary; they are inevitable. How else can we exculpate our shame except by the spectacle of profuse and abject apology revealed through cultural redemption?" Obviously a food connoisseur, he found "a bubbling bouillabaisse of political correctness, multiculturalism, and New Left protest" spawning a whole series of "new" histories in the field, with ideology generally winning out over depth. All this has impacted the general culture as well, with Hollywood either following along, or helping to further such trends. As Gressley puts it, "the great unwashed will go along with a recasting and a redefinition of their mythology of the West.... [So] today's *Unforgiven*, *Tombstone*, *Lonesome Dove*, and *Dances with Wolves* [he could now throw in films like *No Country for Old Men*] are the flip side of yesterday's *Fort Apache*, *She Wore a Yellow Ribbon*, and *Rio Grande*."[34]

Another "old-timer" in the field, Gerald D. Nash, saluting the influence of a once-great name, John D. Hicks, also sees the '60s as the great dividing line in Western historiography, bringing an ever more "drastic change of mood. Whereas historians between 1890 and 1960"—including figures like Frederick Jackson Turner and Bernard DeVoto—"had viewed the [Western] region as a positive and constructive force in American civilization, the generation after 1960 reflected a profound negativism and disenchantment." Nash adds that modern scholars perhaps take for granted the onset of academic "affluence, federal grants, loans, and affirmative action programs," paradoxically enhancing their "far more pessimistic perspective." The result was that "they wrote at length about the destruction of earlier native cultures" (one of the important subjects we also treat below); "of ethnic and racial conflicts; of white Anglo exploitation of blacks, Indians, and Hispanics; of the suppression of Orientals; and the subordination of women at the hands of men. Nor did they ignore the wanton destruction of the West's natural environment. It was a bleak indictment, indeed," Nash concludes.[35]

Not to climb on some fashionable bandwagon, we nonetheless originally found Abigail Scott Duniway, Anna Louise Strong, and other important "activist" women in Northwest cultural history worthy of extended analysis, and of quite a primary source dip here. But when it comes to ethnic/racial history, we cannot match the tremendous monographic efflorescence in that field or genre, which shows no signs of abating.

On older minorities in the Northwest, we have had numerous fine monographs; but now, Scandinavians, Russians, or Germans in the region have become mostly historically passé.[36] Even passé to some degree are studies of African-Americans in the Northwest, such as Quintard Taylor's *The Forging of a Black Community: Seattle's Central District from 1870 Through the Civil Rights Era*,[37] arguing the city's comparative distinctiveness. More recently, we have had a surge on Hispanics, including among others, Lorane A. West's *Latino Voices in the Pacific Northwest*,[38] by an "advocate" who has culled material from Spanish language immigrants; and Philip Garrison's *Because I Don't Have Wings: Stories of Mexican Immigrant Life*,[39] on agricultural workers in the Northwest—responding once again, to contemporary concerns.

But the group that certainly in California is gaining ever more prominence, Asians, will doubtless become foremost in ethnic/racial studies on the Northwest, too. The initial vogue was for studies of the Japanese, including Linda Tamura's *The Hood River Issei: An Oral History of Japanese Settlers in Oregon's Hood River Valley*,[40] on the first generation of Japanese immigrants to this region in the period 1890–1924, after which immigration was then shut off (for a time). These are in the main, beautifully done profiles. But on the more bitter problems affecting the second generation, particularly in World War II, there are books such as Yasuko I. Takezawa's *Breaking the Silence*,[41] with much on these second-generation "Nisei," then third-generation, post-war Sansei, who tried at once to remember and forget.

On another Asian group, we have Dorothy B. Fujita-Rony, *American Workers, Colonial Power: Philippine Seattle and the Transpacific West, 1919–1941*,[42] a meticulous scholarly monograph on identity problems among this contingent. But during the past ten or twenty years—at first little considered by historians, or even Americans generally—there came the momentous opening of China, a country where before 1990 or so citizens were essentially locked up. Now the dust has cleared, and California is a good 30 percent Asian, with most of those being Chinese; and the Northwest will doubtless catch up, as this massive immigration trend shows no signs of abating (and can be seen in many other places in the world, from Paris to Auckland). The result is that this part of Northwest history—work on Asians—will doubtless continue as a growing sub-field, where the demand for "visibility," for the hearing of hitherto unheard voices will become ever more major and marketable in the scholarly world.[43]

We confess that some of these newer trends go beyond our scope of inquiry here, though again, we *do* have a fair amount on Indians—their various cultures and tragedies; and that field will continue to be important, and is important to our own story here. But *most* significant for us here is the growth of a regional civilization. If that makes us to a degree traditional, we nonetheless think our work distinguishes us even from the many article collections that treat the Northwest's developing regional consciousness in a traditional way as well at times, often emanating from scholarly symposia.[44]

If the following chapters concerned British or American general history, our introduction could end here. But this is a work on the Pacific Northwest, and we cannot presume that all our readers will have enough context in time and place to follow our analysis. So with the indulgence of those already familiar with or living in the region, let us briefly summarize this context here.

The heart of the Northwest is the Columbia River system, though we exclude from the region those portions of the system in Canada, and in southeastern Idaho. To the Columbia drainage must be added the Puget Sound area in northwestern Washington, where over half the regional population lived by the 1970s around, essentially, an inland sea; the jumbled hills and valleys of southwestern Oregon; portions of "the Great Basin" in southern Oregon; and the shallow coastal valleys both north and south of the Columbia's mouth. The region is obviously marked by wide variations in climate. Along the coast one finds extremely wet coastal valleys backed by the Coast Range in Oregon and which rise into the imposing mass of the Olympic Mountains in Washington. This strip is succeeded by a trough, containing both the Willamette Valley and the (partially drowned) Puget Sound area. Most Northwesterners still live along this trough, and its cool, mild, often wet climate has helped establish the regional image. East of the trough are the high Cascades with their volcanic peaks, such as Mount Baker and iconic Rainier in Washington, and Oregon's Mount Hood. Beyond this range is the dry, high plateau of the Columbia, an "inland empire," resembling much of the interior West; and to the east, the plateau steps up gradually into the Rocky Mountains. The reader will note that the Columbia flows in most of its course through a relatively dry area. Yet it *is* a great river, the only one in the Northwest that breaks through the Cascades (with the partial exception of the Klamath); and one drawing on a very large area, including the snows of the eastern Cascades and the Rockies.[45]

By the time Europeans came here, three major lifestyles could be found among the region's Native Americans. Most primitive were the sparse cultures of the interior—of hunters and gatherers. Frequently moving, they had minimal dwellings and few possessions, and lived in small bands. To this cultural base Native Americans of the coast and inland along the Columbia had added a borrowed Indian culture centered in modern British Columbia and southeastern Alaska. Here the abundance of salmon and other seafood made possible, among a pre-agricultural people, more sophistication, including large communal houses of cedar, excellent canoes, and developed patterns of material display. East of the Cascades, a third group of Native American cultures had added, by the eighteenth and nineteenth centuries, the use of the horse, and with the horse those features of the late plains culture that for most of us, have seemed quintessentially "Indian." Indeed, the mounted Plateau Indians had begun to depend upon expeditions through the passes of the Rockies to prey on the buffalo herds of the Plains.[46]

White European or British entrants approached the region both from land and sea. The first significant maritime explorers in the 1770s were the Spaniards, followed closely by the British, notably George Vancouver in the 1790s. Contacts between Indians and whites rapidly increased as ships regularly visited the coast to buy furs, especially those of the sea otter. This trade flourished between 1787 and 1812, falling progressively into the hands of Americans (whom the Indians called the "Bostons").

Overland contact began with the stirring Lewis and Clark expedition that crossed the Columbia River, reaching the Pacific in 1805. Since several ships had wintered in the lower Columbia, Lewis and Clark found an Indian contingent already enriched, diseased, and in part, corrupted by whites. Shortly after this famed expedition, American trappers entered the region in competition with Canadian trappers from the Northeast. American enthusiasm was dampened when John Jacob Astor was compelled to sell Astoria, the chief American fur-trading post in the lower Columbia, to a competing British company in 1814. Nevertheless, after the War of 1812 the British and Americans agreed on "joint occupation," and soon the Hudson Bay Company monopolized trade in all but the eastern fringes of the region. The Company established permanent trading posts at Fort Walla Walla, Fort Colville, and Fort Vancouver in the 1820s, and this Vancouver (on the Columbia River, not the later Vancouver of British Columbia) became the center of white civilization in the Northwest. The fort quickly became self-supporting, stable family life developed, and before 1830, lumber was even shipped to the Hawaiian Islands. Soon Fort Nisqually on Puget Sound had begun to develop into an agricultural center, while farming spread southward into Oregon's Willamette Valley.

Under "joint occupation," not more than 150 American trappers, merchants, and missionaries resided in the Northwest in 1840. But with the opening of the Oregon Trail to wagon trains, the "Great Migration" of 1843 shifted the balance. Soon the American farmers of the Willamette Valley were pressing for self-government, and in 1846 the United States gained control of the Northwest as we know it today. Fort Vancouver lost its sway; nearby Oregon City and later Portland took over as the focal points of pioneer life; and American merchants and homesteaders became dominant forces here. The Native American population was quickly outnumbered, although in the 1850s and 1870s there were desperate Indian outbreaks of violence throughout the less settled parts of the region. Washington Territory, meanwhile, separated from Oregon in 1853 and from Idaho ten years later.[47]

Settlement in the Northwest came in several waves: the homesteading frontier period, especially in the lower Columbia and Willamette valleys, from roughly 1840 to 1880; the interior mining and agricultural booms, and general urban growth from approximately 1880 to 1920; and then, during a period of lumber, fishing, manufacturing, and agricultural expansion up to the 1970s. Portland reached a population of 10,000 in 1870 and 46,000 in 1890. On Puget Sound, Seattle started more slowly, but exploded after 1890 to pass Portland, and together with nearby Tacoma, and Spokane in eastern Washington, shifted the Northwest center away from the original heartland of the lower Columbia and Willamette valleys.

Overwhelmingly, the Northwest's inhabitants came (to the 1970s) from the Middle West—Ohio, Missouri, Illinois, and Iowa, and later from Minnesota, Wisconsin, and the Dakotas as well. The Upper South had a more important role to play than this indicates, especially at first; and more recently, California became an important (and sometimes feared) source of population. These statistical generalizations should not obscure the fact that the educational, financial, and business elites were generally (even into the 1960s) directly or indirectly of mostly New England origin. From 1860 or so, the area was overwhelmingly Protestant and white, but that included Scandinavians, Germans, and Canadians. However, non-white races such as American Indians, Chinese, Japanese, and Negroes were significant, too. Aside from Indians, Northwesterners were usually newcomers. The percentage of the population born in the region was below 50 percent in 1870 and surprisingly, lower in 1910 (after the second surge of population), and still at 1870 levels in 1950 (following much movement during World War II out to the coast). As the novelist H. L. Davis said of Oregon: "Its population turnover gives an illusion of newness.... However, this *is* the illusion, the same as in the beginning, and an illusion is enough if it can be made to last."[48]

Chapter 1

The Bitter Spiritual Harvest of Displacement

THE FIRST AND MAJOR intellectual problem of American civilization in the Northwest was spiritually to manage the fact that its accomplishments *only* became possible with the displacement of Indian civilization that had preceded it. Of course, many civilizations in history have developed and expanded through the destruction of others. Still, universality is hardly comforting, especially when the victims of change continued to emphasize this great tragedy. Although in the Northwest there have been periods of comparative inattention, the theme of white and Indian have mainly persisted, and we must begin our search for a regional consciousness by summarizing the problem of the two civilizations' interactions, as perceived by people on the frontier and by more contemporary scholars as well.

In the Northwest these brilliantly disturbing words of Chief Seattle to the white conquerors are often quoted—from a speech he purportedly gave to Governor Isaac Stevens in the 1850s, and printed in 1887; and their echo still bears repetition:

> Every part of this earth is sacred to my people.... The ground beneath your feet responds more lovingly to our steps than yours, because it is the ashes of our grandfathers. Our bare feet know the kindred touch. The earth is rich with the lives of our kin. The young men, the mothers, and girls, the little children who once lived and were happy here, still love these lonely places. And at evening the forests are dark with the presence of the dead. When the last dead man has vanished from this earth, and his memory is only a story among the whites, these shores will still swarm with the invisible dead of my people. And when your children's children think they are alone in the fields, the forests, the shops, the highways, or the quiet of the woods, they will not be alone. There is no place in this country where a man can be alone. At night when the streets of your towns and

> cities are quiet, and you think they are empty, they will throng with the returning spirits that once thronged them, and that still love these places. The white man will never be alone.[1]

However debatable the speech's origins, this version of Seattle's words certainly made some sense.[2] The regional memory has long been haunted by the Indian, by a sense of injustice and by a large sense of loss. Non-Indian Northwesterners generally believed that Native American cultures were inevitably swept away by a superior civilization. And yet in guilt and dissatisfaction, they also looked back, recreating Indian backgrounds that would better serve a more "modern" consciousness. Too often that selective memory and guilt have obscured the historical record and reality.

In order to evaluate a civilization one needs to work on two levels—those of ideal standards and those of average behavior. Both are important, although we would argue that the greatest differences among people are in the ideals of their cultures, and it is on this plane that the advances of mankind have proceeded.[3] Yet the two levels are seldom totally distinct, for the average behavior of a group generally reflects the group's ideals, even as it fails perhaps to live up to them.

Again, the basic assumption of the Indian–white confrontation was that white success was based on their own demonstrated superiority.[4] Let us now examine this putative superiority. First, no one doubts that whites descended from the British Isles or Europe became rapidly superior materially; and indeed, Indian desire for the material goods of the whites played an important role in the impoverishment and deliquescence of their own cultures. Related to this superiority was the fact that the whites were stronger militarily because of better arms. But more important was agricultural technology, fostering such a large population in white Euro-America that Indian opposition became ultimately futile. Chiefs such as Seattle most often mentioned the endless stream of white immigration as the main reason for their ultimate surrender. A Modoc chief put it this way:

> I thought if we killed all the white men we saw, that no more would come. We killed all we could; but they come more and more like new grass in the Spring. I looked around and saw that many of our young men were dead and could not come back to fight. My heart was sick. My people were few. I threw down my gun. I said, "I will not fight again." I made friends with the white man.[5]

Secondly, in intellectual life the Indians had not reached the point of organized, rationalized knowledge, although of course they had many myths and tales, and could "think" as well as uneducated whites of the day. But by and large, they had not achieved the critical detachment that first occurred in ancient Greece, and that in spite of its continued and ever-growing rarity, has played a crucial role in the progress of civilization.

The third weakness of Indian civilization was the absence of political organizations that could establish peace under law beyond village or local group boundaries. Authority and rank were much prized in Indian societies of the Northwest, but even on the local level, authority was indefinite, and relations between groups often hostile and deadly. The result was continual warfare and shifting of groups, including their occasional extermination. In difficult periods bands could weld themselves into tribes, but nothing was sure about the process, and when the going got tough—as when there was pressure to make treaties with white authorities and be removed—half of, say, the Spokanes were for it, half against. Low in population, the Flatheads lost precious men to war with the Blackfoot tribes. The heroic story of the flight through Wyoming and Montana toward Canada of the last free bands of Nez Percé in 1877 most poignantly illustrates the inability of Indians to work together, even when there were close and friendly relations among these bands. Even previously, the Nez Percé had been scattered in southwest Washington, northeast Oregon, north-central Idaho, and their population numbers were quite low. Faced with the onslaught of Protestant missionaries, they had also become divided between Christians and anti–White American nativists right through the late 1850s. Now in 1877 that same disunity worked against them; for here were Nez Percé and other Indians assisting white soldiers in their final campaign against the bands around Chief Joseph, just as the Nez Percé had as a tribe sent warriors to aid the white subjugation of other Indians east of the Cascades in the 1850s. And there was the sad peacemaking of the Salish Chief Moses, who could have helped the Nez Percés. It was an old story repeated in different parts of the country, a story contrasting sharply with the relative unity of white Americans across several thousand miles.[6]

The pre-contact record in most of the primitive world suggests that the main barrier to both population growth and civilizational development may well have been warfare. As elsewhere in the primitive world, there were clever and innovative Northwest Indians, but without written records, inventions frequently died with their inventors in societies where there might be only one or two people practicing a specialty at a time, and where death due to warfare constituted an ever present intrusion.

Beyond these three major shortcomings—disunity, unadvanced technology, and pre–Hellenic standards of rationality—other attributes negatively impressed those who first commented on Northwestern Indians. One of these was cruelty to captives, slaves, and animals. By modern lights, of course, many whites of this period were *also* extremely crude in these matters (witness the tragic fate of the bisons, not to mention of many Indians!). It hardly needs stressing that *both* Indians and whites too often treated one another with the cruelty of people who did not accept each other's humanity. Yet there was surely a difference between Indian and white attitudes toward life and pain. For example, Native Americans kept, captured, and sold slaves. Whites in the American South also held slaves before 1860, yet since this was a pattern decisively rejected by settlers on the Northwest frontier, and long given a bad conscience in the nation as a whole, slavery did little to raise the status of the Indians from the optic of a new settler people. The Chinooks of the lower Columbia were the most sedulous slavers of the Northwest, raiding elsewhere, then trading at huge marts for prized possessions such as Nootka canoes. Slaves were often mistreated, even strangled or starved to death, and at the least, considered akin to untouchables. It was a mark of Veblenian conspicuous consumption for Indian chiefs and aristocrats to own plenty of them—this reinforced status, and the practice was not easily given up, even when the U.S. government legislated against it.[7]

The position of Indian women varied, but generally, it, too, was more depressed than in white society; the gain for an Indian woman in marrying a white man was therefore great, and not simply for the material benefits it brought.[8] It is true, however, that regarding traits such as honesty, diligence, bravery, and reliability, whites of the frontier tended to give higher moral praise to certain tribes—at different times, Flatheads, Nez Percé, and Klickitats; and lower marks to others, such as the Chinook.[9] In particular, the Nez Percé of northeastern Oregon, southeastern Washington, and north-central Idaho were perceived to exhibit a nobility of character and unexpectedly pronounced moral sense—both in those groups that seriously adhered to Christianity, and in those that fervently rejected it. But despite our guilt over the many crimes and injustices that attended displacement of the Indians, it is a mistake to transfer the reported qualities of particular groups onto Northwest Indians in a definitive, generalized manner.

Of course, these issues were not the sole reasons why many early settlers often judged the Indian to be inferior. What stood out in their minds were differences that educated Americans would now judge very differently. To many whites of earlier times, Indians were physically ugly, and this impression was not enhanced by head flattening, practiced especially on the lower Columbia. Indians were despised by puritanical whites of that era because in many groups little clothing was worn for the purpose of modesty, and because Indian dwellings were often untidy and even dirty by again, puritanical white standards. A pervasive odor of decaying fish did not disabuse many of this impression. And far preceding our sexual revolution of the 1960s and '70s, differing standards of sexual morality (for women) also lowered the white view of the Indian.[10] In addition, Native Americans were despised by most settlers for their lack of Christianity (when this religion was a *sine qua non* among almost all white incomers), and agriculture. More generally, there was between Indian and white that lack of understanding and too often, a mutual dislike common to people in contact, which easily led to prejudice-confirming conflicts.

Perhaps most important was the simple psychological need of one people displacing another to justify their success in terms of a much-advertised and pervasively assumed superiority. This despite the fact that many positive features of Northwest Indians *were* noticed and valued by early visitors, if only much more recently assessed in an adequate way. Most important were the achievements in woodworking and other decorative arts of Northwest Coast Indians. The great monuments of this development lay to the north of the region, but among the Makah and Quinaults of the Olympic peninsula, and in a more altered form along the lower Columbia, artistic achievement in this tradition was also significant. Elsewhere, too, basketry (using a variety of often sophisticated weaving techniques) was the outstanding artistic medium of the people, as it was in so much of North America. Among the practical arts, canoes of the coast, Puget Sound, and the lower Columbia represented important triumphs of both art and patience, as did great wooden longhouses with their transportable siding. Although quite recently borrowed, the equestrian display and war games of tribes such as the Nez Percé and some Shoshone groups were the most remarkable features of Northwest culture to many of the first white incomers.[11]

In common with many so-called primitive groups, Northwest Indians had an extensive oral literature. Although it is difficult to recapture the background needed to evaluate it comparatively, at its best it seems to have achieved significant dramatic meaning.[12] These were oral cultures in which formal oratory reflected the intense pride of Indian leaders—pride too often forced by events into traits of bitterness, sullenness, and revenge; but just as often informed by a calm acquiescence in change, and a desire to do as well as they could with what little power was left to them.

Most of all, Native Americans represented a way of life that *belonged* to the region in a sense that no Northwesterner has since quite belonged. While some Indian groups knew that their own ancestors were recent immigrants, taken as a whole the Indians *were* the native inhabitants, and they often scorned whites as transients, as "those who live on the water."[13] Here again, remember the purported, gentle derogation of Chief Seattle:

> To us the ashes of our fathers are sacred. Their graves are holy ground. But you are wanderers, you leave your father's graves behind you, and you do not care.... Your dead forget you and the country of their birth as soon as they go beyond the grave and walk among the stars. They are quickly forgotten and they never return. Our dead never forget this beautiful earth. They always love and remem-

> ber her rivers, her great mountains, her valleys. They long for the living, who are lonely too and who long for the dead. And their spirits often return to visit and console us.[14]

The memory that remained for many Northwesterners was one of degradation, of the shock of change, of a chasm between races, of killing and injustice, and of the ravages of introduced diseases. More, there soon spread among Indians that same sense of hopelessness that had caused the decline of primitive people biologically less ravaged, such as in Hawaii.[15] Seattle's speech accepting the removal of his people (a kind of death chant) both rejects the possibility of a bridge between two such different peoples, and reminds us that our civilization must also decline in due course, which to any but the most blithe relativists, it has indeed begun to do. In this irreversible succession, he adds, "We may be brothers, after all. We shall see."[16]

Seattle's words were supposedly rendered in the Duwamish language, for he refused to speak in the jargon which had originated as a bridge between white fur traders and Indians; *or* in English. Therefore, we have only a local doctor's translation. But, however embroidered the phraseology, and however questionable the speech's origins may be, that message became a central theme of regional mythology and memory, enunciating a principle that later ages have had to deal with, no matter how much they also rejected it. Some Indians did, of course, follow a different path, becoming much like whites culturally. But so many others persisted, sometimes in an alcoholic haze, to see the world in Chief Seattle's terms, and to chant spiritually in Duwamish long after they had forgotten it as a language of life. And then after our period came the great irony of Indian-run casinos, but that irony belongs in a different book than ours.

Returning to a chronological focus, we concentrate first on the early period of trader and trapper, best known through Washington Irving's *Astoria*, depicting the struggle of American and British trappers, traders, and explorers in the early 1800s. In that period John Jacob Astor, mentioned in our introduction, was the guiding entrepreneurial presence for both exploration of the Northwest coast and planning of a fur-trading base there, for which he sought and received support back east from major figures like Governor De Witt Clinton of New York and President Jefferson himself.[17] With the subsequent ordering of the region under the Hudson Bay Company and its chief factor, John McLoughlin, the Northwest attained its first synthesis and sense of unity, a period of comparative tranquility from 1825 to 1846, ending in the creation of an American Washington and Oregon, and of British Columbia, in what became Canada.[18] McLoughlin was both a man and a myth, the representative of a great commercial and imperial system, but was also the first incarnator of "civilized" tradition to reside in the region.

Of Scottish, Irish, and French-Canadian background, McLoughlin was related by birth to people in or near the fur trade, being a nephew of Alexander and Simon Fraser. Trained as a doctor, he took positions early on in the North West Company.[19] On the frontier, he then married a part–Indian fur trader's daughter, the widow of another well-known trader, Alexander McKay; their marriage produced four children, and was honored throughout his life. (Although this was a common practice among trappers and traders in the West, many of whom were part–Indian, the practice was not accepted by the next generation of Americans.)

McLoughlin was a large man—ambitious, irritable, very conscious of his rights—but competent and moral, too. Even though a known dissident, he was named Chief Factor for the huge Columbia region when it was reorganized in 1825. His task was to make the division of the company self-supporting by producing more of its own supplies, and to resist the encroachments of Americans. At first he brilliantly succeeded through his establishment of Fort Vancouver, as well as a string of lesser forts; the regularization of trade through the region; the establishment of extensive farms on both sides of the Columbia near Vancouver, along the Cowlitz River, and on Puget Sound; the maintenance of peaceful relations with Indians; and the trapping out of the Snake River to cut off the advance of American trappers.

McLoughlin ruled his empire with the zeal of a Louis XIV. From California, he imported cattle and pointed the way to a great Oregon ranching industry. He had his own cooperage, his own blacksmiths and tinsmiths, his own shipyards and salt works. Fishing was developed into an export industry through a special form of salting salmon, while the Columbia and Willamette rivers powered flour and sawmills. The fur trade under men such as Peter Skene Ogden provided steady profits. Nor was the feudal or manorial aspect of Fort Vancouver reflected merely in its agricultural and industrial economy, for the ceremony and show mounted for visitors there was often recorded. The courtly atmosphere at the fort was enhanced by outward marks of luxury, doubly impressive on the frontier: silk and lace for fur traders' wives, Limoges and other fine china, imported wine and sherry on the tables. When visitors entered the fort, Highlanders piped their arrival. McLoughlin's elaborate Christmas ceremony was a civilized version of the picturesque rendezvous of mountain men and Indians on the plains. Oregon grape and other greenery hung from the ceiling, expensive candles lit up the rooms, elk roasts and grizzly meat filled huge appetites, while female singers and harpists soothed the stomach after dinner.[20]

McLoughlin and coterie knew the power of a certain mystique, and such ceremony greatly contributed to his image as a great white father reigning over some 80,000 Indians. It was also necessary to impress immigrants with a kind of powerful majesty. From his outpost on the Columbia, McLoughlin ran the Hudson's Bay empire for twenty-four years, thoroughly grasping the practical, day-to-day problems affecting the area. He had to placate Indians, Canadian superiors in the Company, and American immigrants. McLoughlin's superiors especially deplored his humane treatment of the Americans. He aided Nathaniel Wyeth's unsuccessful attempts to establish American commerce on the river; helped American Methodists establish the first missions here; and welcomed early settlers with boats, emergency supplies, and protection. The founding of Fort Walla Walla and Fort Boise, important connecting points for westward American immigration, came under his direction. He advised settlers on agricultural methods suitable to Oregon, and he and associates read many scientific treatises written by British farming experts, passing on that knowledge.

McLoughlin, in other words, helped give early form to a regional consciousness. The White-Headed Eagle to local Indians, he became the great chief they had lacked, and also helped establish a chain of lesser "chiefs" at the forts and stations of the Company. Gradually, these company officers took the place of actual chiefs among Indian groups, many of which had been disorganized by losses from recent epidemics.[21] McLoughlin could play this role in part because he and many of his men had Indian or part–Indian wives. His sons were, after all, part–Indian (one later married the daughter of a Kootenai chief and settled in Idaho).[22] He could also rule because he offered Native Americans trade goods they had come to greatly desire. And he provided peace for them as well as peace for his stations. Though he punished Indians for killing whites, at times severely, peaceful groups had nothing to fear, and most of the time a combination of justice backed by power seemed to suffice.

Regarding McLoughlin's treatment of Indians, Alvin Josephy summed up the results:

> Under that colonial policy, benign and fair to its subjects, the roaming Nez Perces had gradually acclimated themselves to conforming to the standards of relations that the British traders demanded. At the heart of the Indians' change were such things as a continued desire for access to the white man and his trade and alliance with him against common enemies, as well as a wish to avoid trouble—all of which were guaranteed only by the stoppage of horse thefts, pilfering, threats with arms, and other acts that angered the traders. As the Indians had abandoned those traits, their relations with the British had grown more harmonious; and by February 1833 an American who was traveling with a Hudson's Bay Company group through Sahaptin country could visit the area at the junction of the Palouse and Snake rivers, where John Clarke had once hanged an Indian, and write, "these people who are most used to this country are so little afraid of the Indians that they either travel without guns or with them unloaded."[23]

Of course Josephy also points in a later book to the dangers represented by these fur traders paving the way for missionaries who then wished ardently to convert Indians to Christianity—figures like Marcus Whitman, with whom we will deal here, and the temperamental Henry Spalding. More generally, the traders also prepared the way for ever more aggressive settlers and for what Josephy would call "the gathering storm."[24]

In a shorter run, success also changed McLoughlin himself, and he became more and more reluctant to follow his superiors' directives in the Company. They insisted on maintaining coastal trade by boats, while he preferred forts, and they pushed him to move his headquarters when American pressures become overwhelming. For his part, McLoughlin was angered at the Company's treatment of the outposts, in one of which his son was murdered; and he also ascribed his son-in-law's suicide, in another Company position, to the firm's negligence. At last he was forced to quit, moving across the river in 1846 to a new life on properties he had developed in Oregon City. As founder of that town, its industry and stores, McLoughlin himself became a settled American citizen, and was briefly the mayor there in 1851. The Whitman massacre at the hands of Cayuses in 1847, discussed below, found McLoughlin in retirement, and though the Company lent its services, the new Oregonians themselves punished the killers. The territory was quickly organized; Joseph Lane, an American frontiersman from Indiana, and McLoughlin's antithesis, became the territory's first governor in 1849.[25]

All the while, local authorities attempted to deny McLoughlin's right to his properties, rights only finally returned to him after his death. Opposition to him was in part opposition to the Company and to Britain, but also to his reconverted Catholicism (1842), and to his own unconsecrated marriage with an Indian. McLoughlin's most determined opponents were W. P. Bryant, first territorial chief justice in Oregon, and Samuel R. Thurston, a new immigrant of 1847. The latter, representing the view of Protestant missionaries, was elected to Congress in 1849 as Oregon's first territorial delegate. In Congress, Thurston pushed through the Oregon Donation Land law which would make it impossible for McLoughlin to retain his land. The wording of the law was ingenious, forbidding someone who claimed land as a British subject (under a law of 1846) to do so as an American under the new legislation. So, although he remained in de facto possession until his death, McLoughlin's right to his claim as a Briton was cancelled by his new American citizenship![26]

Finally came loneliness—the fur trade having ebbed, and McLoughlin's friends mostly gone. Peter Ogden, Duncan McDonald, and James Douglas—his famous associates—had left Oregon for the area around Fort Victoria, the new hub of Hudson's Bay activity. In his last letters, McLoughlin conveyed a strong sense of betrayal and isolation. No longer British, indeed castigated by his old countrymen, neither was he accepted by American settlers, the denizens of a new dream. He was truly a broken patriarch. For someone used to the exercise of power, this letting out to pasture must have been as hard to bear as the loss of his land. Embittered by personal loss, betrayed by his company and by his adopted country, McLoughlin died in 1857 in Oregon City.

As noted, early Americans in the Northwest were sea traders or trappers, or an occasional entrepreneur like McLoughlin's New England friend Nathaniel Wyeth. But the first permanent American colonies were those of the missionaries. Isolated Methodists led by another New Englander, Jason Lee, struggled to establish schools and churches in the lower Columbia and Willamette valleys.[27] However, since they came after great plagues had decimated the tribes, they soon turned their primary attention to the new white and half-breed population, among which they converted even the mountain man Joseph Meek.[28] Their real accomplishments, such as the establishment of Willamette University, are often forgotten in the maze of petty disputes of the 1840s and '50s, and the alliance of these Methodists against the British and the Company. Jason Lee himself lost two wives in the wilderness, and bitter (and probably unfair) attacks on him as a profiteer forced him to return to the East.

This left it to a second incoming, missionary wave, that of Boston-based Presbyterians and Congregationalists, to leave a greater impression on an emerging regional consciousness. One of the most important historical events of this era was the massacre of the missionary Dr. Marcus Whitman, his wife Narcissa, and their followers at Waiilatpu, near modern Walla Walla, Washington in 1847. How did this occur? In 1834 a Presbyterian and Congregational New England mission board had sent Samuel Parker and Whitman to survey the field, and particularly, to contact the Nez Percé and Flatheads, who had expressed interest in receiving missionaries. The inclinations of both these men were at once pro–Indian and pro–Christian proselytization. Indeed, after his trip Parker concluded that Indians were as good as any other people and, in fact, had the best claim to the Northwest.[29] Parker was too old to go into the field, but Dr. Whitman returned home and prepared for permanent missionary work in the Pacific Northwest. To have his plans accepted by the board, however, he needed to be married and to find another couple to accompany him. He met and married a woman who became Narcissa Whitman, then recruited Henry Spalding, a minister who had also recently married. However, he later found that Spalding loathed Narcissa for having rejected his own earlier proposal! This was a hatred that was to flare up again and again, embittering the relations of the four missionary families that struggled together in this challenging wilderness. Nevertheless, Spalding successfully established a mission amongst the Nez Percé and patiently taught them agriculture and religion.

However, the main establishment was that of the Whitmans at Waiilatpu on the Oregon trail. From the beginning, Whitman had much against him. The Cayuse around his mission had not been interested in having a missionary here, and Whitman's concentration on medicine was a direct challenge to local religious leaders, themselves primarily healers.[30] And of course even the best conventional medicine did not always work against different scourges of the time, like measles and influenza epidemics, or smallpox. One of the worst such epidemics, mentioned above, and nicknamed "The Cold Sick," had spread its ugly course beginning in the very decade of Whitman's mission, the 1830s, and continued through that decade. Against such scourges Indians wanted results from missionaries that could not be delivered. So while Whitman's mission developed materially, it never thrived beyond what the Cayuse could obtain from it, and there were few real converts. As the mission work expanded, feuding among missionaries also grew, especially with Spalding, a man who would not teach English or learn Nez Percé, yet succeeded in transmitting American Protestant culture more successfully than any of the other missionaries. Whitman fought to hold the fractured effort together, and in a famous trip back East in the early 1840s, obtained renewed support for the mission and also helped to stir up growing interest in Oregon.[31]

Returning West with the Oregon migration of 1843, Whitman's mission soon became an important stopping point for white settlers. The Indians were now disturbed by this continual influx of whites, while some among them (one a Delaware) pointed out that eastern Indians had seen all this happen before—and that the missionary was often a forerunner of mass displacement. And again, the immigrants brought diseases, diseases that Whitman could sometimes treat successfully in whites, but which when transmitted to the Cayuse, generally brought death, despite his best efforts. Since in Indian belief a healer could also *cause* illnesses, these deaths were charged against him.

It was against this background that the Whitmans were then murdered in 1847. And although the Indians were decisively defeated in the Cayuse War of retribution, white settlement east of the Cascade Mountains stopped for years. The other Indians did not come to the aid of the guilty Cayuse, yet the events left a tradition of hatred throughout the region that swept away much that McLoughlin had accomplished. And because the Catholics had just entered the burgeoning mission field (at the time of his death, Whitman was discussing sale of his spread to a nearby Catholic mission) and seemed to play an ambiguous role in the massacre, it became part of local lore among many devoted Protestants that these Catholics had actually helped plot the massacre—another legacy of hate for what might have been perhaps an enduring testament to a certain love and self-sacrifice.

It should be mentioned that the Cayuse were no mean foe—their very name meant "superior people," and their great horsemanship and courage in war had long been renowned in the region. Among Indian tribes they were military *crème de la crème*, and to them Whitman's pacifistic religion made little sense; nor did his rejection of superstitions that had always been a comfort to them. (When, for example, Mount St. Helens blew in 1842, they considered it the manifestation of divine anger against these upstart Christians.)[32]

On the other side there were myths made too, more debatable ones; and in the very generation of the Whitman massacre, one such myth coalesced into dogma—that Marcus Whitman, no mere missionary, had "saved Oregon" by riding, à la Paul Revere, to Washington, D.C., where he told the government of the necessity to stymie the British by rapid American settlement. Without Whitman, no Oregon, ran this myth. Ironically, Spalding became one of the main defenders of the legend of Whitman's greatness, thus minimizing dissension within the ranks seen during Whitman's own lifetime! The story was then codified by Spalding's contentious associate, W. H. Gray, in his *History of Oregon*.[33] Although widely disliked, Gray claimed both personal and documentary evidence of Dr. Whitman's intentions in going east, and of his effect on the government and on subsequent immigration.

By the 1880s, the story was being questioned. The first great revisionist was Francis Fuller Victor, always a controversial writer, treated extensively in one of our future chapters. Victor and Elwood Evans wrote articles in *The Oregonian* in 1884, attacking the Whitman legend, and the ensuing controversy these articles provoked is both interesting for the light it sheds on Whitman, and on the Northwest's developing regional consciousness forty years after the doctor's death. *The Oregonian* threw open its columns to rejoinders that make interesting reading even today. In its issue of December 9, 1884, Edward C. Ross first vented his hatred of Mrs. Victor, summarizing the findings of her November 7 article as follows:

> She therein accuses Dr. Whitman [of] falsehood, deception, office-seeking, trying to deprive the Indians of their lands, trying to enrich himself at their expense, and at the expense of the emigrants.... In her ghoulish work Mrs. Victor outdoes all other calumniators of the dead.[34]

According to this observer, Victor had unjustly shifted all the credit for the arduous overland trek of 1836 to Joe Meek. In reply to her accusation that Whitman had given little help to Native Americans, Ross cited books he had printed in an Indian tongue, and noted how he showed them how to raise cattle, sheep, hogs, and fowl.[35] In conclusion:

> Time will vindicate Dr. Whitman, and when all calumnies, and their inventors, shall have been forgotten, his name, and that of his devoted noble wife, will stand forth in history as martyrs to the cause of God and their country.[36]

The Reverend M. Eels, writing in *The Oregonian* for January 11, 1885, also criticized Victor's assertion that "he [Dr. Whitman] had been six years in the Cayuse country without either having benefited or conciliated the Indians." His rejoinder was founded on religious grounds: there were still, he averred, Indian Presbyterians in the area harking back to the doctor's missionary efforts. Eels also found no evidence for Mrs. Victor's speculations that Whitman's personal ambition was to obtain a government office in the forthcoming territory of Oregon.[37]

The most passionate rejoinder came from the pen of W. H. Gray, appearing in *The Oregonian* of February 1, 1885. Gray, the only surviving person who had met Whitman and Spalding (on the Missouri River in 1836), said, "It would be thought strange if I did not come forward to defend them against a slanderer who has filled four columns of your valuable paper."[38] Gray first went to what he thought was the root of Victor's antipathy to the Whitman mission: her prejudice against all such "Protestant Christian efforts."[39] Given the intense religious coloration of the period, and also doubts raised by Social Darwinism, he was probably not wrong to focus on religion as a source of ideological differentiation in the Northwest. He then went on to deal with Victor's substantive accusations. Whitman *did* ride to Washington in 1842 out of fear that the United States would lose Oregon to the British—so he had told Gray.[40] And this was *not* just a "patriotic fable," as Victor had confidently called it.[41]

But the revisionists continued on with Professor Edward G. Bourne's diatribe against Whitman legendizers at the American Historical Association meeting of 1900. Grand interpretations on the West were in the air, the most famous being the recent Turner frontier thesis; historians, having seen the country grow to modern form, felt sure enough now to challenge or refine central myths. With respect to Whitman himself, the process was a cyclical one—of ebb and flow. From Bourne his posthumous reputation took an almost mortal blow and so did that of the Reverend Spalding, seen as the legend's chief propagator. Much was made of Spalding's derangement, both in Bourne's paper and in William Marshall's enthusiastic emendation to it, published as a book in 1911. What the Whitman tale also glossed over, according to these authors, was tension and discord among the missionaries who, far from being real patriots, were not even perfect Christians! The ride was necessitated by petty quarreling; it was no higher patriotic purpose that had set Whitman on his horse. The real Dr. Marcus Whitman? As Bourne's adherent Marshall declared, he was essentially a mediocrity, with which Bourne, in language not quite so blunt, had agreed.[42]

In 1937, Clifford Drury, a churchman, revived the viewpoint that Whitman was a great Christian gentleman. He also defended the doctor from a modern scientific viewpoint—that he had brought medicine to savages. In 1832 Whitman, at the risk of his life, cared for victims of cholera—in a year when the disease killed off a French prime minister and whole sections of Manchester. Such an effort could therefore not be underestimated. As a surgeon on the frontier, Whitman also removed an arrow that had been embedded for three years in Mountain Man Jim Bridger. Even Native Americans were impressed by this.

Historians know from archaeological evidence that Whitman also filled teeth and replaced them at Waiilatpu—the piles of false teeth having been excavated. We know that he ran a gunsmithery at the mission, for remnants of this too have been found. He had a fine collection of stones and was interested in geology, then a still relatively young scientific discipline. With an associate Whitman designed and constructed a pair of granite millstones in order to produce flour from wheat; he accumulated and sold pork, beans, squash, and other foods, and offered generous hospitality—much as did McLoughlin at Vancouver—to incoming people. According to Drury, Whitman was also a linguist who cared about the "heathens" he was about to convert, while his wife, Narcissa, was indeed the warm-hearted, compassionate woman who still deserves our sympathy. The evidence shows that many of the amenities were from her inspiration. As Thomas Garth writes, "Mrs. Whitman was fond of nice things. Possibly they compensated in some part for her feeling of loneliness in being so far from her family and from civilization."[43] At Waiilatpu, the doors were nicely painted, there were fine tables and chairs and good English china, and a beautiful flower garden. The magnificent red poppies she planted there could still be seen growing as late as 1872. But it is also true that contemporaries traced part of the failure of the mission to Narcissa's inability to get over the culture shock of meeting Indians who had very different standards of hygiene, a fact these Indians knew and resented.[44]

Drury finally sees the massacre of Whitman in 1847 as a foolhardy act committed against the very man who was trying to save them. According to Drury, Whitman had become increasingly convinced that the whites would not only displace the Indians but would wipe them out. This genuinely bothered him. He was caught between two worlds: Indians began suspecting the falsity of his position, and "rascally half-breeds" spread false rumors about his supposedly inimical intentions. The straw that broke the camel's back was a virulent outbreak of measles and dysentery brought to Native Americans by the immigrants of 1847.[45]

Attempting to restore Whitman's reputation, Nard Jones (whom we discuss in Chapter 7) tried to paint a more balanced picture, sketching Whitman's naiveté—the feeling that the Cayuse would never betray him and that the threatening faction which would ultimately kill him was not really to be feared. Diversionary strains were added by the presence of Père Blanchet and the fear of Catholicism. There was also the arrival of a sinister half-breed Joe Lewis (Indian and French-Canadian). There were too many guests at the mission; Narcissa was overworked and exhausted. Measles were rampant, while the Reverend Spalding was engaging in heated arguments with Blanchet over transubstantiation—"changing the biscuit into God," as Spalding derisively put it. People whispered that Joe Lewis was spreading tales of Indians poisoned at Whitman's hands, but Whitman ignored the warnings. Finally on his last ride out to the sick, Whitman began to be philosophical about death, and almost resigned, according to third-hand sources. When Joe Lewis and the Cayuse—Tilaukait, Tomakas, Tamsucky—swept in for the kill, November 29, 1847, Whitman was not so lost in thought as to put up no resistance; but it was too late. And so he and his wife, along with twelve others, perished. The Reverend Brouillet came upon the scene the next day and beheld "bodies lying here and there, covered with blood and bearing the marks of the most atrocious cruelty—some pierced with balls, others more or less gashed by the hatchet.... Three others had their skulls crushed...."[46]

Jones, not to mention Drury, was undoubtedly exaggerating Whitman's positive character traits, though earlier revisions were also unduly harsh. Whitman surely knew that tribal medicine required success, and more success, and that inability to cure could mean the loss of life. He could be alternately obstinate or even harsh—particularly with petty Indian thieves—or too tolerant and meek. Nor can we praise unreservedly his religious stance, for it was fueled by an unreasoning sense of righteousness and by a militant anti–Catholicism that created much dissension. Whitman and his associates strike us as too certain of having the right God on their side. They saw the Presbyterian gospel as not only right, but as the one thing that could prevent Indian extinction at the hands of a superior race, or from the equally sad end of falling under the "Romish influence."[47] Yet with all their human foibles and failings, these men were not philistines, and it is anachronistic to condemn historical figures for *either* the idealism or ignorance of their time.

One may conclude that though Whitman did not save Oregon for the United States, he played a major role in encouraging many Americans to come out in 1843, and in convincing Washington of the area's value. His death was undoubtedly a key stimulus for Oregon's incorporation into the Union in the late 1840s. Immediately after the massacre, Oregon's makeshift legislature chose a committee to petition Congress for territorial organization. The document stressed the need for protection, protection that could only be adequately afforded by the Federal Government. Joe Meek and nine associates carried the petition to Washington in 1848. It was the era of Manifest Destiny and of the Mexican War, and Meek was himself a cousin of President Polk. Graphic details of the Whitman massacre were presented, and by a close vote, Congress passed a bill in August 1848 setting up the Oregon Territory.

Like McLoughlin, Marcus Whitman's life lacked a sense of closure; he knew he had fallen short of his ideals even before the fatal blow fell—perhaps this is one reason he deliberately ignored the warning signs. His dreams were realized by others and not in the exclusively Christian manner he had envisioned. Among others, there is still a Whitman County and a Whitman College, and a Whitman National Forest in the Blue Mountains of eastern Oregon. There are highways and monuments named after him in the East. But some of this has surely constituted America's search for a usable past, and centennial observances were largely promoted by the Presbyterians. Drury claimed in 1937 that Whitman's Christian influence continued widely to inspire. Unfortunately, however, this inspiration was no longer available to the Cayuse.

Despite all this white activity, one is struck by the degree to which the lower Columbia region of the 1850s and '60s still remained an Indian society. The transition from the "Indianness" of McLoughlin's world to the thoroughly Americanized one of the next century was a slow one. A dialectical relationship between the two worlds is seen in the persistence of Chinook jargon in Oregon and Washington through the frontier period.[48] This jargon, originating as a linguistic bridge between white fur traders and Indians, consisted of perhaps 250 Chinook words, along with a roughly equal number of Nootkan, English, French, and other Indian words. Inflections and tenses were almost absent, and complex expressions required lengthy compounds. Although there has been scholarly discussion of the language's infidelity, one great authority on Northwest tongues found it an idiosyncratically useable way of communicating, pointing out, however, that the jargon employed in its lower Columbia homeland was superior to that spoken in the north and east.[49]

From the period of the earliest white contacts, use of the jargon was promoted by the diversity of Native American languages in the Northwest, and the limited number of speakers of any one, especially at the heart of the Indian trading zone on the lower Columbia. The jargon became widely accepted by whites between 1810 and 1845, because their small numbers and their own division into two language groups made the Indians slow to learn white languages; while whites had little motivation to learn any one Indian tongue. As a result, by 1870 there were perhaps one hundred thousand white and Indian speakers of jargon.[50]

For the period between 1840 and 1870 in the lower Willamette Valley, the "jargon" was essential for communication between American settlers and Indians. But the Indians decreased or melted into the white population so rapidly, and the whites increased so fast, that after 1870 it should quickly have gone out of use, except in rural areas east of the Cascade mountains. However, Chinook jargon remained a cult language of white Northwesterners, particularly the better off and more literate, into the twentieth century. This could be variously explained by regional pride, the desire to be different, and the argot's simplicity. Unfortunately, the latter also meshed with the average Northwesterner's opinion of the Indian as a simple child of nature, and therefore helped justify the community's disposition of his lands. But the influence of jargon went farther afield. Certain words such as *siwash* (Indian, from the French *sauvage*), *tyee* (chief), *muckamuck* (food), *cultus* (bad), *tillikum* (people), and *potlatch* (gift) came to be widely used in Western literature and are still employed in Northwestern writing about the nineteenth century.

If we confine ourselves to the nineteenth century, the curious fact remains that in the period when Native American culture was entering white tradition, Indians themselves became equated with disorder and disarray. This symbolism is easy to understand. According to Josephy, the combination of defeat and the sudden appearance of material goods caused many Indians east of the Cascades to fall quickly to the standards of the worst whites.

> The tribes were broken and powerless; the headmen and military leaders were weak, venal, and without authority; the Indians lacked cultural standards and self-respect. As village life and traditional traits disintegrated, many of the Indians turned from hunting, fishing, and root-gathering to hanging around white men and farms and settlements, begging, trading, and selling their labor. Liquor was plentiful, and a large number of Indians found an escape in alcohol from their unhappy existence.[51]

Josephy, it should be noted, was a sympathetic historian of the Nez Percé, again, perhaps the most highly regarded Indians of the Northwest.

If missionaries and newspapers of the frontier thundered against evil, there was surely much evil to denote among whites as well as Indians. We cannot treat the intellectual development of the Northwest without recalling the violence and dissolute ways of a large portion of the frontier population.

Although McLoughlin had generally favored the immigrants and travelers who came to him, he had written:

> Again, we had to guard against the designs of many desperate and reckless characters,—men acknowledging no law and feeling not the restraints of conscience, the outcasts of society who have sought a refuge in the wilds of Oregon. With their natural turpitude of disposition embittered by national hostility, such men would not shrink from the connivance of any crime; they were determined at all risks to intrude upon the Company's land claim and they made no secret of their plans if ejected by force.[52]

It is often pointed out that troubles with Indian groups were due to the depredations of the frontiersmen, particularly unattached miners who at times preyed on Indian women, and sometimes led expeditions of extermination. For example, in the 1850s, bands of white miners and drifters were largely responsible for the Rogue River War.[53] A similar lack of order was found by Guy Waring in the Okanogan country of Washington in the 1880s. The violence of whites was directed as much at one another as at Indians, but Waring found that convictions for crimes were almost impossible to obtain. To this New Englander, conditions seemed far better across the border in British Columbia.[54]

On the political and business level, the level of white behavior was not uniformly exemplary either. Certain equitable judges, and leaders such as Jesse Applegate, stand out in a field without too many obvious high points.[55] The political situation in Oregon and Washington was, however, better than in Idaho when in 1866 both the Governor and his Secretary of State there absconded with public funds.[56] On a lesser scale, petty self-seeking was widely charged against leaders in all sectors of the populace. More common was the leader too puffed up about himself, too much in a hurry to produce results. The poet William Stafford (see Chapter 8) reminded us of this Northwestern type when he wrote in one poem ("Deerslayer's Campfire Talk") about solipsistic windbags.

Something of an example was Washington's first territorial governor and Indian agent, Isaac Stevens. Although Stevens left a string of accomplishments in his few years in the region, he deliberately took on too many jobs, and his hasty, far-ranging treaties left a bitter heritage among Indians. The companion of Whitman, W. H. Gray—carpenter, missionary, historian, newspaperman, promoter—also wanted too much, talked too often, and was overly self-absorbed.[57]

Certainly no one figure inherited the wide-ranging power laid down by McLoughlin; but the man who perhaps came closest was Joseph Lane. Although the kind of ambitious politician for whom Oregon—an area just opening up—seemed made, Lane had a quality of permanence in this transitory age.

Lane emanated from a typical frontier background. Born in 1801, he had gone from North Carolina to Kentucky to Indiana. His background, his handsome looks, and his ambition would all be future points in his favor, but most important was his Mexican war record as General Joe Lane. When the war was over, Lane, along with Winfield Scott, Franklin Pierce, and Zachary Taylor, found himself nationally prominent. The Oregon fever and the Whitman massacre brought the Northwest into the national spotlight. Mountain man Joe Meek, Polk's personal agent, approached Lane in August 1848—would he like to be governor of the new territory of Oregon? According to Meek, Lane's answer and packing took only about fifteen minutes.

Lane's political image was then carefully manufactured, and he quite consciously took as his model "Old Hickory," Andrew Jackson. Contemporaries attest that he was quite successful at it; for example, the Raleigh (North Carolina) *Standard*, during Lane's later career, noted: "General Lane is nearer what our imagination has ever conceived General Jackson to have been than any man we ever have or ever expect to see. He is a tall, muscular, bony man of sixty, possessed of all the vigor of thirty...; very plain and very agreeable."[58] The same half-mythical characteristics that people assigned to Jackson were present in Lane. Elwood Evans, a kind of valedictorian of the Northwest, wrote the following epitaph for Lane, and again it reveals a good deal about Northwest values in the prenational era:

> He was a product of pioneer civilization. Nature had been more lavish to him in her bounties than had the schools. He had gained great distinction in the military service of the country, yet simplicity of character, honesty and directness of purpose, sympathy with the people, were his great characteristics. He was a brave, unselfish patriot, whose chief, nay whose only desire was the welfare of his fellow citizens.[59]

Lane's wife, meanwhile, dipped her own candles, at least in her earlier married life; made her own soap; washed clothes; carded, spun, and dyed wool; salted pork; baked bread. Just as Narcissa Whitman civilized, or at least prettified, the doctor's fort, so women like Mrs. Lane carried on the civilizing function in the next period—the last era before the rise of standardized products like bottles and "store-bought" clothes made that function less necessary.[60]

General Lane not only symbolized simple and blunt authority, but also movement and the bustle of a young section. After narrowly failing to receive the Democratic presidential nomination for 1852, he devoted himself unabashedly to raising money for Oregon, giving it a necessary connection to the Eastern or federal money which played such a large role in the area's development. As James Hendrickson notes, "Lane was important because he was the best vote-getter in the territory and because—through his acquaintance with Presidents Pierce and Buchanan—he controlled patronage, the *elan vital* of territorial life."[61] To pay for the Rogue River War he got $200,000 from the Federal Government. He also obtained substantial raises for judges and secretaries of the Oregon territory while he was the area's delegate in Washington. He could get his own men into posts such as Indian Agent. Road money poured into Oregon at his bidding, while back home, through the "Salem Ring," he controlled local politics of the 1850s.

Before the *Oregonian*'s heyday, the Oregon city *Statesman* was almost Lane's house organ.[62] *The Statesman* issue of June 9, 1855, called Lane "emphatically a self-made man." His speeches were reprinted in the newspaper's columns, trumpeting the ideals of a young region. Like many of his generation, Lane saw Oregon as the legitimate object of a generous, Christianizing, Westernizing, American impulse. He thought Oregon possessed special qualities and that it could breed a new and special person, a second Crevecoeurian *homo Americanus*. When he was back in Indiana in 1851, he wrote: "The people [here], though as clever as any in the world, don't look as healthy as they do in Oregon; nor is the country like Oregon. I long to be there.... Oregon is my country, my home."[63] As its delegate to Congress, Lane asserted that Oregon could easily support five million people, and that it would only become increasingly prosperous.[64] Speaking at a banquet for the Jackson Democratic Association in Washington, D.C., he discussed Oregon in terms of Manifest Destiny, announcing:

> We are now upon the far west; we can go no further. Many would regret that the coast did not extend two thousand miles further, that our institutions might be extended over them. They will be extended to the islands, and ultimately, I trust, they will be extended over the whole world. Democracy is progressive, our republican institutions are progressive, and they must prevail, for they are adapted to the happiness of man.[65]

This optimistic Lane became Oregon's first senator in 1853 and continued to rake in patronage for his region. Some considered him the new Cincinnatus, and others saw him as the father of Oregon itself.

Indeed, along with another man, Lane gave a very stirring speech on the admission of Oregon into the Union—the reverse of "the Oregon desert" theme. Here Oregon becomes the beacon that beckons an entire nation. Ironically, of course, this position is quite different from today's Oregonian progressives who have been environmentally conscious:

> There for a time in that valley—that land of corn and wine—the tide of emigration stopped; and the narrow contractionists of this Government—the surly sentries on the outposts of our borders to keep the citizen from escaping to new and fresh fields of enterprise beyond—flattered themselves, and unctiously comforted their illiberal hearts with the belief and hope that our expansion and progress had reached its *ultima thule* on this continent.... The tide of progress obeys no human

voice, but swallows up every creature of the hour—every ephemeral mote in the political atmosphere that arrays itself in its pathway. The eternal fitness of things governs this as it does every other question of substantial national development.

"Westward the star of empire takes its way;" but *westward* now no longer. The orbit of this planet has been traversed in that direction. By its light the pioneer has been guided from ocean to ocean. Under its benign rays waste places have been made glad, and the wilderness has been caused to bloom and blossom as the rose.[66]

As Governor of Oregon, Lane continued to exhort the region forward in this same celebrationist manner. He was an indefatigable stumper who preferred riding out to meet the people to remaining in his office shuffling papers. His inaugural gubernatorial message has the same ring as much of V.L.O. Chittick's collection *Northwest Harvest* a century later—that a great region is *just* around the corner:

We can recognize in Oregon the material for her future greatness. A climate and soil extraordinarily productive eminently characterise it, the prolific growth of grain, vegetables, and grasses ... inexhaustible forests of the finest fir and cedar in the world, never-failing streams, which furnish water power of unlimited capacity, shows how lavishly nature has bestowed her blessings upon the favored land.[67]

After his term in office, Lane continued to take an active role in his beloved Northwest by fighting in its Indian wars. But an extra-regional development—the coming of America's Civil War—suddenly ended his political career. Having come from the South, Lane still felt some allegiance to that section, while yet loving the Union. It was an insoluble dilemma. Finally in 1860 he was enticed to run for vice-president on the Breckenridge Democratic ticket, although Oregon was already going Republican. Harvey Scott and *The Oregonian* (see next chapter) would vanquish the Democratic *Statesman* and the Salem Clique behind it, and Lane's services were no longer wanted.

He then spent the next twenty-seven years in retirement on a farm seven miles east of Roseburg, Oregon—with a commanding mountain view. In 1867 he became a Roman Catholic. In 1878 he moved to Roseburg proper, and two years later, at seventy-nine and in failing health, was persuaded by old cronies to run once again for office. So he stood for the state senate, and lost. In 1881, Lane died, largely neglected in the region which he had much impacted. As with Astor, Wyeth, Jason Lee, Whitman, and McLoughlin, the Northwest turned out to be an alluring mirage that had promised more than, in the end, it could provide. In this ultimate disappointment they may have been joined, as H. L. Davis was to assert a century later, by most of those pioneers who had also followed the sun out to Oregon. Finally, and not least, their sometimes martial ideals *also* wrought much disappointment and disarray among the region's Native American dispossessed!

CHAPTER 2

The Business and Moral Notables: Respectability, Refinement, Enlightenment

WE CONCENTRATE IN THIS CHAPTER on the importance of elites in the Northwest for a developing regional consciousness. Starting with John McLoughlin, he had certainly been a pragmatic businessman, for otherwise he couldn't have played the roles he did. But he differed from his superiors in the Company by coming to identify with the Columbia River area (and the entire Northwest) as *his* region. McLoughlin's business decisions were therefore tempered by a longer-term regional interest than was the case with those above him. Also important was the profound concern he had for his family and legacy: sense of region and sense of family in his case, closely intertwined. McLoughlin's deep feelings of responsibility, we argue here, distinguish the man of regional allegiance from the simple promoter.

McLoughlin was the precursor of a long line of solid, regional bourgeois and as such, should be honored for helping to pour the form. The Applegates perhaps come closer than any other family to exemplifying the "family farm respectability" which Dorothy Johansen considered a key differentiator between pioneer Oregon and pioneer California.[1] With his two brothers, Jesse Applegate came to Oregon from Kentucky by way of Missouri in the migration of 1843.[2] He summed up his experience as a leader of that expedition in "A Day with the Cow Column," a simple description that nonetheless caught the imagination of Oregonians. As a surveyor, Applegate surveyed McLoughlin's Oregon City, and as a trailblazer, went east again to develop a new wagon trail through southern Oregon that would avoid the hazards of the Columbia. Meanwhile, he and his brothers established a farm near Salem,

Oregon, but tiring of this, Jesse moved into new territory to build a mansion of classical splendor over the Umpqua River, not far from the retirement home of Joe Lane. A literate and well-read pioneer, Applegate, the "sage of Yoncalla," became a leader in political affairs, as he had been in family, travel, and economic life. But he was not a true "politician." Identified completely with the Willamette country, he also spoke out for the right of those north of the Columbia to their own territory.[3]

Notions of Pacific Northwest respectability generally went back to New England origins. Representative of these are the namesakes of Thomas Nelson Strong, whose *Cathlamet on the Columbia*, dealing largely with Indian neighbors, is one of the most attractive reminiscences of the period. Of Vermont and upstate New York background, William Strong brought his family to the small town of Cathlamet north of the Columbia River in 1849, upon his appointment as Associate Justice. (He was so impressed with the territorial Chief Justice Thomas Nelson, a man of outstanding reputation, that he named his son after him.) From the base of Cathlamet, Strong aided in the establishment of Washington Territory, though he later became a permanent Oregon resident and a highly esteemed one.[4] The Strong family long persisted in Oregon, retaining its interest in Native Americans down to the 1970s. William Duncan Strong, born in Portland in 1899, was to become a world-famous archaeologist at Columbia University.

Returning to the mid–nineteenth century, the Northwest's major developing area and its heart was undoubtedly the Willamette Valley—"the nursery of civilization" in the region, according to J. Orin Oliphant.[5] To this valley, religious societies, the custodians of frontier culture, brought the seeds of future educational harvests. As early as 1842, the Oregon Institute was created, becoming in 1853, Willamette University. Congregationalists founded Pacific University at Forest Grove in 1854, while Linfield College, under the Baptist aegis, followed in 1857 at McMinnville.[6]

Representative of urban respectability was the son of the president of the University of Vermont, the Rev. Sidney Marsh. Appointed in 1854 as first president of Pacific University, he remained in this position until his death in 1879 (sometimes with the added responsibility of the local Congregational church). The Reverend Marsh promoted with unflagging zeal both the ideals of the old Puritans and those of a liberal college in the Northwest. His struggle was a long, hard one. Since raising money in a young region seemed next to impossible, his job often required long trips to the East for additional funds. Though his purpose was to develop an institution of New England quality in the Northwest, arresting the yearly migration of the region's best minds to the East, Marsh remained dependent on the older section. He made no concessions to the practical-minded spirit of the public universities, but compromised, in the Western spirit, on the question of coeducation. Yet his struggle for educational excellence was a slow one, for by the time of his death, Pacific University had graduated only forty-nine persons;[7] and it never did achieve his goals.

The Willamette Valley also set standards on the Northwest frontier for another institution—the press. Churches and newspapers almost monopolized mid-century cultural life, and it is no accident that so many regional notables of the kind treated here were connected with one or the other avenue of advancement. The elites struggled to educate settlers, but also furthered a democratic consciousness-raising that would imperil their *own* positions. As Kent Richards pointed out about one group, "ironically the same frontier conditions which provided the Methodists with the opportunity to attempt an ideal society also attracted the new settlers who proved their undoing."[8]

Newspapers in the 1850s were moral organs that tried to make citizens more useful and productive. The first authentic one in the Northwest, the Oregon City *Spectator*, was founded in 1846, ostensibly "in order to promote science, temperance, morality, and general intelligence."[9] As was typically the case in frontier areas, newspapers celebrated regional distinctiveness, as novelists would do in the next century. Thus the *Spectator*, February 5, 1846, noted that the Northwest was "happily situated in a healthy and fertile part of the continent, with a salubrious climate, the soil yielding a rich reward to the industrious cultivator...." There was, at the same time, much admonition of settlers to live up to the area's great potential. As Joseph Lane had said several times, it was better to plant trees than to be seduced by the gold mania. According to *The Oregonian* of November 3, 1855, the area along the Columbia could become the "finest fruit-growing country in the world." But people would have to be sober and industrious to exploit adequately the area's fine possibilities. Already there were too many slackers in the region—so noted T. R. Dryer in a vehement editorial in *The Oregonian* of July 1, 1854:

> If the people of Oregon would put forth the same efforts and adopt the same methods to become a producing people that they do in the eastern states, we should hear no more complaint of "hard times" except from the lips of *universal grumblers* [his italics].... There are too many speculators, gentlemen of leisure, and men who live by their wits among us ... the *anti-sweat society* [his italics]. We have entirely too many lawyers, squires, generals, colonels, majors and captains.... We have a large surplus of men skilled in the science of ten-pins, billiards and the sciences generally....[10]

The reader will notice here the theme of inferiority to the East, an often-repeated and persistent belief that people worked harder there than in the Northwest. William Strong's characterization of inhabitants of the area at mid-century was little different—Strong's Northwesterners were mainly honest, "not very fond of work," cared little about luxuries, and led very good lives.[11] A century later, the same view was bruited about in certain Northwest university circles—sentiments that Bernard Malamud, among others, placed in the mouth of a faculty wife in *A New Life*, as noted in our introduction. It is interesting to see the viewpoint present so early in Northwest history.

The key figures of the press in the nineteenth century were Harvey Scott, editor of *The Oregonian* for forty years, Henry Pittock, who both preceded and outlasted him as publisher of that paper, and Scott's sister, Abigail Scott Duniway, founder and then for sixteen years, editor of the suffragette journal, *The New Northwest*. To those key figures—along with extended swaths on Simeon Gannett Reed, quintessential business notable, and Thomas Lamb Eliot, a moral notable—we turn in the rest of this chapter.

Harvey Scott was born February 1, 1838, near Peoria, Illinois, in pioneer country and of pioneer people who had come on a well-traveled route from North Carolina to Kentucky to the Midwest. In 1852, at age fourteen, Scott migrated to Oregon with his family, finally ending up on land subsequently called Scott's Prairie near present-day Shelton, Washington. Scott fought in the Indian war of 1855–56, then became a laborer in the Willamette Valley, prior to entering Pacific University under its new president, Sidney Marsh. While a student, he also had to cut wood, drive teams, and teach school. After receiving the first B.A. granted by Pacific University, Scott began contributing to *The Oregonian* (with his initial editorial on Abraham Lincoln's assassination). He was admitted to the bar in September 1865 and soon became *The Oregonian's* editor.[12]

Scott saw himself at a unique time and place in history. He knew that the pioneer age was in his own lifetime drawing to a close and that this had been an unusual epic in human history, "the last effort," as he put it, "of that profound impulse which, from a time far preceding the dawn of history, has pushed the race, to which we belong, to discovery and occupation of Western lands."[13] Implicitly, Scott identified with a passing Oregon, for in his own view, he *was* Oregon. Yet he was also wracked by the ambivalence of those whose regions found themselves prey to rapid development, evincing nostalgia for the old, but a genuine optimism vis-à-vis the new.

Compete, compete, compete! So Scott might have subtitled his many urgent, hortatory articles on Oregon. Why *not* have better railway connections? Why *not* attain Washington's level of population and material well-being? Why *not* become literarily sophisticated? On the possibilities given to his region, Scott echoed the optimism of the *Spectator* editor. A speech he gave late in his career at the Portland Commercial Club (1900) ended in punctuated bursts:

Note our situation on the Pacific seaboard. Note also that the changes of recent times have virtually made the Pacific an American sea. The active theatre of the world's new effort is now in Asia and Western America. The two hemispheres, heretofore in communication only across the Atlantic, are now rapidly developing an intercourse over the Pacific. Many steamships, and an increasing number, on regular lines, now sail between our Pacific ports and the ports of the Orient ... a large and continually growing fleet.... We are in touch, then, with a movement that includes more than one-half the human race.... Where now are four millions of people there may be fifty million by the close of this century, with every kind of intellectual and moral development comparable with the material prosperity.[14]

Too many ironies suggest themselves for us to point them out here. But the ironies were there in Scott's own lifetime and must have existed in his own mind. The man who heard figurative bands of progressive people marching through Oregon and moving it toward modernity *also* wanted to hold onto that old pioneer flavor that had made the region unique. This was and remains a characteristically Northwestern dilemma.

In Scott's compendium, *History of Portland, Oregon*, he made a bold declaration of regional independence, asking why Portland could not become the hub of a great civilization.[15] Why should it play second fiddle to other centers of culture? True, "the Roman Empire without Rome would be like Hamlet without Hamlet. But America without New York City would still be America, lacking only some million and a half people."[16] Once this declaration of independence was made, Scott went on to stress the uniqueness of the Northwest's physical character and the perfect geographical position of Portland within that microcosm. Much like the nineteenth-century French, taught to believe their country was a perfect hexagon, Scott writes:

Now to focalize our view, if we draw a line from the Gulf of California to Mt. St. Elias in Alaska, by this chain of valleys and waterways, where do we find a cross line opening from the ocean to the Rocky Mountains, and allowing trade and travel to pass east and west as well as north and south? This cross line has been determined by the channel of flowing waters drawn from the Rocky Mountains across the Cascade and Coast Ranges to the Pacific—the Columbia River. A line of two thousand miles, a cross line of five hundred miles—these will ever be the thoroughfares of commerce for the commercial metropolis of the region. At the point of intersection of the two [,] this is the geographical position of Portland. Although on the banks of the Willamette, she is also, practically on the banks of the Columbia, her business portion constantly extending towards the imperial river. This, then is the most comprehensive description of Portland's geographical situation—at the crossroads of a natural depression from California to Alaska and of the pathway of the Columbia from the Rocky Mountains to the Pacific Ocean.

To define her position in more particular terms, she is located in latitude forty-five degrees and thirty minutes north; longitude one hundred and twenty-two degrees and twenty-seven minutes west on the left bank of the Willamette River, twelve miles below the Falls of that stream at Oregon City, and ten miles above

> its confluence with the Columbia. It is one hundred and ten miles from the city by the Willamette and Columbia Rivers to the debouchure of the latter stream into the Pacific. As for distance to other well known points, it is about seven hundred miles to San Francisco by water, six hundred by rail; to the Cascades of the Columbia it is sixty miles; to the Dalles, ninety miles; to Walla Walla, two hundred and forty-five miles; to Spokane Falls, three hundred and seventy; to Lewiston, three hundred and fifty; to Salt Lake City, nine hundred; to Helena, Montana, seven hundred and fifty; to Chicago....[17]

Scott is here both a loving regionalist *and* a universalist. He loves his province and defends it, yet wants the area to absorb all the amenities of Western civilization. To support his own idea of stern pioneer morality, he daily read the most timeless and placeless writer, William Shakespeare, drowning himself in what he considered the playwright's "oceanic" mind.

Scott, to be sure, was a rationalizer of the first order, and like anyone who uses received opinions to support his own, he did with Shakespeare what Shakespeare would surely never have permitted. A passage from *Richard III* was marshaled to prove the great moral force of modern newspaper publicity (1887); while Hamlet ("Lying, in Hamlet's Day and Now") provided a takeoff for criticism of prevaricating Washington politicians (1910). But Scott was also something of a scholar. In *The Oregonian* he reviewed and evaluated Shakespeare critics of his own day, as well as viewpoints as diverse as Arnold's, Swinburne's, or Coleridge's on the playwright. In fact, he had a brawny, unquestioning devotion to all masters, from Homer to Stendhal. As he put it in one *Oregonian* article, "No one expects another Isaiah or Shakespeare or Molière or Milton. Men may appear again whose power will astonish the world, but they will not be like those who have preceded."[18] This "Great Book" mentality was at once ingenuous and worthwhile, giving a useable cultural past to people in a region which seemed to lack one.

In a review of Scott's record, Lee Nash discussed the multiple impact of his literary influence on the region. Scott's editorials repeatedly told readers what to read and how to read it, and these same editorials were then assigned by grammarians in local schools as models of writing for their students. To Nash, four attitudes came through in Scott's criticism. There was his frontier braggadocio, the parading of scholarship by an amateur intellectual; and there was the fighter, the man of strong opinion, abjuring the present for the past. Third, there was his individualism—Shakespeare a key symbol to Scott and his readers of what *one* great person, dependent only upon his own abilities, might do. Finally, there was in Scott the love of region and a certain nineteenth-century boosterism. Incongruously, however, Scott gave little support to local attempts at literature. In part this attitude may have been justified, but one cannot help but feel that it was difficult for Scott to see in concrete cases what he praised in the abstract or disembodied.[19]

A stern Presbyterian background could lead either to self-doubt or, as in Scott's case, to a vigorous *assertion* of that self. For Scott, his position implied the absolute right to furnish moral guidance, and he was one whose ego reinforced the requirements of the position. His religiosity was bound up with reverence for education and with his own brand of Oregonian patriotism. On moral grounds, Scott was a constant critic of state normal and primary schools; he wanted education to accentuate the Oregon character, as he perceived it, and even more, to coincide with natural law. As he put it in one address: "And therefore the education of our race, in the highest sense, consists in and requires the bringing of the conduct of man as an individual, and of man in society, into harmony with the moral law of the universe."[20]

Scott had a belief (still strong through much of the twentieth century) that his region existed as a refuge from evil. As he wrote:

> The social and moral coordination which is so notable of Oregon life ... is a direct achievement of the pioneer spirit.... It is, too, the pioneer spirit that makes the fine social austerity which so pervades the moral atmosphere. It frowns upon a sensational and unclean press; it banishes gambling, even in its minor forms, from respectable circles; it knows not the lottery ticket; it ostracizes the trade in liquors and all who have to do with it. Of course, all this is provincial, that is undeniable; but a provincialism which has saved Oregon from public extravagance ... such a provincialism is a saving salt which any community may thank God for. Oregon has it, and it is to the pioneer spirit that Oregon owes it.[21]

The Oregonian became Scott's own moral trumpet; journalism, he contended, was an educational science, and morality was scientific in the highest sense of the term.[22] Any erroneous ideas of his readers he would root out single-handedly and with no holds barred! Doubtful Harvey Scott was not! But he was not the only Northwest notable of this kind.

As a monument to the Northwest bourgeoisie, Henry Pittock's mansion high on a bluff over Portland would be sufficient to place this figure as well in the regional pantheon. Founder of the *Oregonian*, then publisher and sometime combatant with Harvey Scott, Pittock had a career encompassing a broad spectrum of urban leadership in a developing region. Both he and Scott were pioneers, but the Pittock family had come from England;[23] both were literate, but Pittock was not so informal as Scott. Where Scott quoted Horace or *Paradise Lost* while drinking hard liquor, Pittock was always sober and correct. Scott was tall; Pittock short. Photographs of the two, placed side by side in a special issue of *The Oregonian*, February 4, 1911, show a serene Pittock beside a feisty, serious Scott, and more youthful photographs of the two reveal the same palpable difference.

Raised in Pittsburgh, Pittock had also come West (in 1852) to seek his fortune. As he put it, he arrived "barefoot and without a cent,"[24] but because of prior printing experience, received a job with *The Oregonian* in 1853. Extremely industrious, he worked his way quickly through foremanship and then partnership, and at the outset of the Civil War, became sole publisher of the newspaper, making it a morning daily. By 1875 he and Scott were the owners of what was already and continued to be the great newspaper of the Northwest; but quarrels with the dynamic Shakespeare scholar would mar their relationship. As Pittock noted laconically, "My association with Mr. Scott from 1877 to 1910 was close and uninterrupted, though I did not always find myself in full harmony with his attitude or policies on public questions."[25] But these were problems mostly of personality, for Pittock was generally in tune with Scott's political views. Together they supported the Union during the Civil War, fought Chinese deportations in the 1880s, and opposed William Jennings Bryan's populist campaigns for free silver in 1896.[26] Both were of the same pioneer-booster generation, and both were committed to defeating journalistic competitors (which they did successfully—their efforts helping to eliminate a half-dozen Oregon newspapers in the 1880s).

In common with many leading personalities of the region, Pittock's life was multidimensional. According to one edition of the *Dictionary of National Biography*, he helped found the Northwestern National Bank; became president of the Portland Trust Company of Oregon; was associated with various logging and lumbering operations; was a railroad builder; became principal owner of the Baldwin Sheep and Land Company in eastern Oregon; was an organizer of the Haskins Transportation Company that ran steamboats on the Columbia and Willamette Rivers, and of the Clearwater Irrigation Power and Boom Company at Lewiston, Idaho; was a builder of several paper plants, among the first in Oregon, in the 1860s; and organized the Columbia Paper Company, later to become part of the Crown Zellerbach Corporation. Pittock was also a Mason and a member of many other clubs and societies.

Outside of its Central Library, the Pittock Mansion is probably the best-known building in Portland. It took five years to build during the years 1909 to 1914. A celebrated San Francisco architect, avoiding crude ostentation, gave Pittock a home here of refined elegance—French Renaissance on the outside, central staircase inside in L'Opéra tradition, Jacobean oak-carved library, Turkish smoking room, Edwardian-style suites. Standing 1000 feet above the city, the red terra-cotta roof distinguished the mansion from all competitors. Nevertheless, by 1964 it was menaced with extinction, run-down, and up for sale to wreckers and subdividers. After a spirited public campaign, the mansion was thankfully saved by popular subscription and administered by the city under a Pittock Mansion Advisory Commission.[27]

Was Pittock the typical capitalist, topping off his life with stone? To some extent he was, but he also exemplified a multivalent kind of entrepreneurial energy found in the Northwest of the late nineteenth century. Was his professional versatility due in part to the region's retardation? Certainly Eastern business was already far more specialized and on the road toward conglomeration. But let us also reemphasize the peculiar position between pioneer and modern urban society which figures like Pittock and Scott occupied. That their talents and directions were so varied was partially due to a frontier heritage where do-it-yourselfness was a cardinal necessity. As Daniel Boorstin wrote of an earlier frontier:

> Where a rapid-flowing life informed a man of his tasks, he would be lost if he anchored himself to any fixed role. No prudent man dared to be too certain of exactly who he was or what he was about; everyone had to be prepared to become someone else. To be ready for such perilous transmigration was to become an American.[28]

Our focus on a developing Northwest civilization via its elites may perhaps now be out of fashion, if once facilitated by studies of Eugene Semple, Judge Thomas Burke, and other important figures (such as we treat here) in the nineteenth and early twentieth-century Northwest.[29] We now discuss at length, two *contrastive* (and unstudied) Northwest notables of the nineteenth and early twentieth centuries—Simeon Reed, business notable, and Thomas Lamb Eliot, moral notable. In part our meaning of the word "notable" is derived from studies of nineteenth-century French elites, particularly André Tudesq's groundbreaking *Les Grands Notables en France (1840–1849)*, and from Singer's own work on local French notables of a lower order than Tudesq's, but also important as providers of values and guidance at the grassroots.[30] The Pacific Northwest, of course, had its own specific conditions in the nineteenth century, being a new and frontier society, and the opportunities for mobility within growing institutions of civilization in the area were legion. There are so many typical examples whom we can only note hastily here; for example, George Law Curry, born in 1820 in Philadelphia, an apprentice printer in Boston at eleven, an immigrant (after reading adventure tales) on the Oregon Trail in 1846, then editor of the *Spectator* and after forced resignation, publisher of the rival *Free Press* in Oregon. By 1854 he was territorial governor—a full-fledged Oregonian notable. Another typical career rise was seen in Eugene Semple, from a more affluent family in Illinois, migrating West in 1863 and becoming, among other things, lawyer, journalist, amateur engineer, farmer, and land speculator, as well as territorial governor of Washington in the late 1880s.[31]

As for Simeon Gannett Reed and Thomas Lamb Eliot, they fared better than most at this game of Northwestern ascent. By the end of the nineteenth century, their names could already be counted among the most important in Oregon's young history. Yet their successes, as will be shown, both symbolized the close of an era and helped doom their own types to extinction. Commentators like Daniel Bell have wondered even whether the capitalist system that figures like Reed embodied would survive in our future; and as for moral norms such as the Reverend Eliot dispensed in his sermons, these have become increasingly uncertain in our own period. Both figures were extremely hardworking and found gratification in their work; but today the work ethic is of lower priority and America finds itself in the throes of a more hedonistic mindset. Both expended their energies in part for their family, but the family, too, is threatened as a sacred American institution. Both seized new opportunities and like earlier Northwest explorers, outdid their fathers; today opportunities for mobility in a regimented, fragile, competitive world are more restricted. But the main issue is the concept of a directing minority. Today the notions of deference and of calibration of statuses are under intense attack, and Tocqueville's predictions here now seem prophetic. But onward to these archetypal Northwest figures of that era....

Simeon Gannett Reed was born in East Albington (now Rockland), Massachusetts, April 23, 1830.[32] His schooling lasted until age fifteen, and he subsequently acquired experience in dry goods, shoe cutting, and the grain and flour trade. A wealthy marriage helped improve his condition, and in 1852 Reed went out as a merchant to California and thence to Oregon, where he would reside almost permanently after 1853. At first his business interests were in lumber and flour, which he shipped at great profit to San Francisco, and then he opened a general merchandise store at Rainier on the Cowlitz River, dealing in sundry items, mainly liquor. In 1855 he hired on with the Portland investment concern of W. S. Ladd and Company as a clerk, and by 1859 had become, in Algeresque fashion, a partner with the Ladd brothers in banking. Their main focus of investment was the burgeoning Columbia River steamer trade, and Reed rapidly attained vice-presidency of the firm that would control that trade and which included the Ladds on its board: the Oregon Steam and Navigation Company. From there Reed branched off into other transportation concerns, especially railways and "electric railways," becoming president of both the Oregon Central Railroad Company and the Electric Railways of the United States. He also purchased mines and invested in stocks and Portland real estate, at the same time divesting himself of certain concerns listed above when they turned sour. Reed also bought up some very large farms—one in the Willamette Valley, on which he raised imported sheep and cattle of top quality, extending for over 3,000 acres. He spent the latter part of his life on activities like race-horse breeding, took his wife on a grand tour of Europe, and began to enjoy the various accouterments of his station. Having moved to Pasadena, California, in 1892, he died there of a stroke in 1895.

The era during which Reed and other Northwest entrepreneurs like Pittock came into prominence was one of great transformation in America as a whole. It is tempting, of course, to describe every era as a kind of watershed, but the post–Civil War industrial boom seems indisputably crucial in American history. Railway expansion that linked up far-flung towns of the continent and brought homogenization came in a rapid burst of activity; in the eight years following the Civil War, 35,000 miles of new track were laid, and soon the nation's railroad map rather resembled a Jackson Pollock painting. The communications revolution also included telegraph, telephones (widespread by the 1880s), linotype, better ocean steamers, refrigerator railway cars, dependable and cheap postal service, and of course electricity.[33] A cluster of figures came to prominence in these enterprises, people who were Reed's contemporaries and, in some cases, model providers: Leland Stanford, Jay Cooke, Mark Hopkins, and Commodore Vanderbilt, among others.

But of course Reed did not start on steel, he started on water. And he did not start out in a metropolis, he began in the Portland area—the city itself containing no more than 1,000 people at the outset of the 1850s. And he represented a vigorous capitalist minority in Oregon, of New England stock, and differentiated from the larger run of farmers that was frequently midwestern or southern in origin.[34] We might indeed call this a rural capitalism, one that benefited from the need for supplies in the new gold-struck areas of eastern Washington, Oregon, and the Fraser River Valley, a kind of capitalism that stimulated other, complementary rural industries such as woodcutting (for steamers) and boatbuilding. Atypical in its independence from eastern financing, the Oregon Steam and Navigation Company—until sold in 1879—was all western-owned, apart from a brief period in the early 1870s under Jay Cooke's partial control. Still, the way the company came to monopolize the Columbia trade places it firmly within the Gilded Age. If the brilliant inheritor of "Drake's folly" charged "all that the traffic would bear," so the small-time Reeds emulated the Rockefellers—molasses that cost 70 cents a gallon in Portland traveled the Columbia by steamer (and then by portage) and retailed for $6.00 a gallon in Boise. Oregon Steam men bought up individual steam boats as rapaciously as Rockefeller did oil drillers, and despite great expenses (the *Shoshone* alone cost $100,000 to build), large profits were reaped, especially when completion of mechanical locks at Oregon City assured continuous Willamette Valley transportation to Portland.[35] These monopoly profits aroused the ire of the press and of groups like the Grangers in the Willamette Valley. Meanwhile, as early as 1866 Reed was lobbying for the company back in Washington, D.C., which in turn introduced him to railway interests and to wider possibilities for making money. Reed greatly admired these railway magnates—on the officers of the Union

Pacific he wrote to J. C. Ainsworth: "The fact is this Company... [is] a live institution and such men as Oakes Ames, T. C. Durant, Glidden and Williams... are getting *big* rich out of it."[36] For Reed the name of his work—and of the era itself—was expansion.

It would be distortion, however, to skip to the profit and omit the hard work involved. Reed's meticulous business letters, accounts, and private notebooks reveal the man behind the wealth. They are filled with figures, excerpts from technical journals, information on pipes, mines, compressed air processes, Henderson grass seed, average consumption of charcoal per ton, the cost of making pig iron, production of the Ashland blast furnaces, new elevators, machine grease, the hiring of stone masons, the quality of farm animals, and so on. It is clear that efficient money-making was the focus of his existence. Efficiency and precision characterize almost every page of his voluminous business correspondence. In 1884 Reed bought a passenger coach in excellent repair from Northern Pacific, noting that it cost $2,400 dollars, was forty-eight feet, eight inches long, and seated forty-eight people.[37] In a letter of the next year he sought a bull of the following description: "Horns not heavy, short legs and heavy body. Good behind the shoulders. Good back and loins and *excell* in hind quarters. For a Bull answering this description I am willing to pay a fair price, but not a fancy price."[38]

Reed was always on the lookout for new equipment and techniques, providing the cost factor was not prohibitive. In 1872, having read *The Handy Book of Husbandry*, he learned of steam plows and wondered whether they could be adapted to his farms. Immediately, he sent a letter to an English manufacturer asking the cost, weight, fuel requirements, and capabilities of the machine: how many men were needed to handle it, how much land it could plow in twelve hours, etc. An article in *Scientific American* of 1890 led him to the new Stevenson's Shaft Lighter, which he hoped could be installed in the elevator shaft of a five-storey building he owned. And when he hired a new employee, Reed was just as careful, always trying to get quality at a good price. (For example: "There is an Italian here named 'Canuto,' a stone Mason and one of the best men *I ever saw* to handle men but he has one or two jobs on hand and could not leave just now.")[39] Reed's balance sheets are neat, his notations to the point, and there are no frills in this day-to-day record, no sense of self-irony or play.

When ordering for private consumption Reed also sought out "the best." This applied to spring carriages, horses' harnesses, cigars, which he got from P. Pohalski, New York, and to his business suits. One of his letters to V. P. Despierres, New York, on the matter of suits, somewhat reminds one of a capitalist calling a bookstore for "a load of books" to fill his new library: Reed wanted a suit "of fashionable cut and material suitable for Fall and Winter wear"—period.[40] Pohalski sent Reed 2,000 "assorted" cigars as ordered, and added another 3,000, making "the *prices* as low as they are sold to the largest jobbers, hoping through you to introduce them in your section without trouble and expense."[41]

The contradictions here are obvious. Where Reed could make huge transportation concerns run so well and raise prize race horses and sheep, his private life and tastes invite our irony. Certainly his taste in art was classic nouveau riche. In his large house big statues abounded, and pictures of subjects like racehorses dwarfed the occasional small painting of worth he owned (such as a Titian). When Simeon and wife Amanda toured Europe they had a "courrier" guide them around in the required fashion, though Amanda did get to visit Paris *couturières*. And Simeon jotted down ribald jokes in his notebooks so he could shine for the boys, and also titles of songs (he would sing both at church and at parties).[42] Reed's other extracurricular activities included hunting, for which he procured the finest of guns and dogs, and of course his horses. He also loved children and with Amanda, would give parties and stereopticon slide shows for them.[43] His wife's nephew, Martin Winch, who became chief manager of his interests by the 1880s and who figured prominently in the business correspondence, was a surrogate son. So was his nephew Arthur, whom Reed supplied with money and advised along the lines of a Polonius. In a letter of 1883 Reed told Arthur not to bother his own father for money; Reed himself would pay for schooling, board, and clothes, and offer an allowance as well, provided Arthur remained sensible and worked at self-improvement. Demanding a detailed statement of Arthur's expenses, he concluded as follows: "I *do* hope Arthur you will try and improve your present opportunity, and above *all* choose suitable companions."[44] Reed implicitly offered himself here as a role model, as do many self-made successes; and in all his private notebooks there is little that shows him with his guard down.

Mainly, those notebooks are filled with business details—mundane, practical details. There is, however, an entry entitled "Data of early times in Oregon" that shows real feeling for his section, as well as for his own part played in its fortunes. And when a railroad was being discussed for the Willamette Valley in the late 1860s, Reed demonstrated a regional affiliation, hoping that the line here would profit Portland and Oregon, and *not* Californians.

If one can find in Reed a kind of business idealism and details of a certain human interest, his life was mostly concerned with profits, and in the unabashed manner one would expect of his age. To E. C. Darley in 1890 he wrote about Portland real estate: "It is hardly necessary for me to tell you that there is *big* money in this property if properly handled.... There are three

(3) propositions in connection with this property, either one of which is *first class* in itself, viz—a Real Estate proposition—a Water Power proposition—and third an Iron proposition."[45] To the railway mogul Henry Villard in the same year, on more financial possibilities in a growing Portland, Reed noted:

> The time is coming when they have got to do away with horses, and adopt either the cable system or the electric system, as it strikes me. The former is too expensive, and if the latter is adopted in this city, then it seems to me that the water power of the Oregon Iron and Steel Co., at Oswego is almost a key to the situation. If you could send some one out here upon whose judgement you could rely, to act quietly in these matters, without being known, I think you could bring matters about that would be satisfactory, and afford you a large margin of profit for future operations.[46]

Along with this naked profit motive, one detects here the economic influence on politics that so aroused Northwest progressive theorists like J. Allen Smith and Vernon Parrington (see chapters 4 and 5), as well as political reformers of the La Follette stamp. Reed went from steamer monopolist to railway monopolist when he joined the board of the Northern Pacific in the early, scandal-ridden 1870s. He had joined thereby a concern that would become a monster controller of timberlands and of mines, and W. S. King, in a letter to Reed, also stressed the political possibilities. As he put it, "the almost supreme control of the great Enterprise ... properly Manipulated will Enable you to dictate the politics of your North West."[47] A year later Reed's brother Edward made a veiled criticism of Reed's activities, saying that when he read of the Credit Mobile scandal he was glad *he* didn't belong to the Republican party.[48] On trips back East Reed met important politicians, among them the pro-railway expansion Congressman Thaddeus Stevens, and at one point ate lunch with President Grant. To promote a certain candidate for an Idaho judgeship, Reed said (in a letter of 1891) that he had talked to several senators.[49] There were many other letters to government officials about land and river privileges and appropriations. Reed was involved in failing companies, mining baths, political squabbles with stockholders (one of whom tried to blackmail him), the granting of monopolies (as to Villard in Portland), stringent rent collection (though his nephew called him one of Portland's fairest landlords), and so on.[50] He thus formed part of that plutocratic contingent that furnished ample grist for the mills of the Age of Reform, itself just beginning to boom when he died in 1895.

Reed's very will typifies the age. Leaving an unspecified portion of his estate for the enhancement of Portland, the Northwest notable Reed, like Rockefeller and Carnegie, if on a smaller scale, was using his money in an acceptable way—for stewardship and improvement of civilization. As he put it, his object was "the cultivation, illustration or development of the fine arts in the city of Portland, or to some other suitable purpose, which shall be of permanent value and contribute to the beauty of the city and to the intelligence, prosperity and happiness of the inhabitants."[51] He had already been persuaded by the minister of the church where he prayed to give money to an Old Ladies' Home and to a Boys' and Girls' Aid Society. That minister then prevailed on Amanda Reed to leave some of Reed's money for what would become a Northwest institution of higher liberal arts education intended mainly for intelligent offspring of the region's middle class: Reed College. After Amanda's death in 1904, Martin Winch, a trustee of her will, toured technological and trade institutions of the country for possible models, then called in a distinguished educator, Wallace Buttrick, as a consultant. Buttrick's opinion was that what Portland and the Northwest needed was a small liberal arts college, and that was the college which duly opened its doors September 18, 1911. Its guiding intelligence and president of the trustees was the minister who had procured the Reed money—a man whom Rabbi Jonah Wise would call "the most valuable citizen Oregon has ever had," Thomas Lamb Eliot.[52]

Like Reed and much of the Portland elite of his time, Eliot was a New Englander by origins. He hailed from a very long and distinguished family line, which also produced his famous nephew, the poet T. S. Eliot. Thomas Lamb could trace himself back to the original Puritans and to an English family that included, among others, the martyr for civil liberties who had died in the Tower of London under Charles I, Sir John Eliot. Thomas' father was the Rev. William Greenleaf Eliot, founder of the first Unitarian church west of the Mississippi and almost sole founder of Washington University, both in St. Louis. Thomas was the eldest son and one of a minority of fourteen children who survived into adult life. Like so many he would be a sickly, yet long-lived person. A member of the first graduating class at Washington University (1862), a graduate of Harvard Divinity School (1865), and then an apprentice minister under the elder Eliot, Thomas left for Portland to found the Northwest's first Unitarian church in 1867. Thanks to the opportunity afforded by frontier fluidity he had broken with his father in a constructive manner. Newly married to Henrietta Mack, and finding himself in a town of 7,000 souls eager for institution-building, he was equipped to act in a region that offered much scope for it. Eliot's activities in the next thirty years included work with juvenile delinquents, Indians, foundlings, the insane, and criminals, as well as support for a galaxy of progressive causes of his time—a child labor bill, temperance, prison reform, equal suffrage, and educational expansion.

By organizing lecture series with featured speakers like William S. U'Ren (discussed in our Chapter 4), Eliot played a role in bringing the Australian ballot and a direct primary to Oregon. He also brought in lecturers on controversial subjects such as cremation. He was one of the founders of the Portland Arts Association and of the Oregon Humane Society, a director of the Portland Library Association, and the prime inspiration for the building and stocking of the Portland Public Library. He served on its Park Commission and was in close contact with the famous Olmsted brothers. Then there were his many sermons and lectures, his articles for *The Oregonian*, his missionary trips and visits to the poor, and his own family responsibilities—he and his wife had eight children. And not least, Reed College! The founding in Portland of "the Reed Institute," as Amanda's $2,000,000 will labeled it, was indeed Eliot's pet project, and the growth and functioning of the college was his main concern through the latter part of his life. The progression was significant: from 1867 to 1892 he had been a pastor, and then his focus in the Northwest shifted to education.

One can, in fact, place Eliot within an intermediary generation that began renouncing religious dogma and espoused liberalism, yet still held onto high moralizing standards. No modern liberal would express, as Eliot did, a faith in the Indian's "capacity for enlightened, useful citizenship," nor say that "The final object is to make the Indian an American citizen, merging him into the mass."[53] More symptomatic of Eliot's "intermediary" tenor of thought was his view of education—at once progressive and deeply moral. As he wrote, "No greater mistake can be made than that of supposing that non-religious institutions are therefore irreligious. The atmosphere of schools, strictly secular, can be charged with the highest morality."[54] To be liberal-secular on one hand and religiously moral on the other was a configuration only a man of Eliot's time in the Pacific Northwest could achieve. That time is no longer with us.

In the setting up of what John Scheck referred to as "pattern states" out West, education was obviously a prime instrument of cultural formation. But Thomas Eliot wanted not only to replicate but to move forward with the times. So he touted the methods of Pestalozzi in the Northwest during the 1870s, sponsored phonetic and musical instruction, and became a fierce admirer and partisan of John Dewey in the early 1900s. Education would civilize, it would socialize, as we now say; but it would also find new progressive answers to human problems while remaining within an ethical rubric.

Eliot's own classical education, harmonizing with religious training, also constituted a claim to Northwest moral leadership in an era before such credentials became less necessary. His sermons, some of which were reprinted in *The Oregonian*, are full of quotations from his favorites like Homer or Cervantes, the latter's Don Quixote a character with whom Eliot identified. On trips away from home he carried around Homer, once exulting, "I am reading my *Odyssey* and it never seemed finer, it is full of the sea itself."[55] And of the *Iliad* on another occasion: "That is the greatest book ever written."[56] This love of great books suggests a relationship to the classics very different from that which prevailed among many nineteenth-century orators, lawyers, and politicians. Classics, for Eliot, were *not* simply one part of a conventional snobbery; rather, he enjoyed a genuine European culture, once again in the transitional period before this culture would become routinized among America's growing educated class. Eliot loved symphonies and could play piano. He could quote Trollope and Walter Scott, Ibsen and Zola. Plutarch was another favorite, and Shakespeare was as dear to him as he was to Harvey Scott.[57]

It is interesting to linger on this Northwesterner's reverential attitude toward books. A long, almost manic sermon Eliot wrote in June of 1895, called "A Plea for the Old Authors," is a defense of serious reading that can be read unironically today.[58] He says first that he had always loved old things since he was a boy. Reading classics, particularly on vacations in the country, was Eliot's attempt to "atone for the hours I have wasted within the city with the daily Morning Convulsion, or the Monthly Cataclysm—in vain attempts to keep up with the times." Contrasting Plutarch or the Bible with "whole libraries of ephemera," not to mention journalistic products, he wondered whether too much bad would drive out the good; "whether we are not breeding a whole race of mental dyspeptics and imbeciles, upon the prodigious indiscriminate diet of written words—a surfeit in quantity and quality of mental food." Eliot goes on, bursting with energy and riddling his prose with Dreiser-like dashes, to deplore

> the congested imaginations, the crowded consciences—of this reading herd. This means more than mischief. It is disease—It means intellectual putrefaction or dry rot. Does it not augur for our children the loss of mental fibre, the lapse of healthy imagination,—the access of morbid feeling—the total inability to think ... distaste for the healthy thoughts and emotions of natural life?

So the old books get supplanted by more accessible diversions, and minds themselves become "like the newspapers—a hash—a kaleidoscope—a sewer." Himself? Eliot stayed back with his classical authors, rereading them carefully and considering them part of the family.[59] From this standpoint, he was truly educated, and this was a part of his very real notability in Oregon.

So, more obviously, was his physical image. Handsome and noble-looking, his mien connoted ethical direction: he had a fine, chiseled face, cropped white hair escaping in curls, a beard, a sturdy build, and naturally, the august clothes of his station. Due to overwork Eliot was a victim of endemic ill health, but the serene look of self-mastery never deserted him. One of the oratorical delights of the region, he thoroughly captivated his auditors, whether urban or rural.

Eliot's sermons were not usually so frenzied as "A Plea for the Old Authors," cited above; more typical and orthodox is "To the Worship of God," delivered in San Francisco and Portland. He did, however, speak on subjects like "Modoc Murder Victims" (first given April 1873) and on women's rights (first delivered in October 1871). The latter sermon, as befitted a friend of Abigail Scott Duniway, noted "nothing extraordinary in the request of individual women to be physicians, professors, ministers or lawyers. It seems to me only the legitimate widening of the circle." And in one of those statements that unknowingly undermined the patriarchal ground upon which the Eliots themselves stood, he added, "We owe it to our daughters to make them independent of the necessity of marriage."[60]

Eliot's relations with his own wife were rather romantic for the time, as one discovers from their letters to each other. He loved trips to Northwestern wild country, but from the top of Mary's Peak near Corvallis, he wrote an enthusiastic letter home, wishing his wife Henrietta were there beside him. Then his mind instinctively raced to his children: "Every trout stream I cross, I think of Willy, every good fat cow, I think of Mick and Don. Every new flower, of Nelly 'your little flower wild,' every lamb, of Grace, and every chipmunk of little Etta. The doves and quail with their broods—big Etta!"[61] To "big Etta" (sometimes referred to as "my darling wife") he also confessed his depression when he visited the less fortunate or diseased, writing, for example, from a hospital near Olympia in August of 1883: "I am so overcast by their condition, at times, that words seem a mockery."[62] And whenever Henrietta herself felt ill he seems to have been very kind toward her. But he was protective economically as well. In a letter of 1887 he mentions holding onto some viewfront property that would increase in value, hoping "some day, maybe, our ship will come in, with a moderate load, against our old age."[63] (He would unload it at considerable profit in 1906.) From the other side Henrietta invariably wrote to "My own dear Tom."[64]

Eliot, like Simeon Reed, remained an indefatigable worker. He rose early each day of the week and often worked late at night. When he visited different areas of the Northwest he would routinely ride horseback thirty-five miles a day. His hiking trips were no flat two-milers, but often uncharted and difficult climbs in the Cascade glaciers, one of which was named for him. He also loved to fish in the Hood River. These vigorous outdoor trips were a response to a workload that took him several times to the brink of a breakdown. His conscience seems to have been a constant self-prodder, as even his daily prayers suggest: "Dear God, help me to be thoughtful, and helpful, and unselfish;" but it did not prevent him from acting efficiently nor from noticing the trees amidst life's forest.[65] On board ship to Japan in 1903 he wrote some of his highest letters to Henrietta: "A splendid breeze, blue sky and indigo sea with white caps. It is inexpressibly exhilarating to me."[66] Each morning he took a salt bath on board, then lit into a hearty breakfast where he met with great interest travelers from Boston, Philadelphia, San Francisco. A stern moralist, a crusading teetotaler, a sponsor of antitobacco legislation, a disciplined, over-conscientious man, Eliot still found ways to channel his exuberance in a human way.

Predictably, he could not delegate that pitch of civilizing impulse to his successors. Of his three sons the eldest, William Greenleaf, took over at the Portland Church in 1906 after three other pastorates; Samuel, one of the first Rhodes scholars, went to Pittsburgh to work with the poor; and Thomas became a professor of sociology at Northwestern University. The daughters all married, and one of them, Dorothea Dix, became the spouse of a Unitarian churchman Earl Morse Wilbur, who was Eliot's first biographer. Eliot would also have many grandchildren, although four died between 1919 and 1934, among them a Thomas Greenleaf Eliot and a Thomas Eliot Wilbur.

Here then are portraits of the quintessential business notable and moral notable of the nineteenth and early twentieth-century Pacific Northwest. Well before Eliot's death in 1936, the advent of mass media had spelled the demise and devaluation of such notables. They had helped build up a regional civilization, but that civilization would no longer need them so badly. No individual could quite measure up to the collective sources of power in a more modern time, or at least not in the same way. The great "intermediary era" was supplanted by an era of abundant expertise. Many voices came to resound in the academy and many in the media and churches; but increasingly, these voices have become isolated from one another.

The academy, however, was the point of confluence between the two notables discussed, for Reed College resulted from their combination of business and intellectual-spiritual proclivities. This was to be the ideal regional college—an Oberlin or Amherst of the Pacific Northwest. Its first president, William Foster, a Keynesian economist before his time, wanted liberal education at Reed "to meet new situations, analyze them, discover the issues involved, and develop new solutions in new crises."[67] Students were asked "to share in a high adventure"—to participate in the government of the university, live in the same dormitories as teachers, share the same activities. When Dorothy Johansen wrote a play on Simeon Reed for students in 1937, the romantic ideal belonged to the Swing era, but the optimism about education still reflected the tail end of the American Enlightenment and a certain sense of tradition.[68] A more contemporary scene at Reed is another matter. Reed and Eliot long appeared on the masthead of the college newspaper, there was still pride in learning, and fine work being done; but at Reed, as elsewhere, few in our time believe the contents of the library stacks will significantly help to create a better world.

Eliot and Reed had helped build their section, enjoyed working in the area, and were definitely Northwestern; but to call them regionalists in the modern sense would be an anachronistic distortion. Regionalism later became a pulling away process—whether one studies Brittany, Wales, or Tom McCall's Northwest; but these nineteenth-century Oregon notables were expanding, forming, amalgamating. The contemporary regional impulse—which deserves more critical definition than it has gotten—does not seem to be part of that outlook.

Moving finally to a last kind of Northwest notable, we have Harvey Scott's sister, Abigail Scott Duniway, suffragist and modern woman before her time, and typical of a puritanical, serious elite of women that arose there in the late nineteenth century to preach its own brand of ideals. Her life and work therefore deserve serious consideration in this study.

Scott Duniway was well prepared for her vocation and orientation by a deeply pietist family that had already been involved in a variety of reform movements (prohibitionist, anti-slavery, pro–Indian) *before* coming to Oregon from Illinois. Abigail's marriage at eighteen purposely left out the word "obey" from the ceremony, and she also pointedly refused to take up land in her name, so that she might avoid the implications of having been a "land bride."[69]

A woman who could write in the nineteenth century that "I enjoy a controversy with an enemy [,] I like to puncture his pet prejudices and play havoc with his hoary sophistries"[70] was not of the ordinary sort. Abigail shared brother Harvey's pioneer experience, but that is hardly sufficient explanation for her tough-mindedness and iconoclasm. A more important environmental stimulus was the settlement around Silverton, Oregon, where she and her husband owned a farm in the 1850s. There, the settlers were independent and questioning, critical of the Methodists of Salem, and of the Baptists of the McMinnville area, along with the Santiam high country. Husband Benjamin would never restrain his wife from expressing her views, and yet she found time enough for five children and for farm work. When her husband was forced to sell his farm, Abigail decided to open an elementary school in the Willamette Valley, choosing Albany for its site, which was, by the close of the Civil War, Oregon's third largest town. Next she opened a millinery business, where she learned through contact with a wide variety of women about the inequality that they seemed to suffer in that era. In the postwar civil rights fervor, she now became caught up in the women's movement to which she truly devoted the rest of her life.[71]

In 1871 Duniway founded *The New Northwest*, and published it successfully as a news, reform, and literary weekly concentrating on women's rights, until she sold it in 1887, when family commitments forced a move to Idaho. For a woman to start a newspaper devoted to women's rights seemed unusual even to the most advanced minds of the region. Abigail herself remembered receiving a valentine in these years, depicting a henpecked husband trembling before a broom-carrying harridan of a wife. The poem accompanying the valentine brought tears to her eyes, including these lines:

> Fiend, devil's imp, or what you will
> You surely your poor man will kill....[72]

Behind Abigail's drive for women's rights was also a deep sense of religiosity, and in the women's movement more generally there was then an important religious element. It was thus no accident that ministers composed a formidable contingent among her earliest supporters. There was the Rev. Isaac Dillon, editor of the *Pacific Christian Advocate*; the Rev. J. H. D. Henderson in Eugene, "at whose home I was entertained in the early 70's, when few women besides his faithful wife had openly dared to espouse my mission"; one Reverend Spencer, a Methodist Episcopalian; the Rev. G. H. Greer, a Unitarian; and a group of Congregationalist ministers from Portland who were also helpful to the movement.[73] Abigail's paper campaigned against perceived evil in all its forms—court rings, prostitution, and the refusal of Pacific University to admit an illegitimate child. It would not publish news of sexual misdeeds and never allowed a woman to be defamed without equal defamation of the man. One of its first causes was championing the abandoned Minnie Myrtle (by the poet Joaquin Miller), which we discuss in our next chapter.[74] *The New Northwest* also campaigned for a wide variety of the new movements of its day.

The general goal of women's liberation in Abigail's time was to use equality to reform society as had not occurred, they felt, in terms of the real interests of women. This accounts for the important link of women's suffrage with prohibition, one Abigail ardently promoted. The women's revolution was definitely middle class, but also what one might call a puritanical counterculture of the era.

In the 1870s, women's suffrage associations sprang up in many places, thanks to Duniway's work. One opened in Portland, one in Seattle, another in Olympia. Going from lecture to lecture, Abigail barnstormed in even the smallest Willamette Valley towns, challenging recalcitrant men to debate, including one lawyer who raised the specter of "women deserting their homes for lawyers' offices and judges' seats, leaving the deserted men to quiet the babies, as best they could, with rubber substitutes."[75] According to her account, Abigail verbally eviscerated the lawyer, and for the next forty years of his life "he ... never entered a hall or church where a woman was to be the speaker, and he considers debates on the 'Women Question' nothing else but 'vanity and vexation of spirit.'"[76] Meanwhile, newspapers like *The Oregonian* featured columns, usually by people of the cloth (the region's literati), supporting Abigail's cause. And Abigail herself wrote a weekly column in *The New Northwest*. Around her journal she gathered her sister, then her three eldest sons. Suffrage societies grew as though fertilized directly by this journalistic humus, and Abigail would undertake long railway trips to address even a dozen members of the most far-flung groups. By the 1880s this work was conjoined with that of the newly-founded Women's Christian Temperance Union.

Finally in 1883 the Washington Territorial legislature passed a women's suffrage bill (only to be revoked four years later). Henceforth, reform legislation centered on Oregon, but these resolutions also failed as the century drew to a close. Besides a lack of money, Abigail flatly blamed the alliance with prohibitionists, realizing too late that she had been mistaken in throwing in her lot with the WCTU.[77] Among other things, that alliance forced those against prohibition, including the liquor interests, to oppose women's suffrage.

In 1905 Duniway published an historical work to celebrate the (passed) pioneer epic: *From the West to the West: Across the Plains to Oregon*, a sequel to her much earlier effort, *Captain Gray's Company or Crossing the Plains and Living in Oregon*. Now old, she looked back with nostalgia both to that earlier time and earlier book. She saw *West to West* as a capping effort; she had risen from being "an illiterate, inexperienced settler, a busy, overworked child-mother and housewife ..."[78] and had grown with the century.

Abigail was better known as a poet than as a novelist, and especially for a book-length epic, *David and Anna Matson* (1870). Just as Harvey Scott felt that he and his generation could never equal Shakespeare, so Duniway begins with this apology:

> Presumptuous dreamer, vain am I,
> To dare attempt Parnassus' heights,
> My Pegasus untrained and shy,
> My Muse unnerved to lofty flights.[79]

She also apologized to Lord Tennyson, fearing "great Clio's classic ire."[80] Was this hero-worship merely decorous, or did it have actual meaning? Like her brother Harvey, Abigail had a weakness for great models. Aside from Lincoln, whose speeches she loved, Horace Greeley of the *New York Tribune* was her earliest idol, for the *New York Tribune* had been her first link to the outside world. Greeley's abolitionist stance was the initial form of radical thought she emulated, but that idolatry ended abruptly in 1871 when she met Greeley and found he disliked the idea of women's suffrage! In *The New*

Northwest, June 30, 1871, she called him "low, coarse, unscrupulous, and bigoted."[81]

Ministers also inspired her and it cannot be too often stressed how important religion remained in Abigail's life. The poem *David and Anna Matson* was an essentially *religious* poem. The crucifixion, prayer books, numerous parsons, including a fire and brimstone deacon, and a final prayerlike ending testify to the overriding spiritual concern of the work. In fact it is hard to find a page of the epic that does not mention something to do with religion. This religiosity only exaggerated Abigail's sense of self-assurance.[82]

After her husband's early accident, she fairly dominated the family, although she complained throughout her life of ill health. She certainly dominated her sons for, from the first, they worked with her on the paper, and in 1879 both became partners. Her family was, however, sickly, and her husband was the nurse. After a beloved daughter died, and a son became ill in the '80s, Benjamin's desire to get back to farming was then revived. Abigail sold the paper and they all went off to an Idaho farm, and she did not fully return to the women's movement until after her husband Ben's death in 1896. There ensued predictable disappointment with her sons for being far less committed to her cause than she was.[83]

Abigail was a true radical for her period, while her celebrated brother Harvey was more "establishment"; so these siblings were inevitably slated to clash. The battle pitted Shakespeare's custodian against a lady who in old age came to be called "Oregon's Grand Old Woman." Abigail considered it patriotic to bring new cultural trends to the Northwest, most important of which (to her) was obviously the issue of female suffrage. Harvey, on the other hand, was never a supporter of women's voting rights, taking a jaundiced view of his sister's activity. He also disliked her flirtations with anti-rational and puritanical sects. Then, when the Populists rode into full view, Abigail again ran afoul of her brother: predictably, she was pro–Populist, pro-free silver, and hence, anti–Eastern money conspiracy. A reader of Donnelly's *Caesar's Column*, she introduced to the Northwest the fiery orator Mary Ellen Lease of Kansas (whose famous exhortation was "Raise less corn and more hell!"). Her brother meanwhile, simply wrote off populism as a short-lived phenomenon not worthy of consideration.

Harvey's forward-looking views were primarily business-oriented, while Abigail championed the new in a more completely ideological manner. Here were different ways of looking at the region, both containing all the while a palpable nostalgia for pioneer origins. Together, however, the Scotts, along with others of the types discussed in this chapter, helped create significant strands of a Pacific Northwest identity in the late nineteenth and early twentieth centuries.

CHAPTER 3

Literature of the Frontier

ALTHOUGH THERE WERE A surprising number of would-be authors in the Northwest in the nineteenth century, the era produced little writing that is remembered today. Many of the original settlers wrote diaries or reminiscences of their treks to Oregon or their initial years in the region.[1] The first work of fiction from the frontier period of settlement was *The Prairie Flower*, written en route to Oregon by Sidney W. Moss and published as the work of Emerson Bennett in 1849. It sold over 90,000 copies, inspiring the young with its romance, but was, in fact, tritely sentimental. In this respect it differed little from two other novels published by women in the 1850s. All featured the life of the crossing to Oregon and domestic bliss at its end.[2]

More often read locally was the newspaper writing we discussed in Chapter 2, including the virulent satire and invective that came to be known as characteristic of Oregon journalism. One of the most interesting journalists was William Adams, who brought his books and family to Yamhill in 1848, where he became a successful teacher and writer of newspaper barbs. His satiric verse play, published under the pen name "Breakspear,"[3] was based on the Portland scene of his day, arousing great interest and controversy. After various newspaper and political ventures, Adams went at age fifty-two to Philadelphia, and in a year picked up an M.D. and LL.D., and a gold medal for eminent attainments in medical science. He came back out West to begin a thriving medical practice, and in 1888 published his *History of Medicine and Surgery from the Earliest Times*, a well-reviewed book on the history of medical frauds.

It is remarkable that during this period there were almost no known songs in the region, a record that begins with the lack of voyageur ditties related to the Columbia Basin. Even the colleges of the Northwest seem to have been surprisingly late in developing any college song traditions.[4]

Although the writing of poetry or verse and its publication was much more common than we can imagine today, little of that cultural enterprise remains enduring either. One of the most notable poets was Sam Simpson, who worked on a variety of newspapers, but died in his forties as an alcoholic, never repeating the renown of an early poem he wrote while at Willamette University. The most widely quoted of Northwestern poems by succeeding generations, it begins:

From the Cascades' frozen gorges,
Leaping like a child at play,
Winding, widening through the valley
Bright Willamette glides away;
Onward ever,
Lovely River,
Softly calling to the sea,
Time, that scars us,
Maims and mars us,
Leaves no track or trench on thee.[5]

Another sometime poet, Samuel Clarke, who helped incorporate Portland in 1851, became a leading member of Portland's literate elite. He undertook a series of moves and ventures throughout the state, including editorships of the *Oregonian*, the Salem *Statesman*, and the *Willamette Farmer*, as well as promotion of several railroad enterprises. Clarke spent the last ten years of his long life as librarian of the General Land Office in Washington, D.C., and during this time had the opportunity to put into final form a two-volume history of Oregon. But at age forty-five, he had also hoped to transform himself into a poet. In 1872 he privately published *Sounds by the Western Sea* at Salem. *Harper's New Monthly* published one of the long poems, *Legend of the Cascades*, as a featured contribution in February 1874, but this was all that went beyond the Northwest. In these poems Clarke attempted to use the history and legends of his region as the basis for creating a significant body of Northwest mythology; however, it attained neither popular nor critical notice.[6]

Against the background of attempts such as those of Simpson and Clarke, three nineteenth-century writers did make significant contributions to a developing Northwest cultural tradition: Joaquin Miller, Frances Fuller Victor, and F. H. Balch. Consideration of their lives, writing, and interactions with the region becomes the starting point for appraisal of and a search for meaning in Northwest literature.

Before the 1920s, the outstanding literary figure to whom the Northwest had legitimate claim was Joaquin Miller.[7] Born Cincinnatus Hiner (or Heine)

Miller in 1837, Miller moved from Indiana to Oregon with his family in the early 1850s, settling on a McKenzie River ranch above Eugene. His father was a sometime school teacher, farmer, merchant, and laborer; his mother a woman of some pretensions, yet subject to recurring fits of mental illness. His father's Quaker ideals of pacifism and concern for the underdog, and of humans being essentially good, remained with Joaquin all his life, as did his model of instability—that jack-of-all-trades mentality so typical of frontier life.

Joaquin's life itself became a kaleidoscopic series of wanderings. As a teenager, he ran away to the gold mines of the Mount Shasta region, where he held a variety of jobs, taking part in several scrapes and Indian skirmishes. Gradually he became part of the life of Shasta Indians still struggling against the overpowering waves of American incursion. For about a year he inhabited an Indian village, and in Native American fashion, married and had a daughter, Cali-Shasta, and another child as well. This period of his life also involved an intermittent Robin Hood attitude toward authority, and when he permanently left the mountains to regain Oregon five years later, the law was breathing down Miller's neck. Yet Joaquin found time and leisure to attend a semester at a small college in Eugene and to teach in Vancouver, Washington. His education in Eugene was the only real higher education he would have.

Back in Eugene in 1860, Miller studied law, then went to eastern Oregon and Idaho with his brothers and cousins. In two years, mining and an express route gave him enough money to return to Eugene, buy a house for his parents, and like so many notables of the time, invest in a newspaper. In the next year and a half he edited the paper, and then a literary journal, the *Eugene City Review*. Both efforts were short-lived and both highly sympathetic to the Southern side in the Civil War, apparently due to Joaquin's penchant for supporting unpopular causes.[8] During this period he married a young poetess, "Minnie Myrtle" (real name Theresa Dyer), and after closing of the *Review*, the couple went to San Francisco to live as writers, for acceptance of their work had given them some encouragement. However, they soon found they couldn't live by writing and quickly returned to the Northwest. Joaquin went again to the boondocks of eastern Oregon, this time to a mining town, Canyon City, to set up a law practice and do some mining as well. But his first notable deed was to lead a posse against a Paiute band that had cut off supplies to the town. The Indians led the posse into the wilderness and nearly wiped it out near Harney Lake; however, the siege was then broken.

After visiting the Willamette Valley in 1864, Miller brought his wife, cattle, roses, and fruit seedlings back to Canyon City over the McKenzie Pass.

In 1866, he was elected judge of Canyon City's Grant County, acquiring a reputation for forcing people to listen to his poetry, and a better reputation for a series of vulgarly comic newspaper columns and letters.

After having two children, his wife left Joaquin, apparently disgruntled, and soon she had a third child. This separation became the cause célèbre of the Portland women's movement in that era, though Joaquin may have actually played the more honorable role, for in public recriminations that followed, he did not point out that the third child may not have been his; nor the fact that the court by his suggestion had taken the children away from Minnie, placing them in the care of his mother-in-law.

There was also a literary aftermath to this scandalous divorce. One of Joaquin's most effective and much-cited poems is a parting ode to Minnie, entitled "Myrrh," beginning:

Farewell! For here the ways at last
Divide—diverge, like delta'd Nile,
Which after desert dangers pass'd
Of many and many a thousand mile,
As constant as a column stone,
Seeks out the sea, divorced—alone.[9]

In answer, Minnie wrote the poem "Sacrifice Impetro," widely published in Oregon papers of the time, with sentimental lines such as:

Why did I dream of thee, darling,
    In the sweet wild hours of the night;
...
In this world where there's no one to love me,
    Making me long to die?

Followed farther on by a more public accusation:

What was my troth to him?
    A stepping stone at best
My face was proud and my smiles were sweet,
    And his gold could do the rest.[10]

Yet Minnie Myrtle did not fully accept the campaign against Miller of which she became a part. Although she gave public lectures in Oregon and California on his wrongdoings, she also said that if their divorce made possible his success, and helped him do well poetically, then it was all worth it. After their divorce and the unsuccessful remarriage of both to others, they would eventually have a tearful reunion in New York City in the early 1880s just before her sudden death.

At his own expense Miller brought out his first two books of poetry in 1868 and 1869 in Portland. In 1870 he went off to England, worshiping at the graves of Lord Byron and Robert Burns, and again was forced to publish poetry with his own funds. But this time it "hit," and with a new printing of work called *Songs of the Sierras*, his reputation was established overnight. Miller was now lionized by London literary society, including a rhapsodic Anthony Trollope. He was compared with figures like Robert Browning, and dubbed "the Byron of the Rockies." Spending his next years in London and Europe, where poetry on the Père Lachaise cemetery or Roman ruins reflects his peregrinations, then New York, Washington, D.C., and San Francisco, among other places, he continued writing not only more poetry, but also novels, an autobiography, and plays. His *The Danites in the Sierras* ran for years on the New York and London stages and made a small fortune. Returning, comfortably fixed, to San Francisco in 1887, Joaquin established an estate in the Oakland hills overlooking the bay, where he remained until his death in 1913. This life was broken up only by a summer as a reporter in the Yukon at the height of the gold fever, and a reporter's trip to China in order to cover the Boxer Rebellion.[11]

It is hard today to appreciate the work of Miller as literature; or to understand why, when a mature Hamlin Garland visited California, the one thing he wanted most was to see where the great Joaquin had lived, rhapsodizing, "the mountains, the streams, the pines were his."[12] Our problem, of course, is that much writing of even greater authors of his day now seems dated. At his best, Miller could certainly be memorable, as in the *Columbus* that was the favorite piece of at least two generations of school children, with its beat of:

> Behind him lay the grey Azores,
> Behind the Gates of Hercules;
> Before him not the ghost of shores;
> Before him only shoreless seas.[13]

Yet some of Miller's work was marked by a striking carelessness or sentimentality, as in:

> She turn'd to me and sudden cried,
> "Come, come!" and plunged into the tide.
> I plunged into the dimpled wave:
> I had no thought but 'twas my grave;
> But faith had never follower
> More true than I to follow her.[14]

What was attractive to his age was Miller's romantic spirit, breaking out at times into a mystical vision. His prose was sometimes even less disciplined than his poetry, yet when his later poems failed to satisfy England, Miller's *Unwritten History* of the Shasta Indians renewed his reputation. His reportage was also eagerly read, and his best plays were fast-paced and entertaining. Of course his reception in Britain in the 1870s was also due to his role as an exotic primitive there, getting him accepted in the literary world mostly for that reason.[15]

But Miller was a man of so many sides and aspects as almost to defy understanding. He was something of a literary amateur; however, unlike most of his contemporaries, he made money out of his writing, including even the poetry. And Miller deliberately created mystery and uncertainty about himself. His outlandish Mexican cowboy attire, in the persona of the Spanish-American bandit Joaquin Murietta, pasted onto his identification with a lost Indian tribe, set a style that caught the period's imagination, particularly for audiences far removed from the West. Miller also played an important role in forming a new way of treating Indians in literature, and may also have established the model of the naive American girl later struck off by Henry James in *Daisy Miller*.

Joaquin was the dauntless hero of his own existence and of most of his writings. Yet his continual distortions in what he insisted unnecessarily were "true-life accounts" suggest that his romantic dream existence became so much a part of him that he literally could not distinguish fact from fiction. Indeed, he may well have been putting himself on as much as he was putting on others!

Yet Miller could also be a practical man; he did fight in several battles and was well enough valued for his real actions in northern California to be chosen by his old friends in Canyon City to lead the aforementioned posse against the Paiutes. He was a man who in two years could build up considerable capital from nothing. (He was likely also one of those gold miners who could successfully hide his find and thereby finance the rest of his life.) Miller may have had impossible dreams, but basically, he made them come true.

The chaos and inconsistency in his character can be seen throughout his works, but especially in *Unwritten History: Life Among the Modocs*—a semi-fictional autobiography of his years with the Shastas. Miller penned his *Unwritten History* ostensibly to bring the plight of Native Americans to the public's attention; yet on several occasions, as seen, he himself participated in bloody attacks *against* Indians. In part, this was because he was also a Nietzschean hero, or worshipper of heroes, an admirer of strength applied for its own sake. But he also pointed out that courage and goodness did *not* usually go together. Finally, in his later years above San Francisco Bay, Miller settled down to campaign against the unnatural urban world of his day, and to develop on his own estate a model environment for the future. Appearing to lack self-criticism, he yet revised his works frequently and spent his last years shortening and improving the body of his poetry.

Although his romantic-literary focus came to be international, Miller's first writing *had* been closely associated with the Northwest and with the northern fringe of California. After Washington Irving, he was the first internationally-known writer to take this general region seriously for his subject matter. Miller's feelings were more than literary; he had a sense that to leave Oregon's Willamette Valley somehow constituted treason. In Athens (1870) we find him writing:

... My land of the sun,
Am I not true? have I not done
All things for thine, for thee alone,
...
And sung thy scenes, surpassing skies,
Till Europe lifted up her face
And marvelled at thy matchless grace,
...
Salute my mountains,—clouded Hood,
St. Helens in its sea of wood,—
Where sweeps the Oregon, and where
White storms are in the feathered fir.[16]

It is significant that *Oregon*, a long poem eulogizing the Willamette world of his family, was Miller's first important poem, his chief effort in the short history of the *Eugene City Review*. The four installments in which he presented the poem were part of an effort to make Oregon a center of poetry inspired by its magnificent scenery.[17]

Yet Miller also helped establish the Northwest pattern of people leaving the region after initial successes. Within months of *Oregon's* composition, Miller and his wife departed to make San Francisco their literary home, and after his later success in London in 1870, he spent little time back in the Northwest. His later poetry and prose had less and less to do with the region, and despite all his rewriting and reissuing of his early work, he never reprinted *Oregon*.

One reason was that the people of the Northwest and especially of Oregon had rejected him. Except in some very early reviews, he was not well accepted by what few literary critics there were in the state. After his divorce and fame, he became the center of controversy in Oregon, such as literary figures would be unlikely to excite today. Abigail Scott Duniway's *New Northwest* took up the cause of his former wife (even beyond her wishes),[18] blackening Joaquin's name; while literary circles further from home were less affected. Harvey Scott, who had first praised Miller, now harshly criticized him, both as a person and a writer.[19] Samuel Clarke, at once a leading Portland businessman and poet, also panned Miller's work when it first came out.[20] But Miller had to some extent brought all this on himself. He had never really liked Portland, lamenting its existence in the poem *Oregon*, and had outraged its Republican elite by his support of the Southern cause. To Portland he was but an outlander, a downstater, and how could he *dare* succeed when much of Portland's culture had failed to attract the world's attention? So it was with California's Bay Area that Miller eventually came to be identified by cultural commentators.[21]

After the passing of a Portland society that had spurned him, and of the kind of West he purported to describe, Oregon for a time began to take more posthumous notice of Miller.[22] Three twentieth-century poems praising him, quoted in a regional literary history of the 1930s, rank Miller as the leading poet produced by the Pacific Northwest (as did the author himself).[23] After World War II, Miller again fell out of fashion, but in the 1970s there was a rebirth of interest in him on the basis of his Indian-ecological primitivism expressed so well in *Unwritten History*. It was a period that valued individuality and the natural, and Miller, the misfit who hadn't been able to adapt to "normal" society, was suddenly rediscovered.[24]

By contrast, Frances Fuller Victor has always had an honored position in the Northwest intellectual tradition; for as one of the first to take the area's history seriously and to spend her life in its study, she did much to establish the regional image. At the same time, her prejudices and causes, in particular her contributions to the women's and temperance movements in the 1870s and '90s, also constitute an important aspect of the period's history.

Mrs. Victor, as she was called, was the author of several travel accounts on the Northwest; a history-biography of Joe Meek, the mountain man, called *River of the West* (1870), her first major work; many essays on historical matters like the Whitman ride or the beginning of steamboat traffic on the Columbia, especially in the *Oregon Historical Quarterly*; poems, novels, and short stories—some highly regarded; and a good part of six of the celebrated Bancroft histories of the West. Unfortunately, since her major historical work appeared under Bancroft's name, she received little credit or money from its national success, another in a long line of bittersweet Northwest careers of note treated here.

Frances Fuller was born into a respectable family in the extended New England of upstate New York on May 23, 1826.[25] She and her family moved to Erie, Pennsylvania, and then she attended a young ladies' seminary in Wooster, Ohio; but she was already bitten by the writing and publishing bug,

and never relinquished this propensity. With her sister, Metta, she became quite well known in Eastern literary circles, including in New York City, which seemed for a while congenial to her. (Frances had previously contracted a marriage to a man who wanted to try out frontier living with her in Nebraska, but it ended in the 1850s.) Re-embracing the life of a feted writer in New York, she then met Henry Clay Victor, a naval engineer, whom she married in May 1862. In 1863, Fuller Victor traveled with her husband to San Francisco, charmed en route by the stirring literary atmosphere of Mexico. In California she quickly came under the influence of a young, interesting American region, and of noted authors on San Francisco's "literary frontier," and ever quick to adapt, was soon a contributing member of that society. (Its influence, as seen, played a key role in the life of Joaquin Miller, too.)[26]

But partly due to his seaman's wanderlust, and to ill health, Victor's husband next moved up to a new job in Portland, Oregon, and there Frances arrived in late December 1864 to a climate of inveterate winter rains, and an area that seemed enticingly off the beaten track, even to Californians—not to mention Easterners.[27] Never one to live by the lamp, she stumped all over the region, scribbling as she went, and met notables like Samuel Clarke, Jesse Applegate, whom she liked despite his opposition to women's rights, and Elwood Evans, with whom she conceived the idea of writing about the area, including its history. Typically she brought along stirring books to help her feel the regional past, including parts of Lewis and Clark's journals, and Washington Irving's *Astoria*. By the late 1860s, Mrs. Victor had become a frequent interlocutor of the legendary Joe Meek, and in 1870 she published *The River of the West* based upon his life. The book made a splash both positive, and mainly among missionaries, negative—a portent of the "dark side" that would follow her enthusiastic embrace of the American West to the end of her days, making her a quite typical, if idiosyncratic part of our regional story.

Victor wrote a good deal through the 1870s, and in some ways this was her most interesting period, fueled initially by more travels around the Northwest, including British Columbia, and she produced a book drawn from those travels, *All Over Washington and Oregon*, which she later revised and tried to reissue. She was also at the same time writing many fascinating letters and stories.[28] But as the '70s wore on, she also became more interested in substantive issues, particularly the temperance problem, if allied to her more overarching interest in the subjugation of women. Victor's *The Women's War with Whiskey, or Crusading in Portland*[29] certainly shed light on the puritanism of the women's movement, the connection between suffragism and prohibition; and the connection, too, between certain middle-class female literati like Scott Duniway and Victor herself in the 1870s, an important transitional time in Northwest cultural history. Victor was quick to generalize, and always on the basis of a golden Arcadia, compared to the insidious, creeping corruption apparently rampant in the present. As she wrote:

> Ever since the close of our late civil war the morals of the country seemed to have been going from bad to worse with frightful impetus, until those who had the good of humanity at heart felt inclined to cry out, that our God was as deaf as the stone gods of the pagans. He was not deaf; He was only long-suffering. Men, it is true, had sinned past the power of redeeming their errors. They had consented to a corruption of public morals and private living that began at least to terrify themselves. In this emergency God breathed upon the hearts of women, and with one impulse and accord they thankfully accepted the trust.[30]

Perhaps there was a perpetual conflict between the purer self Victor wanted to be, and the bubbling energy within, which she had to keep from boiling over. Not just a tract, *The Women's War* was a lively example of on-the-spot reportage. Women tried to close saloons in Portland, got hooted at, and finally arrested—materials in her skilled hands which provided good reading. Here is Victor on a typical confrontation:

> At one German saloon the proprietor rushed out, when he saw the ladies coming, swinging his arms and shaking his fists in the most excited manner, and exclaiming: "Vat you want here? You shust go vay! Git off mine sidevalk! Vat for you come here so mooch, braying und singing, und making my license so pig? You shust go vay—I bill not haf it! Vat you vant? You make a church of mine house!—ruin my pizness! No, no, you can't do dat; you moose come here no more. You shust come here vonce more, you vill see vat I vill do mit you! My piple says you moost not bray on de street corners, but you moost bray at home. You go home to bray!"[31]

Mrs. Victor may be at her best while faithfully transcribing, but her generalizations can also be quaintly attractive to contemporary readers. For example, "If anyone supposes it does not require an utter consecration to what is conceived to be the highest duty, to prepare pure-minded ladies to encounter such base and ruffianly assaults as these, that person is in error."[32] She states off the cuff that all reforms generally originate in the middle class, the same idea that was later to permeate the Bancroft works.[33] Here she is both historian and advocate, and it is as advocate that she writes:

> The radical difference between masculine and feminine methods is just the difference between indirectness and directness. An observing woman once said to the writer, "When women come to making laws, they will not be all 'whereases' and 'aforesaid.' Men call women's directness *instinct*, and their own indirectness *reason*; and then say that instinct is safer than reason. It is their way of acknowledging that the direct way is the right way, without any disparagement to their reason!"[34]

Front and center, and with no indirectness whatever, Victor embraced the women's movement of her time, and with Scott Duniway, wrote "Shoulder to Shoulder" in full support of those liberationist values. She melded this, too, with a critique of Christianity, and as a Unitarian felt free to cry out against the male God in these lines from "Magdalena":

> You say there's a Being all-loving,
> Whose nature is justice and pity;
> Could you say where you think he is roving?
> We have sought him from city to city,
> But he never is where we can find him,
> When outrage and sorrow beset us;
> It is strange we are always behind him,
> Or that He should forever forget us.
> But being a god, he is thinking
> Of the masculine side of the Human;
> And though just, it would surely be sinking
> The God to be thoughtful for woman.
> For him and by him was man made:
> Sole heir of the earth and its treasures;
> An after-thought, woman—the handmaid,
> Not of God, but of man and his pleasures.[35]

Elsewhere she condemned fifth-century B.C. Athens for its treatment of women, tracing the decline of its civilization to a one-dimensional standard of values. And in "The New Penelope," Victor developed the same theme in the story of a pioneer woman forced by unequal laws and attitudes to live under the thumb of a bigamist in Portland. Written in a relaxed Jamesian manner (except when her feminism was aroused), it may be the best Northwest short story of the nineteenth century.[36] Victor also wrote a good deal about unequal educational opportunities for the sexes, and about the problems more generally of women in her society achieving, yet at the same time, being wives and mothers. The latter role, however, was already long gone for her, given that she and her husband had separated in the late 1860s, primarily over his inability to handle money. Full closure came tragically when Henry Victor, along with some 200 others on board, perished in a Pacific Mail Company vessel disaster off the northern Washington coast on November 9, 1875.

After her husband's death at sea in 1875, Frances needed a dependable source of support, a need that was answered by a life-changing offer (again, both positively and negatively) from Herbert Howe Bancroft in 1878. As a result, Victor moved to California with her files to work until 1890 as a writer of Bancroft histories of the West. Since the Bancroft volumes were the unique accomplishment of western historiography in the nineteenth century, on both popular and scientific levels this became her most significant life's work. However, Victor was rightly disgruntled that her name did not even appear on these volumes. That disappointment, as well as the sheer toil involved in writing these tomes (in an era when the equivalent of "photocopying" was tedious: twelve Spaniards worked a year copying just the Spanish sources about early San Francisco!) embittered her through the latter part of her life. Lack of credit and low pay (versus the higher rates of remuneration Bancroft kept promising her) were hardship enough; but worse was the knowledge that Bancroft's additions and strictures had marred what could have been a definitive Northwest cultural product. As Victor wrote to Judge Matthew P. Deady, a careful vetter of both her volumes on Oregon's history, November 3, 1886:

> ... I labored under the disadvantage of having my ms. [Bancroft's *History of Oregon*] reduced by another—Mr. B[...] performing this editorial work. As he did not always take in the value of certain matter, and as my ms. overran terribly, he slashed in the wrong places often, and I knew nothing of it until it came before me in the galleys and could be changed but slightly afterwards. But considering all things I do believe the history is more nearly correct than any original history you can point to before the Bancroft series was begun....[37]

In another statement she noted:

> The second volume on Oregon was made up more from matter in the Bancroft library and newspaper files, and is not quite the perfect work I would have made it if I had prepared for it as I did for the first volume. Its errors, however, are not numerous or important. It happened that sometimes when Mr. Bancroft was reading [the] manuscript he altered what I had said to make [it] suit some opinion of his own, or for some other reason.[38]

How much of the Bancroft histories of the Northwest *did* Frances Victor write? The historian William Morris claimed that the *History of Oregon* was completely her work. This certitude has led certain Northwest libraries to put in her name as author of the volumes she claimed. But Morris was prejudiced. He stayed in the same boarding house as Mrs. Victor in Portland and became her confidant and uncritical adherent. His article is based largely on discussions with an embittered Victor, whose death by that time was close at hand. He also used her clippings, scrapbooks and letters, and a lot of this evidence has simply vanished.

On the other hand, the California historian John Caughey concluded a discussion of these claims by suggesting that while Bancroft erred in not acknowledging his assistants' work in the prefaces, "they could not with propriety claim authorship of individual volumes."[39] However, Caughey's conclusion applied overall to many collaborators. As he admitted, Victor was the only one of Bancroft's workers to have had previous experience as an author.[40]

Caughey's conclusion also suffers from the fact that it was contained in a book on Bancroft largely dedicated to his memory and the contribution of his library, and his work is now dated.

We know that there was an elaborate note-taking and indexing system at the Bancroft Library under Henry L. Oak, the Swede Nemus, and an eccentric German-Jewish translator named Goldschmidt, among others. Thus, Victor had to fit into a preconceived mold. One year she worked fifty-one weeks, every day except Sunday, from eight to six, and with but an hour off for lunch and exercise.[41] On the other hand, Victor was herself no mean innovator, and her system for the histories of Oregon—the first volume running from 1834–1848 and the second 1848–1888—helped form a pattern for other books in the series.

No one doubts that Bancroft *did* edit, and often well. Caughey compared certain manuscripts with final versions, noting approvingly Bancroft's tendency to succinctness—with *others'* writing. His own insertions, paradoxically, could at times, be long-winded and extraneous to the issue. Some are famous—one being that "man is a preposterous pig; the greediest animal that crawls upon this planet."[42] Over Victor's strenuous objections, he made Joseph Lane simply into an "Indian butcher."[43] The extent of such interjections, and Bancroft's influence on the general conclusions, nonetheless remain hard to evaluate.

One path toward a more informed opinion on Victor's contribution to the volumes is a comparison of the Bancroft histories of Oregon (volumes I and II), or the *History of Washington, Idaho, and Montana*, for which Mrs. Victor claimed essentially to be sole author, with other specimens of her published work. And especially, with those published previously.

Turning first to *The River of the West*, we find historical material here that would be developed in the Bancroft histories. It is probable that in interviews with Meek, Victor developed the point of view on regional history that was to color her subsequent work. There is a continuity from *River* to the Bancroft histories through to her *Early Indian Wars* (1890s), although *River of the West* is a more popular, less careful work. The subject is the intrepid Joe Meek, mountain man, and later Oregon sheriff and politician, and certainly Mrs. Victor admired her fearless hero—in fact, she was apparently entranced by personal contact with this aging interviewee.[44] She was both repelled and fascinated by details like Meek receiving his alphabet printed on a paddle from a teacher, then pounding the teacher over the head with it![45] The same held true for other primary facets of mountain man life—all stemming from their wildness and uncivilized behavior. She noted in one passage how four trappers calmly played a game of cards on the dead body of a comrade.[46] Victor liked Meek's untutored way of learning—such as the fact that he finally taught himself to read an old Shakespeare book and a Bible by firelight.[47] She was also a booster for the Northwest environment, particularly in the last part of *River of the West*, and this informs all her travel writing, and is also a general feature of her Bancroft volumes. Manifest Destiny and the necessity of overwhelming Native Americans are other recurring themes.

Turning to specifics, Victor spends pages extolling Joseph Lane's treatment of Native Americans in all her volumes, in spite of Bancroft's feelings on the subject.[48] Another clue to her authorship is her quite tolerant view of Catholicism. In the long section Bancroft devoted to the Whitman Massacre, Blanchet and cohorts are given remarkably fair treatment and the Protestant missionaries less so. Yet we know from Caughey that Bancroft was himself anti–Catholic.[49] And in other volumes he sometimes edited that prejudice into the text—not so, however, in those of Victor.

Another obvious method for estimating contributions is to compare the writing in volumes obviously unconnected to Victor with those she allegedly wrote. As an example, we find in the midst of a Bancroft/Victor discussion of Jason Lee:

> In the work of colonization the way was oftentimes difficult, and seemed at times exceedingly slow, yet he could not but feel that though the soft air bites the granite never so gently, the rock will crumble beneath constant effort.
>
> He felt uneasy at the thought of meeting his brethren. Surely there were enough redskins in the west who knew not God. What should he say to those who had sent him forth, when they should ask why he had not converted the heathen? Though he might wrap himself in a newly slain bullock's hide, after the manner of the Scotchman, and lie down beside a water-fall or at the foot of a precipice, and there meditate until the thoughts engendered by the wild surroundings should become inspiration, yet could he not fathom the mystery why God's creatures, whom he had been sent by God to instruct, should wither and die at his touch![50]

At the end of a paragraph, two pages later: "Taken all in all, and I should say, Honor to the memory of Jason Lee."[51] These may well be interjections of an editor anxious to give his imprint to Victor's work. For if one opens the volume entitled *Literary Industries*, largely Bancroft's, and certainly autobiographical, one notices a style more florid than Victor's and with a greater disposition to philosophizing. One sees references here to Cicero, to Dickens, and to the Bible—reminiscent of Harvey Scott and of the literary display common to the age. But what one notices particularly is an almost passionate use of exclamation marks and a pronounced tendency toward nostalgia in his explanatory asides. (For example, "Lovely little Granville! Dear, Open up the California Volume II written by Oak, quiet home-nook"), and one notices again what appear to be dramatic inserts.[52]

There is, however, a remarkable similarity of treatment in the Bancroft volumes, with and without Victor. In part this is due to the fact that the thinking, style, and interests of Bancroft and Victor mainly converged. Both *were* moralizers; both enjoyed and employed classical allusions; both believed in Manifest Destiny, the superior rights of settlers, and the nobility of strength. Without further evidence, we can only conclude that the truth of authorship lies somewhere between the now dated assertions of Morris and Caughey.

After her return to Oregon, Victor was commissioned by the state to write *Early Indian Wars of Oregon*, a commendable work, although covering much of the ground of the Bancroft volumes. The book is careful and detailed, consolidating her place as the first serious historian of the Pacific Northwest. Her view of Native Americans, however, had hardened from *River of the West* to *Early Indian Wars*. Victor seems never to have really understood Indians (or missionaries). More than ever she sees the Indian here as a savage who needed to be dealt with fairly but firmly in the manner of a Joe Lane. Chivalry and the putatively higher Western virtues were lost on such "savages" who proceeded only on instinct, and who had a natural propensity for casual violence or thievery, as well as cowardice.[53] But she often deplored white barbarities toward Indians, too, admiring those who acted with a proper noblesse oblige.

The Early Indian Wars of Oregon is Victor's most disciplined historical product. It does not suffer from the anecdotal quality of her early work on Meek, nor from the unevenness of the Bancroft volumes. There is close attention to chronology and a sure narrative pace, and although unconsciously she selects what favors the whites, the work shows a real unity and coherence—more so than do her earlier ones. Best, the writing surges as actively as the wars themselves. Here is a segment from the "Yakima War":

> Following the fearful yells came the crack, crack, crack of many rifles, white puffs of blue smoke burst out from every clump of bushes, revealing the lurking places of the foe in a line extending from Rock Creek to the head of the rapids, where the men had just begun their day's work on the bridge in front of the store. Along the whole line fell their victims. At the mill, B. U. Brown, his eighteen-year-old wife, and her younger brother were slain, scalped, and thrown into the river, and the teamster at the mill wounded, who, however, escaped to the steamer Olary.[54]

We are reading here a narrative historian the equal of almost any then writing, and certainly the best the Northwest had to offer—one subsequent Northwest historians would certainly have to read and take into account.

Victor's life, however, became more melancholy as time went on, and her last years were the worst of all. There was already a considerable newspaper literature on her sufferings at the hands of Bancroft. But near the end of her life she no longer benefited from the sympathy the story had previously aroused. Having been among the first to discover cracks in the Whitman legend, Mrs. Victor offered an article on the subject to the *American Historical Review* in 1900, only to be beaten to the punch by Professor Bourne, whose position essentially was based on hers! She had also completed a book-length manuscript on the Whitman myth in 1898 but could not get it published. After Bourne's article came out, she revised that manuscript, completing it on the eve of her death in March 1902. But it never found a publisher and disappeared from view.

During her last two years Victor lived in a Portland rooming house, struggling along for lack of income, and hatching a half-dozen publishing projects that never eventuated. On February 18, 1902, she made a bitter inventory of the latter:

> At the moment there lies before me all this:
>
> 1. Chittenden's book to be reviewed *in extenso*.
> 2. Notes for the article on the *Astoria*, etc.
> 3. References for the article on the Oregon Question (English)
> 4. Material for a novel—half done—
> 5. A half written book on the Whitman Legend.
> 6. Material for an article on Oregon Literature.
> 7. Notes on books for Newberry Library—and many incidentals, correspondence, etc. And nothing to show for it! "All work and no *pay*."[55]

Meanwhile Victor eked out a small living in part by composing articles for the *Oregon Historical Quarterly*. Near the end she could look forward to participation in the Lewis and Clark Centennial, but it was not to be. In September 1902, she moved to another rooming house on Portland's Yamhill Street. The moving cost her a breakdown. She was hard pressed to complete a manuscript on steam transportation—in fact, pressed on all sides. She then died November 14, 1902, and was buried in the First Unitarian Church of Portland a few days later, another part of the Northwest's cultural tradition of promise, achievement—and disappointment.[56]

Moving to the region's most significant nineteenth-century novelist, Frederick Balch, we encounter a very different figure from either Frances Fuller Victor or Joaquin Miller.[57] While they produced an enormous quantity of writing, Balch wrote only two short novels. His reputation is based entirely on *The Bridge of the Gods*, a romance on the mythological history of the Northwest that became widely known in the region, and was later made the basis of a pageant.

At first reading, Balch's novels are easy to dismiss. Descriptions are quite thin, and his romanticism seems derivative of Scott, Hawthorne, and more popular writers of his day. Briefly, *The Bridge of the Gods* is based on the Indian myth that there was once a natural bridge across the lower Columbia

River, subsequently destroyed by the gods. The protagonist of Balch's story is Cecil Grey, a young New England preacher who, at the end of the seventeenth century, feels called into the wilderness to preach to the Indians. After years of wandering, the missionary reaches the lodges of Multnomah, chief of a powerful Indian confederacy ruled over by the Willamettes. Multnomah summons these confederated tribes to council, using the occasion to break the power of his disaffected confederates and to cement relations with loyal chieftains. During the council, Grey falls in love with Wallulah, daughter of Multnomah and a shipwrecked Asian princess. But their love is impossible—she has been promised to another chieftain for reasons of state, while eloping would make a joke of Grey's years of missionary work. As the council ends, an eruption of Mount Hood and collapse of the fabled bridge over the Columbia are taken as signs of the collapse of Willamette power, while the killing of Indians by a white landing party on the coast is seen as a portent that all Native Americans will inevitably be replaced by whites. Grey is sentenced to death as partial retribution for the murdered Indians, but soon *all* the protagonists are dead, each faithful to his/her ideals to the end.

Balch's little-read *Genevieve* was written at about the same time but not published until forty years later. One of the Northwest's first "second-generation" stories, it describes a part–Indian, Guido Colonna, who, after worldly education and travel, returns to live with his half-sister on the lower Columbia. Guido sinks into dissipation, but after reaching bottom decides to make a name as a writer. Ultimately, his internal turmoil forces him to renounce the ambition in favor of a life of Christian love. Interwoven with Colonna's struggle for a more meaningful existence is his attempt to win Genevieve, his childhood sweetheart, despite fierce jealousy that continually threatens the relationship. A third strand is the fanatic desire of Winemah, a paralyzed Indian chieftainess, to persuade Colonna to lead her people in one last, desperate war against the whites; and the development of her plan to kill him when he refuses. Winemah embodies Native American antipathy toward incomers that Balch must have known well. For throughout the years Indians had "silently nursed their wrath to keep it warm."[58] At the story's climax, Colonna is trapped by Winemah's conspiracy, and is tried, convicted, and nearly executed for a murder he did not commit. But in the end Colonna marries Genevieve, and the two go off as missionaries to Italy!

On one plane, Frederick Balch was writing rather conventional romance, but on another, he was presenting two different versions of his own life. Born in the Willamette Valley in 1861, he inhabited a variety of homes on the lower Columbia. Although he had only six months of formal schooling and was steadily employed in ranching and construction, he read continuously. Evidently much absorbed by nature, he became so inward as to be considered odd by those around him. Aside from reading, working, and wandering alone, he spent much time collecting Indian lore, especially from the Klickitats who lived near his home. At about nineteen he began to write the novel *Wallulah*, based on Indian lore; but study of the writings of Darwin and the atheist Ingersoll led Balch to concentrate on his religious position, and finally, to announce his conversion at age twenty-one in 1882. Over his family's objections, he burned the manuscript of *Wallulah*, becoming a new man, no longer emotionally and spiritually isolated from his neighbors.

He was soon a preacher and over the next few years established several congregations, serving in more than one church at the same time. Unlike most rural preachers of his day, Balch espoused a liberal congregational doctrine, delivering short, subdued sermons with only casual references to the fires of hell. Although initially he received little or no pay, he finally had two years of fairly prosperous ministry at Hood River (1887–89). In 1889 Balch went to Oakland, California, for theological studies, but became ill, returned to the Northwest, and entered a hospital in Portland early in 1891. Within a few weeks he was dead. Until his death he had continued to revise *Genevieve* and to sketch out further works on the Northwest.

Central in the mythology of Balch was his love for Genevra Whitcomb, the "Genevieve" of his novel. Scanty evidence suggests that he had no more than a few chaperoned conversations with her in the early 1880s, and that they soon quarreled. Nevertheless, when Balch, the only minister in rural Lyle, had to hold a funeral service for Genevra in 1886, he was overcome, and his subsequent emotional life was dominated by her memory.

Although his conversion had impelled him to burn a manuscript, a year after that Balch was at work on his novel *Genevieve*. He never quite got it right—perhaps because *Genevieve* was too close to his own life, and too derived from thinly-disguised relationships in his own community. So in the summer of 1887, he began *The Bridge of the Gods*, which he completed quite rapidly. Since the heroine of this novel is named Wallulah and it is largely a description of the Indian past, *The Bridge* appears to be a reworking of the destroyed novel (rather than of *Genevieve*, as others have alleged).[59] Balch submitted it to publishers many times, with no result, composed a "Ballad of the Rejected Manuscript," and turned to other interests. Finally, the novel came out in 1890, about six months before his death.

Frederick Balch was the prototype of the isolated Northwestern intellectual that H. L. Davis (see Chapter 6) portrays so well in the character of Preston Shively. Davis makes Shively the author of *Winemah: A Tale of Eagle Valley*, a title which obviously echoes Balch's work.[60] The extent of this isolation is hard to imagine today, but when we read Balch's poem in praise of Beethoven, and especially of the Ninth Symphony, we must wonder when and how he could have heard the symphonies, and how much his love of them could have meant to his neighbors on the Columbia![61] Like Davis' Shively, Balch had to study everything by himself, for his community was culturally challenged. But unlike Shively, Balch eventually found in the ministry one of the few intellectual roles such a community could accept.

His writing was a way to self-understanding and self-improvement—intensely autobiographical, mirroring the struggle between on one hand, hedonism, contempt of others, and mysticism; and on the other, an overwhelming desire to live up to the responsibilities of family, church, and society. As with his character Guido Colonna, writing enabled Balch to overcome his own materialism, to replace wine, women, and song with "nobler intoxicants," and to live in "intellectual luxuriousness."[62] Yet Colonna is tormented by doubts and sinks into a world of spirits and ever-deepening gloom, from which only prayer can save him. This world of gloom may be a reflection of Social Darwinism, but it is also possible that for a time Balch himself had entered a Native American world of spirits, from which only the burning of *Wallulah* had freed him.

Beyond his own identity struggles, Balch's work reinforced dark imagery of the Northwest; as in the lines, "Where rolls the Oregon, and hears no sound, / Save his own dashings—yet the dead are there...."[63] Although the theme of natural beauty also runs through his work, Balch emphasizes the Northwest's melancholy side when Cecil Grey first views the Columbia, noting: "It is the very river of death and desolation.... It looks lonely, forsaken, as if no eye had beheld it from the day of creation until now"; or when Wallulah cries out: "This land is a grave.... The clouds lie black and heavy on the spirit that longs for the sunlight and cannot reach it."[64] Balch memorializes a glum, brooding view of the Northwest extending from the general desolation of wilderness to that of the Columbia, with its islands of the dead, to the oppressiveness of the weather that would reach later popular expression in the mordant comedy of *The Egg and I* (1945), set in rain-sodden coastal mountain country. (This is Betty MacDonald's famous comic memoir-novel of a coddled girl off to struggle with her husband on a godforsaken chicken farm in the Olympic Peninsula. Unlike so many Northwest literary products, however, the book sold well, leading to a movie and the Ma and Pa Kettle series; but typically, MacDonald did not stay the course either with the farm life there—or this first marriage. She ended up moving back nearer to Seattle, and predictably, to California.)

However spiritual, Balch did not *himself* turn his back on Northwest cities, particularly Portland. As much as Joaquin Miller disliked that city, Balch honored it. To him, Portland was a cosmopolitan center, and he took seriously what Northwestern literature there was here. In chapter "mottos" of his works, we find alongside Scott and Lowell, Poe and Rosetti, regional classics from Irving's *Astoria* to Gray's *History* to Bancroft, Frances Victor, Sam Simpson, and yes, Joaquin Miller—repeatedly, Joaquin Miller! Balch's intention was, in fact, to memorialize the region. In his teens he had wished,

> to make Oregon as famous as Scott made Scotland, to make the Cascades as widely known as the Highlands; the Santiam as celebrated as the Ayer of Tweed; to make the splendid scenery of the Columbia and Willamette, a background for romance.[65]

His goal—to build a civilization here—was similar to that of the young Joaquin Miller in establishing the *Eugene City Review* during the early 1860s;[66] or of Samuel Clarke in writing the "Legend of the Cascades."

However, for the righteous Northwesterner of sensitivity in an age when Chinook Jargon continued to be widely known and Indians commonly encountered, a major historical problem to be morally resolved was the partially violent process by which these Native Americans had been despoiled of their land. Confirmed Christians needed to confront the sad ineffectiveness of the missionaries' efforts. The first generation of settlers had fought Indians or watched helplessly while they died of white man's diseases. They had been so immersed in their own struggles that their actions almost compelled devaluation of the Indian. But for those who came to consciousness in the generation after the settlement, there had to be better answers. Those of the first generation had needed no myth of the Northwest, for they were the outsiders; their myths were centered elsewhere. But for Balch's generation, the Northwest *was* their world, and they strove to develop a regional tradition with as much depth and continuity as possible. This was among the central intellectual preoccupations that Balch himself had and requires sustained explanation and shading here.

The earliest Northwest chronicles had given few coherent accounts of Indian cultures, and most of what they did offer was not complimentary. Since their writers were not scholars deeply interested in Native American ways, when they did turn to the subject it was to reject the romanticization of Indian life. Such an effort at squaring the record included *Traits of American Indian Life and Character*, ascribed to Peter Skene Ogden, John McLoughlin's one-time lieutenant. Ogden was a serious man, and this is a serious book; yet he was also a man with a job to do and was no reformer. To carry on his work and preserve his reputation, he felt he must refute easy, hazy shibboleths of Easterners who had never met Indians on the frontier.[67] Literary people who came next were generally missionaries, utterly opposed to the Indian way of life on theological grounds. The fact that these two groups dominated intellectual life until the progressive period is one reason we know too little of the feel of Native American life before it was overwhelmed by white influences.

In later periods, some of the record of Indian life was filled in, but to a large extent what was presented now on a literary plane remained a romantic, guilt-ridden retrospective, and hardly an adequate base for a deeper understanding of Northwestern roots.

In sum, Balch had to assimilate these historical givens and received ideas, dealing as best he could with them. Protestant missionaries had come to the Northwest to convert Indians and for them, conversion to a particular religion and to the way of life of settled white farmers were linked. To missionaries, the "enemy" remained the Indians' wandering ways and wicked beliefs, as well as those of trappers and other castoffs along the frontier. But when missionaries were unable to save Indians from mortal white diseases in the Willamette Valley and along the lower Columbia, and when these Native Americans seemed to reject their mission through the massacre of the Whitmans, the charge to reclaim the "savages" became increasingly meaningless and superfluous. As a result, the religious-missionary community that became the intellectual backbone of early settled life in the region allowed its prejudices to exclude the Indian spirit from the new society. Severe condemnation of Indian-white marriages[68] was a condemnation of the way of life the community identified with both trapper and Indian, as well as with an earlier English and/or Catholic world of McLoughlin. This attitude was still current in Balch's time, for when the materialist Colonna chose to attend a dance rather than a camp meeting, it was symbolically referred to as a "half-caste dance," even though it was an American-style dance and many of the participants were not half-breeds.[69]

In order to get on with life, there were three ways for the Northwesterner to understand what had happened to the Indian. The first was to describe the Native American as so subhuman and intractable that it made no difference what happened to him or her. In this view, the Indians deserved what they got. The second was to describe Indians sympathetically as wild, untamed, Rousseauan primitives who were unjustly crushed, as all individuality and authenticity are so often obliterated by "civilization." The third was to accept Indians as members of less advanced societies who were brought low by injustice, cruelty, introduced germs, and alcohol. Significantly, all three versions see this story of the passing of Native American cultures as more or less inevitable. Only the third approach, however, accorded closely enough with history and reality to lay a basis for improvement of the Indian condition. As one of the Bancroft histories put it:

> [Indians] were martyrs to a destiny too strong for them, to the Juggernaut of an incompressible civilization, before whose wheels they were compelled to prostrate themselves, to that relentless law, the survival of the fittest, before which, in spite of religion or science, we all in time go down.[70]

Frances Victor's *Indian Wars* codified for the Northwestern conscience the first and most common interpretation. This was a harsh version, according to which the white man was so superior, and the Indian so inferior, that concern for the suffering and injustice inflicted on Native Americans was dismissed as sentimentality. In deliberately downplaying the horrors of extermination wars in southeastern Oregon,[71] Victor could coldly write such passages as:

> When the volunteers were in the vicinity of Tule Lake ... they found a number of canoes filled with Modoc women and children, and containing fireplaces of stone and mud, at which were cooked the fish on which they subsisted. On the Indian children was found the blood-stained clothing taken from murdered immigrant children. These families, hiding from the justly apprehended wrath of white men, were made to pay the penalty of blood without process of law, or the law's delays.[72]

Or:

> Early in October a party of roving reservation Indians were discovered encamped near the mouth of Butte creek, ... and it was suspected that among them were some who had been annoying the settlers. Upon this suspicion a company of about thirty men, ... proceeded before daybreak on the eight of October to attack this camp, which was surprised and terribly chastised, twenty-three being killed and many wounded before it was learned that the majority of the victims were non-combatants, or old men, women, and children.[73]

At the opposite extreme, the early writings of Joaquin Miller gave regional form to the mythological "wild Indian" of the "Western Novel" described by Leslie Fiedler.[74] In this Edenic myth, the Indian was used as a literary foil for civilization, as a natural person rejecting the artificialities of overly civilized life for the realities of life in nature. Miller wrote his *Unwritten History* to bring the condition of the Shasta Indians, including destruction of their environment, to the public's attention. Yet within the book, and in life, he fought both *for* Indians and *against* them. In real life and in fantasy he became a primitive man of the frontier, refusing to take on the responsibilities of a settled life—among either Indians or whites. To a degree, Miller's life and work remind us of Ken Kesey, Fiedler's candidate for the writer of the true western a hundred years later (see Chapter 6).

Existence in the later nineteenth century of a third approach to the Indian may be inferred from published memoirs or memoir-histories of the period, such as Thomas Strong's *Cathlamet on the Columbia*, Samuel Clarke's *Pioneer Days of Oregon History*, or Orange Jacobs' *Memoirs*.[75] In these writings, Native Americans appear as primitive but intelligent people of a wide variety of types that still had to be supplanted. But they did *not* merit the cruelty and injustice exacted by man and nature during the settlement period. The Indian, in this view, had a deserving place in the regional history, and a modest, if assimilated, role in its fiction.[76]

In sum, Balch's work may be partially seen as a development and expansion of this third approach. His *Bridge* placed Indian-white relations in a precontact period that made possible a symbolic transcendence of actual events during the period of settlement. The geographical region of the *Bridge* is explicitly the historical Northwest region, as we have defined it. Balch's great Indian confederacy, with its "capital" near Portland, ranged from the coast to the Nez Percé, from the Klamath on the California border to the Okanagan and Puget Sound. While standard written accounts available to Balch painted an unattractive picture of many of these tribes, Balch ascribed a certain grandeur to fabled Willamettes who conveniently disappeared before historical accounts were written. (When the hero of *Genevieve*, Guido Colonna, begins to write, he decides on an Indian story to describe the way they *had* been, rather than their current degraded state.) Balch makes of the Indians a confederacy, for in this way Native American history could become more assimilable to a mainstream American past. At the same time he attempts fictionally to explain the missionaries' stubborn beliefs, the reasons for their general rejection by Indians, and the final, inevitable destruction of one civilization by another. In his effort at fusion, Balch's Northwest is made up of Asiatics, whites, and Indians, and his hero of one novel and heroine of the other are half-breeds.

In developing his mythological Indian, Balch rejected elements of both the harshly negative view of Native Americans then current in the region, *and* the romantic, individualistic view of Fiedler's "Western novelist." He rejected the latter in two ways. First, his Indians are nearly always pictured in groups, striving for group goals under quasi-settled conditions. Second, he believed that white ideals and beliefs, if not necessarily their actions, were superior to those of Indians. Balch saw white superiority in more evolved political order and scientific knowledge, as well as in the more favorable treatment of women and animals we discussed in Chapter 1. In theory, whites offered the gift of a new civilization that might compensate Native Americans for the loss of their own.

In taking this position, Balch avoided the message of primitives with whom Fiedler seemed to identify in more recent fiction. To Balch, the mythic Indian either did not exist, or *should* not have. In subduing the primitive in himself, Balch incorporated elements of a historic clash of peoples and of types of peoples in all societies within his own regional myth of progress. Christianizing Indians seemed no more or less necessary to Balch and his generation than their own personal conversion; much as marriage was thought to be a primary means to make young men "settle down"—a process the Keseys and Fiedlers of the world would prefer to call loss of independence.

On the other hand, Balch also rejected as unjust and unChristian the harsh and destructive views of the Indian. Not that Indians had been falsely accused of murder or of harboring an undying hatred of white men; but rather that, given their cultures and experience of the whites, they could not have acted or felt otherwise. Balch was as fully aware of the evil of anti–Indian feeling in his own time as Don Berry would be much later in *Moontrap* and *To Build a Ship* (see Chapter 6). As Colonna says at his sentencing: "The counsel for the prosecution has often alluded to my Indian blood; having it, perhaps it is fit that I should die unjustly, for wherever the men of my race have faced an American tribunal, injustice and death have ever been their lot."[77] And so he justified the undying hatred of the paralyzed Winemah who had brought him to this trial, echoing the words of the seer Tohomish, who, at the denouement of *Bridge*, proposes in these words to execute Cecil Grey:

> Slay the white man as the white man will slay your children in the time to come. Peace? Love? There can only be war and hate. Striking back blow for blow like a wounded rattlesnake, shall the red man pass....[78]

To Balch, the Indian record, including even their hate, remained an integral, and important, part of regional tradition.

In "working through" this Indian regional heritage, Balch was wrestling with elements of both his own personal experience and local history. We must remember that as an adolescent he had to an extent identified with the Native American world. (He remembered his own Welsh ancestry and was still irritated that his ancestors had been conquered by the English.[79]) Significantly, he lived by the Klickitats, and the Klickitats were to Samuel Clarke, Pacific Northwest Iroquois, admired by whites as a superior tribe. Although the Klickitats lived east of the mountains on the Columbia, they managed to exact tribute from tribes from the Umpqua River to Puget Sound, even after the coming of the whites. In the 1850s, chief Kamiakin was thought to have put together a loose alliance of hostile tribes from southern Oregon to the Canadian border that waged war for three years against the whites. Historically, Kamiakin's role is overstressed, but it is true that for a brief period the Northwest Indians saw their destinies as linked in a way they had never before realized. Kamiakin was more a Yakima than a Klickitat chief, but he had Klickitat wives, and was related to groups throughout the Columbia Basin, including the Spokane, Palouse, and Nez Percé. At the same time, he had developed a large farm with several hired hands near the Yakima.[80] Balch had also heard of a great tribe in the Portland area referred to as the "Multnomahs" or "Wankanississe," that had been wiped out almost overnight in a measles epidemic after the coming of the whites.

Balch's Willamettes, then, are the Multnomahs of history, but with the ascribed military virtues of the Klickitats. Their great chief "Multnomah," the organizer, is surely modeled on the story of Kamiakin, while the aged and paralyzed Winemah of the more historical *Genevieve* is almost explicitly the daughter of our historical Kamiakin, whose real and historical hatred she fictionally represents. These two, and Tohomish, the seer and advisor of Multnomah, are the most memorable of Balch's literary creations. To sum up, the literary heart of Balch remained firmly in the Indian world.

Yet in the end, this world was allowed to fade out. Both the spiritually half-breed Balch and his half-breed hero Colonna fused into the post-conversion Balch. Balch finally wrote of Colonna:

> He cast his lot with a leading Protestant church, a church that believes in liberal Christianity, ... the universal brotherhood of man regardless of creed, and in the final redemption of the whole human race.[81]
>
> ... He lived down the race prejudice.... He proved that here in Oregon a man of Indian blood can so live as to win trust and honor, as though he were of the purest Saxon race.[82] [Balch, of course, was Welsh, not Saxon.]

For his generation, Balch began to lay a basis for a literature of regional pride, incorporating the contrasting symbols of natural beauty and pervasive gloom that have characterized the Northwestern experience. He strove for a combination of literature and didactic message that was appreciated by the local public—a public soon to be steeped in the regional literature of Eva Emery Dye or Ella Higginson, whom we later treat. Yet interest in Balch and his work soon waned, for he had written in an age of Northwest self-confidence and a certain incipient brand of regionalism that was en route to passing.

After 1900 new people came in so fast that as emphasized here, a smaller percentage of the population of Oregon in 1910 was recorded as born in the state than in 1870.[83] And these new people bore no responsibility for the destruction of the Indians. In addition, a shift of migration patterns to Puget Sound meant that Portland was no longer the obvious center of regional life. So the regional writer must now be more sophisticated, a professional living in a world of other, increasingly cosmopolitan professionals. Balch's idea of a revived sense of the ancient confederation—from the Okanagan to the Klamath, the Makah to the Nez Percé—was a Northwest myth that would remain in cold storage, but which contributed to a collective regional memory.

CHAPTER 4

Populists, Progressives, and Radicals

THERE HAVE BEEN MANY catchwords for the period beginning around 1890 in the U.S. and cresting with the end of World War I, but one that has lasted is certainly "the age of reform." In fact, with the squeezing of farms by railroads and big business and the concomitant rise of Populist protest; with changes attendant upon massive immigration, depressing wage scales and broadening of the culture; with consequent pressures of urban growth and corruption; with the increase of cosmopolitan values radiating from New York City; and finally, with a new radicalism enhanced by World War I, industrial unrest, and the Russian example, the age cannot be summarized by any simple expression. The many lines of social and ideological change make a mockery of neat boundaries, and we have clear oppositions here, such as educated elite progressive versus anti-city populist; puritan prohibitionist versus liberal, even anarchist champion of personal freedom; or anti-foreigner versus internationalist. Sometimes a key issue like women's suffrage could unite reformers of most tendencies, but just as often, reformers were unable to agree on fundamental directions of change. In the Pacific Northwest, however, the period was one of surprising vitality and achievement.

One of the characteristic products of "the age of reform" here was the "Oregon system." Inaugurating direct democracy on the state and local level, the Oregon system became widely emulated. Legislatively, in Oregon it included the Initiative and Referendum passed in 1902 (and extended in 1906), the Direct Primary Law in 1904, the Corrupt Practices Act and the Recall Amendment in 1908, and finally, in 1913, a law on the presidential primary. Equally important was the use of a clause in the Direct Primary Law to force legislative candidates to support the people's choice for senator, a device initiated by twenty-one states before the Seventeenth Amendment (1913) made it unnecessary.[1] Closely linked with this system were often the movements for labor, farm, and railroad reform, as well as those of women's suffrage and prohibition. Evil, inequality, and the bosses were equally the enemies of the time.

It does not unduly stretch the historical record to say that the Oregon system, as we know it, was made possible by the Lewelling family, an exemplar of Dorothy Johansen's enduring characterization of Oregon in terms of family farm respectability. The Lewellings were Welsh Quakers who had migrated to North Carolina in the eighteenth century.[2] Meschach Lewelling, a physician and nurseryman, had inherited several slaves from a relative and in 1825, moved to Indiana so that he might free them outside the South. Here he reestablished his business and profession. In 1836 his son Henderson moved to Iowa where he set up a nursery on the frontier, prospered, and became a leader in Friends meetings. But in 1847 he took his large family and a collection of 700 grafted trees to Oregon in a wagon so heavy and slow that they had to travel alone most of the way. After seven months on the road they settled near Portland, and by 1851 were again thriving in a nursery business, the first in the Far West. Henderson later went on to more adventures in California and Central America, but by this time his brother Seth had arrived from Indiana, and became primarily responsible for the nursery until his death in 1896. During this time he developed a wide variety of fruits, the most famous being the Bing cherry.

Seth had always supported the Republican Party, the Grange, and other reform movements; but not until the early 1880s, following the death of his only son and first wife, and influenced by a second spouse, did he make his home the meeting place for Oregon's leading intellectuals and reformers, especially ones in the Populist Alliance. During this period a spiritualist friend of Mrs. Lewelling often brought destitute young men to live in the cabins at the nursery and take meals with the family. In 1891 one such, destitute and asthmatic, was William U'Ren, important to our story of a developing Northwest culture.

William U'Ren was born in 1859 in Wisconsin, of a line of Dutch and Cornish blacksmiths and preachers. His parents had recently come to the U.S. to find liberty, and they hated slavery. Not wishing to be tied down to blacksmithing for a large outfit, his father tried homesteading and ranching in a variety of places in the West and upper Midwest, but without positive results. Against this background, young U'Ren tried law and newspaper work in Denver, but becoming very ill, gave this up to travel for several years in search of better health in California and Hawaii. Finally he came to Oregon, where his father was, for the moment, trying ranching near

Prineville. William was a rather weak young man, used to being alone a good deal, and in his early thirties, still considered odd; but he was also interested in ideas and hoped especially to aid the poor. His ideas derived from those of the day's reformers, particularly Henry George and his single tax. When he arrived at the Lewellings, U'Ren's confidence had just been raised by successful participation in the Portland campaign for the Australian ballot.

U'Ren became a leader in discussions at the Lewelling home, and was soon made a business partner on generous terms. Then one evening Alfred Lewelling, Seth's nephew and also a partner, brought to an Alliance meeting a copy of J. W. Sullivan's work on the Swiss system of initiative and referendum, and its possible application in this country. The group immediately saw the Swiss system as the tool they were looking for to break the power of professional politicians. They put together a joint state committee of the Grange and labor, U'Ren became its secretary, and the Lewelling family home was henceforth a center of the resultant educational campaign. (The many Swiss in the area were, of course, eager to help.)

U'Ren plunged into this life of educational and political activity, and though he served only one term in the Oregon legislature, the initiative and referendum were firmly incorporated into law by 1902. He then used that stepping stone to achieve a direct primary in 1904, and later the direct election of senators. His creation of the statement No. 1 for the Direct Primary Law of 1904, presaging direct election of senators, was "a genuine invention, the rarest of phenomena in politics."[3] In Washington, U'Ren helped create a counterpart to the People's Power League, and the ensuing Direct Legislation League accomplished many of the same results—results soon echoed in Idaho. But he failed to attain further political positions himself, and also in his attempts to use "I. and R." to achieve single tax legislation. The people liked the tools but had other ideas of how to use them.

To achieve all this, meanwhile, the Lewelling nursery had been bankrupted, both by inattention and through Seth's donations. After Seth's death in 1896, and machinations by U'Ren in the 1897 legislature that horrified many of his supporters but made success possible, Seth's widow turned violently against U'Ren, fighting him the rest of the way. However, he never profited financially, remaining a poor, part-time country lawyer, and did not reciprocate the disappointed widow's hatred.

In Washington State, John R. Rogers represented the populist spirit in a different guise. Before coming to the Northwest in middle age (1890), Rogers had edited a reformist newspaper in Kansas, and his heroes of the day were the populist leaders he had known. His attacks on capitalism were as severe as any Bolshevik's, for he based his arguments on the idea that wage slavery and southern black slavery were essentially the same. However, his intellectual god was not Marx, but Jefferson, and he always insisted on American-style freedoms.[4] An environmental determinist, Rogers felt that conditions made the person, but also believed that such conditions could be changed, and he found the Northwest of the boom-and-bust 1890s in an angry mood to do so, via a farm-labor coalition, strikes, and the creation of a Washington State Peoples' Party, which he joined. Somewhat in the spirit of Harvey Scott, Rogers insisted on the virtues of diversity, individuality, competition, and hard work.[5] And as an agrarian, he emphatically rejected U'Ren's interest in the single tax, for it was a tax on land. Rogers proposed instead that there should be *no* tax on farm land or on citizens' improvements up to a value of $2500. He wanted every man to have a guaranteed farm of his own, an achievement he saw as particularly easy to bring about in Washington State, which might then serve as a national model. Although Rogers' proposed amendments to the state constitution in order to achieve this failed to pass, he was elected Populist governor of Washington in 1896. And he continued to try to educate the people through his writings until his death in 1901. But this was not the end of his influence, for Rogers' campaign manager, Ernest Lister, conserved these ideas, and upon election as Washington's governor in 1912, proudly announced his goal as enhancement of rural civilization in the Northwest.[6] This was to be achieved through cooperatives and credit systems, county agents, new irrigation projects, and the clearing of logged-off lands by county governments for homesteads. Again, family farm respectability was to be the model, for Lister mainly rejected a future based on logging or industry. Unhappily, the problems that arose for Lister were those of labor and urban unrest, and soon the economy was fundamentally affected by World War I as well. After 1916, Lister based his support on labor and talked little more of the agrarian dream.

Another achievement in the populist-progressive upsurge that brought John Rogers to regional power in 1896 was the summoning of a radical, J. Allen Smith, to the University of Washington as professor of political science in 1897. Smith's courses there were mainly conceived as exposés of those who oppressed the people. Anticipating Charles Beard's economic interpretation of the Constitution, Smith's *The Spirit of American Government* (1907) attacked that document as a betrayal of the American dream, a dream he hoped might be resurrected by direct democracy. Smith saw the separation of powers enshrined in the Constitution as a device to protect privilege against the assertion of rights that had been adumbrated in the Declaration of Independence.[7] He was also a local activist who took on conservatives at the university, as well as the Seattle Electric Company, which he considered a prime example of capitalist excess.[8]

In this age of reform, two burning issues were those of women's suffrage and prohibition—issues naturally linked, in a time when women still aspired not so much to become indistinguishable from men, as to use their moral superiority to *uplift* the wayward opposite sex. Closely identified with these movements was George Cotterill, who came from New Jersey in 1892 to work under the engineer R. H. Thomson, Seattle's Robert Moses. A follower of William Jennings Bryan, Cotterill quickly became involved in causes of the day, including the public ownership of power and water that was to become so important in the Northwest. He then entered the state senate where he began to fight the railroads, and as a friend of William U'Ren, promoted use of the Oregon System in Washington. And in 1909, he *also* got the Woman Suffrage Amendment through the legislature. But closer to his heart was the attempt to achieve initiative and referendum in Washington through the Direct Legislation League. In this effort, the intellectual stimulus was J. Allen Smith, who played a major part in the League's efforts. Under their combined pressure, the state legislature passed the initiative and referendum in 1911, along with a variety of other reform measures (including ratification of the federal income tax.) Cotterill then became Seattle's reform mayor, where he fought liquor and big business. And he considered his greatest achievement to be the Anti-Saloon Initiative, a precursor of prohibition, which he successfully sponsored in 1914.[9]

Before leaving the agrarians, it is well to remember that around the turn of the century people had come from all parts of the nation to Puget Sound in order to establish five major utopian agrarian communities.[10] Unlike many would-be utopias, founders of Washington's were fired by secular ideals, ranging from the cooperative movement through socialism to anarchism. The first utopian colony grew out of reform movements and labor agitation in Seattle during the 1880s; in a few years it became simply another section of Port Angeles across the water from Victoria, B.C. More ideological was the Equality colony, near La Conner in the Skagit Valley north of Seattle. The site was chosen by a national organization hoping to use it as a base from which to radicalize the state and later the nation. The cooperative or Rochdale movement of the day was responsible for the establishment of Freeland near Anacortes, and Burley, west of Tacoma, had a similar moderate impulse. South at Longbranch the community of Home became famous nationally through its advocacy of complete individualism within a kind of philosophical anarchy. Most dramatic were accusations of bathing in scanty attire there, eliciting the ire of Tacoma's good citizens. But Home also attracted leading radicals of the day such as Emma Goldman, Elizabeth Gurley Flynn, "Big Bill" Haywood of the IWW, and William Z. Foster, and others with explicit Communist Party connections. Nationally, the communities were famous as experiments and as the places of publication of short-lived, but widely distributed radical or communitarian periodicals. In time, these utopian communities unraveled, to be rewoven into the Northwestern fabric, but they did add to the leaven of the region's social thought. The utopias no doubt helped spark interest in the Bolshevik Revolution that would lead Northwesterners to organize migrations to the U.S.S.R., or to contribute to the "Seyatel Commune," established in the Caucasus with the aid of eighty-seven Seattle residents in 1922. In 1961, when the name of Seyatel was changed, five of the original Seattle founders were still residents there.[11] In the 1920s, the Finnish people of Astoria, Oregon, also set up a commune in the far north of the Soviet Union.[12]

Yet the Northwest, and particularly Seattle, gained a reputation for radicalism largely due to labor troubles in the region that had begun with the struggle against Asian workers. The early twentieth century was marked by the concentration of the Industrial Workers of the World, the most radical labor union in the country, among miners, lumberjacks, and woodworkers of the Northwest. Unlike other labor movements, the IWW (or "Wobblies") saw themselves as a class apart. This led them to intervene beyond the arena of the local strike. In 1909 so many invaded Spokane to jeer and speak and sing for free speech that over 1200 were jailed before the city council revoked its ordinance against public meetings.[13] In 1916, after a series of mass rallies, Wobblies were excluded forcibly from further interference in a tense Everett strike. Finally, after a Seattle Wobbly group was cruelly beaten in Everett, they decided to make this a test case, chartering a boat in Seattle with 250 men to intensify the effort. Met on the dock, the resulting gun battle, or "Everett Massacre," left several dead on each side. Although what started the shooting is unclear, Mayor Hiram Gill of Seattle publicly announced that the cowards at Everett had fired into the boat, and that many in the IWW had every right to go armed.[14] This was the tenor of thinking in Seattle in 1916, the same year the formidable, egregious Anna Louise Strong was elected to the School Board.

Like V. L. Parrington, discussed in our next chapter, and many other Northwest figures of note, Strong hailed from the Midwest. She was born November 24, 1885, in Friend, Nebraska, where her father was a Congregationalist minister of that same moral elite class as Frances Fuller Victor or Abigail Scott Duniway.[15] Intelligent, aggressive, ambitious, Strong garnered high grades in a Cincinnati elementary school and then in a Chicago high school. The more she achieved scholastically, the more she found herself isolated. Not only her academic performance, but her multiple ambitions set her off from fellow students, and particularly, from other girls. In her autobiography she recalled her high school years:

> I wanted to be a North Pole explorer, and an airman, and a great writer, and a mother of ten—one child wasn't worth the time! There were at least ten lives that I simply had to live, and I knew if I started to think, I could make it a thousand.[16]

Add to this ambition and intelligence a pronounced penchant for religious mysticism, and acute guilt about her comfortable suburban life in Oak Park, and one has an interesting characterological mix. Impelled by her mother to see how the other half lived, Strong became involved in Chicago social work, yet also continued her elite, and for a woman of that era, pathbreaking studies—learning languages like Greek and Latin, but also modern ones in Germany and Switzerland, before embracing higher education at Bryn Mawr in 1903, along with Oberlin College in Ohio.

To prove herself, Strong spent the rest of her life passing self-imposed tests. The first was a doctorate of philosophy at the University of Chicago, which she garnered in two-and-a-half years at age twenty-three. Her thesis, "A Study of Prayer from the Standpoint of Social Psychology," was abstract and theoretical, but she was soon to reject further study of this kind.

Coming to Seattle in the immediate prewar years, Strong worked with her father on a typical progressive project there, the "Know Your City Institutes"—lectures, discussions, and excursions intended to stimulate urban awareness. Versions of these "Know Your City Institutes" rapidly spread to other West Coast cities.[17] Anna then sunk herself into welfare and children's bureau work in New York, where she also liberated herself in bohemian circles. She subsequently hit Kansas City and Louisville, becoming a traveling Jane Addams. More and more she became convinced that America needed a fundamental series of reforms. She had first learned the word "socialism," like many others, reading Edward Bellamy's famous *Looking Backward*. Her view of the ideology was thoroughly American—as a new, more efficient way of allocating resources and granting just wages to workers.

Back in the Northwest after her peripatetic life had begun to depress her, the wildness and ruggedness of nature there aroused her will to conquest, the same will that took her later to Russia and China. In a manner reminiscent of the older and more sedate Parrington, Strong wrote in her autobiography:

> This new-found wilderness became for me a passion; I began to seek more and more difficult climbs, new peaks to conquer. I organized in November 1915 the first winter climb of Mount Hood, in which we four participants were all but swept away in an unexpected blizzard.[18]

Based again in the reformist Northwest, Strong found herself in an intellectual ambiance which best suited her. As her most recent biographers put it, "Seattle was one of the most progressive cities in America" and "an ideal place for her talents."[19] It was also ideal for her continuing tests in a bracing physical environment. For the next five years, there would be summer hikes on Mount Rainier, treks in the Puget Sound area, and other outdoor experiences, "my new form of opium."[20]

Near the mountains and wilderness, Seattle was also suitable ideologically and was fast "becoming a paradise of public ownership...."[21] Here there were a vigorous Central Labor Council, burgeoning cooperative groups, a liberal university movement, and an alternative chamber of commerce, called the Commercial Club. (Progressive businessmen in this contingent had clambakes and beach get-togethers with workers, educating each other in the new issues of municipal politics.) The main issue was public ownership of utilities, and the main foe was Seattle Electric, the same monopoly J. Allen Smith had fought. Anna Louise enthusiastically joined the forces of righteousness and in 1916 entered city politics, running for the school board. Seeing herself as an educated woman fighting ignorant interests (the University clubs supporting her used the phrase "a really educated woman against those self-made men of business"[22]), she won easily—the first female elected to the board in twenty years. Strong had been one of a tiny minority of women Ph.D.s, then among the first to climb Mount Hood in winter; and now she was one of the leading radicals in Seattle.

Soon, the vigorous labor movement in Seattle attracted her interest. Near the end of 1916, while still on the school board, Strong became the *New York Evening Post*'s correspondent on the trial of IWW workers indicted as rabble-rousers during the Everett riot.[23] With her usual enthusiasm she lionized these Wobbly workers as the true inheritors of pioneer freedom. There was also, concomitantly, the problem of imminent war, which her pacifist father adamantly opposed. Anna Louise joined Seattle branches of the Anti-Preparedness League, the Union against Militarism, and the Emergency Peace Federation, and wrote angry pacifist articles in *The Call*. Early on she opposed the so-called merchants of death, the international capitalists—a revulsion which would have widespread currency only after the conflict in Europe. Soon she was preaching the anti-war message on editorial pages of the *Union Record*, a more solid newspaper than the now-bankrupt *Call*. And yet she still resisted the term "radical." As Strong described her attitude:

> We progressives resented the term "radical"; we were not digging anything up by the roots; we were merely continuing the good old American tradition of inevitable progress, a country getting better and better forever—a tradition which the interests had attacked.[24]

By late 1917, Anna's enthusiasm was pointing toward Russia, then the hope of many in the western world. Her articles poured out in support of the new Soviet government and she interviewed touring Bolshevist lecturers who happened upon Seattle, like Albert Rhys Williams and Portland's Louise Bryant, John Reed's fiery consort. What was Strong's impression of the globetrotting Louise? Apparently she was very taken with her. "I remember," she wrote, "when Louise Bryant returned from the revolution in Russia to dazzle the smoke-laden air of the close-packed longshoremen's hall with her gorgeous amber beads and the glamor of the forbidden border."[25]

Strong was nothing if not florid and passionate, and this is also reflected in the proletarian verse she wrote in these Seattle years.[26] Published under the pseudonym "Anise," her satirical verses had a national impact on the labor and socialist scene. Verse was still a legitimate activity for a variety of intellectuals, especially in the Pacific Northwest. Abigail Scott Duniway, Ben Hur Lampman, Edmond S. Meany (see Chapter 7), John Reed, C.E.S. Wood—all wrote poetry taken seriously in their day. Strong's poems in fact read like sermons. The blaring capitals she used even in her prose are found in abundance in her verse as well. Even in nature poetry, celebrating the hikes she led, Anna capitalizes words like MOUNTAIN and FOG, or contrasting words like CIVILIZATION and NEWSPAPERS, to show how life felt on Mount Rainier and then back in Seattle. Later she wrote fiction, which, although propagandistic, remains more enduring than her poetry.

Primarily she was a journalist of causes, and as an editor of the *Union Record*, became a leader of the more radical working people in Seattle. When they decided to call a general strike in 1919, dissatisfied over wages and unemployment in the aftermath of war, she hurried back from Chicago to write a famous editorial outlining their intentions and purposes. Yet those goals remained unclear, even to her. When the strike came, it successfully and nonviolently shut down the city for four days, only to ebb as the men went back to work.

As historian of the General Strike Committee, Anna wrote a passionate account of the demonstration.[27] Again, she used a didactic, intermittently capitalized poem to show her ideological colors at the book's beginning:

What scares them most is
That NOTHING HAPPENS
They are ready
For DISTURBANCES
They have machine guns
And soldiers,
But this SMILING SILENCE
Is uncanny.[28]

The author then surprises the reader by giving a detailed, cogent recitation of the strike, creditably sketching the fearful atmosphere of Seattle on the brink of the crisis—small businessmen rushing to get riot insurance, people stockpiling groceries, and so on. She is precise, too, on workers' wage demands, and one is reminded how really badly workers were then paid. She lists the various unions—Musicians, Carpenters, Hotel Maids—won over to the strike, and then goes into an hour-by-hour account, taking care to discuss both sides (though perhaps not *all* businessmen wanted to shoot down strikers, as Strong avers here).[29]

After the strike petered out, the good feeling and sense of community among workers in Seattle rapidly declined as well. With the ruin of her "Seattle Utopia" (as she entitles a chapter of her autobiography), Strong was glad for an opportunity to meet Lincoln Steffens in 1920 at Blanc's Cafe—"the place to which Seattle artists, authors, and members of the left-wing generally ... used to take important visitors whom we wished to favor with good food and quiet talk...."[30] When she explained to Steffens that the radical movement in Seattle was now bankrupt, a dead-end,[31] he suggested that she go to Russia as a reporter and explain its new vision to the world. Having read Lenin's *Soviets at Work*, Strong was quite favorable to Steffens' idea of a pilgrimage there. Moscow sounded glamorous, particularly when described by Steffens, whose *Shame of the Cities* had once stirred her deeply. That very evening Strong sent a letter to the American Friends' Service to obtain a correspondent's job in Russia.

Traveling first to Poland, Strong finally reached Russia, bearing Quaker food for the starving city of Samara. In the Soviet Union she exhausted herself and caught typhus, but by 1923 had become "guardian" of a new farm colony for homeless children on the Volga—named, appropriately, for Portland's John Reed. In Soviet communism she had located a new faith, one strong enough to erase the more critical spirit of her youth. Her life would henceforth be an alternation of lecture tours in the United States to raise funds for the Russians, and extended travels to the Soviet Union, along with others to important countries in the communist future, such as China. Besides lectures, a plethora of books and articles resulted. One of her main roles became that of "interpreter and defender of the Soviet Union,"[32] and particularly of Stalin, whom she never saw fit to criticize even after the purges of the 1930s! Strong's own (de facto) husband of that decade, an American Jew named Joel Shubin, editor of the touchingly titled *Peasant's Gazette*, based in Russia, ultimately died there in the early '40s; yet her viewpoint scarcely changed. Her novel of 1943, *Wild River*, still criticized the *kulaks*, though by that time a great many had been liquidated. By then Strong was helping to put together screenplays on Russia in the more idyllic environs of Hollywood—ahead of her time in what Tom Wolfe later dubbed "radical chic."[33]

After the Second World War, she spent increasing time in China, becoming more interested in the soon-triumphant Mao than in an ever more paranoid Stalin. Always keeping one foot in the U.S., she did the good American thing by smuggling boxes of Oh Henry! chocolate bars into China for the Communists! On trips back to America she naturally aroused the interest of the F.B.I. The McCarthy era found her in Altadena, California, recuperating from nervous pressures, but preparing yet another Chinese voyage. Her final years included trips to Vietnam during America's war there, and stays in a China where she kept fortuitously alive, even during its Cultural Revolution. Of course Strong was willing to toe the ideological line, despite atrocities there that would rival Stalin's. In 1970 at age eighty-four Strong died of a heart attack in a Peking hospital, a quirky Northwest figure who had derived much from that American region, but also went well beyond it in her radicalism.[34]

If Seattle was no longer at the Northwest center of radical ideas after 1919 or so, as it was before and during World War I, neither was Portland; for in that year its most famous intellectual radical, Charles Erskine Scott Wood (1852–1944), also left the region. To this major figure we now turn.

Raised in a cultured home in Pennsylvania and Maryland, Wood had been forced reluctantly through West Point into a military career. Posted to the Northwest in the 1870s, he was present at the surrender of Chief Joseph, recording the Chief's famous declaration and aiding in its popularization.[35] He then returned to the East, married, and took a law degree from Columbia University; but bitten by the Northwest, he returned with his wife and two children to begin a law practice in Portland. At this enterprise he was steadily successful—especially, and ironically, representing large corporations. Wood raised five children in Portland and moved in its most elite circles. However, after the First World War, he departed the city for California. For some years he had wanted to leave his conventional wife and children to live more freely with a younger, more intellectual woman; and in 1919 a million-dollar commission from a big land sale made this move possible. Wood now had enough to secure the life of his wife and children in Oregon *and* to establish a new one for himself. In his flamboyant style, proclivity for poetry, and rejection of Portland for a remarkable estate at Los Gatos, California, it seemed as though Wood was somewhat imitating, a generation later, the less-educated Joaquin Miller.

Aside from law and family, Wood had already lived other lives in Portland. One was as a writer and painter ensconced in a secret office in the Chamber of Commerce building. Here he wrote continuously, although for long periods he published little. His primary outlet was Portland's *Pacific Monthly* (1898–1911), to which he contributed profusely, both under his own name and various pseudonyms. His other best-known publications came later—in poetry, the slender *Poems from the Ranges* and the long *Poet in the Desert*; and in prose, the *Heavenly Discourse* and a less famous sequel, *Earthly Discourse*. Except for the latter, all this writing was done in Portland, though the *Heavenly Discourse* was not published as a unit until the late 1920s. The *Poet in the Desert* had a great impact at the time, especially in revolutionary circles where it was distributed as a tract; however, Wood's national reputation rests on the satirical *Heavenly Discourse*, which was then reprinted many times.

Colonel Wood was also a well-known speaker and inveterate letter writer for the causes of his day. He was always a rebel, active in leftist movements during his era—including that of U'Ren; but his corporate connections inevitably led to charges of hypocrisy. Eventually a philosophical anarchist, Wood's interests encompassed both Leninism and liberal politics of a more conventional hue.[36] A pacifist, he yet liked the idea of bloody revolution—he seemed to see breaking down of the old order as an end unto itself. Wood was an early and continuing advisor of the young John Reed, and by 1917, was also writing for *The Masses*. His friend Emma Goldman, the celebrated anarchist, had *Poet in the Desert* printed cheaply for distribution at her meetings. After moving to California to devote himself more thoroughly to his literary pursuits, Wood continued to develop as a pamphleteer and gadfly. But after his Portland period, the *Earthly Discourse*—directed to issues of the thirties, as *Heavenly Discourse* had been to those of the century's teens—was his only major new work.

What we have in published form of Wood is, nonetheless, but the tip of the proverbial iceberg, and here he was better served than by the *too* prolific publishing of Joaquin Miller. What remains in print is nonetheless uneven. Although he lived in Portland, Wood was previously fascinated and inspired by the Northwest's interior, especially the range and desert life of Harney Valley—also a favorite of Miller's. His poetry is mostly free verse, at times almost common prose, and often marked by cloying sentiment. It also suggests a desire to parade a classical education, or to play with various poetic affectations of his youth.

In Wood, aesthetics and the contemplation of nature bumped up against his desire to change the world, and perhaps assuage, through a violent expression of revolt, the guilt he felt at living a life of ease, supported by great corporations; while ordinary people with whom he identified lived much more poorly. Ultimately, the Northwest nature aesthetic simply wouldn't suffice, or as Wood put it poetically:

> But when young Evening on the hill-top lingers
> And I, couched on a lichen-covered boulder,

Choke with world-beauty, I know it cannot slake
The unrest in me, deeper far, and older,
The unanswered question; unforgetful ache.[37]

The result is that while many writers lose aesthetically when they try too strongly to mix ideology with art, Wood, like Frances Victor, *only* came alive when deeply involved. In his most successful work, the *Poet in the Desert*, the desert is only background, not a goal. Although a confused montage, the pieces increasingly cohere, so that the reader feels this poem on an opulent but thoughtless nature, the inevitability of progress, the odium of war, the ugliness of religion and moral codes, and the rising anger of the revolutionary masses, somehow holds together. To Wood the desert is a voluptuous, mystic siren:

I know the Desert is beautiful
I have lain in her arms.
She has kissed me.
I have come to lie on her breast
And breathe the virginal air
Of primal conditions.
I have come out from the haunts of men;
From the struggle of wolves upon a carcass
To be melted in creation's crucible
And be made clean.[38]

The poet goes to the desert to find Truth, to escape; and the truth of that desert is terrifying, a simulacrum of his own dilemma:

Where are you, Truth? Let me behold you.
Shadowy, appearing, disappearing, ever retreating
As the Mirage of the Desert which lures to the glittering
Death-spaces beyond; advancing, never overtaken;
Your smile serene as death, your hand comforting.[39]

In his quest, Wood becomes at times akin to a Sufi or Zen Buddhist, glorying alternately in man's insignificance, but also in the significance he achieves through spiritual union with the universe. In his mystical mood, Wood offers this kind of warning:

If [Man] will not swim with the benevolent current,
as the willow leaf, in September,
Floats happily on the force of the river,
the resistless flood shall strangle him.[40]

More commonly, Wood's personal philosophy glorified a Nietzchean brand of egotism, where the highest morality is immorality, and man's duty becomes the elevation of himself to unencumbered godhood. Like William Blake, Wood wanted "To express myself fully, absolutely, cruelly, / Or I am a dead thing."[41] In this sense, he reminds us both of Joaquin Miller, and of James Stevens and Ken Kesey in subsequent generations (see Chapter 6). This ideal of limitless self-expression would conflict with Wood's solicitude for the poor and wretched in accompanying verses; but then he was a poet, not an academic.

In service of revolutionary social protest, the desert perspective allowed Wood to see the putative shame and injustice of a conventional life. Oppression was everywhere: in inherited custom, in authorities, in people of wealth, in private property. Although himself both urban and urbane, like Northwest figures such as Rogers and Lister Wood, he paints the city as the enemy.[42] A man who was soon to make a million-dollar commission on a land deal could write from a populist perspective:

> I had rather taste the common lot and be
> A man full statured,
> Than live like a louse on the backs of the poor.[43]

This confusion in Wood's life and work was reinforced by the paradox of his rejection of Christianity, coexisting with a Christian kind of guilt he felt for his good fortune! Wood held that guilt, along with his environmental determinism, in common with Rogers and Parrington, and it was mirrored when he poetically addressed criminals and prostitutes:

> Before you were born, I prepared you
> For the brothel and the gallows,
> And before you were born,
> I prepared the brothel and gallows for you.
> I have consented to the conditions
> Which lay with you in your mother's womb,
> I have made you murderers, thieves, prostitutes.[44]

There are further paradoxes. Here was a military man who retained the title "Colonel Wood" all his life; yet in some of its most graphic and moving stanzas, the *Poet in the Desert* truly condemns war. Wood builds his case by reciting the names of great Native Americans he had known, and the horrors of their bloody defeat. He then goes on to attack war, which only profits the few who always lead the sheep to slaughter. Yet this pacifist affirmation is followed by a paean to the masses marching forward to do themselves bloody conflict—in a *good* war, of struggle for meaningful change:

> They cover the earth, and like the rustle of leaves
> Is their breathing:
> "Revolution! Revolution!"
> ...
> (They) are pressing forward ready to die and to kill
> ...
> They have beaten their picks into swords,
> Their saws into knives.
> ...
> Come with agony and bloody rain,
> ... utterly destroy
> This distorted and misshapen world,
> That another may rise in beauty,
> And the little children be born into joy.[45]

No wonder the poet in the desert had early on complained that none could understand the soul of another, nor even his own. For as he put it, "[My soul] eludes me: dissolves and flies / Like a mist in deep canyons, where I cannot follow."[46]

Wood's best known work, *Heavenly Discourse*, though an important Northwest product of its time, reads today as a collection of rather simplistic anti-bourgeois, anti-war, and anti-capitalist tracts. The sense of awe before the unknown, and feeling for aesthetic or mystical experience of *Poet in the Desert* vanish here in one-dimensional discussions which Wood puts in the mouths of well-known personages of the past and present, gathered about God's throne. There is little bite to all this, and nothing, either in argument or emotion, that would convince a person not *already* convinced by positions Wood espouses here. (Of whom plenty then existed in a Northwest searching for ideals.) Important for understanding Wood's elitism is the persistent claim of the book's discussants that the enemy of man is ignorance and his greatest crime, stupidity.

Perhaps the most significant aspect of *Heavenly Discourse* is the contrast between God, a liberal but somewhat cynical and indifferent symbol of Nature, and Jesus, the idealist son who pleads continually for humankind, reminding God of His promise to perpetuate man's arduous development toward understanding. Although one commentator sees God here as a thinly-disguised Wood,[47] the contrast of Jesus and God more plausibly reflects a tension in Wood's own thinking—between a passive, pacifist position, and an active revolutionary one. The contrast is illustrated by the Mark Twain of the *Discourse*, who tells the story of an idealist using his moral authority to bring order into a mining camp. When his property is pilfered, the idealist turns the other cheek, but in his name, the other miners hang the offender to preserve the order his idealism had created.[48] Ambiguously, as in much revolutionary rhetoric, violent means are rejected by the theoretician, but eventually, his goals *are* achieved through violence. It is unclear whether Wood ever faced and understood this dilemma of all idealistic movements—a dilemma that, in the end, may also have crushed John Reed.[49]

Growing up with Colonel Wood's children, and receiving emotional and critical support from him throughout his life, the revolutionary writer John Reed—more than any Northwest figure—would become a gray eminence for radical movements of the 1930s; but had he lived longer and repudiated Bolshevism, as he showed signs of doing before his death, this apotheosis might not have occurred. However, the fact that Reed did become a kind of icon makes him important. Granville Hicks' *One of Us: The Story of John Reed,*[50] published in 1935, just before Hicks himself deserted communism, is a fairy-tale narrative of Reed's life; on every few pages there are childlike lithographs showing a clean-cut, muscular American fighting injustice on many fronts—a Lone Ranger of the left. The book is pure idolatry, but this should not obscure the fact that for a whole generation of radicals, and even certain liberals, Reed's *Ten Days that Shook the World* was required reading.

Born in Portland in 1887, Reed passed an ideal youth at a West Hills mansion exploring the surrounding woods.[51] Although his family boasted one of the city's pioneering businessmen (in gas works), was solidly Episcopalian, and employed Chinese servants, Reed also had a nonconformist grandmother, and an Uncle Ray full of stirring adventure stories about Guatemala. John took a strictly private school education, first at Portland Academy, and then in the East, at Morristown, New Jersey. A true romantic he loved medieval history (particularly the Crusades), and was already writing in his mid-teens, publishing work alongside Wood's in the *Pacific Monthly*. He then went to his father's choice of Harvard and began to blossom there. At first Reed felt outside the mainstream, consorting in particular with a Jewish boy who felt the same way; but increasingly, he garnered self-confidence and aplomb. He wrote poetry, stories, jokes, lyrics, and became editor of the *Lampoon*, captain of the water polo team, and vice-president of the Drama Club—to name only his most prominent activities. In sports Reed was trying à la Theodore Roosevelt to overcome feelings of inferiority stemming from youthful health problems—in his case, bad kidneys. Drawn to pranksters and radicals, Reed also evinced, at one point, the good old American desire to make a million dollars.[52] Of his teachers, only one had any real influence—Charles Townsend Copeland, the legendary "Copey," to whom he would dedicate his first book, *Insurgent Mexico*. As Hicks noted, "there were only three men who could say to John Reed [the] things that needed to be said."[53] These were "Copey," C.E.S. Wood, and a giant of the era, Lincoln Steffens.

A net of relationships connects the lives of Reed, Wood, and the Portland environment that played a role in producing them both. John came early to Wood through the colonel's children, and letters indicate continuing influence after Reed left town. When Reed's future wife, Louise Bryant, was deciding to leave her first husband, she turned for support to an equally emancipated suffragist, Sara Field, who was Wood's mistress.[54] In 1918, when Reed resigned on principle from a radical magazine, Wood wrote to support his actions, offering financial aid.[55] The anarchist Emma Goldman, who popularized Wood's *Poet in the Desert*, became a close acquaintance of Reed and one of the authorities on his last years in Russia. Finally, Floyd Dell, an editor of Reed and intimate associate, was also editor of the initial version of *Heavenly Discourses* in *The Masses*.[56] Steffens, who was perhaps most responsible for Reed's post–Harvard success in the New York literary world, was also a long-time friend of both Reed's father and Colonel Wood. (One of Wood's best poems is dedicated to Steffens' memory.)[57]

Although not a Northwesterner, Lincoln Steffens' role relates to our story. Born in San Francisco of parents who had come west, well educated at the University of California and abroad, he became a top New York reporter, keenly observing the seething poverty of the city's immigrant labor. At the same time, Steffens was a ubiquitous promoter of progressive reform, and increasingly, of leftist causes. He communicated to Reed the importance of direct observation, showing him how to get inside phenomena, and both of them shared an intense enthusiasm for other peoples and subcultures. A remarkable passage by Steffens in his famous autobiography shows this ability to empathize with and, indeed, live other cultures:

> ... I at that time was almost a Jew. I had become as infatuated with the Ghetto as eastern boys were with the wild west, and nailed a mazuza on my office door; I went to the synagogue on all the great Jewish holy days; on Yom Kippur I spent the whole twenty-four hours fasting and going from one synagogue to another. The music moved me most, but I knew and could follow with the awful feelings of a Jew the beautiful old ceremonies of the ancient orthodox services.[58]

Steffens almost incarnated this age of reform. He had gotten in on the ground floor of the new magazine boom, becoming editor of *McClure's* in 1901, which pioneered a spate of muckraking imitators like *Collier's* and the *Independent*. He then investigated and wrote about corruption in cities ranging from St. Louis to Pittsburgh to Boston, and exposed the New Jersey "trust factory." But he did not always tear down: he lauded La Follette's Wisconsin system of reforms, and in *The Upbuilders*, wrote the stories of five people who, he felt, had done a great deal for the country. William U'Ren was one of these, and Steffens' account remains a good source on that Northwest figure.[59] Finally, after a stint on *Everybody's* magazine, Steffens became caught up in New York's revolutionary scene of 1910–11.

Into this maelstrom of the new pranced John Reed, fresh from Harvard and a trip to Europe, where the Mediterranean seascape had aroused his dreams. Here was a handsome, stylish romantic, brimming with energy and very willing to learn. Steffens was duly impressed. Reed took a room right above Steffens' in the same house (42 Washington Square) and soon met the cream of radical and bohemian New York—Max Eastman, Floyd Dell, Big Bill Haywood, Mabel Dodge Luhan, Alfred Stieglitz. At the bidding of Reed's father, Steffens tried to keep an eye on the impetuous boy; yet he also told him to mix with New York, to "dive into life."[60] An encouraged Reed toured the slums, ate with bums, even slept in a basket of squid. He talked nonstop to Steffens about each experience, and Steffens wisely told him "to write it down." To Reed, "everything was the most wonderful thing in the world," writes Steffens, but "Jack and his crazy friends were indeed the most wonderful thing in the world."[61]

Steffens was rather puritanical, typical of one progressive wing; but another stream of reform pointed in the direction of Freudian self-liberation. John Reed fell easily into this liberationist ethic and became a lover of the bohemian leader, Mabel Dodge. He continued to write poetry and also penned a satirical play that parodied popular monthlies in the same fashion as C.E.S. Wood's satires. Reed could mix with lower-class denizens of pushcart New York, then, dressed to the nines, with the stylish. He could be a radical, but also the husky, good-looking All-American boy who, if he hadn't played college football, at least looked like he could have. He could indulge in the frivolities of bohemian life while also immixing himself in strikes, revolutionary activity, and, finally, war.

By 1913, Reed had become interested in the class struggle, locating an example of it close at hand—the Paterson silk-workers' strike. He went to see it, got arrested for four days along with Bill Haywood, then staged a pageant in Madison Square Gardens to dramatize the strike for a large New York audience. After a short trip to Italy with Mabel Dodge, he returned to New York to become managing editor of *The Masses*, still uncertain of his eventual calling.

At this juncture, the *Metropolitan Magazine*, on Steffens' advice, chose Reed to chart the Mexican Revolution led by Pancho Villa. That episode allowed him to learn what he truly was—a journalist; but what some ignore is that *Insurgent Mexico* is not simply the precursor to *Ten Days That Shook the World*, but a masterpiece in its own right. In Mexico, Reed would risk his life many times and along with this immersion in daily realities of war, bring both a poet's viewpoint and a mind that could cull hard detail. Composed from a series of dispatches sent to the *Metropolitan* and the *New York World*, *Insurgent Mexico* offers stunning portraits of Villa and the other Mexican leaders. The atmosphere of day-to-day immediacy is, astonishingly, the same as what we sometimes think to be caricature in later movies: women starving yet passionate, children milling at generals' feet chewing on bullets, murders as casual and gratuitous as spitting; and poverty, beauty, warmth, desert vastness all commingled. The vivid Reed surrounds goings-on with effulgent descriptions of fiery sunsets, velvety hills, bloody primitive hospitals, but permits actions and anecdotes to speak mainly for themselves. In sum, the book still deserves to be read, not least by journalists.

In his time, *Insurgent Mexico* already gave Reed a national reputation. A much larger conflagration then elicited another book of his, *The War in Western Europe*; but that extended conflict did not really interest Reed from a military point of view. It struck him rather as an impersonal capitalist war, a view that his visit to the Western front merely confirmed. According to Daniel Lehman, this period constituted an important turning point in Reed's thinking, buttressed of course by a heavy dose of Marxian pacifism.[62]

Disillusionment with European and American socialists, and their acquiescence in this lethal conflict, then helped impel Reed toward Russia in 1917. He left in August of that year, during the Menshevik era of the Revolution, to report for *The Masses* and *The Call*; and the enduring product of his trip was *Ten Days that Shook the World*, which became the best-known firsthand account of the Bolshevik takeover, both in the West and the U.S.S.R.

To Russia, Reed carried both an enthusiastic Marxism and at least some journalistic rigor born of his Mexican experiences. (However, Robert Rosenstone argues that he never quite reconciled the gap between his romantic and realistic sides, and David C. Duke has found factual errors in the work of this literary journalist.) By this period Reed was assisted and often accompanied by an ardent female admirer who was first his lover, then his wife—Louise Bryant. Bryant, herself a romantic who had lived in Reed's home town and attended the University of Oregon, abandoned her successful Portland husband to be with Reed. When both became involved with Eugene O'Neill's developing career, she also developed for a time a liaison with the playwright. But Louise grew into a passionate socialist, enthusiastically supporting Reed's trip to Russia. Later she went there herself and wrote an alternative *Ten Days* (*Six Months in Russia*), before returning to conduct an extensive lecture tour in America. After Reed's death, Bryant would marry the Russian expert who later became America's first ambassador to the Soviet Union, William Bullitt. Soon divorced, and separated from the child she had given Bullitt, she died in her late forties as an alcoholic in Paris. Despite infidelities, Bryant's romance with Reed had been the high point of her life.[63]

Reed's *Ten Days* chronicles the political maneuvers and street-fighting in Petrograd of November 1917, culminating in the Bolsheviks' success. Compared to *Insurgent Mexico*, this book is more rigidly organized, less romantic, and also less balanced. The novelist's sensibility is readily apparent, as in this typical description of the street atmosphere:

> It was on November 18th that the snow came. In the morning we woke to window-ledges heaped white, and snowflakes falling so whirling thick that it was impossible to see ten feet ahead. The mud was gone; in a twinkling the gloomy city became white, dazzling. The *droshki* with their padded coachmen turned into sleighs, bounding along the uneven street at headlong speed, their drivers' beards stiff and frozen.... In spite of Revolution, all Russia plunging dizzily into the unknown and terrible future, joy swept the city with the coming of the snow. Everybody was smiling; people ran into the streets, holding out their arms to the soft, falling flakes, laughing. Hidden was all the greyness; only the gold and colored spires and cupolas, with heightened barbaric splendour, gleamed through the white snow.
>
> Even the sun came out, pale and watery, at noon. The colds and rheumatism of the rainy months vanished. The life of the city grew gay, and the very Revolution ran swifter....[64]

The book builds on actual speeches by Lenin, interviews with leaders like Trotsky, and statistics, such as the crucial rise in bread prices. Still, beyond the factualism, Reed's specific ardor carries the reader here. For example:

> Think of the poorly-clad people, standing on the iron-white streets of Petrograd whole days in the Russian winter! I have listened in the bread-lines, hearing the bitter, acrid note of discontent which from time to time burst up through the miraculous good nature of the Russian crowd....[65]

Some have called Reed a transitional link between social reform of the Steffens stamp, and the subsequent hard-line communism of "scientific" Marxists; that is, between old-style progressivism and the vogue of proletarian revolution that reached its peak in the 1930s.[66] Upton Sinclair would call Reed the playboy of the revolution—specifically, a playboy of millionaire stock. But Reed's involvement with the Russian Revolution was certainly to have a significant effect on American intellectual history. It also made daring, on-the-spot journalism henceforth legitimate, helping galvanize writers like Hemingway into becoming participants as well as authors.

Returning to the U.S. in the spring of 1918, Reed found the anti–Communist winds beginning to blow hard there, and along with other left-wing radicals, he was excoriated for his pro–Soviet lectures. His notes for *Ten Days* were temporarily confiscated and the book only saw the light of day in March 1920, selling 9,000 copies in its first three months. Meanwhile, the Palmer raids were commencing and Reed had already decided to sail back to Russia. Perhaps he was trying to live down Sinclair's epithet—certainly he was stung by the word "playboy." Wishing to show his seriousness, the following statement is typical of this autumnal period (as it turned out) of Reed's life: "It is not only necessary to plan the political downfall of the capitalist class [in America], but also to get into the minds of the workers some conception of the industrial framework which will underlie the new Socialist political commonwealth."[67]

Back in Russia of the terrible Civil War era, Reed traveled widely, and met Lenin several times again, along with Kamenev, Zinoviev, Radek, and others doomed to be eliminated by their own. He observed the effects of revolution on Russian society, but rather like Arthur Koestler in 1933, was still tarnished with an illusionary optimism that perhaps went back to his idyllic Northwest origins. No "God that Failed" for Reed—in any event, time was lacking for such a reappraisal. When the American Communist parties seemed about to fuse, Reed decided to go back to the States, but twice was stopped. He spent three awful months in Finland, exposed to disease there because of confinement and a poor diet. Unable to identify his incarcerators, and waiting for help from East or West, he became more and more depressed. Perhaps Reed suspected the Bolshevik Zinoviev, whom he came to distrust, of engineering the prison sentence, but he couldn't confirm this. The Russians finally liberated him, and in August 1920 permitted him to attend a congress of Oriental nations at Baku. After a long separation, his wife, Louise, again returned to him; but still weakened by prison scurvy, Reed caught typhus during their reunion in Moscow. (In the wake of a world-wide flu epidemic, doctors at first mistakenly diagnosed his symptoms as influenza.) Reed passed away on October 17, 1920, three days before his thirty-third birthday.

This death coincided with the ending of an era. At home the complications of extending revolutionary notions to all spheres of life had led other radicals to a general retrenchment. Many who were for railroad reform found they could not also countenance free love. As we will see, this was probably the case with Vernon Parrington, who took a dim view of literary radicals or of hedonistic novelists such as F. Scott Fitzgerald. Perceptively, Parrington's colleague, J. Allen Smith, came, near the end of his life, to write this epitaph for his progressive generation: "The real trouble with us reformers is that we made reform a crusade against standards. Well, we smashed them all and now neither we nor anybody else have anything left."[68]

Chapter 5

The Northwest Achievement of V. L. Parrington

INTELLECTUALLY, THE BRIGHTEST LIGHT to appear in this regional firmament of reformism was Vernon Louis Parrington. Of all the Populist and Progressive intellectuals in the Pacific Northwest, this historian of ideas contributed the most substantial, interesting, and widely-received scholarly work, one whose influence in its field was never matched. Parrington was a man who, despite two years at Harvard, was largely self-educated, and who taught in Emporia, Kansas, and at the University of Oklahoma, before coming to Seattle's University of Washington as a teacher of rhetoric in 1908. Somewhat *sub rosa*, and energized by the Northwest environment, he then devoted himself to a work which would become his masterpiece: *Main Currents in American Thought*, the first two volumes of which appeared in 1927 (the third appeared in incomplete form after his sudden death in 1929). At the end of his life, an obscure Seattle professor had suddenly become a major influence in American thought. Charles Beard, the historian, and Henry Seidel Canby, a famous critic, were both highly enthusiastic, while the *New York Times* and *Dallas News* gave equal applause.[1] In 1928, Parrington received the Pulitzer prize for history, having produced in *Main Currents* a work that was useful and acceptable to specialists in a variety of fields, but insightful and vivid enough to impact a wider cultural world.

During the 1930s, Parrington's *magnum opus* was broadly accepted, especially on the Left, as a part of his generation's heritage. Richard Hofstadter, in his *Progressive Historians*, conveyed this great sense of connecting to one of "us" on first reading Parrington in 1938. The sociologist, Lewis Feuer, in a letter, said "we all" read Parrington, along with other Northwest figures like Anna Louise Strong, C.E.S. Wood (*Heavenly Discourse*), and

John Reed. Lionel Trilling in the *Partisan Review* (1940) was effusive, and so was Alfred Kazin in his *On Native Grounds* (1942).[2] To be sure, there was an intellectual group in the late thirties—socialists *à outrance*—who reproached Parrington either for not being sufficiently Marxist, or for hiding his allegiance to that creed in Jeffersonian garb. Representative here was Bernard Smith's article "Parrington's Main Currents in American Thought," in *Books that Changed Our Minds*. Smith conceded that the time had not been ripe in the '20s for a genuine Marxist,[3] but also declared that Parrington's definite tinges of the philosophy had "been overlooked by those metropolitan intellectuals who were charmed by his agrarian leanings."[4] It was therefore wrong to call him a mere Populist, for "I can state dogmatically that he had some acquaintance with Marxism, had been influenced by it, and knew that his method was related to it. I have seen a letter by him in which he said as much."[5] But E. H. Eby, who knew Parrington well, noted that by the late '20s at least, Parrington, like other Northwest intellectuals, feared the decline of American individual liberalism before the onslaught of collectivist creeds like Marxism.[6]

Although both were leaders of liberal opinion in their day, the contrast between the Jeffersonian progressive Parrington and the elitist-socialist Wood reflected a split within American reform movements and their ideologies. Fundamentally, Parrington loved the past and simple values—values he saw as corrupted and lost through changes in America stemming from capitalism and modern technology; whereas the socialist Wood saw the past as imperfect, looking instead to a future that would throw off not only historical chains that clearly included capitalism, but also other popularly cherished traditions.

With the passing of the Depression and increasing academic specialization after World War II, Parrington's work was downgraded. Leading the reaction was the group known as the New Critics, who held that a literary work was autonomous, a work of the individual imagination, and not a mere cultural byproduct or artifact. They ranged themselves against "proletarian" critics like Kazin or Edmund Wilson, whose viewpoint more resembled Parrington's on the importance of socioeconomic background in literature. In the Northwest there was a local uprising of New Critics even at Parrington's own University of Washington, causing his reputation to decline there. Robert Heilmann, brought to the U.W.'s English department as its chair after the war, was a leading critic not only of Parrington, but of American Studies generally.[7]

Not to disparage the original insights of the New Critics, they missed the point that Parrington was no crude determinist, but rather a fuser of form and substance, and one to whom aesthetics were undoubtedly important. This partly explained Parrington's "notorious eulogy," as Trilling saw it, of the stylist James Branch Cabell.[8] On the other hand, historians of ideas continued to deal sympathetically with Parrington, because they saw him as one of the early legitimators of their discipline. In *The American Mind* (1950), Henry Commager praised Parrington by acknowledging his great debts to him; and in 1952, a sample of some 100 American historians chose his *Main Currents* as their favorite among *all* American histories published between 1920 and 1935! Much more recently, there seems to have been a mini-rediscovery of Parrington in a variety of articles or short pieces, some by major intellectual figures. But he has never quite gotten his long-term due.[9]

Where do *we* place V. L. Parrington—part of a Northwest age of reform in both its academic and literal environment—within the history of American ideas? Surprisingly, few American intellectual historians came before him, and of those who did there was no real consciousness of being one. Edward Eggleston (1837–1902) and Moses Coit Tyler (1835–1900) were probably Parrington's two most important predecessors. The former resembled Parrington in his environmentalism, the latter in his florid style and adverse treatment of specific figures in American history like Cotton Mather. Both, however, were essentially colonial historians who largely ignored the great explosion of romanticism, realism, social thought, and agrarian views in the nineteenth and early twentieth century.

The first course in American intellectual history, and the first intimation that it was a subject worthy of study, was James Harvey Robinson's seminar on it in the early 1900s at Columbia University. A group of fine progressive historians followed in the furrow of Robinson's new direction; yet Parrington's conception and execution of a truly comprehensive history of American ideas remains unique. He was one of those rare historians who could actually make his intense prejudices work for him. In *Main Currents* his loves—above all, agrarianism and liberalism—are pitted violently against his hates, including preeminently, Puritanism and big business. His *oeuvre*, as Kazin first pointed out, was a battleground of ideas. Parrington's heart went out to those who had rebelled in the name of American justice and freedom: Roger Williams, Henry Thoreau, Walt Whitman, John Calhoun. Mainly, American history was a tale of the pure going inevitably sour. Even the Declaration of Independence had soon been betrayed by the Constitution, and in this story Alexander Hamilton was nothing less than a satan who had wormed his way into the rosy American apple. More and more of these worms appeared, and against them were ranged brave reformers, like Andrew Jackson, considered, like many Parrington heroes, an epigone of Jefferson. Everyone on Parrington's pages is alive and moving, even warring, toward either Good or Evil. And here the Northwest intellectual environment of his time (including proximity to J. Allen Smith) truly played a role. Take, for example, Parrington's sympathy for James Fenimore Cooper: "A materialistic middle class with its gospel of progress interpreted in terms of exploitation seemed to him the hateful progeny of a period of 'moral occultation'; and against this 'Yankee' philosophy [Cooper] waged an unrelenting warfare."[10]

In Parrington's world, moral figures tried hard to warn complacent Americans about the evils of commercialism (for a later age, read industrialism), but were often ignored. Empathizing with these independent thinkers, he depicted them writhing in a philistine environment that simply could not recognize their worth. Here is Parrington in a vivid passage on Herman Melville—"Pessimist":

> Lifelong he was lacerated by the coldly moral in his environment, and harrassed by the crudely practical; and without forcing the comparison, one may feel that Bryant and Greeley embodied in nobler form the twin forces that seized upon his bold and rich nature, and bound it to the rocks to be fed on by eagles. Like Jacob he wrestled all night with an angel, yet got no blessing from the touched thigh. Instead, his free spirit was tormented and his adventurous heart seared with fire.... All the powers of darkness fought over him, all the devils plagued him. They drove him down into the gloom of his tormented soul, and if they did not conquer, they left him maimed and stricken.... There is no other tragedy in American letters comparable to the tragedy of Herman Melville.[11]

Sometimes, however, Parrington's moralism became too naive, and on no subject was he more simplistic or one-dimensional than religion. In particular, he seems distinctly old-fashioned treating the Puritanism we know played a formative role in the growth of American democracy. Puritanism, in Parrington's view, was antidemocratic, and he gratuitously wedded it to conservatism of all stripes. Thus, John Winthrop added "Hebraic twists to aristocratic prejudices,"[12] while Thomas Hutchinson was "a stiff-necked official of scrupulous principle," and "grossly reactionary."[13] Even John Adams' mildly skeptical outlook (including distrust of people's foibles) smacked of Calvinism, as contrasted to the boundless, generous doctrines of a Paine or Jefferson;[14] while George Washington's anti–Jacobinism was mere "*odium theologicum*."[15] Occasionally, Parrington's obsession about Puritanism located worthwhile insights; for example, John Calhoun's Southern proslavery stance and sternness were placed against the background of Puritan Scotch-Irishness.[16] But generally, Parrington dealt poorly with the Puritans, and his first volume suffers for that.

This view of the Puritans seems to have been strongly influenced by one of Parrington's few intellectual predecessors—Moses Coit Tyler. Textual comparison may not prove an influence, but certain Parrington and Tyler passages sound interchangeable, both in style and attitude. In Cotton Mather, Tyler saw

> a person whose intellectual endowments were quite remarkable, but inflated and perverted by egoism; himself imposed upon by his own moral affectations, ... [he] stretched, every instant of his life, on the rack of ostentatious exertion, intellectual and religious ... in deference to a dreadful system of ascetic and pharasaic formalism, in which his nature was hopelessly enmeshed.[17]

In Parrington's Mather,

> Religious exaltation flowered from the root of egoism. His vanity was cosmic.... What a crooked and debased mind lay back of those eyes that were forever spying out occasions to magnify self! He grovels in proud self-abasement. He distorts the most obvious reality.[18]

Who then did this Northwest historian of ideas praise? He praised anyone who furthered the march of democracy—especially, agrarian, Jeffersonian democracy—including characters now not always viewed as democratic, such as Roger Williams of Rhode Island and Thomas Hooker of Connecticut. Arriving at Jefferson himself, the author seems to cut loose, and the writing here—with partiality on parade—reveals Parrington at his most characteristic (and possibly prescient): "As [Jefferson] looked into the future he saw great cities rising to breed their Roman mobs, duped and exploited by demagogues, the convenient tools of autocracy; and counting the cost in social well-being he set his face like flint against the rising capitalism."[19]

With Volume II and the nineteenth century, Parrington comes most alive, charting the bracing struggles of agrarianism and capitalism in an America finally freed from Puritan dogma. The contrast between the sunshiny Volume II and a more dour Volume I is striking. It may be that Parrington had developed an increasingly relaxed routine in Seattle, which he certainly preferred to any other place he had inhabited. Of course he continued to be prejudiced, dismissing even major writers like Poe with a mere page or two. ("The problem of Poe ... may be left with the psychologist and belletrist with whom it belongs."[20]) And sometimes his phrases outrun meaningfulness, as on the Southern Greek revival: "It was no vagrant eddy but a broadening current of tendency."[21] On figures like Andrew Jackson he sounds distinctly old-fashioned and conventional, taking at face value the president's manly backwoods exterior and ignoring his urban support. Many first-rate works from Arthur Schlesinger, Jr.'s pioneering *The Age of Jackson* onward make Parrington's treatment here seem dated.

But in Volume II he becomes surer stylistically, and here, for example, is a superb Parringtonian evocation of Washington Irving's mindset:

> An incorrigible *flâneur*, Irving's business in life was to loaf and invite the picturesque. A confirmed rambler in pleasant places in the many lands he visited, he

> was a lover of the past rather than the present, seeking to recreate the golden days of the Alhambra or live over the adventurous mood of the fur trader. The immediate and the actual was an unsatisfying diet for his dreams. There was in him nothing of the calm aloofness of the intellectual that stands apart to clarify its critical estimate, and none of the reforming zeal of the Puritan that is at peace only in the thick of a moral crusade.... Revolutions seemed to him somewhat vulgar affairs. The French Revolution had brought destruction to many lovely things, and the industrial revolution was taking too heavy a toll of the picturesque to please him. He thought it a pity that steam should drive the clipper ship from the seas and put an end to snug posting in the tally-ho. Progress might be bought at too dear a price. The bluff squire with his hounds, the great hall with its ancient yuletide customs, the patriarchal relations between master and man, seemed to him more worthwhile than the things progress was substituting for them; so he turned away from the new and gently ingratiated himself into the past in order to gather up such fragments of the picturesque as progress had not yet destroyed.[22]

In his unfinished Volume III, Parrington finally began to touch his own experience, and his populist pique, bred of harsh Kansas farm life, makes this excitingly felt history. On populism and its corresponding opposite, the monopolists' Gilded Age (and/or the East), he is again superb. Partly, Parrington's very pessimism makes his writing so forceful. There are wistful pangs here for the Hamlin Garland frontier of his youth, gone as in a puff. ("The prairie fires have long since died out, the prairie chickens have left forever fields that have fallen to the base servitude of the plough—so much is gone definitely out of my life to its loss."[23]) Pangs, too, for the plight of individual liberalism, succumbing to the use of Hamiltonian government as a control on big business. And sadness over the final victory of huge, standardizing forces over the little man. For Parrington definitely loved the individual and the average person, seething over the rise of a mass society in America. Treating Walt Whitman from his own perspective of the '20s as a regretted throwback to an older era, he writes: "Certainly in the welter of today, with science become the drab and slut of war and industrialism, with sterile money-slaves instead of men, Whitman's expansive hopes seem grotesque enough."[24]

The modern context, and Volume III, began for Parrington in the post–Civil War period, when the face of America changed radically from an agrarian to an industrial one. Opposed though he was to the Gilded Age, Parrington yet writes some of his most stimulating pages on that phenomenon—perhaps affected by the era's undeniable energy. Lurking behind his tone of condemnation is one of good humor, and that combination is partly what makes these pages so readable. Of course, Rabelaisian detail was here for the asking, and Parrington had a sure instinct for it. With people around like Jay Cooke, whom he reckoned "the first modern American,"[25] or General Grant, who accepted bribes "as a child would accept gifts from a fairy godmother,"[26] or Barnum the Showman, "growing rich on the profession of humbuggery, a vulgar greasy genius, pure brass without any gilding, yet in picturesque and capable effrontery the very embodiment of the age,"[27] Parrington had ample material to exploit. His ambivalence toward material progress spills over here into the literary realm as well. He shows a qualified admiration for the naturalists, yet fails to realize that modern urban life was the necessary grist for their mills. Despising vulgar newness, he yet gives genteel writers of the 1870s, guardians of the old, short shrift on his pages. Having treated Whitman in Volume II, he brings him in again for Volume III, placing him under the rubric of "The Afterglow of the Enlightenment." Parrington treats too many good things in the modern age as mere lucky atavisms, and even Mark Twain fits within a subsection called "The Backwash of the Frontier."

On Twain, Parrington demonstrates both his insight and prejudices. Having placed the celebrated writer within a frontier past, he then acknowledges another, deep-down Mark Twain, different from the folksy joker—"the artist, the chivalrous lover of justice, the simple child puzzled at life...."[28] Next, he derides Twain's anti-medievalism (Parrington's own cult of the Middle Ages bordering at times on silly);[29] and as a radical, misreads *A Connecticut Yankee* as "a flame that sears and shrivels the mean property-consciousness which lays a blight on every civilization."[30] (Parrington by the way, owned a nice house in Seattle and a cabin on Puget Sound!) But he ends by getting at the heart of Twain's final isolation.

The acme of Parrington's power comes in the part on populist revolts, collected in a subsection called "The Plight of the Farmer." Here, his own rural background is woven into the prose, as he pits farmers against capitalism in an ineluctable struggle to the death. Note the verbiage he uses for his farmer-victim: "And now in the middle eighties he began to feel the rope about his neck.... It was the money-power of the East, the grip of Wall Street, that was strangling him...."[31]

On Hamlin Garland, in particular, Parrington is on his own turf, and the whole historian and person—aching Jeffersonian, witness of the dying frontier, lover of style—works well here. Unfortunately, this was one of Parrington's last completed sections before his untimely death:

> At bottom [Garland] is an idealist of the old Jeffersonian breed, an earnest soul devoid of humor, who loves beauty and is mightily concerned about justice, and who, discovering little beauty and finding scant justice in the world where fate first set him, turned rebel and threw in his lot with the poor and the exploited.[32]

Parrington sees Garland as a *last* type, a relic, as he may well have felt himself to be in the declining age of reform, particularly in the Northwest:

> The vast bleak chemical cosmos that bewildered Theodore Dreiser did not rise before [Garland] to dwarf the individual nor overwhelm his aspirations. Like a French romantic of a hundred years before, he remained a confirmed optimist

> who believed that the future will correct the mistakes of the past, and the peace and beauty for which the human race longs lie immediately ahead. The art of the young man was becoming old-fashioned in the world of Stephen Crane; his ideals were Victorian in the days of Mark Hanna. And so after the agrarian revolt had failed and America lay fat and contented in the lap of McKinley prosperity, he found himself a man without a country, an alien in an industrializing order....[33]

Parrington here sounds like a romantic pessimist. Not only did he fear for the survival of American liberalism, but he also felt isolated from the new literary vogues, and in the 1920s felt alienated from the alienated themselves! His notes for the unfinished part of *Main Currents* discount F. Scott Fitzgerald as "a bad boy who loves to smash things to show how naughty he is; ... Precocious, ignorant—a short candle already burnt out";[34] and on the new currents of bohemian protest, inspired by the war, Freud, and Babbitry, he writes disdainfully of "luminaries of the school which holds that the sufficient tests of intellectual emancipation are rolled hose, midnight discussions, black coffee, and the discarding of wedding rings."[35] There was a seriousness to Parrington that in the Harding and Coolidge era must have appeared to some as odd (though of course the more earnest '30s were just around the corner).

How did Parrington's background, then the Northwest environment in adulthood help form this unique cultural commentator and reformist? The origins of his ideas can partially be found in certain writers such as the Socialist and anti-modern writer William Morris; but they can *also* be located in a particular strand of personal development to which the Northwest made a distinct contribution.

Parrington was born at the outset of the new industrial era, in 1871 at Aurora, Illinois, to which his family had come, like Hamlin Garland's, from rural Maine. Six years later, he moved to a farm in eastern Kansas to be brought up in drab, tiny Americus. To understand Parrington, one must treat the influence of this farm background less one-dimensionally than in, say, Richard Hofstadter's emphasis on its harshness.[36] Certainly Parrington revolted against his cramping background by escaping its thin soil (as he would say); and to a degree he *was* the typical angry young man frowning on the provinces and putting his anger into ideology. But the fact is that Parrington never quite shed the farm either. At college in Emporia he referred contemptuously to poorly clothed "country jakes" and "clodhoppers," realizing his own clothes had only just removed him from that milieu. At Harvard he suffered because he thought himself (or feared being) a rube; in Chicago he peered up at skyscrapers, surveying the city's bustle with the fascination of a recently emancipated but no less rural person.[37] He had a visceral distrust of the city that was fueled by the populist era of protest and reform, but which also stemmed from his boyhood.

Parrington, in sum, departed the farm, thankful to leave a tough, stultifying setting; but the farm never really left him. We know how deeply rural imagery infused his *magnus opus*—form complementing theme. Nature allusions—reefs and barriers, natural fruit and rotten fruit, thin soil and deep soil—punctuate the book. Sometimes, as Hofstadter put it, these allusions "come along so fast that they seem to trip over each other...."[38] But decoding of Parrington's profuse imagery remains interesting: for example, barnyard, cider house, or granary frequently standing for good things; narrow, crooked, stinking city street milieus for bad.[39]

Parrington's mind was so concrete that he could not discourse on a complex subject until he had found a central organizational, down-to-earth term for it.[40] The period that stumped him most was the Gilded Age, and he ultimately hit upon a famed tagline for the era—"the Great Barbecue." Barbecue connotes abundance, even feast, and Parrington despised luxury because it was soft and bourgeois, the worst outgrowth of urban civilization.[41] Captains of industry who smoked cigars wrapped in fifty-dollar bills provided as ample a target as Trimalchio with his silver toothpicks had for Rome's Petronius. The Great Barbecue was the most venomous epithet a man of frugal background could summon up.

This continuing rural residue in Parrington is most clearly seen in his vibrant treatment of Midwestern populism. The description of a depressed Middle Border (in Volume III), along with the following parts on writers like Garland, reveal Parrington at his warmest and most searing. There is an odor of glamour and of drama, as he pits the innocent farm against Wall Street. And his sympathies are openly telegraphed: "With his feet on the sobering earth the farmer was no middle-class adventurer, no buccaneer lying in wait for the golden argosies of Spain, but a sober realist kept sane by wind and weather and kept honest by his daily occupation of tilling and reaping."[42]

Like a painter with his blood up, Parrington depicts sunburned farmers tilting their heads out of cornfields to hear the rousing speeches of Mary Ellen Lease or Sockless Jerry Simpson—populist appeals to the discontented in their own idiom which set the countryside on fire.[43] The ultimate struggle of dying agrarianism and triumphant capitalism was the paroxysmal climax of Parrington's whole enterprise (and of its "main currents"). But it also showed that his philosophy, as with all philosophies, went back to a specific formative experience, a certain primary vision that could never be effaced.

To infuse that vision with content, Parrington especially drew upon Hamlin Garland. "Hamlin Garland," he wrote in a memoir, "has pictured truly the life that I knew and lived."[44] Garland's *Son of the Middle Border* was not only redolent of Parrington's background, but also directed him to its underlying poetic possibilities. Parrington might dismiss this ("much of the poetry of my youth is woven of things that have passed with the border"[45]); but clearly that quality remained in his mature Northwest writing. Compare Parrington, in his memoir:

> To go to bed with the pleasant acrid smell of the freshly burnt-off land in the nostrils, with the mind full of the excitement of backfiring, of watching the low flame running before the wind, of wielding the broom against all dangerous vagrant tendencies; and then to wake in the morning to the call of the prairie cock from a low ridge half a mile away—a call that was compact of the dawns and freedoms of the untamed places—was not that to sleep and wake in the very Land of Desire, the changing seasons of which will bring each its wonders?[46]

with Garland:

> The grasshoppers move in clouds with snap and buzz and out of the luxurious stagnant marshes comes the ever-thickening chorus of the toads, while above them the kildees and the snipe shuttle to and fro in sounding flight. The blackbirds on the cat-tails sway and swing, uttering through lifted throats their liquid gurgle, mad with delight of the sun and the season—and over all, and laving all, moves the slow wind, heavy with the breath of the far-off blooms of other lands, a wind which covers the sunset plain with a golden entrancing haze.
>
> At such times it seemed to me that we had reached the "sunset region" of our song, and that we were indeed "lords of the soil."[47]

Both Garland and Parrington knew the drudgery of farm life and used strong prose to capture it. But each finally lamented, and was deeply haunted by, the passing of a rural America.

Parrington's personal experience also made him acutely aware of exploitation. He had seen produce rotting while money-lenders closed in for the kill.[48] He had seen his mother, like Garland's, do backbreaking work for paltry gain, while middlemen raked in profits from behind a desk. He had watched buyers' testers make fresh butter seem rancid and cut the price before his outraged parents. And to cap it all, his father was swindled in a shady timber-stock promotion.[49] Again, Parrington's radicalism was in good part engendered by bitter experience.

Meanwhile, there were Christian philistines to stimulate his anticlericalism and special hatred for predestinarian religion. Paradoxically, Parrington may have been indebted to Midwestern revivalism—to its oratorical expansiveness, in particular—for his ability to mint phrases was born of the same background as a William Jennings Bryan's.[50] And, again, there *is* ambivalence in Parrington's attitude toward religion. With the coming of Mammon (in his third volume), he notes a little wistfully that "the transcendental theologian was soon to be as extinct as the passenger pigeon."[51]

Returning to his life chronology and influences, Emporia College had been a dismal undergraduate wasteland, making the Victorian novels Parrington consumed by the bushelful at the public library heady by comparison.

Harvard came next and intensified Parrington's distaste for New England. His years in Boston wrought an all-important hyphenation process, whereby Puritan, Brahmin, Tory, genteel would all be somewhat thrown together. And he vowed *never* to send his own son to undemocratic Harvard.[52]

Back at Emporia for teaching, the twenty-two year-old Parrington was caught up in the populist wave, as seen; and he would vote for Bryan in 1896.[53] The Panic of '93 and ensuing hard times had driven him to a serious viewpoint, from which all religion seemed banished as unpardonable nonsense. Then, in 1897, he moved to the University of Oklahoma, where a heavy load included football coaching (at which he shone), and where the blunt, drab campus kept him an angry struggler. However, when the territory became a state in 1907, a new group insinuated itself into political control of the university at Norman. The clique was theologically conservative and thanks to its influence, Parrington and other progressive faculty were dismissed.

Had he remained at Oklahoma, however, Parrington probably never would have given us his master work. His appointment to Seattle's University of Washington in 1908, as assistant professor of rhetoric, allowed him to leave the fundamentalists behind; and he now found himself in an area of vigorous, burgeoning progressivism, and could work in a congenial physical environment.[54] Suddenly his mental windows were thrown open—as fresh as the bracing down-lake views of Mount Rainier. Certainly he now became surer of his directions. In Parrington's words, "The change from Oklahoma to Washington marks the shift with me from the older cultural interpretation of life to the later economic."[55] Secondly, Parrington finally opted for American literature as a legitimate field of study in itself—this in a period when it was still submerged beneath the discipline of "English literature." Third, he derived from the Washington faculty about the mix of confirmation and distance that he required. Too many splendid intellects, at a better-known university such as Yale or Wisconsin, might well have affected him adversely.[56] On the other hand, there were now bright Northwest progressives with whom he could talk without fighting—J. Allen Smith, Edward MacMahon, and later, Joseph Harrison and E. H. Eby.

Most important to Parrington's development in Seattle was his contact with the political scientist Smith, to whom *Main Currents* is dedicated (for a "Scholar, Teacher, Democrat, Gentleman"). To Parrington, Smith was a key intellectual whose early-warning radar had helped turn America reform-minded and specifically, toward an attitude of vigilance vis-à-vis the excesses of big business. Smith seemed, above all, realistic, helping to invest liberalism with a necessary solidity. Thanks to his efforts, "the blowsy romanticisms that earlier had befuddled the American mind were pretty much dissipated."[57] From Smith, Parrington derived a *conscious* view of American history. Both, of course, had grown up in the crucible of Midwestern populism—it is interesting how close Smith's pre–Washington experience comes to Parrington's; but Smith could take the unfocused resentment many of his generation felt and put it into usable theory. Parrington made Smith's view of the Constitution his own, and Smith's practical struggles against oppression and conservatism in the Northwest, and at the sylvan university in Seattle added to the attraction of his theories. In setting about to write his own history, Parrington drew upon his older colleague's moral fire. Only many years later would Parrington begin to question the application of Hamiltonian constraints for Jeffersonian ends,[58] one of the central dilemmas, as it turned out, of modern liberalism.

But Smith's general viewpoint offered Parrington an architectural foundation for his own work that placed all American political history into a streamlined structure. All struggles became essentially Declaration of Independence (rights of people) versus Constitution (rights of property). Democratic movements could *only* be restorative—attempts at recovering the Declaration's spirit. As seen, Parrington lumped together Roger Williams' religious independence movement, Jeffersonianism, Jacksonianism, and finally, the third-party revolts of his own time. Progressivism and its practical reforms—initiative, referendum, recall, Australian ballot—only cap off and culminate a long struggle.[59]

The Northwest's Smith thus helped solidify Parrington's Manichaean separation of contrastive elements, including romantic fluff, as he saw it, contrasted to forthright realism in American literature.[60] Thus, Henry James, Hawthorne, and Poe—to take only the most prominent examples—are notoriously short-changed in the Parrington landscape because they refused to see what was important! Parrington finds James the most petty—"like modern scholarship he came to deal more and more with less and less."[61] In the shadow of Herbert Spencer, Parrington saw life basically as force and struggle; it was not, or should not be, supernatural speculation, subtle dinner table interplay, or cool, narrow-headed Puritan strictures.[62]

Parrington may have profited from participation in the departmental struggles of a still young university in Seattle. The liberal arts faculty at Washington was then split roughly along the lines conservative versus progressive. Among the conservatives were Edmond S. Meany and Frederick Padelford, head of the U.W. English department and subsequently, dean of the graduate school.[63] Parrington became embroiled with Padelford over language requirements, which included Anglo-Saxon, Middle English, Latin, and several modern languages, and over the place of American literature generally in the university.[64] He had to fight hard to get library money, and only after *Main Currents* was published did he receive as much as six hundred dollars to purchase American literature books.[65] Meanwhile, he served on an architecture committee at the university and would vociferously criticize the new Suzzallo library building. He backed Smith in his altercations with president and community, and as an ardent conservationist, ranged himself against the state's powerful lumber interests.[66]

For daily reinforcement, his classes did wonders. Parrington's Socratically-taught courses, much more discussion than lecture, became a hit on campus.[67] Despite a fondness for ribbing certain students,[68] that popularity grew by leaps and bounds. Not only was he bright and stimulating, but also quite handsome, with distinguished-looking hair and a sturdy figure. A contemporary student estimate of Parrington stresses all this:

> You've heard tell of Professor Parrington—his court is worthy of Mr. Bloom's consternation. Not only are the coeds adoring followers, but young men who would swallow their English requirement tout suite [sic] are given to lingering at his feet ...
>
> Mrs. Parrington doesn't worry about her popular husband. She realizes there is safety in numbers. She's very used to hearing folks say they just love Mr. Parrington. She's very used to them remarking about his wonderful hair and his charming manners.[69]

Parrington was indeed a stylish man and took pride in being one. Says Harrison: "His dress, his carriage, his speech, his meticulous literary style were exact but natural expressions of himself.... Photographers greeted him as a privilege."[70] But Parrington's sure demeanor was also a result of being in the right conditions. He even enjoyed playing billiards at the faculty club with conservative faculty.[71] However, he still knew how to maintain needed reserve, and was so unobtrusive about his brilliance and scholarly intentions that both his family and most of the faculty were greatly astonished by the appearance of *Main Currents*—"none save those who have read the manuscript were prepared for the event."[72] Indeed, the whole history profession and the literary U.S. would be stunned by this thunderbolt from the West. Seattle's very remoteness was the *sine qua non* for this element of surprise; as David Noble put it,

> Seen from the viewpoint of the historical profession, Parrington, the unknown outsider whose life was almost over, was a voice crying from the wilderness. And this is the fundamental significance of Parrington: his was a voice crying out to this people to return to the ways of their ancestors, to reform, to purify themselves before it was too late.[73]

Parrington had certainly been impatient with foot-dragging colleagues, but again, for our benefit that pique was ultimately displaced into his major project. A quirky essay[74] he wrote, assailing the English Literature department at Washington, was withdrawn from publication, probably because Parrington was ashamed of it; and only thirty-five years later did it appear in print. Though ostensibly the essay asked colleagues to be more economic-minded or hard-headed, it was also a critique of mere antiquarianism. Parrington was pleading here for scholarship that counted; and still quietly working at his own, could only exhort at this point, rather than show the way. The pent-up, self-righteous fury testify to his own frustration. Sinking one's life into a huge literary effort for fifteen exhausting years is not calculated to stimulate equanimity! Not that Parrington was entirely devoid of publications before *Main Currents*. He contributed a chapter to the *Cambridge History of Literature* and several literary essays, notably on Sinclair Lewis,[75] whom he considered a first-rate satirist, and James Branch Cabell. He was indeed one of the first to champion Cabell, putting him in the highest American rank. "A self-reliant intellectual," wrote Parrington in 1921, "rich in the spoils of all literatures, one of the great masters of English prose ... [Cabell] stands apart from the throng of lesser American novelists, as Mark Twain stood apart, individual and incomparable."[76]

Finally Parrington, himself "individual and incomparable," brought it all together, putting life, heart, and ideas to fine creative use. The immediate response was overwhelming, from the admired Charles Beard on down, even if Professor Meany nearer home devoted only one perfunctory paragraph to *Main Currents* in the *Washington Historical Review*. Teaching offers now poured in, but Parrington spurned them. Almost single-handedly he had made American literature academically respectable, and now he could complete a third volume, and eventually a fourth, in peace. He was off to England for relaxation amidst the gardens he adored. (He had always hoped Seattle would become a garden-city *à l'anglaise*.[77]) He looked forward, at the last, to meeting British intellectuals like Harold Laski and Bertrand Russell.[78] Then angina struck, and suddenly in 1929, V. L. Parrington was dead, at the height of his power.

The dedication for the 1929 U. W. annual, *Tyee*, expressed what many felt:

> To Dr. Vernon L. Parrington, whose study of literature has won him national recognition; whose charm of manner has made him the most beloved of University professors and whose study of the past is infused with the spirit of modernity, the 1929 modern Tyee is dedicated.

In 1930, Parrington Hall was built in his honor on the Washington campus, and his colleague, Professor Eby, brought out the posthumous third volume of *Main Currents*. His son, Vernon Parrington, Jr., used some of his father's work as a basis for his own on utopian American writers,[79] and continued to teach a critical brand of American history to the elite at Seattle's Lakeside school, until his death in 1974. V. L. Parrington had left a good deal to the world, and not least, to his own region; however, the Pacific Northwest had given him much in return!

CHAPTER 6

Literature and the Development of the Northwest Novel

SERIOUS LITERATURE IN THE REGION developed slowly, and until the 1930s, some felt that it had little or none. Doubts continued to persist. The critical record includes Edmond Meany's article, "Has Puget Sound a Literature?" (1889),[1] to which question he answered "no"; the churlish manifesto about regional writing, *Status Rerum*, written by James Stevens and H. L. Davis[2] in 1926; the Reed College Writers' Conference of 1948, searching with only modest success for the foundations of Northwest literature;[3] more "culture is just around the corner" articles in the 1950s, such as John H. Binns' "Northwest Region—Fact or Fiction?"[4] in which the author faulted its literary complacency; remarks such as the one made by Theodore Roethke's English department chair at Washington, that there wasn't another poet of worth for a thousand miles;[5] and summations by the like of Roger Sale, a Northwesterner who found only two novels from the area worthy of outside scrutiny—Jack Leahy's *Shadows on the Water* and Allis McKay's *They Came to a River*;[6] or of Robert Cantwell, finding in this region a reasonable amount of good writing but little distinguishable as Northwestern.[7]

However, when H. L. Davis became a favorite of Henry Mencken, and his *Honey in the Horn* received the Pulitzer Prize in the 1930s, many believed the Northwest had entered a new age—an age in which it made sense at least to consider the inception of literate civilization here. To evaluate the development of Northwest literature, we will step back and pick up the record after Balch and Victor, then go on to consider the evolution of its fiction since the call to arms of *Status Rerum*.

The story of regional literature in the period roughly from 1890 to 1930 is, to a surprising extent, a story of women.[8] At the turn of the century the places of Frances Victor and A. S. Duniway were immediately filled by female writers such as Eva Emery Dye and Ella Higginson. Dye's best work was in historical novels, beginning with *McLoughlin and Old Oregon*, written in the mid–1890s and published in 1900; and it continued with others based on library research, journals or letter collections she unearthed, and oral memories of a vanishing Oregon and West. Dye was at once ahead of her time, and yet a woman of her era. Born in Prophetstown, Illinois, she lost her mother before age two, but a strong, literate, inventive father helped fill the gap, though a difficult step-mother did not. Overcoming her father's opprobrium, Dye went to Ohio's Oberlin College at age 19, where she was part of an advance guard of college women, educated in French, German, maths, sciences, and in the classical Latin and Greek literature which affected her subsequent literary life. At Oberlin Eva met Charles Henry Dye, a Congregationalist with similar interests, who complemented her well. They graduated in June 1882 and married the next month. Spending time in Iowa, Nebraska, and South Dakota, the growing family, eventually with four children, found the lure of a booming Northwest worth pursuing. They arrived in Oregon City at the beginning of the 1890s, where both Charles, succeeding economically as an attorney, and Eva blossomed. Eva's taste for an heroic, pioneering American past seemed confirmed around her by statues, lore she heard, and by the general atmosphere. She was duly inspired to write an historical novel on McLoughlin and his era, including the missionary impulse of the time. Given her interest in women's issues such as temperance and suffrage, she devoted much space in this study to McLoughlin's wife, along with prominent missionary spouses such as Narcissa Whitman and Eliza Spalding, whom she considered important in the making of her adopted region. The American western past Dye embraced felt like an Homeric epic to her; but when the McLoughlin book appeared in 1900, it met with quibbling reviews from sticklers like Frances Fuller Victor, due to its subtle blur between fiction and history. Well in advance of Doctorow's *Ragtime* and other books of this genre, Dye had nonetheless succeeded in firing the Northwest past with real, readable interest, and her Chicago publisher wanted more.

That "more" became her lasting literary achievement, *The Conquest: The True Story of Lewis and Clark* (1902), blending passion and sincerity with real standards of historical research on the explorers, and on a woman she made larger than life—as the maternal, knowing soul of the expedition, and a true princess-figure, the Shoshone Sacagawea. Dye was encouraged by regional figures like Harvey Scott, by the imminent centennial celebration of the Lewis and Clark trek, and by a current expansionist impulse under Theodore Roosevelt. On a research trip to the East she talked to many descendants of the Clark side, in particular, unearthing new letters and journal material, and bringing her passion to bear on this work of historical fiction that would resonate both in the Northwest and in the wider American public. It helped make Lewis and Clark and Sacagewea iconic figures, and Dye herself a sought-after speaker. But disappointments of her later life—the inability to gain interest in screen adaptations of this work, low sales of her last book, and turn-downs from publishers of an epic she wrote on Hawaii—fit somewhat with other Northwesterners' sometimes bitter search for cultural fulfillment. Dye's wish was to be remembered "as one who loved Oregon and who wanted its people to have the best the world has to offer in history, literature, art, music, and social service." Her own contributions in that regard were noteworthy.[9]

A quite different literary figure was Ella Higginson, who was born in Kansas, but grew up at La Grande, Oregon, and in the lower Willamette Valley. First published in Oregon City at fourteen, Higginson married a druggist and they moved to Bellingham on the northern Washington coast in 1888.[10] There, she maintained contact with the Oregon world of letters, becoming a regular contributor to *West Shore*, as well as to national magazines of the day. Her first book was a collection of stories that was well reviewed in the East. Macmillan then began bringing out her work regularly—mainly, short stories and poems. Her only novel, *Mariella of Out West*, caused many in Bellingham to turn against her for a time, as they saw themselves or their friends maligned in its pages. *Mariella* does not sentimentalize the early life of the region—indeed, it suggests that aside from its abundant natural beauty, the area was no place for a person of sensibility. Unlike in the work of later female novelists we discuss, *Mariella* is a cry against both personal injustice and the cultural poverty of the region's inheritance. However, in her great house on a hill, Higginson eventually became the pride of Bellingham. At least fifty of her poems were set to music, including "Four-Leaf Clover" and "The Lamp in the West." While nationally some saw her as a new Joaquin Miller, her poems and songs were especially well received in Washington and Oregon, and by 1935 she became the poet laureate of Washington State. Her style was highly praised, though to us her poetry seems rather sentimental. However, Higginson had the virtue of tying her readers to a living regional heritage, for she was thoroughly Northwestern. When a girlfriend of Mariella learns to recite a poem in school, it is naturally Sam Simpson's *Willamette*. Also characteristically Northwestern is the fact that the heroine of *Mariella* leaves at the end for a more exalted life in England.[11]

With Higginson one can conveniently bracket Edwin Markham, a newspaper poet around the turn of the century. It is indicative of the Northwest's cultural dependency that although he left Oregon at age five for California, never to return as a resident, Markham was nevertheless made the state's "poet laureate" in 1921. He remained so until his death at an advanced age in 1940 on Staten Island.[12] That Oregon and Oregon City took deep pride in Markham may astonish the reader in our less poetic age. Appealing to populist tastes, his most famous poem, "The Man with a Hoe," was a complaint about the hard life that the average man endured. Like Miller, Markham had little education; he was a man, and versifier, of the people.

The best-known male writers, poets, or even artists were generally *also* newspapermen.[13] For example, John Fleming Wilson wrote widely for magazines and was well known for children's literature. Wilson's *The Land Claimers*, a story of settlement on the Oregon Coast, was typical of popular literature in that era. But the writing is relaxed and effective, particularly on the coast environment. After a few years in the Northwest, including work on the *Oregonian* and a brief editorship of the *Pacific Monthly*, Wilson moved to New York and later became affluent as a scenario writer in Hollywood, where he met an early, accidental death.[14]

In the 1920s perhaps the most famous Northwest literary figure was Opal Whitely of Cottage Grove.[15] Opal was an intelligent high school student with a literary love of nature and a desire to communicate this love to the public. She was also an omnivorous reader and a dreamer who confused reality with fiction. When she brought a manuscript on "The Fairyland Around Us" to the *Atlantic Monthly*, the editor there was so struck by her that he offered to print her diary instead. So she produced it, and in 1920 it ran for several months in the *Atlantic*, becoming an international sensation. In it she claimed to be the daughter of a French nobleman who had been substituted for a child whom her "foster parents" accepted as their own—at age six! The diary was fascinatingly naive, yet highly literate for a journal purporting to go back to the age of six. Despite the story's implausibility, Whitely managed to put it over on most readers, was financed on a world trip, and at last report (in the '30s) had been accepted into the circle of a maharaja in India. We may remember that both Whitely and Joaquin Miller grew up near Eugene, and that in both lives there is the pattern of ambition, fantasy, confusion, and the escape into success—at a distance. Whitely's antipathy toward reality was so strong that she rejected even a biological link to the family that had raised her, a step beyond obfuscation of both age and background wrought by Louise Bryant.[16]

In the early 1930s, Portland and the lower Willamette Valley had become one of the most productive literary centers in the country. There were many writers who continued the success of Higginson and Dye, often as creators of "westerns." Quality is another issue, yet the very fact that there were so many showed a certain collective aspiration and community spirit. The audience was popular, comparable to later TV publics, and again, the best known male writers were often newspapermen.[17] Some of the more famous were Charles Alexander, winner of an O. Henry award in 1923, and Vivian Bretherton, a native of Portland. Alan Hart, a Seattle physician, produced the serious *Dr. Mallory*, set on the Oregon coast. Albert Wetjen, an English sailor who settled in Oregon, wrote fine stories of the sea, often featuring direct reference to Northwest life of his time.[18]

To William Douglas, the great Northwest nature writer of that general period was Ben Hur Lampman.[19] Born in Wisconsin, Lampman grew up in North Dakota as the son of a printer. After a sojourn in Gold Hill, Oregon, he joined the staff of the Portland *Oregonian* in 1916, where he was to remain the rest of his life. He became regionally famous as a columnist, essayist, nature writer, and writer of verse, and much of his writing was collected in books. Unlike later newspaper writers, Lampman took risks with vocabulary, style, and subject matter that carried him far afield, especially into myth and a rhythmic kind of prose that was much better than his poetry. Although to our sensibility some of his writing is, again, overly sentimental, he could at times succeed marvelously in attempts to give significance to the commonplace, whether it be the simplest form of fishing, or the labored movements of the aged.[20] In contrast to Douglas' own descriptive writing, Lampman emphasized the emotional and symbolic content of experiences, weaving a fairytale web around the events and problems of life.

In sum, the Northwest produced a wide variety of publications of more than passing interest.[21] It is also true that in the past non-literary newspapers and magazines generally had their literary side and were a prime outlet for the region's writers. Among the most important periodicals was *The West Shore*, published between 1875 and 1891 at 15,000 copies an issue. Its fields were literature, art, science, and resources of the Northwest. An expensive publication, in the end it couldn't obtain enough advertising. The place of *Out West* was taken by the *Pacific Monthly*, an ambitious Portland magazine published between 1898 and 1911 that printed much of Colonel Wood's work. Since it merged with *Sunset* in 1911, there has been no equivalent publication in the region.

But what of the new direction in Northwest fiction called for by Stevens and Davis in 1926, and following that rough date? If we look at novels that came out since that time, we find progress, but also a certain falling short. Even the best of Northwest novels were beset by recurring difficulties, lacunae too persistent to ignore. Good novels, first off, require good characters; whereas novels here have sometimes failed to provide even one with whom readers could easily empathize. Novels rest on ideas, yet Northwesterners often seemed to ignore (willfully) the great philosophical inheritance of

Western civilization. Novels should have exciting plots, unless they eschew a what-happens-next formula, à la Joyce, in which case they need to be strong in the first two categories mentioned; but Northwest novels too rarely made readers thirst for the next turn—with expectation, fear, or joy. Novels require a strong sense of locale—and here the Northwest has been abundantly represented! Firs and salmon, rain and snow-topped peaks: they are profusely found in the region's fiction. Novel after novel lays out for us the inventory of natural charms the Northwest has offered. In fact, it might well be called inventory-writing; but obviously setting is only setting, and no matter how spectacular, can never make a good novel on its own.[22]

These endemic problems have not afflicted every novel in the same proportion, so we must return to a comparative and specific emphasis if we are to avoid empty dismissals that have too frequently passed for Northwest criticism. Let us begin with Allis McKay's *They Came to a River* (1941) and *The Women at Pine Creek* (1966), best of the whole chain of McKay-like novels, mostly by women, that constitute a typical part of this region's fiction. *They Came to a River* is a growing-up novel—autobiographical, happy, and even saccharine. It is a cozy sort of work, giving the reader, by osmosis, a real empathy for the Wenatchee apple country. McKay was a girl from that area who went off to make her living in Chicago, only to return with heightened regard for the home base.[23] This leads to warm writing here. *River* is a novel that builds slowly, demanding a reader's patience. It is both Northwest and a paradigm of American innocence vis-à-vis the crumbling Europe of the twentieth century. It proceeds by subtle "firsts"—a first dance, first kiss, first forest fire, first job, first marriage, first baby—toward a certain plenitude. Chris, the heroine, a quiet, unflappable person, loves simple things. Indeed, this *bildungsroman* itself has a mute sort of quality shot through it—an unobtrusive style, and mood of silent wonder faithfully reproducing both the viewpoint of Chris and the province she inhabits. Characters, aside from footloose Bernella, Chris' foil, reveal few memorable traits. Even the death of Chris' husband provokes only a dull resignation that lets a reader off the hook as well. The tears aren't wrung from us by any force.[24] Attachments are as much to place and role as to individuals. But for those who have time and patience, there *is* a subtle warmth here, and a budding wealth of environmental detail that make the book worth reading.

Incredibly, twenty years and convulsive changes in postwar America had virtually no influence on McKay's follow-up novel, *The Women at Pine Creek*. Again, the novel is autobiographical, and again the setting is Wenatchee apple country. The plot concerns two sisters who operate an apple farm there, then leave it due to marriage. Mary, the youngest, and the real heroine, becomes a teacher, then goes to another farm run by her husband and loses him to the First World War, only to regain him at the end. He is older, and though she is not really in love with him, she respects him. Somehow she reminds us of Betty MacDonald (*The Egg and I*) as she fumbles with beehives and hay and fruit, and in her resignation, of a continental heroine—like Julie in Rousseau's *Nouvelle Héloïse*. Only discipline permits freedom seems to be the moral here.

Anyone interested in a typology of Northwest writing must read at least *They Came to a River*, for there are so many others like it. In *The Rock and the Wind*, Vivian Bretherton tells an appealing story of a Cornish woman who raises a bourgeois family in Portland. We have Patricia Campbell's *Silver Fruit* (1959) and Evelyn Bolster's first novel *Morning Shows the Day* (1940). Better known are Elizabeth Marion's *The Day Will Come* (1939) and *The Keys to the House* (1944), both on growing up in agricultural Washington. Herself raised on a Palouse wheat farm in the eastern part of the state, Marion writes frankly autobiographical novels, slow, simple, and divorced from the complex world beyond; however, her work is less distinguished than *They Came to a River*. Characters are too often plain and expectable; Marion should have let her private energy onto the page more often, as in this portrait of Rosemary, from *Keys to the House*: "She [was] only an obese slovenly indolent woman who confused bustle with industry, who believed that a dime-store cologne was preferable to a bath, who concealed her inherent inefficiency beneath a beaming exterior of cheerful good nature."[25] This is a fine description, but too rare. Ideas, too, are also somewhat platitudinous; for example: "Time itself was a queer thing, an impressive force in human life ... that living forced upon the most stupid of them awareness of time, consciousness of its passing....[26] Marion forces us to wade through too many pages waiting for resolutions of conflicts that never quite materialize. Will a dog whose virtues we never knew die? Will a character go fishing in the mountains, or not?

The landscape of feminine growing-up novels was, however, not unrelievedly a grey one in the Northwest. One of the few that rival *They Came to a River* is Berenice Thorpe's *Reunion on Strawberry Hill* (1944). True, Northwest tendencies we have been discussing are not absent here. Inventory-writing abounds, as in lists of items that were home-canned (beets, apricots, plums, etc.). The bright creamy world depicted jolts the reader who thinks about grand catastrophes; to Thorpe's characters World War II is "out there" and should be shut off whenever it reaches them via the radio. A certain naiveté is omnipresent, but our own feelings are ambivalent enough not simply to condemn that. Do we like or dislike the following passage, describing a girl from Strawberry Hill in "the city":

> It's the hum, all the noises coming together, symphonically together. The city. It's great to be alive, she tells herself. And attractive. White-collars girls, it's great; maids in uniform, girls in lively wool, new suits, slacks, it's great; here we go gaily; high-stepping feet, vitality, smile of beauty, skin you love to touch....[27]

Of course, Americans once loved movies like *Singin' in the Rain* and perhaps still do, judging from the nostalgia boom. Again, it is not naiveté that rankles here, but dull pages that could easily have been removed. To give Thorpe her due, she writes better and better as the book progresses. The plot runs faster toward the close (unlike *River*'s), and one really becomes immersed in Strawberry Hill, a place from which, on a good day, one could see Mounts Adams, Rainier, and Hood.

Unfortunately, more economical writing or simply, original writing, would have helped here. Meanwhile, many Northwest writers remained documenters of the environment—none moreso than Nard Jones and Archie Binns. In career they differed, for Jones was primarily a newspaperman, while Binns was primarily a professor at the University of Washington—one of those writing teachers against whom Stevens and Davis had directed their ire in the previous generation. Yet they can easily be grouped together, for each began a novel-writing career in the early 1930s. Jones' *Oregon Detour* was a thinly disguised tale of Weston, his hometown in eastern Oregon, a tale that would turn the countryside against him, and even against his college, Whitman. Jones' *Wheat Women* appeared in 1933, Binns' *Lightship* (also based on his own experience) in 1934. Neither is distinguished, yet we would say that *Wheat Women* is more energetic than *Lightship* and more pleasing in the long run. *Lightship*, too realistic and plodding, is not easy to read today, if indeed it ever was; whereas *Wheat Women*, at its best, presents strong environmental writing that adequately conveys the atmosphere of the Palouse wheatland, as in:

> Black and rich and soft to a man's boots. A fine thick soil that looked clean and smelled clean—that even tasted clean when the mares' hoofs tossed it against your mouth as you braced yourself on the harrow....
>
> Up from this had come the thin, green wisps of early grain, growing heavier and taller until the whole countryside was a checkerboard of green and black: ground seeded to wheat, ground lying fallow....[28]

There is, to be sure, a plot in *Wheat Women*, but the novel feels like a document, a document of what life was like (Sears and Roebuck catalogues, marriages, harvests, etc.) in the rural West.

Binns and Jones reached their apogee by the end of the 1930s. Binns' *The Land Is Bright* (1939) dealt in a hortatory fashion with pioneers on the Oregon Trail. This is a bold paean to the big country, but is quite devoid of lasting characters or stylistic distinction. Jones' *Swift Flows the River* (1940) appeared a year later and similarly used an historical setting. The plot concerns the navigation of the upper Columbia River by steamboat. A young boy, as in Conrad's *Youth* and many other such novels, is taken on reluctantly and must prove himself. We get good descriptions here of The Dalles and Walla Walla in the nineteenth century. Two deaths climax the novel, and the steamboat then wheels into the sunset.[29]

More novels followed by these two figures, none of the first rank, though some, such as Binns' *Timber Beast*, interesting because they illuminated a relatively unknown world. Binns also documented the Puget Sound scene later in *The Headwaters* (1957). Here we have the "environmental novel" *par excellence*. A couple about to be married struggles on an island with the elements, as do the central figures of *The Egg and I*. The constant cozy chill of rain and fog permeates our consciousness, but subtlety of vision is notably lacking. Again, the reader derives a relaxed feel for the area, though no vicarious experience of lasting significance.

Robert Cantwell was another Northwest novelist of the 1930s, one who subsequently became known for different endeavors. Few would associate an editor of *Sports Illustrated*, as he became after World War II, with Marxism; but the 1930s were more dire than the '50s, and a younger Cantwell used his utter commitment to the kinds of Northwest workers he had known and admired, and his hostility to capitalist inequities, along with undeniable literary skill to craft at least one fine novel. His *Land of Plenty* (1934) was a literary landmark of "the Pink Decade" in America, selling little, but receiving praise from such as Clifton Fadiman and John Dos Passos.[30] Scenes in a Puget Sound wood mill, clearly modeled on Cantwell's own experience working on plywood veneers in Aberdeen, Washington, an electrical power outage that showcases workers as more noble than management, and a strike, revealing the awful courage it took for desperate, ill-paid laborers to risk loss of pay, job, and even life in such an activity reproduce class realities Cantwell knew directly from his own experience. The conflict of father and son, and other character development, also reveal his psychological side. In actuality, Cantwell had not hailed originally from the lower class, but from the bourgeoisie he derided here. However, his sympathies are clearly telegraphed in *Land of Plenty*, and his pessimism about the American system pervades the novel's conclusion. That whole climate now feels somewhat other-worldly, and even did to Cantwell later on—after he had departed the Soviet-inspired "movement"; but his realist achievement here in a thoroughly Northwestern novel remains significant.

Among the most prolific Northwest writers of this era through to about 1950 was someone very different from Cantwell: Ernest Haycox, born in Portland in 1899, and educated at Reed College and the University of Oregon.

Primarily a popular writer of conventional Westerns of the Greek tragedy genre, Haycox on occasion rose considerably above this level in his historical novels. Though derived from pioneer stock in the Northwest, Haycox was anything but an anachronistic hayseed; he was a sophisticated literary man with political aspirations, very much in touch with his contemporary world, though making good money off the western past. He was very patriotic, a man of libertarian sentiments who nonetheless saw the need for government both to protect abroad (having served in the First World War, he tried to get in again for the Second); and at home, to preserve the Northwest's lavish forests—from wholesale, wanton destruction. Haycox had contemporary marriage problems, was a typical family man of his time, an investor, though not a good one, and as with Maugham, the popular short story master, was ignored or derided by certain critics for sticking to westerns and making such good cash from a trade at which he labored hard. He got a thousand dollars a story in the Depression, and was up to over twice that in wartime; yet those stories or novel serials that appeared in *Collier's* and *The Saturday Evening Post* attracted readers as prestigious as Ernest Hemingway.[31]

Haycox devoted himself to his craft as few other Northwest writers did. He combed the entire region for material, even while on vacations; worked daily at his office in Portland; and took seriously all other ancillary functions, including stints in Hollywood (some of his stories and novels were adapted as films, of which the most celebrated was John Ford's *Stagecoach* of 1939).[32] His own homes, the first in Portland more modest, the second a mansion built in the city's West Hills, were filled with Western artifacts and paintings, and a huge amount of books he used for research.

To certain critics, the impetus of American fiction came most *not* from the regionally rooted, as Haycox was; but from alienated minorities. In the Northwest the few hyphenates we have from the pre–1970s era sometimes provided a racier brand of fiction than their down-the-middle brethren, but generally not *great* novels. Two of the best examples are John Okada, a Japanese-American, and Elizabeth Sales, a transplanted southerner. Okada's *No-no Boy* (1957), which treated a Japanese-American boy just out of internment camp in 1944, avoids admirably the problem of all "shout" novels: it does not become a tract. The hero of *No-no Boy* returns to Seattle, encountering a mother who touts a coming Japanese victory; a father driven to alcoholism by his wife's utter certitude; friends who are fixated on materialism, boosterism, or self-pity; and abortive father-figures (the best portrayed being a professor of engineering at the University of Washington), who all console the boy in measured terms without really listening to him. The writing is peppy and angry from the beginning. On those parents he writes:

> Pa's okay, but he's a nobody. He's a goddamned, fat, grinning, spineless nobody. Ma is the rock that's always hammering, pounding, pounding, pounding in her unobtrusive, determined, fanatical way until there's nothing left to call one's self.[33]

Obviously, the theme of generation gap has now become old, but Okada's character embodies much more. He is a "no-no boy"; in his own anguished words, to his parents, "I am not your son and I am not Japanese and I am not American." He is a character without roots or a country he can hold onto in any sure manner. The despair and drive of the book are its virtues, while the plot, proceeding to no real resolution, ultimately flaws it.[34]

Passion in this cool wet region has too often been absent, but it bubbles up as well in Elizabeth Sales' novels. Sales was frankly Southern, yet she wrote about Tacoma-Seattle, and the mix is, in spots, an appealing one. A series of her novels dealt with the young Fenella Rand growing up. In them we get a sense of evil, or at least of Manicheanism that could only have come out of the South. Her *Recitation from Memory* (1954) has Fenella kiss a greasy fellow (her aunt's term), consort with a part–Italian Indian who entices her into harmless nude bathing, and inspect the goings-on in a prostitutes' quarter of Tacoma. Sales' novel reflects the muscular feel of the booming, turn-of-the-century Northwest, but is so Southern it could also have transpired in Louisville (whence the family migrated). Long-winded, the novel is yet much alive in its best parts, and is particularly good on the effects of loss—of a grandmother, an aunt, and a mother.

Another Northwest writer with a certain pizzazz was Zola Ross. In her *Cassy Scandal* (1954) we have yet another adventurous young girl, placed in Seattle circa 1885, a girl drawn, as her name suggests, to bawdiness and adventure. Her friend, Lavinia, more prudent, is the necessary foil to a main character brimming with vitality. The novel's shortcomings are bound up with its staged quality—the propped-up hustle-and-bustle of the Seattle docks making this, in a way, a diminished *Oklahoma*. Cassy is wooed by tough types who seem to swing onto the scene rather like Gordon MacRae hopping a fence; but the book's energy does jibe with turn-of-the-century Seattle, set to burst into prominence.

History, one notices, figures in many of the above novels and indeed, in a sizable portion of all Northwest writing. This is a young area but, paradoxically, has been a past-thinking one. For those who think the past is only for the old kneeling before statues, the Northwest proves the opposite: that even youth could look back here. Part of this is due to the Western myth, but that does not fully explain a regional emphasis on the past. We take it that novelists who preferred to expend energies on the age of McLoughlin or of Marcus Whitman could not find worthier subjects all about them. Their present seemed somehow too mundane.

So there *is* a plethora of "past" novels here—in real Northwest abundance. Among the best is Don Berry's *Trask* (1960). *Trask* is the story of a mountain man caught between "civilization" and Native Americans, but leaning toward the latter—in this case, the Tillamooks of the 1840s. Trask is, first off, an onomatopoeically right name for this direct, laconic man. He is also given the usual Indian nickname, "the Boston," though we are told he is not a typical Boston. Berry gives us a well-plotted yarn wherein the Boston wins the Indians' trust by passing increasingly difficult tests. Through all these tribulations, Trask retains his composure; he is a genuinely likeable fellow, an unideological man, to whom a favorite Norwegian pipe, a well-brewed cup of coffee, and his own little corner of the earth are vastly more important than changing the world. He rolls easily with the punch. And Berry's writing rolls easily, too. The tone is calm and woodsy, and nature images that are used basically fit well with Berry's preindustrial scene. Yet the author does not resort to "inventory-writing" here, as did so many of his compatriots. Neither does he write so sparingly as to deny his characters their right to live. For once we have an Indian who is not a theme: Trask's guide, Charlie, steers him through the perils of tribal contact, teaches him about nature, but also exists as an (almost slangy) personality himself. He laughs and feels sad, and he explodes in anger. The reader, too, becomes emotional about parts of this novel. There is, for instance, a death on a cliff that gives us the feeling of arrest all good novels can perpetrate upon readers. In short, we have character and plot in *Trask*, and refreshingly, a setting that doesn't overwhelm.

Berry's other novels are set in the same time and place, but certainly *Moontrap* (1962) deserves treatment in its own right.[35] Again, pioneer Oregon is the scene, this time around Oregon City, 1850, and again, a trapper caught between two worlds is the subject. (Trask himself makes another appearance.) There is a curiously close parallel between *Moontrap* and Ernest Haycox's last novel, *The Earthbreakers*,[36] set in the Willamette Valley of the 1840s; but the parallel serves, at least, to highlight the efficacy of Berry's own work. Where *Moontrap* succeeds is in sharp plotting and characterization. Johnson Monday, an ex-trapper, tries to settle down with his common-law Indian wife, an appealing and real person; but having a baby presents problems. From there ensue troubles with politicians and missionaries, and the insertion of another trapper, Webster W. Webb, into the conflict, which ends in senseless violence. Webb is a salty type who constantly swears and interjects "Wagh! Wagh!" (The latter phrase may seem to come from Thomas Wolfe's "wa-waing" Luke in *Look Homeward, Angel*, but in fact was a mountain man expression.)[37] There is also an interesting frontier Frenchman here named Deveaux. Berry's sympathies clearly lie with trappers and Indians of his home region and against the tamers of the wilderness. He himself was apparently for a time difficult to contact, and photographs of him remain quite rare.

We may generalize that closely allied to this historical thrust of many Northwest novels was their primitivistic quality. Of course many of us still look back wistfully to woodsy times, neglecting life expectancies, poor diets, disease, and culturally impoverished wastelands of yore. And perhaps the Northwest had a stronger claim to primitivism than most other sections of the country. Since Indian culture had such a large influence on the Northwest mystique, it is natural that Native Americans continued to figure prominently in the region's post–World War II novels, such as in Jack Leahy's *Shadows on the Water* (1960). This novel, the reader will recall, is the only one besides *They Came to a River* that the critic Roger Sale believed would travel well outside the Northwest. Our own view is a harsher one; we are not certain that it deserved great currency even in its own region. Technique first off: where *Trask* exhibits its own kind of control, prose in *Shadows on the Water* seems standardized from some college creative-writing factory. In terms of characters, the action here is seen from the viewpoint of a little boy in a coast town, and the child's point of view *is* well rendered. Unfortunately, the other main characters, most of whom are Indians, do not come through strongly at all. The most important one, Gooeyduck, a clammer, does little more than creep through the novel. The novel has a theme, but the theme remains too divorced from the story. Leahy is telling us in *Shadows on the Water* how modern civilization's attractions had ruined the Coast Indians; in the end a lovely Indian village turns into an amusement park, after being the prey of anthropologists. One can see where Leahy's heart is, but his storytelling prowess and ability to create pathos are less evident.

There were later primitives of another sort who cared little about Indians, except as material to "groove on"; these are what one might call the metallectuals, connected to the counter-culture of the '60s. In the Northwest the metallectuals were fairly well represented by Gary Snyder, the poet; Frank Herbert, the science fiction writer; David Shetzline, a transplanted novelist and short-story writer; and Tom Robbins, the novelist. The latter attained good paperback sales around the country with *Another Roadside Attraction* (1971). The pity is that Robbins could have written a great hip novel if he himself had only been greater. For one thing, we have here a real sense of fun, albeit pure counter-cultural (and therefore, dated) fun. One of his main characters, an ingénue named Amanda,

> became pregnant during a fierce thunderstorm. Was it the lightning or the lover? she was heard to muse.
>
> When her son was born with electrical eyes, people no longer thought her foolish.[38]

Sometimes Robbins writes in low-level Voltairean tones, but the irony that should be available to more novelists appears only as brief thunder bursts. The area used as backdrop, the Skagit Valley, had great possibilities,[39] yet counter-cultural platitudes intervene to reduce the book's power. F.B.I. agents, Middle Americans in small towns, and anyone viewing the Soviets as even mildly menacing are set up as so many tenpins for Robbins' rather single-minded, literary bowling ball. For instance:

> F.B.I. Agent: "I'm an American and proud of it!"
> Amanda: "I'm a human animal and prepared to accept the consequences."[40]

Sometimes Robbins goes from this sort of universalism to specificity with alarming rapidity: we get pages and pages on butterflies, and the concrete information looks like it came straight from an encyclopedia; it is not integrated as butterflies were in, say, Nabokov's *Lolita.*

Primitive, metallectual, historical mythicologist—all these apply to a person who *almost* wrote "the Great Northwest Novel": Ken Kesey. Kesey's most famous book, *One Flew Over the Cuckoo's Nest*, takes place in Oregon but could well have been set elsewhere. Certainly *Cuckoo*'s regionalism is less apparent than in his next novel, *Sometimes a Great Notion*, yet it forms an implicit part of the work. For one thing, this is a big book—one where outsized individuals in an insane asylum take on "the Combine" and try to win a hopeless battle. (We are aware that both Kesey's novels and their plots will already be familiar to many movie-watchers.[41]) The atmosphere in *Cuckoo's Nest* is not dissimilar to James Stevens'—the tall-tale aura, and the mythical hugeness are very Western, indeed. Chief Bromden, a nominally mad but prescient American Indian, is six-foot-eight and incarnates his wider community, the Indian nation. The Combine literally makes Bromden smaller, and, simultaneously, presses all Native Americans into the tight-fitting clothes of sameness. Bromden's viewpoint remains quite extraordinary. Memories of his tribe expropriated along the Columbia River salmon grounds call up memories all have of a simpler America, and the Chief's animadversions toward the modern at least seem earned. Descriptions of an Oregon coast transformed are nothing less than masterful. Here are the Chief's interior words:

> All up the coast I could see the signs of what the Combine had accomplished since I was last through this country, things like, for example—a train stopping at a station and laying a string of full-grown men in mirrored suits and machined hats, laying them like a hatch of identical insects, half-life things coming pht-pht-pht out of the last car, then hooting its electric whistle and moving on down the spoiled land to deposit another hatch.
>
> Or things like five thousand houses punched out identical by a machine and strung across the hills outside of town, so fresh from the factory they're still linked together like sausages, a sign saying "NEST IN THE WEST HOMES—NO

> DOWN PAYMENT FOR VETS," a playground down the hill from the houses, behind a checker-wire fence and another sign that read "ST. LUKE'S SCHOOL FOR BOYS"—there were five thousand kids in green corduroy pants and white shirts under green pull-over sweaters playing crack-the-whip across an acre of crushed gravel. The line popped and twisted and jerked like a snake, and every crack popped a little kid off the end, sent him rolling up against the fence like a tumbleweed. Every crack. And it was always the same little kid, over and over.[42]

The Chief's opposite number is Big Nurse Ratched, outside world or bureaucracy personified.[43] This might appear an easy target for Kesey, but is redeemed by first-rate characterization.

Other characters in the ward include a garrulous little fellow, Harding, an amateur rural philosopher; and George, an old Swedish fisherman, big like Bromden but amusingly human—his dirt fetish a fine Keseyan touch. The fish they all catch under George's direction is "as big as a leg."[44] This fishing trip of loonies, a collective revolt, is indeed the novel's focal point, representing the collective attempt of Kesey's characters to recover for themselves a sense of Oregon's limitless freedom. The inmates revolt toward what they have lost, and attempt to regain by naive Luddite force what perhaps couldn't be regained. (This Luddism would also pervade *Sometimes a Great Notion.*) George, for example, remembers great times he had forgotten on Puget Sound as he wrestles with the salmon.

But the leader of the ward's revolt and the hero of the story is obviously R. P. McMurphy, a frontier epigone. For him life is a continual wrestling match, and from the start, he contracts out of a world of rules and regulations. This constitutes his mental disease, but for Kesey he is also a throwback to that pioneer individuality Harvey Scott and Orange Jacobs had already seen slipping away seventy-five years earlier. McMurphy must be biggest and baddest—the term he uses for this is "bull goose." He had been bull goose logger, bull goose gambler, bull goose pea weeder at Pendleton, Oregon, and he would now be Bull Goose Loony in the mental ward![45] In Big Nurse, McMurphy is fighting bland homogeneity, and rootless Americans found not only behind government desks, but behind other desks and counters everywhere in the land. For Kesey, making light of things is central, and *Cuckoo's Nest* is still a funny novel, goofy and uninhibited. Certainly Kesey exaggerates, verging on the tall-tale quality mentioned; but it works, precisely because the uncivil McMurphy himself is an exaggerator. To Big Nurse, who tries to deaden him with television, he shouts: "Can't you even ease down on the volume? It ain't like the whole state of Oregon needed to hear Lawrence Welk play 'Tea for Two' three times every hour, all day long! If it was soft enough to hear a man shout his bets across the table I might get a game of poker going..."—to which he receives only the citation of rules and regulations.[46]

The highlight of *One Flew Over the Cuckoo's Nest*, and its most Oregonian part, is again, the crazy men's salmon fishing trip. Here is that fishing scene's climactic moment, where the Northwest myth really lives, and not simply as thesis:

> It started slow and pumped itself full, swelling the men bigger and bigger. I watched, part of them, laughing with them—and somehow not with them. I was off the boat, blown up off the water and skating the wind with those black birds, high above myself, and I could look down and see myself and the rest of the guys, see the boat rocking there in the middle of those diving birds, see McMurphy surrounded by his dozen people, and watch them, us, swinging a laughter that rang out on the water in ever-widening circles, farther and farther, until it crashed up on beaches all over the coast, on beaches all over all coasts, in wave after wave after wave.[47]

Obviously Kesey had his own hankering after a limitless, pioneer Oregon.

However, his next novel, *Sometimes a Great Notion*, is the one that rather like a big fish, *really* got away. For this novel demonstrated the possibilities of a finely wrought, and perhaps quintessential, Northwest literary achievement.

The author wrote *Notion* at a watershed point in American literary history—the era (1963–1964) of Saul Bellow's *Herzog* and John Updike's *The Centaur*, both quite autobiographical. And Kesey's *Sometimes a Great Notion* was also autobiographical. Here again, was a well-defined setting; here, too, a writer who at his best could rival the great stylists of his day. The failure of this novel to quite click is doubly poignant, for not only did the literary moment pass, but Kesey himself passed to the "on the bus, off the bus" bravado of the hip years, years he helped create, according to Tom Wolfe's *Electric Kool-Aid Acid Test*. In the process of discovering new vistas, however, Kesey seemed to have burned himself out. For example, *Garage Sale* (1973) was little more than a miscellaneous collection of counter-culture artifacts, including senseless letters from Neal Cassady, coloring contests, and other innocent stuff that felt stale on its day of release. By this time Kesey had passed his novelistic peak.

That peak came in the first 150-odd pages of *Sometimes a Great Notion*. Here was and is Northwest writing at its best, with an unmistakable flavor of coastal Oregon. And the setting, rather than a literal ball-and-chain, becomes in expert hands almost a character itself. Kesey clearly does something with the elements, and the results are for this short stretch spectacular. The river, so central to the novel, is likened to a scintillating, sometimes placid, but also menacing bird of prey; yet in it, almost innocently, "great chubs lie on [its] bottom like sunken logs."[48] The Oregon scene explodes with life, tugs at the reader's heart. We have read of logging trucks in other accounts but never as "those great growing, gear-grinding log-trucks, charging out of the wilderness with grilled grins...."[49] We realize early on that we are reading a stylist of the first order, and one can quote profusely here. A boat idles on the river "slow as Christmas,"[50] and "there's a silence stretched between [the brothers] like barbed wire."[51]

In addition to nature, the characters, too, are well rendered. The central ones are the Stamper sons, half-brothers, one a tough, individual logger in Wakonda, Oregon, the other a weaker Hamlet type—two sides of Kesey himself, according to interviews. ("For one thing, I want to find out which side of me really is: the woodsy, logger side—complete with homespun homilies and crackerbarrel corniness, a valid side of me that I like—or its opposition. The two Stamper brothers in the novel are each one of the ways I think I am."[52]) The father is a hard-bitten person, and appealingly untutored. *His* father had come to Oregon from Kansas, seduced by advertising signs that said: "There Is Elbow Room For A Man To Be As Big And Important As He Feels It Is In Him To Be!"[53] The novel works out that very Western theme in the age of Eisenhower's presidency.

Since Leslie Fiedler (in *Return of the Vanishing American*) dismissed *Notion* in three or four lines, it is hard to tell precisely *why* he found it so flawed. Perhaps Fiedler's problem was one of ideology. Kesey's hero, Hank Stamper, is another bull goose, only here he is not fighting the nasty Establishment, but rather, the loggers' union. Hank's great notion is to deliver his logs to the mill while other loggers strike. The Stampers' is a family firm, a fossil refusing to become rationalized along "Marxian" lines. But novels must naturally be more than ideology. What makes a novel is the author's own commitment and energy, and Kesey's first 150 pages or so are so energetic one wants to stand back and cry "enough already!" But better a surfeit than a dearth. What hurts the novel is the increasing place awarded to Leland Stanford Stamper, the weaker son, and the shunting away of Hank, whose untutored and fresh viewpoint helped give the book its initial drive. Certainly Kesey could have done better things with Leland (or Lee). The boy is an asthmatic who had lived outside Oregon for health reasons and was called back at a crucial moment in his late teens to replace Henry, Sr., who, though he could still cuss, could no longer cut logs. Unfortunately, Lee remains weak throughout the novel, and worse, the kind who *talks* his weakness, sometimes under the influence of drugs, and always under the influence of an undergraduate slideshow education—Hawthorne today, T.S. Eliot tomorrow, etc. All this ultimately mars the novel.

Kesey, however, can certainly string words together, and his words bring the Northwest alive in fiction as no others' ever have. Sometimes, there is a certain verbal tapdancing; for example: "On all sides, just beyond the fingertips, night hung in thick folds; even when the keen edge of the moon managed to slice itself a brief hole, its crippled light emphasized, more than alleviated, the gloom."[54] But at his best the author deepens and energizes here. When he talks about the "abstract splash of autumn" in the Willamette Valley; or the rain "leveled out to its usual winter-long pace ... not so much a rain as a dreamy smear of blue-gray that wipes over the land instead of falling on it ... an old gray aunt who came to visit every winter and stayed till spring," the Northwest emerges as an almost anthropomorphic section of the country. It lives.[55]

Too, Kesey gives at least some of these characters that same generous breadth one saw in *Cuckoo's Nest*. The Oregon loggers, like McMurphy and Chief Bromden, are his vehicle for a big, uninhibited brand of comedy. Here is one of the Stampers instructing Lee on how to comport himself in the forest: "The main thing," Joe says, "Oh yeah, the *mainest* thing ... is when you fall, fall in the *direction* of your work. *Conserve* yourself." Joe Ben, a cousin of the main characters, is indeed one of the funniest people in the book. Environmentalists might disagree with his defense of hunting, but note the stretched rural humor:

> ... I don't have much respect for this sort of do-good thinking because it's always seemed to me a whole lot *more* cowardly for a man to have nothing to do with the meat he eats except picking it up out of a supermarket meat section all sliced and boned and wrapped in cellophane, looking about as much like a pig or a cute little lamb as a potato does.... I mean, if you're going to eat another living creature, I figure you at least should know he *was once living* and that *somebody* had to kill the poor devil and chop him up.... But people never think that way about hunting; it's always "brute and coward" the hunters are called, by some Eastern prick who thinks pheasants are *found* under glass, plucked and already full of stuffing.[56]

Emotions, too, are well rendered, and we have scenes that for sheer power, rival any we know in Northwest literature. One involves bobcats stolen by one of the Stamper sons, nurtured, domesticated, and then suddenly drowned by the father. In a century when violent death has become statistically dehumanized, it is refreshing to see a novelist who can still bring us back to caring about one person or animal. The novel, in sum, partly succeeds for its vibrancy, a vibrancy again almost unique to Northwest fiction. Unfortunately, as the book goes on, Kesey overwrites, introduces, with alarming frequency, tangential detail, becomes flabby or inward-looking, and worst, slows the action to a walk. The latter part of *Notion* fails to match its early promise, and a moment in Northwest literature that won't return was consequently, and irretrievably lost.

From that missed literary moment, let us segue back to *Status Rerum*, the well-known attack of 1926 on the general characteristics of Northwest writing.[57] This offensive, mounted by James Stevens and H. L. Davis, represented many things—a revolt of working people, cowboys, or country boys against the cities; a revolt against a romantic, derivative tradition then largely dead elsewhere in the country; a revolt against a local literary establishment they believed had not sufficiently credited their work while it was well received nationally—and for all these reasons, a feeling of regional shame they felt when submitting their works in the East. Since no one was willing to publish *Status Rerum*, its authors published it themselves and sent it out to their friends—friends who would soon be chilled, for they felt both themselves and their region much maligned here.

What had these two iconoclasts written or intended to write that permitted them to so skewer their peers? Of the two, James Stevens was by far the better known. Born in Iowa in 1892, Stevens had been brought up from age ten by relatives in western Idaho, and by fifteen was completely on his own in the world of work—as teamster, construction worker, and later lumberjack. By 1926, he already had two important books under his belt—the most significant he was to write.

Stevens will be best remembered for putting together the first compilation of the Paul Bunyan stories.[58] Bunyan was a huge French Canadian of prodigious strength who had fought in a Canadian revolution of the 1830s, and later was to be the leader of a lumber camp. But in the hands of lumbermen south of the border, he became a central character in liars' contests that enlivened camp life, and one teller of these tales in the Northwest was James Stevens himself. There were about a hundred basic plots, within which each was compelled to develop individual elaborations. Thus, Stevens did not simply record tales, but was both creator and collector. In addition, for his first collection, Stevens talked to people in Washington who had known people personally connected with the original Bunyan, and contacted some early raconteurs from the East. H. L. Mencken encouraged Stevens' work on Bunyan, as he also encouraged the real-life sketches Stevens was producing for *American Mercury*, from which a collection was later published.

Beyond Paul Bunyan, Stevens' contribution must finally rest on two curious books: *Brawnyman* (1926) and *Big Jim Turner* (1948). The protagonist of both is Jim Turner, and both begin with largely autobiographical accounts of Stevens' own existence in Idaho, of being thrown out of school and taking off on his own. Both are concerned almost exclusively with the period in his life between age fourteen and twenty-two. Yet the two Jim Turners are quite different personalities. The 1926 Turner is a taciturn tough who hates books, takes pride primarily in his muscles, and thinks women like to be treated roughly. He is surrounded by a cast of memorable characters, one a teller of tales equivalent to those in the Paul Bunyan tradition (although he is a hobo teamster). Indeed, the love story of the Minktums, the bard Gager's creative high point, is one of the most effective asides in the book.[59]

The Jim Turner of 1948 is another strong boy, but one whose interests go well beyond physical work. He is enthralled by libraries, particularly the work found there of writers like Whitman, Dickens, and Jack London; and throughout the book, he persists also in writing poetry. His female heroines seem to be idealists or librarians. The besetting sin of this Jim Turner is an incorrigible tendency to lie, and to throw himself into a fit of revivalist preaching that is pure hypocrisy, yet is convincing to his listeners. The emphasis here is on the struggle in the construction and lumber camps between Christians and radical unionists of the IWW, with Turner's Idaho relatives and female idealists arrayed on both sides. Stevens sympathizes here with the IWW struggle, especially its free-speech aspect, and incidentally, suggests the contrast between liberal Portland, where free speech was upheld by our previously-discussed radical, Colonel Wood; and a more conservative Spokane or Boise. But in neither book does Stevens himself become a true believer. The cruelty of the IWW also repelled him. His most sympathetic models are an uncle converted to Catholicism and his librarian wife. In this regard one of Stevens' explicators, Warren Clare, misrepresented the second Jim Turner, and thus Stevens himself.[60] The 1948 Jim Turner points out that for him "plain friends, good labor, quiet mists, green peace, Poesy are enough."[61]

Both books may be read as paeans to labor, to skill, and to the self-reward of hard, steady work. Many times Turner describes at length the joys of being out on the job and doing something important. Beyond this, the first Jim Turner stays in a rural Northwest, with urban life restricted here to San Francisco and Los Angeles. The second Turner integrates the rural world of western Idaho and the broader Northwest with its cities, primarily Portland, which become for him, centers of civilization. Evidently the post–*Status Rerum* Stevens had made his peace with the urban Northwest, working for years as a public relations counselor for the West Coast Lumberman's Association in Seattle. He was also a founder of the Keep Washington Green Association, occupations the first Turner would not have understood. In his second Jim Turner, Stevens explicitly emphasizes the role of the public library, an institution that had helped him so much.[62] The second Jim Turner was in theory the real James Stevens, yet *both* reveal aspects of the author—the same personal schizophrenia we have seen Kesey expressing through his two brothers in *Sometimes a Great Notion*, Wood through the images of God and Jesus in *Heavenly Discourse*, or Balch with his Indian-white opposition.

To what extent did Stevens fill the gap lamented in *Status Rerum*? Paul Bunyan remains one answer. Indeed, in an addendum to *Status Rerum* Davis tells us that all literature is essentially oral or folk literature.[63] Yet this is not what Davis himself wrote, and beyond Bunyan, Stevens did not really create a literature. As fictionalized reminiscence, as descriptions of the times, and of the working person's world, his novels and short stories are valuable documents. But too much is missing from them. The style is sometimes flat, especially when poetry is introduced, and the writing only works when it moves back to the tall tale.

Curiously, when H. L. Davis joined Stevens in his condemnation of Northwest literature, he had to his credit only a few poems. Yet it was no doubt this younger Davis who was primarily responsible for the celebrated attack. *Status Rerum* is written in the style of hypercritical vituperation that was to become most characteristic of Davis. It doesn't really fit with Stevens' fundamental optimism, or his obvious sympathy with others' foibles. It should not be surprising, therefore, that Davis actually set out to answer his own challenge; and that he did, in fact, work on quite a different plane than that of the literature he had criticized.

Thoroughly Northwestern, H. L. Davis' writings reflect details of his own life, but he wrote no truly autobiographical novel. Born in 1894 or 1896 in southwestern Oregon near Yoncalla, he was the son of East Tennessee mountaineers who had migrated early to the state. The family moved often, and when he was eleven, they were in Antelope, east of the mountains, where he engaged in a variety of rural occupations that were later to influence his work.[64] The Davises then moved to The Dalles, where they achieved local prominence over the next twenty years. Higher education consisted only of the army and some months at Stanford University, and soon Davis was back in the Northwest and a poet, winning almost instant recognition with a prize in the first year he published. Although his poetry was highly praised by Robinson Jeffers and H. L. Mencken, to later readers it might have less appeal. Yet there are moments of special emotion, such as in "The Gypsy Girl," or "October: The Old Eyes."[65]

During the '20s, Davis and his younger brothers worked for their father, the County Assessor, a job thoroughly acquainting him with the tragedies of homestead failure and estate settlement. But in 1928 the people of The Dalles rose against politicians in power, and the Davises lost their jobs. Davis married a hometown girl (a University of Oregon graduate) and moved to Bainbridge Island across from Seattle, where he collaborated with Stevens and Stewart Holbrook on a radio series concerning Paul Bunyan, incidentally singing and playing from his folk song collection.

In 1929 H. L. Mencken, who had published Davis' poetry in *American Mercury*, convinced him to write fiction, and his success as a short story writer was even more instantaneous than his poetic debut. In 1932, Davis left the Northwest on a Guggenheim Fellowship for Mexico; and he resided later in California, Arizona, and again, Mexico, until his death in 1960. He never permanently lived again in the Northwest, although he did visit it; yet his writing continued to be concerned primarily with the Northwest experience. His last published book, *Kettle of Fire* (1959), still consisted of essays and stories set in, or about the Northwest. Why Davis did not return to the Northwest is unclear, but surely the reasons included a love of Mexico, his ambivalence toward the section he had departed, the restlessness he had imbibed as a child, and perhaps uneasiness over what others thought of him after his strong critique of the regional record. He claimed he could not really capture Oregon literarily while in the Northwest; but in fact, some of his best short works were written before he left. What else was eating at him? Rejection of his family in The Dalles? The Northwest's cool reception of his writing? (*Status Rerum* being partly a product of wan local praise.) A feeling that his novel *Honey in the Horn* perhaps represented his peak? Bitter words with his family after *Honey* appeared, because—like Thomas Wolfe's family faced with an explosive *Look Homeward, Angel*—they read into it aspersions on their own lives? Whatever the ultimate reasons, Davis became increasingly gloomy. And that gloominess depressed his wife, who herself would have preferred to regain the Northwest. Finally they separated, and soon after, she died in a car accident.[66]

Returning to genres, after success in the short story form, Davis embraced the novel with equal ease. His best known achievements were the long *Honey in the Horn* that received a Pulitzer Prize in 1936, and *Winds of Morning* (1952), a Book-of-the-Month selection that year. Both were set in the area and time Davis had known directly. *Honey in the Horn* was explicitly meant as a cataloguing of Oregonian ways of life in the early 1900s, and *Winds of Morning* transpired in the wheat and stock country south of the Columbia River in the '20s. Davis also wrote *Harp of a Thousand Strings*, a complicated historical novel that ends up in the Mississippi Valley; *Beulah Land*; and *The Distant Music*, a novel set north of The Dalles in the period 1855 to 1930. Its recounting of a pioneer family's story through several generations is reminiscent of many Southern novels.

To understand Davis' contribution we must look first at his two most critically acclaimed novels.[67] *Honey in the Horn* tells the story of a sixteen-year-old orphan, raised about where Davis had been—a boy forced to set out on a series of wanderings throughout the state. In the course of these he meets a girl, and after an extended series of tribulations finally learns that she had committed two murders he had formerly imputed to her father. Yet by then his experience leads him to feel that since all make mistakes, he can reconcile himself to her and to a world of imperfect people. *Winds of Morn-*

ing is the story of a young deputy sheriff who aids an old man, Hendricks, with a herd of horses. With all his quirks, and though he loathes his children, this old Hendricks represents a different order of responsibility than the deputy had known. The story is essentially that of stages through which Hendricks develops from a bitter outsider to a person willing again to take responsibility for a family that had rejected him.

In both novels Davis uses a picaresque story line, modified by unlikely random encounters that nonetheless keep the plot relatively coherent. However, reading the material through brings many criticisms to mind. In spite of being anti-westerns, with an avowed purpose of demythologizing that entire part of the country, Davis' work here borrows heavily from the westerns' spirit. Although interesting in their detail, neither book causes the reader to identify deeply with its characters or subjects. There is a mordant, dry tone in these novels, and page after page can wear on a reader. Sometimes the descriptive passages seem obligatory interludes, but they can also sing, forming a new reality more engaging than the poetry Davis had left behind.

In an era of proletarian novels, Davis' work of the '30s remained personal, for he would have sneered at the idea that there was "a people"; nor would he have accepted the socialist faith that government officials could ever have the people's real interest at heart. One of his most unconvincing sections of *Honey* is a eulogy to the pioneers and the spirit of group enterprise that at the end breaks though Davis' general suspicion. Abjuring prejudice, Davis intended to treat all races with even-handed justice. He often recorded the white's casual destruction of the Indian, yet his descriptions of Native American ways are frequently so jaundiced that they make us doubt whether he really cared about their displacement. Although there are clever Indian individuals in his work, they are generally pictured there as dirty, stupid, cruel, irresponsible, and without moral standards. The traditions to which they cling seem as silly as the whites' naive belief that they had something they could force down Native-American throats. Davis stood with Frances Victor, unable to be swayed by the mysticism or romance of either Indian *or* missionary; but unlike Victor, he chose the countryside over the city. Spiritually, he could never follow Stevens into Portland and Seattle.

And unlike Victor, Davis' work seems (certainly on initial readings) to exude a rational, fatalistic irresponsibility. In the tradition of the western, he offers us casual murders that are not deeply felt by either character or reader. He inserts obscenities even when they detract from the overall effect. And the practice of interlarding fictional and true anecdotes so overwhelms the writing that even in his nonfiction, Davis' accuracy succumbs to fable, as in giving Seattle fifty-eight inches of rain annually, or in having wild buffalo range independently in the lower Yakima Valley of the mid–twentieth century.[68]

Much of Davis' life, even in autobiographical notes, was fictionalized—à la Joaquin Miller, Louise Bryant, and the angel of Cottage Grove. For instance, he apparently took the birthdate of a deceased younger brother as his own, and imputed to himself jobs, such as an editorship, that he had never held down.[69] This casual dishonesty probably came from his family training, for Davis recounts approvingly how that family stole a deer from hunters with the same slim justification that he often used for the irresponsibility of his fictional characters.[70] With such a background it is easy to see why Davis so resented the moral claims of others. His writing has a certain offhandedness and disenchantment, somewhat reminiscent of Mark Twain's or of Davis' mentor, H. L. Mencken.

But there is more here than the imitation of styles or attitudes. Both Davis' mother and father were from East Tennessee, and his writing commonly deals with people of that background. In one of his last essays, Davis pointed out that Oregon was settled by two kinds of people—those harking back to Missouri and points east and south and settling in the countryside; and those of New England background, who established the towns and cities. The two groups in his view, hadn't had much love for each other, and still didn't.[71] As history, this old story is too simple, especially for the twentieth century, yet for Davis, it was the plain truth. Favoring those of southern provenance, Davis' writing was in a sense a life-long crusade against the hypocrisies and superficialities of urban dwellers, primarily Northerners, whom he almost uniformly constructed from cardboard. His quasi-fictional "A Town in Eastern Oregon"[72] is as bitter an attack on a town and its history as one can find, and the same thread runs through his other works. What he particularly disparaged was the townsmen's desire for respectability, for a "City of Homes," the very quality Dorothy Johansen considered distinctive of those who came to Oregon. In a note at the beginning of *Honey in the Horn*, Davis tells us that he had hoped to represent all lines of work in homesteading Oregon of 1906–1908. He then points out that he had to give up the idea, for there were too many. Yet significantly, every calling he proceeds to mention in the book is a rural one, and the towns encountered are never the equivalents of Portland, or even of Salem or Eugene. Davis' entire Oregon became a kind of frontier backwoods on the Southern border—his view of Northwestern civilization!

Beyond towns, Davis' hatred was directed toward the tribulations of family life. His depicted relations of parents and children are almost uniformly cool or bitter—with children even of relatively good parents often becoming worthless or evil. Again, this probably derived from bitter experiences in his own life. (The depth of that asperity varies—his short stories written more directly for the magazine market after 1932 are much sweeter than the novels, a sweetness that Davis presumably summoned up due to the demands of these popular outlets.) Davis quite apparently used family instability and disappointments to bolster his literary case that what we build up or create almost always turns to ashes. The pioneer struggled, his wife sacrificed, and got precious little for it all besides bitterness. There is a vast difference between hatred of the land and what it had done to those who acquired it in Davis' *Honey in the Horn* and *The Distant Music*; and the picture of reward in the sunny, apple country novels of Allis McKay.[73] Each chose his/her own slice of reality. Paradoxically, Davis was a novelist of settlement who rejected settlement, and in his misanthropy thought it might have been better had the land never been touched. He thus felt, in the homesteader's defeat, a perilous kind of *schadenfreude*. We are very far here from Theodore Winthrop's beatific vision in the Northwest. While certain critics have purported to find in Davis the message that people were more important than the land, more often his message seems to have been the reverse, as when he said (prophetically):

> Civilization in my country meant shifting the balance in favor of people. That was its business. Where people had to live, other things had to die. Someday all other forms of life would be exterminated, and there would be nothing left anywhere but people. Then humanity could settle down with a happy sigh to revel in its triumph. There wouldn't be much of anything else left to do.[74]

This spirit has a startling connection to today's Northwestern preservationists, but it is also the spirit of a region that aged, as Davis often pointed out, with startling rapidity, that flourished so superficially and sporadically that development and growth often seemed to him rather like bad jokes.

As with many Northwesterners, Davis was explicitly concerned with a lack of roots, and he saw the problem of the region's literature as its failure to tie past and present together in a meaningful relationship. At the same time, the writer needed to write what he knew directly. Combining these objectives, Davis set out to describe a West that remained alive in his own time, or in the memories of his contemporaries, and was still something of a frontier place. He himself had come to maturity in an area where homesteading was still occurring. But Davis remained cut off psychologically from his own roots, and in his writing and travels wandered back to his parents' Tennessee homeland, to the Mississippi and Oklahoma frontiers, and finally further, until he tried to assimilate European, Southern, and Indian history with the movement westward. But the novels of this later period are more artificial ones, for they do not grow out of what he knew (or semi-loved?). So Davis' imagination finally returned to experience, and in his last decade, he wrote again of the Northwest, specifically, The Dalles area. He again visited the region, exploring its meaning—although he no longer lived there; and in the end, the meaning fairly consumed him.

Davis had much in common with the best Western writers, of the caliber of a Twain or Stegner; but he is much removed from stereotypical, Greek tragedy "westerns" or typical heroes, shootouts, and predictable resolutions. Like other Western novelists, he wrote epically and mythically, and went easy on intensive, subjective analysis.[75] Certainly, too, he had the Western desire to explore the past. Critics have pointed out the degree to which Davis worked within a western historical-literary tradition, where "man is seen as inherently imperfect, but with universal possibilities for redemption and reconciliation."[76] But of course this does not tell us how such redemption was to be achieved. One critic believed Davis' major theme was the search for a purpose and goal in a life where that search itself was what mattered.[77]

However, a deeper reading of Davis shows the growth of rather more important ideas. While the relationship between maturity and accepting responsibility is superficially tacked on to the end of *Honey in the Horn*, the theme becomes an integral part of Davis' work after "Beach Squatter" (1936). Stories such as "The Stubborn Spearman" and *The Distant Music* itself are *bildungsromane*, tales of growth through acceptance of the evil in humans, including one's own, and then the responsibility that one has for one's life—a tragic responsibility, since people are often incapable of controlling impulses and natures. This is the meaning of old Hendricks' character development in *Winds of Morning*, a character akin to Pop Appling's in the Davis story "Open Winter"[78] from years before.

Responsibility was a hard taskmaster, but in Davis' more optimistic moods, it existed alongside a deep and enduring Grant Wood kind of love. The attachments of Clay for the young Indian and later for Luce in *Honey in the Horn* were exceptional. Stronger and more insistent were the father-son relationship in "The Homestead Orchard," or that of old Hendricks and daughter in *Winds of Morning*. Finally, one realizes that Davis tells us of this numb, mute love in nearly every tale. The Lydia (in *Distant Music*) who as a child held her family together, who spends years caring for her husband, and who in the end, talks her old acquaintance through his illness is not only responsible, but she has also loved those people and is repaid by the knowledge of it.

The most explicit and persistent development of the concept is, however, in *Beulah Land*, a Davis novel linking the Cherokee removal to the Northwest's settling, and in so doing, also tying Davis' Southern inheritance to the region.[79] But primarily, *Beulah Land* is the story of the love that emerges along each side of a triangle: father, daughter, and foster son. Nowhere else in Davis' work does a man's life mean so much after death as after that of this father; and nowhere does the father try so hard to insure his children's future. After his death, the two offspring imperceptibly mature, finally marry one another and have children of their own; but the changes of role are hardly noted. To Davis biological relations might or might not be important. Often they seem simply meaningless, or as Grandma Luttrell says, "[Children] are all well enough for a while, but then they grow up and git like everybody else. I wouldn't want to have 'em again."[80] But sometimes there develop spiritual relations among those close together in life (usually within the family), and these are the relations that ultimately provide meaning. For over two hundred pages *Beulah Land* is bound up with the fear and insecurity of the young. As the daughter thinks to herself:

> It was love people were punished for hardest.... There should be a place somewhere in which people could love without being shamed or frightened or exterminated for it. There must be such a place, it must be ahead, somewhere beyond the river, beyond the settlement....[81]

But in the end she realizes,

> Love did hurt people. It punished and maimed them sometimes, but in the end it reached down to things worth finding out, worth keeping. The important thing was to hold out to the end, to believe in love through its shifts and changes and cruelties. And the end was not an end at all, only a change. It shed and sprouted again, and went on.[82]

This is the love Lydia realizes at the end of *Distant Music*, and through it, the rationality that is central to Davis' critique of humans is transcended:

> The sun had lifted clear of the hills to strike down on the gray rocks and bleached grass and moving water, shimmering through tree-leaves and weed-tangles and telephone wires and flaming from window to window as it moved across the living things stirring under it to begin another day. If the people were right, it meant that her reasoning was mistaken.... If they were right, the places she had lived and left behind, and all the lives she had touched and lost had not been wasted, and nothing of all she had gathered was either dead or useless. If they were right, the deep swell of tears and rest and sweetness from which reason had tried to hold her back was peace.[83]

Davis, it turns out, catches us unaware here; his customary cynicism dissolves into an affirmation reminiscent of a McKay or Berenice Thorpe. Out of the most unlikely materials, and a garrulous pessimism, emerges this hopeful faith. It could not easily have been predicted.

That faith may have derived from a long submerged religious interest, and perhaps out of struggle with an overpowering sense of guilt. It may have related to Davis' long-time interest in the Catholic Church, which he joined just before his death.[84] For whatever reason, Davis ultimately discovered a significant meaning, one much deepened by the doubt that had preceded it.

Significantly, this is a level Davis achieved in his work only when the action centered on the old, rather than the young.

We conclude, then, that there were at least four Northwest authors (to the 1970s) whose work still deserves the attention of modern readers; each was a true representative of Northwest writing that mattered in the formation of a regional civilization. Allis McKay was outstanding among a long line of autobiographical family novelists of settlement, often women. Don Berry brought the Northwest historical novel a long way from preceding works of that genre (though we must give more than a polite nod in this genre to the pioneering, passionate, well-researched work of Eva Emery Dye); while H. L. Davis successfully used fiction to cut through the patina of a ranchers' and homesteaders' world to show the rewards of human effort. Finally, Ken Kesey brought to the setting of western Oregon social and psychological dilemmas and literary style of the modern world with an effectiveness never before equaled. Their achievements cannot be mocked. The literary region each created may be in varying degrees, remote from today's Northwest. Yet neither was the South of Faulkner an acceptable South to most Southerners, and certainly its relevance to modern life is now obscure, too. Yet Faulkner's South helped create what we know as Southern literature. Outside of another *War and Peace*, perhaps *the* national or regional novel can never be written; but there can be regional literatures, and the Northwest certainly has had one that was (and is) noteworthy.

Chapter 7

Reflecting the Northwest: Historical and Other Non-Fiction Writing

Serious history in the Pacific Northwest really began only with Frances Victor's Bancroft histories; and because of their reliance on primary material, sound historical sense, and literary ability, they provided a more adequate basis for Northwestern self-understanding than many academic and popular histories that succeeded them. Beyond the Victor Bancroft work, we may quickly pass over ceremonial nineteenth-century books, such as Elwood Evans' two-volume *History of the Pacific Northwest*. Evans was a booster and jack-of-all-trades notable, of a type we have met frequently here. He was colorful, but not a serious or major historian. Other reminiscent historians included the Oregonian W. H. Gray, Samuel Clarke, and, of course, Harvey Scott. Sometimes such historians have much to give us, but more as personal, primary source documents than as secondary authority.

After Victor, the Northwest's best-known regional historian was an academic, Edmond S. Meany, the successor in many ways to Elwood Evans. Meany is hard to evaluate fairly, for he was a pioneer in the field, and was akin to scholars in the third-century Roman Empire who also had little competition. Dorothy Johansen in her text, *Empire of the Columbia*, wrote him off with a phrase: "Edmond S. Meany's *History of the State of Washington* (1909) breathed local patriotism...." Meany was bracketed with other parochial Northwest writers of the turn of the century, and given short shrift, too much so, given a more recent scholarly reappraisal.[1]

That he *was* a local patriot, and a booster of the Harvey Scott variety, none would deny. Meany was also a literal pioneer, coming from Michigan to Washington State at about Scott's age (fifteen), though twenty-odd years later—in 1877. Scott graduated from Pacific University at Forest Grove, Oregon, Meany from the University of Washington, at age twenty-three. There he taught the rest of his life, until his death at seventy-three, growing with both the university and region.

Meany certainly derived some of his character from a preindustrial era. The homespun poetry by which he solemnized various occasions can definitely be described as folksy. In 1913 he delivered a commencement address at the University of Washington, preparing a poetic tear jerker on Marcus Whitman for the occasion. It is interesting that professors of history still composed poetry, and also that Meany's emotions seem authentically homemade and not simply obligatory. But the following elegiac conclusion to "Whitman" remains as foreign to the modern reader as the work of Joaquin Miller:

> He did not seek to glorify a church;
> No thought had he or time for laureled name,
> Nor wealth or power or flitting tinsel fame;
> His steady aim
> Knew leap nor lurch,
> Nor aught did flinch from chast'ning rod;
> He loved his fellows, humbly served his God.
> He served and loved, and always by his side,—
> His equal martyr, singing, fair haired bride.
> When giant states build lofty tower on tower
> To house the teeming millions' throbbing power,
> Ah, memory's tardy flame!
> On Whitman's lonely grave this tribute flower![2]

When Harvey Scott died in 1910, Meany wrote another memorial poem, a eulogy that again soars well above the subject himself. It was printed in the *Oregonian* and reprinted by the University of Washington *Daily*. Meany concludes on Scott as follows:

> One law and one condition:
> No personal ambition
> For him whose pen would mould a mighty State:
> No boastful brandishings,
> No empty vanishings,
> But words that range 'twixt love and hate.
> As engine wheels increasing whirled
> And noise of life full throbbed each hour,

Glad Hope's new banners quick unfurled,
He led the hosts to fresh found power.
Then Oh, the end of Life's allotted span!
Blow ye the glowing embers
Till every child remembers
The West brought forth a rugged, honest man.[3]

But most of the time Meany wrote, compiled, edited, or spoke history in abundance. If it is of varying quality, much is useful and interesting. His edition of *A New Vancouver Journal on the Discovery of Puget Sound*, for instance, has a well-informed, if somewhat cumbrous, introduction. Among other things, Meany wrote articles and books on the origins of geographical names in the Northwest; pamphlets on Chief Joseph and on the Bon Marché department store in Seattle; capsule portraits of Washington's governors; and a book entitled *Mount Rainier, A Record of Exploration*.[4] He gave addresses at the University of Washington, but also at fora such as the Tulalip Indian School (in 1920). He wrote, in short, for both scholar and layman, and even co-authored a text on civics and government for elementary schools. This was not rare, however, in that era, for even great academic French historians like Ernest Lavisse wrote for the primary school as well.

Meany's best known work is his *History of the State of Washington*.[5] Though definitely out-of-date on matters like the controversial Whitman Massacre, and devoid of modern social history, the book is an acceptable forerunner, along with the more comprehensive Bancroft volumes, to the Gates/Johansen work. Meany deserves a prominent place in Northwest historiography, but partly, it must be reiterated, due to academe still being in a fledgling state there.

He also became posthumously, and quite recently, controversial as a memorializer of the tragic Chief Joseph of the removed Nez Percés. In 1901, toward the end of Chief Joseph's life, Meany went to the Colville Reservation to interview the chief there. In photographs of the time, the bearded, sober Meany clad in suit and tie is a foil for the tragic Indian in his fine headdress. Both seem in their way noble, but Joseph's fate, according to Robert McCoy, allowed the myth of the "noble savage" to be perpetuated—both interesting to the Northwest mainstream in that regard, but also not quite up to the standards of white, Christian civilization. When "the Red Napoleon" attended a University of Washington football game in 1903, and enjoyed himself, was this a case of sad, resigned assimilationism, or even tokenism? This remains open to debate. After Chief Joseph's death, Meany supervised the building of a monument on his grave, but again, today's interpreters may see all this as merely patronizing.[6]

Among other historians of that time, Clinton A. Snowden produced a four-volume *History of Washington* (subtitled *The Rise and Progress of an American State*), and Joseph Schafer wrote *A History of the Pacific Northwest.*[7] Snowden's is an old-fashioned, anecdotal narrative without notes or bibliography. The writing is laborious and rather thin, but provides some insights—such as on the haphazard nature of early explorations—into Washington history. Especially valuable are numerous photographs of the nineteenth century moral elite—army captains, lawyers, or governors, all hirsute, all with some degree of girth, all projecting an image of custodianship. Snowden himself idolized the pioneers and significantly, the book was dedicated to his parents, noting simply, "They were Pioneers." Equally attracted to pioneers, Schafer, at the University of Oregon, offered a conventional but not overly moralistic picture of Northwest history. His attitude toward missionaries and the decimation and assimilation of Native Americans remained in the tradition of Evans and Meany. On the Whitman episode he wrote:

> Thus some of the tribes of the interior country were at last brought under the influence of a few men and women wholly devoted to their welfare, and understanding with a fair degree of clearness how to guide these barbarians along the path of civilization. The task was stupendous; but the missionaries believed it was not impossible and labored with exemplary courage.[8]

Where Schafer differed from Meany was in his more liberal outlook on contemporaries, leading him to defend U'Ren and proponents of the Oregon System against charges of radicalism, but in the name of Progressivism.

More readable is George W. Fuller's *A History of the Pacific Northwest: With Special Emphasis on the Inland Empire*, originally published in 1931.[9] Fuller gives us the almost obligatory geographical overview that frequently introduces such texts; but his first chapter, especially strong on geological developments, ranks among the best descriptions of the region. Fuller's genuine interest in the Northwest's marine, mountain, and desert evolution is communicated to the reader with a subtle mix of scientific and literary writing. On Glacier Park he writes evocatively of the artistic beauty wrought by a fault in its northern part that had altered its rock formations. His full treatment of the mysteriously rich Palouse soil gives one a background for Nard Jones' novels on that area. The checkerboard of climates even beyond the Cascades in the Northwest is well outlined here. A second chapter on the "Aborigines" is also clear and strong, going well beyond later general histories in this regard. Various cults and customs are fully explained, and we learn more about matters like Indian food than in other general treatments. Fuller steers nicely between modern romanticization of the Indian and the old condescension of "civilized" people. The book becomes more standard and less unique on McLoughlin, Whitman, and the mid-century, and gives little space to the post–1870 period and to modern reform movements and ideals.

Building on the work of Charles Gates and Oscar Winthur, Dorothy Johansen became the first really modern, comprehensive Northwest historian; and her *Empire of the Columbia* (in different editions) long remained a standard text on the region's history. Johansen was one of a minority of native Northwest historians, though most spent the greater part of their lives there. Born in 1904 at Seaside, Oregon, of a German father and a mother from Astoria, Johansen took her degrees at Northwest institutions—her B.A. at Reed College, and M.A., then Ph.D. at the University of Washington (1941). After teaching in a variety of Northwestern public schools, she spent the remainder of her professional career at Reed College. A director of the Oregon Historical Society and board member of the *Pacific Northwest Quarterly*, her publications dealt exclusively with the region's history, though she dipped into various modes—economic, intellectual, and political—in her specialized work. Hers was the career of a complete Northwestern.

In the Meany tradition, Johansen also edited primary sources—particularly explorer, pioneer, or trapper accounts. She published articles on navigation, Columbia River steamboating, the growth of education and libraries in the region, and the Hudson's Bay records, as well as a few interpretive pieces, such as "Oregon's Role in American History: An Old Theme Recast,"[10] along with numerous reviews. Johansen was a solid, careful historian, and her revision of the text she had co-authored with Gates, *Empire of the Columbia*, became for a time the only one of its kind on Northwest history. Readable, chronologically easy to follow, succinct, it is yet lively in spots. The book is equally adept on McLoughlin, turn-of-the-century Portland, or the more modern context. No scholar can research a subject in Northwest history without beginning with Johansen. The only weak spot is her treatment of cultural history, which—in common with other textbook treatments—is more list than analysis. Intellectual history is still under-represented there.

The intellectual historian who concerned himself most deeply with the region before the 1980s was Edwin Bingham, who taught at the University of Oregon. Born in Denver in 1920, he took his Ph.D. at U.C.L.A. in 1951, and was based in Eugene from 1949. Bingham was important to a Northwest vision of itself by breeding students who took the region's cultural products as serious materials for research. In this respect his teaching, along with publications, had a continuing influence in the area. Just to mention one of his distinguished students: Richard Etulain, later chair of the history department at Idaho State University, and so much else, became the first comprehensive literary historian of the region. From Etulain, one learned what novelists the Northwest possessed, and methods for evaluating their contributions. Bingham himself reviewed novels by writers like Don Berry and H. L. Davis in the *Oregon Historical Quarterly*, and his paper on John Reed and C.E.S. Wood is still one of the more literate examples of Northwest intellectual history.[11]

Earl Pomeroy, Bingham's colleague at the University of Oregon, considered the Northwest past within the larger framework of the American West. Pomeroy was a transplanted Californian, and after short stints at other universities, came to Oregon at the outset of the '50s. He then became one of the most distinguished faculty members in the region, garnering numerous awards. Like Bingham he inspired others, including this book's initial senior author, to investigate the Northwest as a cultural region. He read papers and wrote numerous interpretive articles and reviews that stimulated many scholars. His *In Search of the Golden West* related a history of tourism to the Western myths that had long fired Americans.[12] Pomeroy's *The Pacific Slope* remains an important interpretive history of the West and still a generator of ideas for future research.[13] Concentrating primarily on California, for this is the larger part of the story, his socio-economic history is particularly good on progressivism and the concomitant rise of nativism and anti-union activity in the '20s; on regional reflections of the New Deal in the '30s; and on the rise of aluminum, aircraft, and other core industries during the '40s and '50s. In the preface to one paperback edition, Pomeroy regretted the lack of space devoted to minorities, yet certainly dealt ably in his day with anti–Chinese and anti–Japanese sentiments in the Northwest. Against this background, he offered modestly optimistic, but subtle prognoses for the various subregions of the West, including the region we discuss here.

However, outside of school and college, the Northwestern past was most known through its popular historians. Although such writers have often been more attracted to the random, picturesque, or titillating detail, rather than to a careful recovery and evaluation of earlier times, at their best they have made important contributions.

One of the most widely read was certainly Stewart Holbrook (1893–1964). Born in Vermont as a ninth-generation "Yankee," and educated in New Hampshire, Holbrook arrived in British Columbia in 1920. After experience with logging that would influence his later books, he came down to live in Seattle and Portland, with some stints back East as well. Holbrook contributed a book on *The Columbia* in the Rivers of America Series—a book more ambitious than the title indicates. He wrote on logging history, the iron industry, agricultural machines, war heroes, capitalists of the Gilded Age, and the history of forest fires. This last book, *Burning an Empire*,[14] was dedicated to the writer James Stevens, whom Holbrook admired and touted. To produce his journalism and history, Holbrook combed every corner of the

Northwest, observing both forest fires and the activities and language of oddballs with equal fascination. His writing is, like Stevens,' muscular, yet possesses a taut, sometimes poetic quality as well. Holbrook's Portland is the single workingman's Portland, the Portland of eccentrics, the Portland that heroes of the early Stevens would have visited when they blew their season's pay. Holbrook knew concrete things better than most and made them come alive on his pages—as in this description of logging that led to the massive Tillamook burn in 1933:

> A chokerman set a choker around a big blue butt of fir, the rigging slinger shouted "Hi!" and the punk blew the whistle on the yarding engine once. Up reared the big log, thrashing its way out of the underbrush like some whale of the woods. The main line of steel whipped taut, then slacked, then sung with a long mean whistle as the donkey engine got into the pull. The log jumped, fell, then leaped ahead, and on its way to the landing it ground down hard and long while passing across a wind-felled cedar, matchwood for many years.
>
> An instant later a thin puff of white smoke curled up from the cedar. Another instant it was whiter still, not so thin, and within a couple of minutes the hook tender yelled: "Fire!"
>
> The hooker was right. Fire it was, fire to burn up four centuries of trees, fire to take a life.[15]

Perhaps Holbrook's most affectionate work was his *Far Corner: A Personal View of the Pacific Northwest.* This is popular history cum autobiography of the best sort. We have long passages here on pioneers and logging, but also sensitive swaths on writers such as Opal Whitely and Ben Hur Lampman. There is the usual geographical overview, but also much local lore on place names and people, and a fine chapter on the growth of Portland. Holbrook addresses himself to one of the fundamental questions that faced people here: Who, in this area of transients, *was* a Northwesterner, and how long did it take to become one? Holbrook felt it required roughly ten years to grow into the region in Seattle or Spokane, but as much as twenty-five in Oregon City, Walla Walla, or Portland. Overgeneralized as he might have been here, the reader pardons it in such a writer. Holbrook's prejudices certainly favored the pioneer. As he put it:

> Many a latter-day immigrant has resented the pioneer cult. I rather enjoy it. Its mild snobbism is harmless. It has its foundations in one of the greatest American experiences. What if it does make for parochialism? Most of the descendants of pioneers I happen to know do not allow the fact of their antecedents to affect their own decency as human beings.[16]

But Holbrook remained addicted to progress, seeing the forest, in particular, as both the area's future economic *and* aesthetic focus. Only in later life did he warn against a huge influx of people, who would collectively ruin this lavish environment, and decided to propagandize the "everlasting rain" as "our first line of defense."[17] This balancing act between espousing economic growth derived from generous natural resources, and *protection* of those resources became a distinguishing mark of a developing regional civilization in the Northwest.

Another of Holbrook's well-known books was his *Holy Old Mackinaw: A Natural History of the American Lumberjack*, and among so much else he did, he also contributed the chapter on Oregon for a distinguished photographic essay entitled *The Pacific Northwest*, co-authored by Roderick Haig-Brown and Nard Jones, and edited by the Portland salmon authority, Anthony Netboy. He also brought together a still valuable collection of Northwest writing under the title *Promised Land*, which any beginning student of the region can read with profit (supplemented with a companion volume by Ellis Lucia). Beyond this, Holbrook wandered far afield, but often only to tie a thread of significance back again to the Northwest. In *Yankee Exodus*,[18] he returned to his New England roots, tracing the dispersion of people like himself throughout the nation. For a time Holbrook was probably the Northwest's most famous writer, one whom distinguished literary visitors like William Faulkner, Robert Frost, or H.L. Mencken came to see when they sojourned in the region. And Robert E. Ficken called him a "pioneer of environmental history," well before it became a vogue.[19]

In Washington the analogue of Holbrook in the next generation was Murray Morgan, a journalist who also knew regional history well, and wrote warmly and cogently about it. Born in Tacoma in 1916, and aside from a New York period, a lifelong resident and supporter of the Northwest, Morgan was an ebullient writer who loved to travel to locales, and who wrote as a mature professional (partly due to a formative period at the Columbia School of Journalism and stints on *Time* and *Life* magazines).

Among his voluminous works were books on the Seattle World's Fair, the Grand Coulee Dam, the Klondike Gold Rush, and hospitals. In the tradition of multi-faceted Northwest authors, Morgan even tried his hand at detective fiction with *The Viewless Winds* (1949), a work that used much fog and seascape for its ambiance. Morgan's popular history, *The Northwest Corner: Its Past and Present* (1962), parallels Holbrook's *Far Corner*. It is quite rare for journalists to know history so well, and Morgan's high standards in that department were greatly appreciated in the region.

The feel for the Northwest that charged Morgan's work is best seen in his *The Last Wilderness* (1955), a history of the Olympic Peninsula, and especially in the regional classic, *Skid Road: An Informal Portrait of Seattle*. In the first book Morgan's concern was to take readers back to the land the Indians had known ("In the Time Before Everything Changed"), and transport them via exploration, logging, and white settlement to the creation of a park in the 1930s. Morgan was not one-sided—he knew the logging scene as well as more touristic ones—nor did his nature writing overly intrude, as so often happens in this kind of book. He examined the peninsula from the point of view of Spaniards, Vancouver, and modern people, too, and equally well. Even his contemporaries evinced mixed opinions: "There are those who hate the peninsula on sight and consider it a great wet thicket, and others who covet it as a secret garden."[20] Morgan was also solid on the great allocation struggle, as it might be called, for the Northwest's bounty—salmon fishermen, hikers, farmers, loggers, naturalists, or hunters of the sea otter in a continuing joust that had begun with the first incoming of whites. Much of the bounty was brokered away, but many trees were also saved in a national park. Was beauty not something in itself? Morgan held that it was. Ending positively, but not vehemently, the record he delineates deepens our understanding of the natural Northwest's value.[21]

Skid Road needs scant introduction here. It is a fine example of popular but responsible urban history that has thrilled many readers, and been a bestseller. Given a contract by Viking's Malcolm Cowley, who had been out visiting and wanted Morgan to write the book, the author emphasized the first contacts with Indians, the railroad boom, the growth of dock industries, and of labor organizations, culminating in the General Strike; then Hooverville poverty of the '30s, and the rise of Northwest oddballs like Vic Meyers and Marion Zioncheck. He ended with a look at more modern labor and at the figure of Dave Beck, in particular. The writing is strong and the subject matter often the brawnier side of Northwest life—the life that so fascinated Holbrook and the proletarian novelist Cantwell, too. Morgan's story of the ultimate victory of Seattle's middle class over a colorful, earthier world of labor, waterfront, and Skid Road dereliction reminds one of the message in H. L. Davis' "A Town in Eastern Oregon." Morgan conveys here that Seattle's best traditions lay in its varieties of homegrown lower classes and lumpenproletariat. The city finally grew more "comfortable" (and how much moreso since then!); but not without paying a large price. On this more contemporary Seattle mentality, Morgan remarks: "Some cities glory in their culture, some in their institutions, some in their industries, but Seattle loves its scenery. 'To hear you people talk,' a friend from the East assured me, 'you'd think you *built* Mount Rainier.'"[22]

Aside from history, another lasting literary inheritance of the Northwest is likely to be its record of personal experiences.[23] In the early period we had, of course, the explorers, then the pioneers; and finally, travelers such as James Swan, and Theodore Winthrop in his celebrated *Canoe and the Saddle*.[24] Of writers in the generation that followed, Robert Cantwell especially praised Guy Waring's account of his ranch on the Okanogan—the ranch that his friend Owen Wister also used as a backdrop for "the Virginian."[25] Around the turn of the century a plethora of reminiscences were published. Most famous perhaps is George Waggoner's *Stories of Old Oregon*. A similar type of author was T. T. Geer, born near Silverton, Oregon in 1851. For much of his life Geer was both farmer and author in the eastern part of the state. Naturally he wrote for newspapers, and for a few terms served in the legislature. After becoming Oregon's governor (1899–1903), Geer edited the *Statesman*, then the *Pendleton Tribune*, and spent his last years as a Portland real estate developer. His main literary legacy was a massive book from these last years entitled *Fifty Years in Oregon*, one among a number of similar volumes published about the turn of the century. The book is lighthearted, but also contains a trace "of sadness, peculiarly characteristic of books of reminiscence, as though a deep experience of the country still touche[d] the whites with melancholy as it did the Indians."[26]

Silverton's other gift of the era was the cartoonist Homer Davenport, born seventeen years later. *Country Boy*, reminiscent of his life in Silverton, portrayed in Norman Rockwellian tones the Oregon version of small-town American nostalgia.[27] Davenport became a leading New York cartoonist, but his work retained "...the somberness and melancholy, as a pervading note or in clutching brevity, that seem[ed] inseparable from a deep sensitivity to Oregon."[28] In the early 1900s his life fell apart, he died in 1912, and the body was brought back at the behest of William Randolph Hearst for burial in Oregon.

Succeeding decades saw much additional material emerge, and one can only mention a few such books here. Among the best nature-reminiscences was Hazel Heckman's of the 1960s concerning her life on Anderson Island near Tacoma.[29] One of the most appealing and well-known accounts of Northwest life for the outdoorsman was William O. Douglas' *Of Men and Mountains*, initially published in 1950.[30] Brought up at Yakima in a fatherless, isolated family, Douglas said he struggled against the effects of an early polio attack by developing himself into an ardent outdoorsman, an activity he pursued largely in the Cascades east and southeast of Mount Rainier, and in the Wallowa Mountains of eastern Oregon. Because of this experience, he endowed the love of mountains with a virtuous burden it could not quite represent in the lives of most. It was also significant—and akin to the experience of many Northwest notables—that Douglas left the region to make fame and fortune elsewhere, becoming a powerful U.S. Supreme Court Justice. However, his obvious love of the Northwest's wild country never left him, and few can more effectively entrance the modern reader with details of fishing or the lure of a meadow, or even the terror of a rock climb in its awe-inspiring mountains. Douglas also used both his love of the region and

Eastern clout to help gain wilderness protection for parts of his native area, especially by joining the tendentious fight for an Olympic National Park in Washington.[31]

Among natural scientists Thomas Condon had come to the Northwest as a missionary in 1852, and lived to become its outstanding geologist in the latter half of the century, as an original researcher, professor, and popularizer.[32] An important scientific work of the nineteenth century—though published in 1905—was Thomas Howells' *A Flora of Northwest America*.[33] Coming to Oregon from Missouri as a child, Howells received only three months of schooling! Beginning in 1877, he started a serious plant collection, and for twenty years, pursued this as a sideline to jobs such as one he had working in a small grocery. Knowing he could not afford to hire a printer, Howells learned to set type, then printed the manuscript of eight hundred pages himself.

After Howells' period, university and government research institutions increasingly dominated the area's intellectual product. In presenting this review, we can by no means cover the ground of recent intellectual activity in the Northwest since Vernon Parrington. Centered in academic institutions, within professional schools, and departments in the humanities, social, and natural sciences, that output has often been too specialized for a study of our scope. Most relevant to our interests here is the substantial work emanating from a number of institutions in anthropology, sociology, and geography, particularly as this work relates to the region. On Native American cultures, we have already referred to a number of anthropological works in Chapter 1. Professors such as Luther Cressman at the University of Oregon in archaeology and Erna Gunther in ethnology at the University of Washington devoted their lives to the Northwest. In geography an outstanding work of synthesis was Donald Meinig's *The Great Columbia Plain*.[34] In sociology we have a number of distinguished names, perhaps best known being Washington's George Lundberg,[35] the apostle of a scientifically directed society. The regional sociologist of longest service was Lundberg's colleague, Calvin Schmid, with quantitative publications on the problems of Seattle and Washington State dating from the mid–1920s to at least the late '60s. Schmid's work both in sociological theory and for the immediate public interest demonstrated the degree to which academe and a regional society could work together for mutual enhancement.

For our most recent decades treated here, social thought and historical consciousness were effectively brought to bear on Northwestern problems by Norman H. Clark. Clark came from elsewhere, but like Pomeroy and Bingham, was a Westerner. Born in Mesa, Arizona in 1925, he would arrive in the Northwest in 1948 and ultimately take his doctorate at the University of

Washington in 1964 under Robert Burke. He then taught at Everett Community College and became its president.

Clark's first book, *The Dry Years: Prohibition and Social Change in Washington*, was based on his doctoral dissertation.[36] The book is his most sprawling and uncontrolled work, and that remains both its virtue and its flaw. A compulsive marshaling of detail betrays the dissertation, but the versatile, pleasing digressions do not. In a review Edward Allen complained of undue stress placed here on peripheral data;[37] but in fact, that data often takes the reader into tangential areas that need exploring. The subject allows Clark to touch various Northwest nerves, for anti-alcohol sentiment in this region went back to the age of McLoughlin and Whitman. A fine, nuanced chapter on the degenerating effects of rum on Indians makes this more than just a conventional account of the fall from primitive virtue. With the 1860s and '70s, modern attempts at prohibition really began, says Clark—punctuated by colorful marches on saloons, such as stirred Frances Victor, and lobbies, or stumping lectures. Ancillary motivations, as we have seen, became linked to the temperance issue—anti-immigration, women's suffrage, religion, tax reform, Populist protest, and so on. Perhaps too slavishly, Clark seems to follow Richard Hofstadter's groundbreaking, but now dated, connections between middle-class status loss and progressivism, as adumbrated in *The Age of Reform*. Ultimately, prohibition was rural, Protestant, and Anglo-Saxon, with the rural element transferred to the lower- and middle-middle-class elements in Washington's growing cities. Clark points out that most inveighers against saloons knew not of what they spoke, and he considered prohibitionists as last-gasp Puritans, who before Freud's influence spread, still felt unashamed to advertise that outlook. But he also views saloons themselves as last-gasp institutions, before the modern "god of precision" took over.[38]

In *Mill Town: A Social History of Everett Washington from its Earliest Beginnings on the Shores of Puget Sound to the Tragic and Infamous Event Known as the Everett Massacre*,[39] a new Clark took shape. Though the writing in his earlier book was sprightly, Clark became emphatically more poetic here. The book opens with a passage that could have come from Morgan or Holbrook: a cascading nature description—this one of the Skykomish River—which sets the tone of the entire narrative. Even when Clark describes the most hard-hearted of industrialists, the poetry, the very feel of clinking glasses, is allowed to intervene, though not intrusively. Everett emerges here as a welter of conflicting tendencies, an industrial U.S. in microcosm. Clark is particularly strong on immigrant groups to the Northwest like Danes, Norwegians, and Germans, detailing the range of their clubs and activities, and evoking well the warmth of their existence, as well as their acute fears of unrest, and need to assimilate into an Anglo-Saxon mold. The robber barons are painted in all their cruel regalia, and the many churches which the city could boast are thrown up cheek by jowl with its burgeoning radical contingents. The book culminates in a fair and careful explication of what is known of the massacre itself. Clark is a better painter than explainer, and perhaps that is as it should be; but his fatalistic conclusion does leave one unsatisfied: radical action, he contended, was doomed at that level of industry, and at that time in the timber sector. He felt that monopoly conglomerates of Weyerhaeuser and the rest would paradoxically bring more for workers than strikes. Education along with rising wages would help boost them, and particularly their offspring, into the middle class. In other words, Clark was ultimately unconvinced of the massacre's long-term importance. Its principal actors trickled out lives in a very different era; patriotism revived after World War I and there was only a brief renewal of violence, like that perpetrated against the Wobblies in Centralia. Basically, however, radical activity petered out. So ends the book, but at least the whole trip there is well worth it.

In the 1970s, Clark brought out a fine bicentennial history of Washington.[40] Bicentennial histories were commissioned for each state but commendably, the editors allowed their authors a broad range in the choice of material and style. Clark elected to use a biographical approach, concentrating on figures whose lives typified certain periods or social issues. And the book is beautifully written. Though we might reproach the author with, at times, *too* much fine writing, this exciting brand of narrative history on the Northwest, and by a Northwesterner, was certainly welcome.

When he finally entered the contemporary stream of history, Clark seemed the quintessential liberal idealist of the 1970s. The mindless growth of "Pugetopolis" obviously bothered him, while at the same time, the "saving" of Lake Washington seemed a miraculous, dream-inspired achievement. Conservation efforts and university research on salmon spawning gave him real hope; but much of this idealism had emanated from outside the region. F.D.R., he noted, had as much to do with the creation of an Olympic National Park as any Washingtonian. Like all regionalists, Clark here seemed to fear the loss of Washington's uniqueness. Yet transcendent possibilities remained, and these, he felt, must connect into American ideals of 1776. The conclusion, then, weighs the progressive versus what Clark took to be retrogressive factors that had made Washington's history; and Clark felt that the former had won out. Not a bad state, he concluded—a conclusion that, after all the fire of the text, brings us not much beyond Cantwell. But by the cogency of his presentation, and a unique blend of mood and specifics, Clark still gives readers good reason to look deeper into the region's history—and developing civilization.

Chapter 8

Distinguished Achievement: Northwest Poetry Since World War II

The sentimental theory of scenery might suggest that the Northwest would automatically produce a rich, expressive, even effulgent poetic literature. In the late nineteenth century, as seen, Joaquin Miller emerged from the ranks of the era's poetasters to inspire an age. However, Miller was an exception, and after he departed, or was, to a degree, deregionalized, the Northwest featured few well-known versifiers until the 1930s. Quite telling was the fact that Edwin Markham became the best-known Oregonian poet of the early twentieth century.

In the 1920s and '30s the general level of Northwest fiction extended to poetry. Stoddard King of Spokane's *Spokesman Review* attained a national reputation for light verse, and Portland's Ethel Romig Fuller produced widely appreciated domestic poetry.[1] Often the verse of that era was directed toward illuminating the region. Indeed, Howard Corning's *The Mountain in the Sky* is arranged geographically by sections of the state of Oregon, and one of his best poems describes the moment when Joaquin Miller moved apple trees and cattle from Eugene to eastern Oregon.[2] In 1935 Audrey Wurdemann received the Pulitzer Prize for poetry, with a volume beginning with an undeniably bold style.[3] But although educated in Seattle's best schools, Wurdemann's work seems somewhat unconnected to the regional background. Highly philosophical or moralistic, it strikes a deeper note than most Northwest poetry of the day, yet gets little beyond a Frances Victor. Of the same generation as Mary McCarthy, Wurdemann in the late '30s followed McCarthy's path from the Northwest into permanent Eastern exile.

It has become conventional wisdom to see this relative aridity ending when the thirty-nine-year-old Theodore Roethke arrived in 1947 to teach at Seattle's University of Washington. A Michiganer of German background (his grandfather, Bismarck's chief of forests, having made it to the U.S. in 1870), Roethke took up his appointment in the Northwest with a poor heart. As with Parrington, this was to be the environment where he would come to full maturity; but initially, Roethke had felt condemned, rather like Thorstein Veblen at Stanford, to the comparative sticks; and his invitation to U.W. seemed like a push "even further into the provinces."[4] Initially viewing Greater Seattle as a "vast Scarsdale," and his chair in English considering him "the only serious poet within a thousand miles," Roethke toyed in the manner of academics with alluring offers from elsewhere up until his death in 1963.[5] Many saw him nationally as an author who just happened for a time to reside in Seattle. Yet in this period he became a local legend, helping to engender a poetic renaissance in the region, much as Mark Tobey did for its painters in the 1950s.[6]

A great, dark, depressed poet, Roethke could also be clever, light, ribald, and nostalgic. But he was known, too, for nature poetry of a high order, such as in "The Long Waters," where his vivid lines on a Northwest matutinal landscape of waves pouring over a downed tree certainly bring his region alive; or in "The Rose," where again, he shows poetically, how important the environment—in this case, a maritime seascape complete with screaming birds and powerful, palpable tang in the air—could be to sensitive writers like himself, and thereby, to his readers.[7] Roethke's poetry really makes his adopted region a living thing, and in certain swaths, the distinctive civilization so many had announced for this American section of unusual promise.

Roethke did not gain plaudits and poetry awards on the basis of nature evocation alone.[8] By mood and in direction he was also a love poet, and a meditative one, as well as a renowned teacher and reader of poetry, and a writer of children's verse as well. After a great pouring forth of energy and achievement in the period (1947–53) that culminated in his marriage, he turned beyond Freudian psychology to a deeper study of philosophy and theology, embracing a wider range of poetic experience.[9] The wild dance of emotion with which he had protected his sanity became but an aspect of another reality, with certain lines insistently imploring God's help, a distant, unattainable God, in poems such as "The Marrow." Like so many discussed here, Roethke had an ambivalent, changing, and changeable attitude toward religion; but on the whole, he did come to feel something important called God up, or out there. In an autobiographical piece he noted: "I can't claim the soul, my soul, was absorbed in God. No, God for me still remains someone to be confronted, to be dueled with: that is perhaps my error, my sin of pride. But the oneness, Yes!"[10]

Already in the mid–'50s, before Roethke's sudden death in 1963, Carolyn Kizer had announced that alongside the Northwest School of painting—Tobey, Guy Anderson, Morris Graves, and the painter who most accessibly represented the regional environment in his work, Kenneth Callahan—there had also arisen in poetry a "School of the Pacific Northwest."[11] Quantitatively, Kizer found an unusually strong representation of Northwest poets in the best journals. Things progressed until in 1964 the University of Washington could produce in *Five Poets of the Pacific Northwest* a definitive volume of fine achievement;[12] while in one review of American poetry since 1950, 12 percent of the poets considered were Northwesterners.[13]

The "Five" long defined the region's best. David Wagoner, originally from Ohio and Indiana, was a University of Washington professor from 1954 through the '70s, and beyond. Despite influence from a proximate Roethke, he was a poet of plain song. Having been raised near Gary, Indiana, where his father was a steel smelter, Wagoner's first trip through the Cascades to the coast's marvelous greenery wowed him; but a Northwest impact on this rather careful, subtle, multi-various personality was, in one of his expressed views, gradual. Wagoner's poems to 1970 or so catalogued the varieties of nature and of ordinary lives, an approach rewarding the reader in works such as "A Guide to Dungeness Spit," "The Night of the Sad Woman," and "The Apotheosis of the Garbageman." Predictably, the ecological '70s elicited more environmentally anguished, forthright Wagoner poems, such as "Elegy for a Forest Clear-Cut by the Weyerhaeuser Company," with a poignant evocation there of old trees replaced by a large, ghostly expanse of stumps and sawdust.[14] Here Wagoner seemed typically rooted in his region.

Richard Hugo, born in Seattle, and a student of Roethke's, before teaching at the University of Montana, emphasized rough, natural images in his poetry, with bold, strong, but also clearly vulnerable lines. Of the five, Hugo had the most repulsive childhood, growing up in a poor part of Seattle, where his hard-shell Lutheran grandmother beat him regularly. He translated both those tribulations and ones following in adulthood into his work, and especially, into poetic attempts at establishing a sense of place. Of the five, Hugo was perhaps most concerned with the meaning of specific locales, and in his earlier works, these were in the Puget Sound country. In a typical poem, Hugo revealed the sense of excitement many discover in the San Juan Islands, leading him, however, to a nuanced sense of how personal trouble, not to mention loneliness, can nonetheless find one even in a comparative paradise.[15] (Another significant part of an evolving Northwest civilization—the scenery never quite enough! A propos, Saul Bellow told one of the present authors that he wouldn't want to abandon Chicago for the maritime "paradise" of Victoria, B.C., where he taught for a term during the early '80s.)

However, Hugo did earn his artistic spurs in the real world. An Air Corps bombardier in World War II, then a Boeing employee for years before he became a professor of English, his adult hobbies included—and he wrote of them—fishing, baseball, and liquor. Perhaps his greatest obsession was with boredom. By the time his collection *The Lady in Kicking Horse Reservoir* appeared, most of his work had shifted to Montana, and the Montana he evoked in the '70s was startlingly reminiscent of that described by Mary McCarthy on a visit with school friends decades earlier (in her *Memories of a Catholic Girlhood*).[16] Hugo's renderings also remind one somewhat of haunting scenes devoted to homesteader life in H.L. Davis' eastern Oregon. Examples are the poem "Dixon," where mostly, Hugo's tone is wan and discouraging, and where each day seems a kind of chore; or his "Degrees of Gray in Philipsburg," which seems even angrier, lampooning small-town or regional ways, mill work, and limited horizons (as much as Hugo definitely drew upon all that for his material).[17] However, his "Assumptions" about Northwest town life again shifted his gray, personal obsessions west of the Cascades to the rainy, and for him, melancholy region where he had grown up. Hugo was a Northwest poet who definitely refracted his life experience into his poetry, emphasizing the sadder aspects of regional landscape which he beheld around him; yet he also paid tribute to life's earthier moments derived from his many pursuits, and from his background in the world of work.[18]

Originally from Idaho, Kenneth Hanson, long a professor at Portland's Reed College, emphasized in his work oriental patterns and international backgrounds, making an electrifying entry onto the Northwest poetic scene in the 1960s with his well-sculpted, accessible poem pictures. Similarly influenced by a Northwest gaze toward the Orient has been Carolyn Kizer, a keen student of Chinese and Japanese culture. Ms. Kizer was a Northwest native connected to the societies of both Spokane and Seattle, and played a major cultural role in the region; but for years she also lived in the East, where she was for a time Director of the National Endowment for the Arts. Oriental-flavored, love-remembered, nature-fragrant, her work expresses a delicate evocation of experiences, wrapped in a mantle of tough professionalism and revolt.[19] Form in control of personal emotion became in parts of her poetry, regional tradition precisely because it raised such experiences to a universal human level.

Kizer's world is not only that of oriental art and literature, but also of marriage, children, mother, and parents—*especially* her mother, who had so much to do with Kizer's initiation into a life of culture. The themes of loss of love and of mother are recurrent in her work, and extremely expressed, as in several searing lines of her long poetry-and-prose recitation of an emotionally taxing marital breakup ("A Month in Summer").[20] These direct personal experiences combine well with Japanese tradition here.[21] Despite the piece's familism, the region is to a degree, rejected, particularly Spokane—a place where in desolation the youthful Kizer had obviously dreamed of other, more culturally vibrant places to live and thrive. Not only did Kizer herself wish to exit Spokane, but as an only child, she had also imbibed her mother's frustration in this Eastern Washington city that felt ultra-limited after time spent before marriage in New York and San Francisco. Here again is a typical part of the Northwest cultural experience, though Kizer's renderings of foreign poetry in a variety of tongues and more generally, her eclecticism make her *sui generis*.[22]

In the 1950s, '60s, and early '70s, a plethora of new poets arose, many also under oriental influences, or those of Roethke and academic fashions of that time; but especially, too, came the Friscan, drug-beat inspired poetic analogues of a counter-cultural Ken Kesey. Most famous among the latter group was undoubtedly Gary Snyder. From age two Snyder grew up in what is now a suburb north of Seattle, but the area—then including many clear-cut stumps of massive trees felled near his home—played a major role in his ecologically-aware development. As a boy Snyder loved the Northwest wilderness—gathering blackberries, canoeing, and by the time of his teen years, climbing peaks like Mount Adams or a then intact Saint Helens. He was also bowled over by Chinese landscape paintings he saw at the Seattle Art Museum and read omnivorously at a branch of the Public Library. Comparative poverty in the Depression era made the boy empathize, too, with ordinary workers of the region. When his parents split up, he went with his mother to Portland for high school, continuing his regional development not only on mountains like nearby Hood or in summer camp at Spirit Lake by Saint-Helens; but at a Portland museum, where the Northwest School of Painters—particularly, the art of Graves—became a major influence. Snyder then attended Reed College on a scholarship from the late '40s through to graduation in 1951; and it was not only a heady intellectual experience for him, but it also revealed the magnetism he could already exert on others as a budding poet and intellectual steeped in Joyce, Eliot, Proust et al., and simply as a person. Reminiscences about Snyder are invariably favorable. According to Jerry Crandall: "Most everyone liked Gary, especially those who skied or climbed.... But what I admired most was that he had the courage of his convictions. He was always an individualist." J. Michael Mahar remembers Snyder's powerful, independent mother with Irish in her who drove her boy to professional, yet idiosyncratic standards in all he did. This ran the gamut from academic work, such as Snyder's B.A. thesis on Haida Indian myths, which he later published, to the fact that "he knew a large repertoire of labor and Wobbly songs, which he sang with great vigor while whacking away at the guitar."

A professor at Reed called him a "BMOC" there, again, due to his talent and eclectic mind. (The young Snyder was already well into Buddhism and experimenting, too, with peyote and the like.) One woman, Carol Baker, who lived in the same Portland rooming house as Snyder, said: "He was a critic and a friend. He stimulated us. He was our leader." And his summers working at jobs such as a ranger in the Cascades kept him in touch with a more down-to-earth life—all to end up in his poetry. Baker said she always sensed that he would become famous.[23]

However, that fame was typically attained elsewhere. Like many we have encountered here, Snyder after graduation left the Northwest, mainly for the San Francisco Bay Area and the beat scene, along with stints in the Far East, where he marinated himself in Japanese and Chinese poetry, and various religious orientations. On trips back to his home region, such as to read new beat poems with Allen Ginsberg at University of Washington's Parrington Hall in 1956, he electrified audiences of a still staid America. As Will Baker recalls, "like a big, fresh, cold wind, [Snyder] carried us out of poetry, out of school.... At some moment, in the midst of my intoxication and delight, I was stricken by a disturbing thought. *Maybe this isn't poetry at all. This is too easy. Too clear....* But a moment after that, I knew it was all right...." Baker concludes: "We were there—clapping madly, sighing out loud, behaving in fact more like a crowd at a nightclub than an audience for a poetry reading—because we wanted this to go on and on." Like Kesey's work, Snyder's earlier poetry and prose often reveal a warm, disciplined evocation of his personal experience, and life in the Northwest; but also in East Asia, and in sailor ports of the world (among other things, he worked on tankers). However, his later *oeuvre* lost some of that quality, while taking on ever more accents from the Orient, American Indian mythology, the ecological movement, and Bay Area illuminati. In his simpler work the poetic strength remains, but the pontification also betrays a poet who came to assume himself a kind of prophet, including before it became a buzz word, of global warming. It is significant that the spiritual centers of Snyder were *both* the wilderness and San Francisco—his home region being again, a civilization to draw on, and a place from which to get away. Meanwhile, California became simply a place to be (before the great exodus of more recent years). All this notwithstanding, the spirit of Joaquin Miller's early Northwest work, particularly the Amerindian mysticism of *Unwritten History*, remained alive in Snyder well past the time when he inhabited the region.[24]

A mid–1970s Northwest invitational brought together in one volume a surprisingly good array of largely academic poetry then being produced in the area, or by regional offspring.[25] Judged by Carolyn Kizer, the collection reflected both the established and the new, with considerable continuity revealed in pathways set by Roethkian and other late '40s intellectual immigrants here.

Perhaps most expressive of this continuity was the fifth of the "Five Poets," and for a time, Oregon's poet laureate, William Stafford, a professor at Lewis and Clark College near Portland from 1948. Stafford's world-view was that of the small town, nostalgia, friends and family, and often flowed back to his depression-era roots in Kansas. His pacifism, revealed in conscientious objection during World War II, certainly attracted the late '60s generation, somewhat to his discomfort. For Stafford was always a writer who resisted being pigeon-holed.[26] And through the 1970s, his was an art showing few explicit marks of the oriental heritage common to much other Northwestern work; whereas the theme of accepting one's life, and of achieving sturdy, reliable goals echoed more pervasively throughout his poetry. Here Stafford had received lessons from his own father, mirrored in poems such as "Father's Voice," where he showed the effect of learning a certain self-satisfaction with one's lot.[27]

But that father was also a foil for Stafford's own maturing views, particularly given the fact that as much as he had striven for the simple life, the elder Stafford had also found that existence too much to manage. By contrast, Stafford always wished to stay within himself, and though he would increasingly attain national renown in his field, managed to attain a well-rounded life in the Northwest of comparative stability which seemed to have eluded his father.[28] So Stafford stayed at small, nationally unknown Lewis and Clark; and paraphrasing the words of Jesus, by underplaying his life he informed us in a number of ways that he had, in fact, won it.

Often Stafford's poems appear to be games, a poetry of entertainment and mystification; but always he is leading on, opening up, building a reality with which readers may be better able to co-exist. Despite a superficially standard academic liberalism, he was characteristically a purist, a poet who seldom descended to overt political messages. He knew that the "message" in a poem was always less than the poem itself. He also realized that as he condensed experience within the demands of poetry, he became the "faker inside the poem" who could not take himself too seriously.[29] In this way Stafford avoided both the psychological and mystical claims that add interest to Northwest poetry, but ultimately, have marred it as well.

Most of Stafford's poetry strove toward a soft populist honesty, refusing to employ inaccessible academic language, or to deny the importance of the everyday. He announced this populism in one of his best-known poems, "Traveling through the Dark." In this clear, poignant rendering, the author, driving on a dark, serpentine road, encounters the reality of a dead and obviously pregnant doe, just killed and still almost sentient, and whom he finally has to overturn (*malgré lui*) into the river. Despite being a sensitive, artistic soul, he must *also* grow up in reality around him. In fact, it is difficult to imagine a better synthesis of the poet's tender sentimentality and the pragmatic realism of those who must get on with life in the world as it exists.[30]

Taking this stance, Stafford hoped to make readers aware of dignity and significance in the ordinary person, who simply by doing his/her job, facilitates the lives of others. In "Deerslayer's Campfire Talk" his poem treats the silent division of labor performed, including among traveling Indians of yore; and contrasts that mind-set to the glib who spew and explicate (including via culture parade), in order to make themselves seem important.[31] Stafford's Northwest dignification of ordinary humans and their understated nobility reached a certain apotheosis in his poem "Bess," certainly one of his most accessible. Suffering from cancer, his oddly poetic Bess does her job to the end at a local library with taste and concern, even for those who find fault with frivolous mundanities (in a Northwest January it would naturally be with the rain).[32] Here is Stafford's contribution to regional civilization—via a poetic sense of its humanity, *ordinary* humanity transcending day-to-day events through a consistent, quietly empathetic decency.

Stafford's more recent poetry seemed (from the 1970s or so) not invariably up to his previous standard. Perhaps he remained too long at Lewis and Clark, or went out on too many lecture tours. He himself became an increasingly frequent explicator of his poetic processes, and these exegeses on the writer's strategies now seem dated. More likely, his genius was that of a prudent, relative optimism less sustainable with age and a matured family. In his collection *Someday, Maybe* (1973) the poet set a newer tone, and in three poems included there, "An Introduction to Some Poems," "In a Time of Need," and "Friend," he seemed to embrace with a number of lines a world of loss and of simply carrying on, but *not* with any palpable enthusiasm or even sense of meaning.[33] In such poetic lines we search in vain for the sustaining love of the earlier poet, or even that adumbrated by H. L. Davis. Instead there is at best here, the steely satisfaction of authenticity, or the evanescent pleasure of certain peaceful moments.

Stafford's regionalism was typically that of the convert, of the new settler come to the Northwest, of the post–World War II generation, for whom H. L. Davis said everything was once again new. But if we look closely, we will find deepening echoes of the regional human past that Stafford himself may have missed. As an example, in his poem "A Story That Could Be True," the author mused on the idea that a person might have been exchanged as a baby for someone of a different class, and really be a much greater figure than seemed to be the case. (The poem's last line surmises the person might even be a king.) In writing this poem, Stafford was probably unaware of the best-known literary event of the 1920s in his own Willamette Valley—the purported autobiography of Opal Whitely. He did not, of course, require this background for his poetic imagination, but cognizance of it might have increased a sense of regional connections in his work.[34] However, Stafford, "the convert," did not make such a link.

His own regionalism began with the perhaps jejune, but still significant realization that "you write from where you are."[35] However, Americans have often chosen where they are, and thence they can become regional in deep attachments to the chosen area. This comes out clearly in one of his best poems, "Lake Chelan," set in that area featuring this extremely deep lake as the showpiece of Washington wilderness in the North Cascades.[36]

The region, then, was not primarily something one grew out of, but something people mainly grew *into*—or so Stafford seemed to emphasize in a number of his poems. That sense of place was crucial for the author, as when he wrote:

> All events and experiences are local, somewhere. And all human enhancements of events and experiences—all the arts—are regional in the sense that they derive from immediate relation to felt life.
>
> It is this immediacy that distinguishes art. And paradoxically the more local the feeling in art, the *self* that art has, the more all people can share it; for that vivid encounter with the stuff of the world is our common ground.
>
> Artists, knowing this mutual enrichment that extends everywhere, can act, and praise, and criticize, as insiders:—the means of art is the life of their people. And that life grows and improves by being shared. Hence, it is good to welcome any region you live in or come to or think of, for that is where life happens to be—right where you are.[37]

Yet Stafford was too much of a realist and also too much of a poet to believe that reality ever comes in pure drafts. The landscape of life which he painted was obviously a transmuted one, drawn from something "in dear detail, by ideal light," to cite one of his poem titles.[38] On his pages it remains for us a place of dreams and hopes, the region to become, as well as the region that was and *is*. Or as he put it both poetically and practically in "As Pippa Lilted," the ideal spread in spring will be locatable if only the cash can be found! There is his poetry—beauty and blunt reality in a constant, but ultimately enriching, Northwestern dialectic.[39]

CHAPTER 9

Conclusion

IN THE COURSE OF A PREFACE, introduction, and eight chapters of this book, the reader has been asked to consider the Pacific Northwest experience from a variety of different viewpoints. Yet our explorations crossed relatively lightly a very extensive terrain that could consume several lifetimes before the region was well, or even partially, understood from the cultural-social-historical viewpoint we chose to embrace here. We hope, however, that we have provided an interesting, informative study of a significant, idiosyncratic American region, especially from the human point of view. We have tried to be perhaps old-fashioned, broad-based humanists in an era of fast-increasing and terrifying specialization, and in this field, of micro-history.

Our subject was the growth and meaning of a regional life and civilization—how it was created, experienced, and expressed by the area's notables and by some of its most formidable intellectuals or artists. We began with an examination of the tragic confrontations between white and Indian, a theme that must inevitably be revisited, given the unavoidable fact that people here live on formerly Indian lands. We also examined the dark, grey feelings so often experienced by the region's settlers and dreamers. As an isolated but verdant "far corner" of America, the Northwest has always appeared to offer more perhaps than it could come up with in the final accounting. Yet even if outside the mainstream to a degree, the region has continued to entice people to come and stay, and to thrive within its generous cocoon. We also examined a strong moralist/reformist tradition here, one that at times spawned (and still does) outright radicalism and even utopianism. At its best this tradition played a major role in expanding both regional and national horizons, for example, through the introduction of the Oregon System, or the cultural concerns and contributions of a Parrington, Kizer, or Kesey.

Fundamentally, the reader was asked to take stock, and to become thoroughly aware that people were (in the cliché) here before, that they faced similar problems to ours, particularly in the realm of character and life choices; and that quite often, they moved on and out. Their work was frequently scattered and vitiated, sometimes even as they lived; but something usually remained of it, and we feel at the close of this book that we can point to a significant, and in some cases, fascinating Northwest *Weltanschaaung* and cultural inheritance adumbrated in the past couple of centuries through to the 1970s.

The expression "quality of civilization" can finally be defined only in terms of judgments individuals make on the myriad details that constitute this perhaps hazy concept. Everyone will form different ones—as they would even of the many historical figures we have discussed here; but gradually the attempt of a few to judge and classify could develop into a more generally accepted framework of discussion. We feel that we have provided a kind of inventory here of what the Northwest could offer, mainly in the cultural realm, and we have tried to do so in a manner that was perhaps not as sprightly as much of what these figures themselves achieved. But hopefully the effort would not have thoroughly displeased them, making at least some of their attempts at creating a Northwest cultural consciousness in the end seem a worthwhile and important part of the development of a regional civilization.

Chapter Notes

Preface

1. (Seattle: University of Washington Press, 1975).

2. See, for example, Douglas Todd, ed., *Cascadia: The Elusive Utopia* (Vancouver: Ronsdale Press, 2008).

Introduction

1. These concerns were first discussed in Raymond D. Gastil, "The Pacific Northwest as a Cultural Region," *Pacific Northwest Quarterly* (hereafter *PNQ*) 64 (1973): 147–162 and in Gastil, *Cultural Regions of the United States*, especially ch. 5.

2. The definition of the Northwest as a cultural region is discussed in Gastil, "The Pacific Northwest as a Cultural Region," *passim* and Gastil, *Cultural Regions of the United States*, 264–72.

3. Wallace Stegner, *Angle of Repose* (Greenwich, CT: Fawcett, 1971), 426. On Stegner see also Barnett Singer's "The Historical Ideal in Wallace Stegner's Fiction," in Anthony Arthur, ed., *Critical Essays on Wallace Stegner* (Boston: G.K. Hall, 1982).

4. Ella Higginson, *Mariella of Out West* (New York: Macmillan, 1904).

5. Bernard Malamud, *A New Life* (New York: Farrar, Straus and Cudahy, 1968; copyright 1961), 19. Malamud's take on the Northwest is analyzed in contrast to another important regional novelist we discuss below—in Barnett Singer, "Outsider Versus Insider: Malamud's and Kesey's Pacific Northwest," *South Dakota Review* 13 (Winter 1975-76): 127–144.

6. Thomas Griffith, *The Waist-High Culture* (New York: Harper and Bros., 1959).

7. H. L. Davis, *Kettle of Fire* (New York: Morrow, 1959), 48.

8. Kevin Starr, *Americans and the California Dream, 1850–1915* (New York: Oxford University Press, 1973).

9. Subsequent Starr volumes include *Inventing the Dream: California Through the Progressive Era* (New York: Oxford University Press, 1985) on the rise of a Southern California culture; *Material Dreams: Southern California Through the 1920s* (New York: Oxford University Press, 1990); *Endangered Dreams: The Great Depression in California* (New York: Oxford University Press, 1996); *The Dream Endures: California Enters the 1940s* (New York: Oxford University Press, 1997); *Embattled Dreams: California in War and Peace, 1940–1950* (New York: Oxford University Press, 2002); and *Coast of Dreams: California on the Edge, 1990–2003* (New York: Knopf//Random House, 2004).

10. Robert Cantwell, *The Hidden Northwest* (Philadelphia: Lippincott, 1972).

11. *Ibid.*, 285.

12. Some of the detail provided here emanates from a magisterial study of the fascinating, paradoxical Cantwell: Per Seyersted's *Robert Cantwell: An American 1930s Radical Writer and His Apostasy* (Oslo: Novus Press, 2004).

13. Dodds, *The American Northwest: A History of Oregon and Washington* (Arlington Heights, IL: The Forum Press, 1986), reasonably announcing itself as the first of its kind "in almost twenty years." (ix); and Carlos Arnaldo Schwantes, *The Pacific Northwest: An Interpretive History* (revised edition from 1989 publication; Lincoln: University of Nebraska Press, 1996).

14. (New York: Simon and Schuster, 1995).
15. (New York: HarperCollins, 1995).
16. (New York: Forge, 2000).
17. Golay, *The Tide of Empire: America's March to the Pacific* (Hoboken, NJ: John Wiley and Sons, 2003). As he says of the book: "It might just as well have been subtitled 'How a Nondescript Band of Trappers, Missionaries, and Junior Army Officers Seized a Pacific Empire for the United States.'" *Ibid.*, xiii. For some of the same occurring in a burgeoning French empire, particularly after 1830, see Barnett Singer and John Langdon, *Cultured Force: Makers and Defenders of the French Colonial Empire* (Madison: University of Wisconsin Press, 2004), *passim*.
18. (Yardley, PA: Westholme Publishing, 2007).
19. See Scott Kaufman, *The Pig War: The United States, Britain, and the Balance of Power in the Pacific Northwest, 1846–1872* (Lanham, MD: Lexington Books, 2004) and Michael Vouri's less scholarly *The Pig War: Standoff at Griffin Bay* (Friday Harbor, WA: Griffin Bookstore, 1999).
20. (Pullman: Washington State University Press, 2007).
21. (Corvallis: Oregon State University Press, 2003).
22. *Ibid.*, 8.
23. (Portland: Oregon Historical Society Press, 2005). An earlier account by Terence O'-Donnell, *That Balance So Rare: The Story of Oregon* (Portland: Oregon Historical Society Press, 1988) is spirited, but thinner, in part due to many pictures; and it was frankly aimed at Oregonian schools.
24. (Seattle: University of Washington Press, 1988).
25. (Pullman: Washington State University Press, 2002).
26. (Pullman: Washington State University Press, 2007).
27. (Seattle: University of Washington Press, 1996).
28. (Ithaca: Cornell University Press, 1995).
29. For instance, Jewel Lansing, *Portland: People, Politics, and Power, 1851–2001* (Corvallis: Oregon State University Press, 2003) and Mary C. Wright, ed., *More Voices, New Stories: King County, Washington's First 150 Years* (Seattle: The Pacific Northwest Historians Guild, 2002)—King County amounting to Greater Seattle.
30. (Lawrence: University Press of Kansas, 1997), and see also his specialized articles, such as "The Environment and Settler Society in Western Oregon," *The Pacific Historical Review* 64 (1995): 413–432.
31. Bunting, *Pacific Raincoast*, 2–3.
32. See William G. Robbins, *Hard Times in Paradise: Coos Bay, Oregon, 1850–1986* (Seattle: University of Washington Press, 1988), quotations 4, 5; William Dietrich, *The Final Forest: The Battle for the Last Great Trees of the Pacific Northwest* (New York: Simon and Schuster, 1992); and Sallie Tisdale, *Stepping Westward: The Long Search for Home in the Pacific Northwest* (New York: Henry Holt, 1991). As she writes on this sense of environmental "loss": "No one, Indian or white man alike, could imagine it gone. I have the benefit of hindsight, buckled on every side by clear-cuts and parking lots and the skeletons of malls. I look at such steady loss now and review the losses past: the decimation of the once-populous sea otter down to a few hundred single animals, the near-extirpation of the beaver from the Northwest, the steady disappearance of one thing after another." *Ibid.*, 46. The pioneering work noted here is William Cronon, *Changes in the Land: Indians, Colonists, and the Ecology of New England* (New York: Hill and Wang, 1983). Not only was the field young when Cronon published that book, but so at the time were now much established, mainstream American historians like Cronon himself. Many other works in the field could be mentioned, such as Marc Reisner's *A Dangerous Place: California's Unsettling Fate* (New York: Pantheon Books, 2003), with a good deal on the increasingly massive settlement during the nineteenth and twentieth century of a huge amount of land ecologically unsuited for it. An earlier book by Reisner sounded these dire notes: *Cadillac Desert: The American West and its Disappearing Water* (New York: Viking, 1986). Returning to the Northwest, *sui generis* is Finn Wilcox and Jerry Gorsline, eds., *Working the Woods, Working the Sea: An Anthology of Northwest Writings* (Port Townsend, WA: Empty Bowl, 2008), with marvelous parts illuminating the intersections of environmentalism and the world of work, along with resultant literary reactions, in the Northwest. No contributor does so better here than the courageous tree-planter (in the Olympic Peninsula), Mike Connelly, showing in powerful prose the complicity of virtually everyone in destroying one Northwest mini-environment after another; the utter sadness of salmon depletion; the desperate, counter-cultural heroism of tree-planters on territory that would have remained all clear-gashed or clear-stumped ("clear-cut" not quite enough); and the dilatory, do-nothing committeeism of report makers, consultants, or legislators who have done too little to alter this severe environmental impact. (See *ibid.*, 325–346.) Environmental (including biological and geological) history in the Northwest also figures prominently in elegant

essays by William Dietrich in his *Natural Grace: The Charm, Wonder, and Lessons of Pacific Northwest Animals and Plants* (Seattle: University of Washington Press, 2003).

33. (San Francisco: Lexikos, 1984).

34. Savage quoted in John R. Wunder, "What's Old About the New Western History: Race and Gender Part 1," *PNQ* 85 (1994): 57. A wonderful rescuer of actual doers in the West is Michael Allen in his pathbreaking *Western Rivermen, 1763–1861: Ohio and Mississippi Boatmen and the Myth of the Alligator Horse* (Baton Rouge: Louisiana State University Press, 1990) and *Rodeo Cowboys in the North American Imagination* (Reno: University of Nevada Press, 1998). Quotations in Gene M. Gressley, ed., *Old West/New West* (Norman: University of Oklahoma Press, 1997) are from his introduction, 3, 7, 9, 10, 16. The book itself features very different voices, from Patricia Nelson Limerick to Gerald Nash. On the former, Gressley sums up an extensive *oeuvre* (including in the popular press): "With passionate prose and missionary zeal, Professor Limerick proceeded to turn western history upside down: Where there had been conquerors, there were now victims; where there were triumphs, now there were defeats; where there had been the West of the white settler, there was now the west of minorities—black, Hispanic, women, and the Native Americans." See Limerick's own pathbreaking book *The Legacy of Conquest: The Unbroken Past of the American West* (New York: Norton, 1987, and reissued in Norton paperback in 2006). One may also consult historiographical overviews, such as Susan H. Armitage, "From the Inside Out: Rewriting Regional History," *Frontiers: A Journal of Women Studies* 22 (2001): 32–47 and Laurie Mercier, "Reworking Race, Class, and Gender into Pacific Northwest History," in *ibid.*: 61–74.

35. Gerald D. Nash, *Creating the West: Historical Interpretations 1890–1990* (Albuquerque: University of New Mexico Press, 1991), 158 (part of his ch. 3: "The West as Region, 1890–1990"). Textbooks reflecting the new trends are too numerous to list here, but at least one representative example is Robert V. Hine and John Mack Faragher, *The American West: A New Interpretive History* (New Haven: Yale University Press, 2000).

36. See as examples, Janet E. Rasmussen, *New Land New Lives: Scandinavian Immigrants to the Pacific Northwest* (Northfield, Minn.: Norwegian-American Historical Association and Seattle: University of Washington Press, 1993), part of the oral history genre, too; Susan Wiley Hardwick, *Russian Refuge: Religion, Migration, and Settlement on the North American Pacific Rim* (Chicago: University of Chicago Press, 1993); and on one branch of Germans, Richard Scheuerman and Clifford E. Trafzer, *The Volga Germans: Pioneers of the Northwest* (Moscow: University Press of Idaho, 1980). Also helping to inaugurate the "ethnic" trend were article collections, such as James R. Halseth and Bruce R. Glasrud, eds., *The Northwest Mosaic* (Boulder, CO: Pruett Publishing Co., 1977), including work on the Basques (appropriately by Richard Etulain), Jews, etc.

37. (Seattle: University of Washington Press, 1994).

38. (Pullman: Washington State University Press, 2004).

39. (Tucson: The University of Arizona Press, 2006).

40. (Urbana: University of Illinois Press, 1993).

41. Subtitled *Redress and Japanese American Ethnicity* (Ithaca: Cornell University Press, 1995).

42. (Berkeley: University of California Press, 2003).

43. C.f. Krystyn R. Moon's review essay, "Making Asian American Actors Visible: New Trends in Biography Writing," *Pacific Historical Review* 76 (2007): 615–621. There are of course many more specialized articles on the Chinese in Northwest history, such as Clayton D. Laurie, "'The Chinese Must Go': The United States Army and the Anti-Chinese Riots in Washington Territory, 1885–1886," *PNQ* 81 (1990): 22–29. An interesting monograph on an ultra-specialized "ethnic" subject is Jean Barman and Bruce McIntyre Watson, *Paradise: Indigenous Hawaiians in the Pacific Northwest, 1787–1898* (Honolulu: University of Hawaii Press, 2006).

44. See, for example, David Stratton, ed., *Terra Northwest: Interpreting People and Place* (Pullman: Washington State University Press, 2007); William G. Robbins, ed., *The Great Northwest: The Search for Regional Identity* (Corvallis: Oregon State University Press, 2001), including both articles and stories, and with a bi-country, comparative emphasis; and Paul W. Hirt, ed., *Terra Pacifica: People and Place in the Northwest* (Pullman: Washington State University Press, 1998). There are many other collections with many varied contributions; but though they have been of utility to us, one can only list here: Howard J. Critchfield, ed., *Pacific Northwest Essays in Honor of James W. Scott* (Bellingham: Western Washington University, 1993); Carlos A. Schwantes, ed., *Experiences in a Promised Land: Essays in Pacific Northwest History* (Seattle: University of Washington Press, 1986), some contributions here previously appearing in regional journals; Schwantes, ed., *Encounters with a Distant*

Land: Exploration and the Great Northwest (Moscow: University of Idaho Press, 1994); David Stratton and George A. Frykman, eds., *The Changing Pacific Northwest: Interpreting its Past* (Pullman: Washington State University Press, 1988), almost all from a symposium; William G. Robbins, Robert J. Frank, and Richard J. Ross, eds., *Regionalism and the Pacific Northwest* (Corvallis: Oregon State University Press, 1983), again, based on papers given at an Oregon State University symposium; Edwin R. Bingham and Glen A. Love, eds., *Northwest Perspectives: Essays on the Culture of the Pacific Northwest* (Eugene: University of Oregon Press and Seattle: University of Washington Press, 1979), papers derived from a symposium at University of Oregon; and on more narrowly defined topics, collections such as: David H. Stratton, ed., *Washington Comes of Age: The State in the National Experience* (Pullman: Washington State University Press, 1992); William L. Lang and Robert C. Carriker, eds., *Great River of the West: Essays on the Columbia River* (Seattle: University of Washington Press, 1999), including (as in other collections) a contribution in literary history by Richard Etulain; and anthologies, such as Glen Love, ed., *Fishing the Northwest: An Angler's Reader* (Corvallis: Oregon State University Press, 2000), with some of the key literary figures we discuss below represented.

45. See Richard M. Highsmith, Jr., ed., *Atlas of the Pacific Northwest* (Corvallis: Oregon State University Press, 1968).

46. To start, one could consult on this Robert Spencer et al., *The Native Americans* (New York: Harper and Row, 1965), 168–228, 273–82.

47. Our brief historical background here is based on many books, including the classic of Dorothy O. Johansen (with Charles M. Gates), *Empire of the Columbia*, 2nd ed. (New York: Harper and Row, 1967). One should also consult the recent, comparative overview on this period in Stuart Banner, *Possessing the Pacific: Land, Settlers, and Indigenous People from Australia to Alaska* (Cambridge, MA: Harvard University Press, 2007), especially ch. 6 (on what became British Columbia), and ch. 7 on Oregon and Washington.

48. Davis, *Kettle of Fire*, 25.

Chapter 1

1. William Arrowsmith, "Speech of Chief Seattle," 5 (edited from version of Dr. Henry Smith, *Seattle Star*, October 29, 1887).

2. The best book on Seattle's speech—its hazy origins and different versions, and the regional memory it inspired—is Albert Furtwangler, *Answering Chief Seattle* (Seattle: University of Washington Press, 1997). See also Denise Low, "Contemporary Reinvention of Chief Seattle: Variant Texts of Chief Seattle's 1854 Speech," *American Indian Quarterly* 19 (1995): 407–421.

3. On the more general problem of the humanistic evaluation of civilization, see R. D. Gastil, "Beyond a Theory of Justice," *Ethics* 85 (1975): 183–94.

4. In addition to relevant portions of Spencer et al., *The Native Americans*, Johansen, *Empire of the Columbia*, Dodds, *The American Northwest*, and Schwantes, *The Pacific Northwest*, references used for the following evaluation include Robert H. Ruby and John A. Brown, *A Guide to the Indian Tribes of the Pacific Northwest* (Norman: University of Oklahoma Press, 1986); Philip Drucker, *Indians of the Northwest Coast* (New York: McGraw-Hill, 1955), and *Cultures of the North Pacific Coast* (San Francisco: Chandler, 1965); L. S. Cressman, *The Sandal and the Cave* (Portland: Beaver, 1962); Elizabeth Colson, *The Makah Indians* (Minneapolis: University of Minnesota Press, 1953); Theodore Stern, *The Klamath Tribe* (Seattle: University of Washington Press, 1965); David French, "Wasco–Wishram" in Edward Spicer, ed., *Perspectives in American Indian Culture Change* (Chicago: University of Chicago Press, 1961), 337–430: Melville Jacobs, *Content and Style of an Oral Literature* (Chicago: University of Chicago Press, 1959); Ella E. Clark, *Indian Legends of the Pacific Northwest* (Berkeley: University of California Press, 1969); James G. Swan, *The Northwest Coast* (New York: Harper and Bros., 1857); Erna Gunther, "The Indian Background of Washington History," *PNQ* 54 (1963): 158–65; and Herman Haeberlin and Erna Gunther, *The Indians of Puget Sound* (Seattle: University of Washington Publications in Anthropology 4 (1930): 11–84. On the two historians, Robert Ruby and John Brown, who helped stimulate this whole field of inquiry, see Cary C. Collins and Charles V. Mutschler, "Great Spirits: Ruby and Brown, Pioneering Historians of the Indians of the Pacific Northwest," *PNQ* 95 (2004): 126–129.

5. Quoted in Stern, *Klamath Tribe*, 38–39.

6. See Alvin Josephy, Jr., *The Nez Perce Indians and the Opening of the Northwest* (New Haven: Yale University Press, 1965). Some of the other detail on the Nez Percés here is derived from Philip Weeks' fine survey, *Farewell, My Nation: The American Indian and the United States 1820–1890* (Arlington Heights, IL: Harlan Davidson, 1990), 206–211 and ch. 6 generally, along with Ruby and Brown, *Guide to the Indian Tribes of the Pacific Northwest*, 144–

147. On the Flatheads see *ibid.*, 76–78. On the Spokanes and half-half split of chiefs vis-à-vis Washington Governor Isaac Stevens' treaty pressures, see Robert H. Ruby and John A. Brown, *The Spokane Indians: Children of the Sun* (Norman: University of Oklahoma Press, 1970), 114. Cf. also Swan (in *The Northwest Coast*) on the willingness of the Quinault to sign a treaty with Governor Stevens as long as they received their land, irrespective of other Indian losses. On the dilemmas and actions of Chief Moses, see Robert H. Ruby and John A. Brown, *Half-Sun on the Columbia: A Biography of Chief Moses* (Norman: University of Oklahoma Press, 1965). This noble figure and Chief Joseph ended up reservation friends.

7. The best book on the subject, Robert H. Ruby and John A. Brown, *Indian Slavery in the Pacific Northwest* (Spokane: Arthur H. Clark, 1993), shows that Indian slavery was long rejected by American scholars as worthy of consideration, compared to enslavement of blacks and others.

8. On this issue see David Peterson del Mar's study of Celiast Smith, a Chinook woman of the early nineteenth century, and her "agency" through intermarriage: Peterson del Mar, "Intermarriage and Agency: A Chinookan Case Study," *Ethnohistory* 42 (1995): 1–30.

9. On the Chinooks, see Robert H. Ruby and John A. Brown, *The Chinook Indians: Traders of the Lower Columbia River* (Norman: University of Oklahoma Press, 1976), as well as in earlier accounts, Thomas N. Strong, *Cathlamet on the Columbia* (Portland: Metropolitan Press, 1930 [1906]), 15–19, 93–102; Jacobs, *Content and Style of Oral Literature*, 12; and Josephy, *Nez Perce Indians*, 151, not to mention Swan, *Three Years Residence*, 160.

10. For negative attitudes and the experiences that led to them, see *The Journals of Lewis and Clark* (numerous editions), and Lewis O. Saum, *The Fur Trader and the Indian* (Seattle: University of Washington Press, 1965), *passim*.

11. There is extensive literature on all this which we haven't space to assess or include here; but representative among contemporary estimates of Indian arts is Aldona Jonaitis, *Art of the Northwest Coast* (Seattle: University of Washington Press, 2006)—with much on the variations among different tribes just within the Salish group, male versus female arts, weaving and other techniques, etc. One might add that modern ecological students have also discovered Indian use of controlled fires in the Northwest (again, with distinct regional variations), in order better to hunt deer, promote berry growth, create prairies, and perhaps inadvertently, to maintain a healthy forest environment. All this jibes with a recent altering of previous views favoring the maintenance of stands (with conflict on such "fire suppression" policies still raging). See Robert Boyd, ed., *Indians, Fire, and the Land in the Pacific Northwest* (Corvallis: Oregon State University Press, 1999).

12. Jacobs, *Content and Style of an Oral Literature*, especially 27–36.

13. A derogatory Makah term for whites. See Colson, *Makah Indians*, 119–20. On the impact of incomers on the Salish-speaking Stillaguamish—Roman Catholic priests, Samuel Hancock and others searching for coal deposits, Scandinavian and Portuguese immigrants—see Robert H. Ruby and John A. Brown, *Esther Ross, Stillaguamish Champion* (Norman: University of Oklahoma Press, 2001), ch. 2. Ross' valiant attempts later on to gain recognition and reparations from the government need to be situated against that background.

14. Arrowsmith, "Speech of Chief Seattle," 3. The young chief Joseph echoed these words when he said of his father: "I buried him in that beautiful valley of winding waters. I love that land more than all the rest of the world [;] a man who would not love his father's grave is worse than a wild animal." In Josephy, *Nez Perce Indians*, 450.

15. See Robert Schmitt, *Demographic Statistics of Hawaii* (Honolulu: University of Hawaii Press, 1968).

16. Arrowsmith, "Speech of Chief Seattle," 5.

17. See James P. Ronda, *Astoria and Empire* (Lincoln: University of Nebraska Press, 1990), and Washington Irving, *Astoria* (1836) (Portland: Binfords and Mort, 1967), *passim*.

18. The following is based primarily on Dorothy Nafus Morrison, *Outpost: John McLoughlin and the Far Northwest* (Portland: Oregon Historical Society Press, 1999), the best biographical treatment; Nancy Wilson, *Dr. John McLoughlin: Master of Fort Vancouver Father of Oregon* (Medford, OR: Webb Research Group, 1994); R. G. Montgomery, *The White-Headed Eagle* (New York: Macmillan, 1935); William R. Sampson, ed., *John McLoughlin's Business Correspondence, 1847–48* (Seattle: University of Washington Press, 1973), including the editor's introduction and notes; Burt Brown Barker, *The McLoughlin Empire and its Rulers* (Glendale, CA: Arthur Clark, 1959); Walter N. Sage, "The Place of Fort Vancouver in the History of the Northwest," *PNQ* 39 (1948): 83–102; and H. H. Bancroft (F. Victor), *History of the Northwest Coast* (San Francisco: The History Company, 1886), II, especially 86, 704.

19. On why Dr. McLoughlin left medicine for the fur trade, see Dorothy Morrison and Jean Morrison, "John McLoughlin Reluctant Fur

Trader," *Oregon Historical Quarterly* (hereafter cited as *OHQ*), 81 (1980): 377–389.

20. For a romanticized picture of this aspect of McLoughlin, see Eva Emery Dye, *McLoughlin and Old Oregon* (Chicago: A.C. McClurg and Co., 1900), 124–29. One noted visitor who met with McLoughlin was a great Scottish naturalist, botanist, and ornithologist of the Darwin stamp, David Douglas. (And for whom the Douglas fir was named.) See John Davies, ed., *Douglas of the Forests: The North American Journals of David Douglas* (Edinburgh: Paul Harris Publishing, 1979). On his travels Douglas came to an untimely end, and his journals remained unpublished until the 20th century.

21. This is the view of Strong in his *Cathlamet on the Columbia*.

22. Sampson, ed., *John McLoughlin's Business Correspondence*, 142.

23. Josephy, *Nez Perce Indians*, 74.

24. See Alvin Josephy, Jr., *Nez Percé Country* (Lincoln: University of Nebraska Press, 2007), ch. 3, 4, 5, 6 (the latter titled "The Gathering Storm").

25. As much as we emphasize McLoughlin here as one of the formers of a Northwest consciousness, we should also emphasize the contribution—less well known—of his sometime cohort, Peter Skene Ogden. Skene Ogden was one of those individualists who at different times opposed Americans, Russians, and in combat, Indians. He played a significant role in countering the Hudson's Bay Company, and in exploring the whole region. See Gloria Griffen Cline, *Peter Skene Ogden and the Hudson's Bay Company* (Norman: University of Oklahoma Press, 1974).

26. Factual matter for this latter part is drawn from Montgomery, *White-Headed Eagle*, ch. 20 and relevant parts of the later biographical treatments.

27. The material on Jason Lee is based primarily on Robert J. Loewenberg, *Equality on the Oregon Frontier: Jason Lee and the Methodist Mission 1834–43* (Seattle: University of Washington Press, 1976), arguing that Lee and the Methodists were ambivalent about converting Indians; Cornelius Brosnan, *Jason Lee: Prophet of the New Oregon* (New York: Macmillan, 1932); and Theresa Gray, ed., *Life and Letters of Mrs. Jason Lee* (Portland: Metropolitan Press, 1936), I.

28. Brosnan, *Jason Lee*, 204–5.

29. Josephy, *Nez Perce Indians*, 140. Albert Furtwangler has a sophisticated analysis of various missionary attitudes toward the Indians, particularly their chances of absorbing bookish culture and Christian religion, in *Bringing Indians to the Book* (Seattle: University of Washington Press, 2005). Another sophisticated analysis of missionary differences is in Ferenc M. Szasz, "The Clergy and the Myth of the American West," *Church History* 59 (1990): 497–506. For the enlightenment of some Christians on the dizzying array of Indian tongues, see also Gerald McKevitt, "Jesuit Missionary Linguistics in the Pacific Northwest: A Comparative Study," *The Western Historical Quarterly* 21 (1990): 281–304.

30. This included the "dreamer-prophets" so well described in Robert H. Ruby and John A. Brown, *Dreamer-Prophets of the Columbia Plateau: Smoholla and Skolaskin* (Norman: University of Oklahoma Press, 1989). They were angered not only by the evident failures of white medicine, but by the broken promises of the U.S. government, and presented a contrastive, utopian, cult-like appeal to suffering Indians. See also Elizabeth Vibert, "The Natives Were Strong Enough to Live: Reinterpreting Early Nineteenth-Century Prophetic Movements in the Columbia Plateau," *Ethnohistory* 42 (1995): 197–229. On a later charismatic Indian leader, see also Ruby and Brown, *John Slocum and the Indian Shaker Church* (Norman: University of Oklahoma, 1996).

31. As much as Indians often felt angry and let down by the missionaries' inability to combat disease, Protestant fundamentalists on their side frequently considered plentiful Indian corpses piled up from "The Cold Sick" as evidence of God's punishment of a lower race. See Ruby and Brown, *Chinook Indians*, 186–187.

32. See Robert H. Ruby and John A. Brown, *The Cayuse Indians: Imperial Tribesmen of Old Oregon* (Norman: University of Oklahoma Press, 1972), 70–83, and Ruby and Brown, *Guide to the Indian Tribes of the Pacific Northwest*, 13–15.

33. W. H. Gray, *A History of Oregon* (Portland: Harris and Homan, 1870), 288–91, 480–82.

34. In Ed C. Ross, *The Whitman Controversy* (Portland: G. H. Himes, 1885), 3.

35. *Ibid.*, 6–7.

36. *Ibid.*, 9.

37. *Ibid.*,13.

38. *Ibid.*, 25.

39. *Ibid.*, 25.

40. *Ibid.*, 25–26.

41. *Ibid.*, 26.

42. See the article version by Edward G. Bourne, "The Legend of Marcus Whitman," *American Historical Review* 6 (1901): 276–300, and William I. Marshall, *Acquisition of Oregon and the Long-Suppressed Evidence About Marcus Whitman* (Seattle: Loman and Hanford, 1911), 2 vols.

43. Thomas P. Garth, "A Report on Second Season's Excavations at Waiilatpu," *PNQ* 43 (1949): [295–315] 305–6.

44. "Judge William Strong's Narratives and Comments," 29.

45. See Clifford M. Drury, *Marcus Whitman, M.D.: Pioneer and Martyr* (Caldwell, ID: Caxton Printers, 1937), 390–91, and *passim*. On Drury we have Thomas F. Andrews, "Clifford Merrill Drury, 1897–1984: The Oregon Mission of the American Board and its Historian," *PNQ* (1984): 140–141. On the outbreaks and terrible impact of diseases brought to Native Americans by Europeans, see more generally David Dary, *Frontier Medicine: From the Atlantic to the Pacific, 1492–1941* (New York: Knopf, 2008). For much of his period Dary finds Native American medical procedures less deleterious to patients than those of European or white incomers.

46. Quoted in Jones, *The Great Command* (Boston: Little, Brown, 1959), 316.

47. See Walker's letter to David Greene, October 2, 1881, in Charles Gates, ed., *Readings in Pacific Northwest History* (Seattle: University of Washington Press, 1941), 74–76. More generally, see Francis Paul Prucha, "Two Roads to Conversion: Protestant and Catholic Missionaries in the Pacific Northwest," *PNQ* 79 (1988): 130–137, partly derived from his book-length works, such as *American Indian Policy in Crisis: Christian Reformers and the Indian, 1865–1900* (Norman: University of Oklahoma Press, 1976).

48. On Chinook, see Edward H. Thomas, *Chinook: A History and Dictionary of the Northwest Coast Trade Jargon* (Portland: Metropolitan Press, 1935), and references. Also Rene Grant, "Chinook Jargon," *International Journal of American Linguistics* 11 (1945): 225–33, and Horatio Hale, *An International Idiom: A Manual of the Oregon Trade Language, or "Chinook Jargon"* (London: Whittaker,1890); as well as Alfred Powers, *History of Oregon Literature* (Portland: Metropolitan Press, 1935), 74–88.

49. Melville Jacobs, "Notes on the Structure of Chinook Jargon," *Language* 8 (1932): 27–50. The texts recorded by Jacobs seem to be more complex than those found elsewhere in his general period.

50. Grant, "Chinook Jargon," 227.

51. Josephy, *Nez Perce Indians*, 409, 389, 404–5.

52. Letter, November 20, 1845, quoted in Katherine B. Judson, "Dr. John McLoughlin's Last Letter," *American Historical Review* 21 (1915): 112.

53. Particularly in Southeast Oregon. See Stephen Dow Beckham, *Requiem for a People* (Norman: University of Oklahoma Press, 1971), and Dorothy and Jack Sutton, eds., *Indian Wars of the Rogue River* (Grants Pass, OR: Josephine County Historical Society, 1969), especially 172.

54. Guy Waring, *My Pioneer Past* (Boston: Humphries, 1936), 136–38, 156, 238.

55. See Johansen, *Empire of the Columbia*, 243–44.

56. *Ibid.*, 271.

57. On Stevens and Gray, there are relevant parts in Josephy, *Nez Perce Indians* and Gray, *History of Oregon*.

58. *Ibid.*, 222.

59. Elwood Evans, *History of the Pacific Northwest* (Portland, OR: North Pacific History Company, 1889), 2 vols., 323.

60. For a fairly good re-creation of Mrs. Lane's life, see Victoria Case's historical novel, *The Quiet Life of Mrs. General Lane* (Garden City, NY: Doubleday, 1952).

61. James Hendrickson, *Joe Lane of Oregon: Machine Politics and the Sectional Crisis, 1849–1861* (New Haven: Yale University Press, 1967), viii. But Lane was also important as a human bridge to Indians—in 1850 he was the first white to parley with chiefs of southern Oregon, helping craft a short-lived peace treaty (as "Chief Lane") in 1853. See Nathan Douthit, "Joseph Lane and the Rogue Indians: Personal Relations Across a Cultural Divide," *OHQ* 95 (1994–95): 472–515.

62. For these details, see M. Margaret Jean Kelley, *The Career of Joseph Lane, Frontier Politician* (Washington, D.C.: Catholic University of America Press, 1942), 111–27.

63. Quoted in Hendrickson, *Joe Lane of Oregon*, 38.

64. *Ibid.*, 64. During the 1850s, Lane was already involved in transfers of Indians—to what ultimately became reservations. See for one area, Ronald Spores, "Too Small a Place: The Removal of the Willamette Valley Indians, 1850–1856," *American Indian Quarterly* 17 (1993): 171–191. And on the growing complexities of ethnic mixing, cultural distinctions, and the making of territorial boundaries for another Northwest area, Alexandra Harmon, "Lines in Sand: Shifting Boundaries Between Indians and Non-Indians in the Puget Sound Region," *The Western Historical Quarterly* 26 (1995): 429–453.

65. Quoted in Robert W. Johannsen, *Frontier Politics and the Sectional Conflict: The Pacific Northwest on the Eve of the Civil War* (Seattle: University of Washington Press, 1955), 10.

66. Joseph Lane, et al., *The Admission of Oregon: The Serenades, The Responses* (Washington, D.C.: L. Towers, 1859), 5; in Pacific Northwest Collection, University of Washington Library.

67. Lane quote in Lena Newton, *The Public Career of Joseph Lane of Oregon*, unpublished manuscript, Pacific Northwest Collection, University of Washington Library. This is a com-

pendium of many of Lane's speeches. See also V.L.O. Chittick (or Victor Lovitt Oakes), ed., *Northwest Harvest: A Regional Stock-Taking* (New York: Macmillan, 1948). The papers of Oakes/Chittick are available at the University of Washington.

Chapter 2

1. Dorothy O. Johansen, "A Working Hypothesis for the Study of Migrations," *Pacific Historical Review* 36 (1967): 1–12.

2. See especially Jesse Applegate, *A Day with the Cow Column in 1843* (Chicago: Caxton Club, 1934), especially introduction.

3. Johansen, *Empire of the Columbia*, 244–45 and *passim*. See also appropriate pages (on Applegate and others like him) in Joyce B. Hunsaker, *Seeing the Elephant: The Many Voices of the Oregon Trail* (Lubbock: Texas Tech University Press, 2003).

4. Johansen, *Empire of the Columbia*, 243–47. See also "Judge William Strong's Narratives and Comments" (carbon copy, Pacific Northwest Collection of Verbal Reminiscences at University of Washington, originally recorded in 1878 when Judge Strong was sixty-one). Also, Sidney Teiser, "The Second Chief Justice of Oregon Territory: Thomas Nelson," *OHQ* 48 (1947): 214–24 and an article by Harry M. Strong, "The Adventures of a Pioneer Judge and His Family," *Columbia Magazine* 16 (2002–03): 18–23.

5. J. Orin Oliphant, "Some Neglected Aspects of the History of the Pacific Northwest," *PNQ* 61 (1970): 6.

6. See Jonas A. Jonasson, *Bricks without Straw: The Story of Linfield College* (Caldwell, ID: Caxton, 1938); Henry L. Bates, "Pacific University," *OHQ* 21 (1920): 1–12.

7. *In Memoriam: Rev. S. H. Marsh 1825–1879* (Portland: Himes, 1881); Sidney H. Marsh, *Inaugural Discourse: Pacific University* (Burlington, VT: Free Press, 1854).

8. Kent D. Richards, "The Methodists and the Formation of the Oregonian Provisional Government," *PNQ* 61 (1970): 87–93, 93.

9. Quoted in George Turnbull, "Influence of Newspapers on the Economic, Social, Cultural and Political History of Pioneer Oregon to 1859" (M.A. thesis, University of Washington, 1932), 7.

10. The previous three quotations are cited in Turnbull, "Influence of Newspapers," 20–21, 33, and 52 respectively. It should be noted that it was mostly tougher and more expensive to mount and make a go of newspapers in the nineteenth-century Far West than in the East. As Barbara Cloud notes, "That so many of them [newspaper publishers] did indulge in dragon slaying is all the more remarkable given the more pressing matter of business survival." Cloud, "The Press and Profit: Newspaper Survival in Washington Territory," *PNQ* 79 (1988): 147–156 (quotation 156).

11. "Judge William Strong's Narratives," 11.

12. Biographical details are found in *The Quarterly of the Oregon Historical Society* 14 (1913), Harvey W. Scott Memorial Number, *passim*, a fine collection of articles on his life and work.

13. "The Character of Oregon a Resultant of Pioneer Life" (1901), in *The Pioneer Character of Oregon Progress: Selected Writings of Harvey W. Scott* (Portland: Ivy Press, 1918), 2.

14. In *Ibid.*,14.

15. Harvey Scott, *History of Portland Oregon* (Syracuse, NY: Mason and Company, 1890), ch. 2.

16. *Ibid.*, 53.

17. *Ibid.*, 59.

18. "Shakespeare's Problems of Life and Mind," in Leslie Scott, ed., *Shakespeare: Writings of Harvey W. Scott* (Cambridge, MA: Riverside Press, 1928), 9. The other topics we have noted are found in this collection, 51–52.

19. Lee Nash, "Scott of the Oregonian: Literary Publicist," talk at Pacific Northwest Conference, Seattle, August 1974 (see also his article below).

20. Quoted in Lee Nash, "Harvey Scott's Cure for Drones," *PNQ* 64 (1973): 72.

21. Scott, ed., *Writings of Harvey W. Scott*, 16–17.

22. Nash, "Harvey Scott's Cure for Drones," 76–78; and on Scott's bullying dogmatism concerning one important regional issue, Donald J. Sevetson, "George Atkinson, Harvey Scott, and the Portland High School Controversy of 1880," *OHQ* 108 (2007): 458–473. Atkinson, a compromiser, was Scott's foil in their jousts.

23. There is an article on this in *Time*, October 3, 1938.

24. *Morning Oregonian*, February 4, 1911, 2. On Pittock's career see George Turnbull, *History of Oregon Newspapers* (Portland: Binfords and Mort, 1939), 90–110.

25. *Morning Oregonian*, February 4, 1911, 3.

26. *Ibid.*, 11.

27. See Thomas Vaughan and G. A. McMath, *A Century of Portland Architecture* (Portland: Oregon Historical Society, 1967), 131–33, with pictures.

28. Daniel Boorstin, *The Americans: The Colonial Experience* (New York: Random House, 1958), 194–95.

29. Alan Hynding, *The Public Life of Eugene Semple, Promoter and Politician of the Pacific Northwest* (Seattle: University of Washington Press, 1973); Robert C. Nesbit, "*He Built*

Seattle" (Seattle: University of Washington Press, 1961), on Burke. Nesbit calls such men "business pioneers."

30. André Tudesq, *Les Grands Notables en France (1840–1849)*, 2 vols. (Paris: Presses universitaires de France, 1964); Barnett Singer, *Village Notables in Nineteenth-Century France: Priests, Mayors, Schoolmasters* (Albany: SUNY Press, 1983).

31. On Curry, see Leslie W. Dunlap, "The Oregon Free Press," *PNQ* 33 (1942):171–85. On similar kinds of careers, see Ann Briley, "Hiram F. Smith, First Settler of Okanogan Country," *PNQ* 43 (1952): 226–33 and W. A. Katz, "Public Printers of Washington Territory, 1853–1863," *PNQ* 51 (1960):103–14.

32. A convenient biographical sketch is Dorothy Johansen's "Mr. and Mrs. Simeon G. Reed," in *Reed College Pioneers*, Reed College Bulletin, Vol. 15 (Portland: Reed College, 1931). Singer also used Ms. Johansen's then untitled, unpublished manuscript on the history of Reed, hereafter cited as "Manuscript," and provided by the author.

33. On the various technological "mini-revolutions" that changed American history, see Boorstin, *The Americans: The Democratic Experience* (New York: Random House, 1973), more materially-oriented than the title suggests, and Howard Mumford Jones's overview of the period, *The Age of Energy: Varieties of American Experience 1865–1915* (New York: Viking Press, 1971).

34. Dorothy Johansen, "Capitalism on the Far-Western Frontier: The Oregon Steam Navigation Company" (Dissertation, University of Washington, 1941), 19–31. On Portland, see Joseph Gaston, *Portland, Its History and Builders*, 3 vols. (Chicago: S. J. Clarke Publishing Co., 1911).

35. Johansen, "Oregon Steam Navigation Company," 89, 90, 191, 218.

36. In *ibid.*, 202. This was when Oregon Steam was dickering with Northern Pacific to take over some of its stock.

37. Reed to A. Onderdonk, November 11, 1884 in "The Letters and Private Papers of Simeon Gannett Reed," typed version, prepared by Reed College Project, Division of Professional Service Projects, WPA, Portland, 1940; in Reed College Library, vol. 16, p. 124, hereafter cited as "Letters."

38. Reed to M. H. Cochrane, January 18, 1885, "Letters," Vol. 16, pp. 154–55. All quotations used here from the papers of Simeon Gannett Reed, as well as the T. L. Eliot Papers at Reed College Library, originally appeared in Barnett Singer, "Oregon's Nineteenth-Century Notables: Simeon Gannett Reed and Thomas Lamb Eliot," in Edwin R. Bingham and Glen A. Love, eds., *Northwest Perspectives: Essays on the Culture of the Pacific Northwest* (Seattle: University of Washington Press, 1979), 60–76.

39. Reed to John Fowler and Co., March 4, 1872, "Letters," Vol. 2, 177; Reed to Hugh Stevenson, May 12, 1890, "Letters," Vol. 31, 89; Reed to A. Onderdonk, October 8, 1883, "Letters," Vol. 16, 65.

40. Reed to V. P. Despierres, July 8, 1864, "Letters," Vol. 2, 5.

41. P. Pohalski to Reed, January 21, 1885, "Letters," Vol. 18, 15.

42. Some of the personal detail on Reed came from a conversation Singer had with Dorothy Johansen at Reed College, May 6, 1976.

43. Conversation with Dorothy Johansen; Johansen, "Manuscript," ch. 1, and her *Anniversary Play*, Reed College, which played June 6, 1937.

44. Reed to Arthur, October 12, 1883, "Letters," Vol. 16, 71.

45. Reed to E. C. Darley, February 8, 1890, "Letters," Vol. 30, 47–48.

46. Reed to H. Villard, February 12, 1890, "Letters," Vol. 30, 54. Villard was the chief buyer of Oregon Steam in 1879. That sale alone made over a million dollars for Reed. See Johansen, "Oregon Steam Navigation Company," 277.

47. W. S. King to Reed, November 24, 1872, "Letters," Vol. 5, 19.

48. Edward Reed to Reed, February 16, 1873, "Letters," Vol. 5, 62–63.

49. See Johansen, "Mr. and Mrs. Simeon G. Reed," 5; Reed to Jas. H. Beatty, January 9, 1891, in "Letters," Vol. 30, 173.

50. On blackmail, see Reed to Mr. Mills, September 24, 1884, "Letters," Vol. 16, 111; on granting of monopoly to Villard, see Reed to Villard, December 21, 1889, "Letters," Vol. 30, 27, mentioning "the exclusive right to cross *both* bridges with The Motor and Electric franchises on the other side of the river, *in connection* with the water power of the O.I. & S. Co. at Oswego..."; on rents and reputation, see Martin Winch to Phillip Wasserman, November 21, 1889, "Letters," Vol. 30, 2, averring that Reed "now has the reputation of being one of the fairest and most just landlords in Portland."

51. The will is cited in Johansen, "Manuscript," ch. 1.

52. Jonah Wise in *The First Quarter Century: Retrospect and Appraisal 1911–1936* (Portland: Reed College, 1936), 24. This book gives details on the founding of Reed. Biographical details that follow on Eliot are found in Earl M. Wilbur, *Thomas Lamb Eliot 1841–1936* (Portland: privately printed, 1937) and John Frederick Scheck, "Transplanting a Tradition: Thomas

Lamb Eliot and the Unitarian Conscience in the Pacific Northwest, 1865–1905" (Dissertation, University of Oregon 1969).

53. Cited in Scheck, "Thomas Lamb Eliot and the Unitarian Conscience," 281, 284.

54. From a report of 1876, cited in Johansen, "Manuscript," ch. 2. On the "intermediary generation" and education in France, see Barnett Singer, "Jules Ferry and the Laic Revolution in French Primary Education," *Paedagogica Historica*, 15 (1975): 204–25.

55. Eliot to wife Henrietta, March 12, 1903, in Thomas Lamb Eliot Papers, Reed College Library, hereafter cited as TLE Papers.

56. Quoted in Wilbur, *Thomas Lamb Eliot*, 111.

57. Scott's writings on Shakespeare found in Scott, ed., *Shakespeare: Writings of Harvey W. Scott*.

58. In TLE Papers.

59. All quotations from Eliot, "A Plea for the Old Authors" (unpaginated), in *ibid.*.

60. He goes on to describe "the courageous woman who dares to have an opinion, and is not ashamed that she studied Greek. It seems to me that there is no more significant evidence of the progress of our race, than that women are rapidly obtaining the same facilities of education that men have had." Sermon in TLE Papers.

61. Eliot to Henrietta, July 21, 1881, TLE Papers.

62. Eliot to Henrietta, August 17, 1883, TLE Papers.

63. Eliot to Henrietta, September 30, 1887, TLE Papers.

64. She was also on occasion self-deprecating in these letters back. For example, April 14, 1901: "This is a very stupid letter, but it comes from a very stupid woman." TLE Papers.

65. In Wilbur, *Thomas Lamb Eliot*, 103.

66. Eliot to Henrietta, March 12, 1903, in TLE Papers. The letters and postcards from Japan testify to a continuing interest in new things and in people.

67. Cited in Johansen, "Manuscript," ch. 3.

68. See the hortatory *The First Quarter Century* which has a series of appreciations. The quote on a "high adventure" is in this book, 5. Significantly, the student newspaper was called *The Quest*. Singer remains indebted to Professor Johansen for showing him a copy of her play.

69. Letitia Cappell, "A Biography of Abigail Scott Duniway" (M.A. thesis, University of Oregon, 1934), 23.

70. Abigail Scott Duniway, *Pathbreaking: An Autobiographical History of the Equal Suffrage Movement in Pacific Coast States*, 2nd ed. (Portland: James, Kerns and Abbot, 1914), 189.

71. For biographical details we have, in addition to *Pathbreaking*, used Ruth Barnes Moynihan, *Rebel for Rights: Abigail Scott Duniway* (New Haven: Yale University Press, 1983), Debra Shein, *Abigail Scott Duniway* (Boise, ID: Boise State University Printing, 2002) (in Boise State University Western Writers Series), Cappell, "A Biography of Abigail Scott Duniway," and H. K. Smith, *The Presumptuous Dreamers*, I (Lake Oswego, OR: Smith, Smith, and Smith, 1974). See also Suzanne K. George's chapter on "Abigail Scott Duniway," in Glenda Riley and Richard W. Etulain, eds., *By Grit and Grace: Eleven Women Who Shaped the American West* (Golden, CO: Fulcrum Publishing, 1997); and Elizabeth F. Chittenden's sketch, "By No Means Excluding Women: Abigail Scott Duniway, Western Pioneer in the Struggle for Equal Voting Rights," in Halseth and Glasrud, eds., *The Northwest Mosaic*, 191–196 (originally published in *American West* magazine). And on the larger context of how Northwest womens' history generally has developed, see Karen J. Blair, "The State of Research on Pacific Northwest Women," *Frontiers: A Journal of Women Studies* 22 (2001): 48–56.

72. In Duniway, *Pathbreaking*, 29.

73. *Ibid.*, 34–36.

74. See Powers, *History of Oregon Literature*, 247.

75. Duniway, *Pathbreaking*, 49.

76. *Ibid.*, 70. On the Oregon suffrage movement generally, and Duniway's place in it, see Lauren Kessler, "A Siege of the Citadels: Search for a Public Forum for the Ideas of Oregon Woman Suffrage," *OHQ* 84 (1983): 117–150.

77. Duniway, *Pathbreaking*, 200–10. For a good discussion citing Duniway's fears of the women's suffrage movement being subsumed within a puritanical prohibition movement, see John Putnam, "Racism and Intemperance: The Politics of Class and Gender in Late 19th-Century Seattle," *PNQ* 95 (2004): 75–76. There were other groups whose needs also criss-crossed those of settler suffragists, including Indian women. For problems in this regard, see Gail H. Landsman, "The 'Other' as Political Symbol: Images of Indians in the Woman Suffrage Movement," *Ethnohistory* 39 (1992): 247–284.

78. Duniway, *From the West to the West: Across the Plains to Oregon* (Chicago: A.C. McClurg, 1905), ix. See also on her poem written to open the Lewis and Clark Centennial Exposition in 1905, *and* coincident with the annual Woman Suffrage Association Convention (both held in Portland), Albert Furtwangler, "Reclaiming Jefferson's Ideals: Abigail Scott Duniway's Ode to Lewis and Clark," *PNQ* 98 (2007): 159–167.

79. Duniway, *David and Anna Matson* (New York: S. R. Wells, 1876), 3.

80. *Ibid.*, 3. Debra Shein has tried with some success to resuscitate Duniway's reputation as a novelist, albeit a didactic one, in "Abigail Scott Duniway's Serialized Novels and the Struggle for Women's Rights," *OHQ* 101 (2000): 302–327, and also in her *Abigail Scott Duniway, passim*.

81. Quoted in Cappell, "A Biography of Abigail Scott Duniway," 11. On her split with Greeley, see Moynihan, *Rebel for Rights*, 173.

82. Cappell, "A Biography of Abigail Scott Duniway," 40.

83. On Duniway's disappointment with her sons around the turn of the century, see Moynihan, *Rebel for Rights*, 197–98, 209.

Chapter 3

1. See Powers, *History of Oregon Literature, passim*.

2. *Ibid.*, 195–204, 211–18.

3. *Ibid.*, 204–11.

4. *Ibid.*, 221–28, 470–94.

5. On Simpson see *ibid.*, 295–300, and quotation from poem, 301.

6. *Ibid.*, 339–49.

7. This section is based primarily on O. W. Frost, *Joaquin Miller* (New York: Twayne Publishers, 1967) and Benjamin S. Lawson, *Joaquin Miller* (Boise: Boise State University Printers, 1980)—in the Boise State Western Writers Series. We have also learned from M. Marion Marberry's more critical *Splendid Poseur: Joaquin Miller, American Poet* (New York: Thomas Y. Crowell, 1953). See also Joaquin Miller, *Unwritten History: Life Among the Modocs* (Eugene, OR: Orion Press, 1972), with an introduction by A. H. Rosenus (first published 1873); and Powers, *History of Oregon Literature*, 229–77.

8. He might have also been moved by Quaker pacifism. But Southern sympathy was in the air in the West. Frances Fuller Victor, still in San Francisco, curiously also supported the South. See Franklin Walker, *San Francisco's Literary Frontier* (Seattle: University of Washington Press, 1969 [1939], 110–11.

9. In Joaquin Miller, *The Complete Poetical Works of Joaquin Miller* (San Francisco: Whitaker and Ray, 1902), 55.

10. In Powers, *History of Oregon Literature*, 271, 273.

11. Again, one can follow a good deal of Miller's travels, sympathies, and interests by the poetry collected in *The Complete Poetical Works of Joaquin Miller*. For instance, his "The Poem at the Potomac," or "A Christmas Eve in Cuba." He also saluted deaths of poetic titans with poems such as "The Passing of Tennyson," in *ibid.*, 225–26.

12. Hamlin Garland, *Son of the Middle Border* (New York: Macmillan, 1962), 188, 380–81.

13. In Miller, *The Complete Poetical Works of Joaquin Miller*, 253.

14. In Joaquin Miller, "The Californian" in Miller, *Songs of the Sierras* (Boston: Roberts Brothers, 1871), 101.

15. See Walker, *San Francisco's Literary Frontier*, 324–32, 344–46. As Lawson adds, "the more outlandish [Miller] seemed, the more plaudits he received...." Lawson, *Joaquin Miller*, 5, and also on his reception in England, 17–18. See also Marberry, *Splendid Poseur, passim* for this general theme.

16. Miller, beginning of "Even So," in *Songs of the Sierras*, 278.

17. Frost, *Joaquin Miller*, 47. C.f. also "Where Rolls the Oregon," in *The Complete Poetical Works of Joaquin Miller*, 164–65. Somewhat like Thomas Wolfe, even in Europe aspects of the Northwest came back to him poetically.

18. See Powers, *History of Oregon Literature*, 247–77.

19. From the paper by Nash, "Scott of *The Oregonian*," (Pacific Northwest History Conference, Seattle, Washington, August, 1974).

20. Frost, *Joaquin Miller*, 113–14.

21. See Starr, *Americans and the California Dream 1850–1915*, 288–90 and *passim*. So much is this the case that when Seattle's Vernon L. Parrington, Jr., published a book on Utopianism he discussed Miller condescendingly as a typical California writer. (*American Dreams: A Study of American Utopias* [Providence, Brown University Press, 1947]), 161–63.

22. Apparently Portland never quite recanted its early judgment, for even Johansen (of Portland's Reed College) gave Miller only two sentences in her otherwise admirable history. She failed to mention his relation to Eugene, his *Unwritten History*, or any work after the unnoticed Portland publication in 1869. With uncharacteristic inaccuracy she then added: "The next year he moved to the more receptive intellectual climate of California 'where passions are born, and where blushes gave birth' to his songs of the South." This was the ultimate contempt of a Portland Oregonian for a native backwoodsman. Johansen, *Empire of the Columbia*, 294.

23. Powers, *History of Oregon Literature*, 697–701.

24. See, for example, the review by William Kittredge of a reprint of *Unwritten History* in *Northwest Review*, 13 (1973): 80–82. Miller expressed the origins of his misfit individuality well in that book: "I had never been a boy, that is, an orthodox, old-fashioned boy, for I never

played in my life.... Cattle and horses I understand thoroughly. But somehow I could not understand or get on with my fellow man. He seemed to always want to cheat me....” By contrast, there was his treatment by Native Americans that he knew, and as he puts it, “I could not have been treated more kindly even at home.” This was because the Indian “was a natural; a child of nature; nearer to God than the white man.” Whereas in white society one needed to meld into the mainstream: “Be a big pebble if you can, a small pebble if you must. But be a pebble just like the rest....” One can easily see how Miller's “anti-establishment” prose would appeal to readers of the late 1960s or early 1970s! Quotations in Miller, *Unwritten History*, 22, 29, 30.

25. For the following biographical detail, see especially Hazel Mills and Constance Bordwell (and really, Thomas Vaughan, listed as an editor), *Frances Fuller Victor: The Witness to America's Westerings* (Portland: Peregrine Productions for the Oregon Historical Society Press, 2002), now the best work on her; and Jim Martin, *A Bit of a Blue: The Life and Work of Frances Fuller Victor* (Salem, OR: Deep Well Publishing Co., 1992). We have also benefited from much older studies, such as William A. Morris, “The Origin and Authorship of the Bancroft Pacific States Publications: A History of a History,” *OHQ* 4 (1903), Part I: 287–364; Mills, “Travels of a Lady Correspondent, *PNQ* 45 (1954): 105–15; and Frances Victor's own autobiographical sketch in the Salem *Daily Oregon Statesman*, June 16, 1895.

26. See appropriate parts of Mills and Bordwell, *Frances Fuller Victor* and Martin, *A Bit of a Blue*, as well as Walker, *San Francisco's Literary Frontier*, 127, 137–38, 159, 179, 224.

27. As she later put it, “When I came to Oregon ... nothing was known by my generation in the East, or even in California, about the Pacific Northwest.... The people and their history were in obscurity. The very aloofness and uniqueness of the country interested me, and I began at once to study its characteristics.” Quoted in Martin, *A Bit of a Blue*, 54.

28. Victor, *All Over Washington and Oregon* (San Francisco: J.H. Carmany, 1872). (The subtitle goes on for several lines: “Observations on the country, its scenery, soil, climate, resources, and improvements, with an outline of its early history. Also hints to immigrants and travelers concerning routes, the cost of travel, the price of land, etc., by Frances Fuller Victor....”)

29. Frances Fuller Victor, *The Women's War with Whiskey or Crusading in Portland* (Portland: George H. Hines, 1874).

30. *Ibid.*, 7.

31. *Ibid.*, 14.

32. *Ibid.*, 12.

33. *Ibid.*, 14.

34. *Ibid.*, 51.

35. In F. F. Victor, *The New Penelope and Other Stories and Poems* (San Francisco: A. L. Bancroft, 1877), 284.

36. See *ibid.*, 9–79. The critique of ancient Athens is in her long poem, “Aspasia,” in *ibid.*, 291–296.

37. From the Deady correspondence in the Oregon Historical Society manuscripts collection, quoted in Alfred Powers, “Scrapbook of a Historian—Frances Fuller Victor,” *OHQ*, 42 (1941): 325–31, 328.

38. *Ibid.*, 328.

39. John W. Caughey, *Herbert Howe Bancroft: Historian of the West* (Berkeley: University of California Press, 1946), 267–68 (and full discussion, 253–272).

40. *Ibid.*, 266.

41. See the standard biographies, especially Mills and Bordwell, *Frances Fuller Victor*, ch. 12 (“Holding Her Own in the Bancroft Literary Workshop” [1879–84]) and ch. 13 (“The History Company” [1885–1889]). These chapters offer the best detail on what it took for Victor to work under Bancroft, endure pay offers that never materialized, and yet keep obsessing positively, as she did, on her project, indefatigably fact-checking and writing to people in the know on it. See also Mills' old article on this, “The Emergence of Frances Fuller Victor—Historian,” *OHQ* 62 (1961): 309–56. Martin's book (*A Bit of a Blue*) does not really address front and center the thorny question of how much Victor ought to be credited for her work on these famous histories; nor, more surprisingly, does Mills and Bordwell's *Frances Fuller Victor*, especially eschewing the possibility of textual comparisons.

42. Bancroft, *History of Oregon* I (San Francisco: The History Company, 1886), 592. William Morris says Mrs. Victor often laughed about the insertions. Morris, “The Origin and authorship...,” 357.

43. See Mills, “Emergence of Frances Fuller Victor—Historian,” 329.

44. Mills, “Travels of a Lady Correspondent,” 110; Frances Fuller Victor, *The River of the West* (San Francisco: R.W. Bliss, 1870), vii.

45. Victor, *River of the West*, vi.

46. *Ibid.*, 51.

47. *Ibid.*, 84.

48. See, for example, Bancroft, *History of Oregon* II (San Francisco: The History Company, 1888), 222, 439, 455, 456; Victor, *Early Indian Wars of Oregon* (Salem, OR: Frank C. Baker,1894), 209; and Victor, *River of the West*, 502.

49. Caughey, *Herbert Howe Bancroft*, 275.

50. Bancroft, *History of Oregon* I, 219.

51. *Ibid.*, 221.

52. H. H. Bancroft, *History of the Pacific States of North America*, XXXIV, "Literary Industries" (San Francisco: A.L. Bancroft, 1890), 80 and Caughey, *Herbert Howe Bancroft*, 262–263.

53. Victor, *Early Indian Wars of Oregon*, 411.

54. *Ibid.*, 461.

55. Mills, "Emergence of Frances Fuller Victor—Historian," 335.

56. For the latter part of Victor's life see in addition to the standard biographical treatments noted above, Mills, "Emergence of Frances Fuller Victor—Historian," 355–56.

57. Some basic references are Leonard Wiley, *The Granite Boulder: A Biography of Frederick Balch* (Portland: Dunham, 1970); Powers, *History of Oregon Literature*, 317–32; Delia Coon, "Frederick Homer Balch," *Washington Historical Quarterly* 15 (1924): 32–42; Robert Ballou, *Early Klickitat Valley Days* (Goldendale, WA: Goldendale *Sentinel*, 1938); and F. H. Balch's own *Genevieve: A Tale of Oregon* (Portland: Metropolitan, 1932). Richard Etulain fits him with others into a Northwest literary tradition that helped create a regional consciousness: Etulain, "Inventing the Pacific Northwest: Novelists and the Region's History," in Hirt, ed., *Terra Pacifica*, 25–52.

58. The phrase of Orange Jacobs in his characterization of Indians after fifty-five years of contact (*Memoirs of Orange Jacobs* [Seattle: Cowan and Hanford, 1908], 59).

59. This seems much more likely than Leonard Wiley's suggestion in *The Granite Boulder* (74) that *Genevieve* is a rewriting of *Wallulah*.

60. H. L. Davis, *Honey in the Horn* (New York: Harper and Brothers, 1935), especially 8–9.

61. In F. H. Balch, *Memaloose: Three Poems and Two Prose Sketches* (Portland: Ricketts and Binford, 1934).

62. Balch, *Genevieve*, 128.

63. Cantwell, *The Hidden Northwest*, quotation from *Thanatopsis*, 66.

64. Balch, *The Bridge of the Gods*, 112, 163.

65. Wiley, *Granite Boulder*, 23.

66. Frost, *Joaquin Miller*, 47.

67. A Fur Trader (Peter Skene Ogden), *Traits of American Indian Life and Character* (London: Smith, Elder, 1853). Ogden apparently represented a rather polite version of the trappers' and traders' view. See Saum, *Fur Trader and the Indian*, *passim*.

68. Powers, *History of Oregon Literature*, 218–252. This is, of course, a central theme of Don Berry's *Moontrap* (to be discussed in Chapter 6). On the symbolic identification of a people with devalued ways of life, see R. D. Gastil, "Lower Class Behavior: Cultural and Biosocial," *Human Organization* 32 (1973): 349–62.

69. Balch, *Genevieve*, 113–14.

70. H. H. Bancroft, *History of Oregon* II (San Francisco: The History Company, 1888), 99. These may of course have been Victor's words. See her *Early Indian Wars of Oregon*, 424, for another "survival of the fittest" explanation.

71. See Dorothy and Jack Sutton, eds., *Indian Wars of the Rogue River* (Grants Pass, OR: Josephine County Historical Society, 1969), 172. The book is a heavily annotated reprinting of part of Victor's *Early Indian Wars of Oregon*. For comparison see Stephen D. Beckham, *Requiem for a People* (Norman: University of Oklahoma Press, 1971), a more modern history of the Rogue Indians in this same period. The Suttons remark that Victor was more anti–Indian than Bancroft, and this may be why there seems to be a different spirit in Bancroft (cf. H. H. Bancroft, *History of Oregon* II, 412; *History of the Northwest Coast* II [San Francisco: The History Company, 1886], 650). However, Bancroft's condemnation of miscegenation is equally harsh (*ibid.*, 650–51) and makes a clear contrast to Balch's work and views.

72. Victor, *Early Indian Wars of Oregon*, 318.

73. *Ibid.*, 343.

74. Leslie Fiedler, *The Return of the Vanishing American* (New York: Stein and Day, 1968).

75. Samuel A. Clarke, *Pioneer Days of Oregon History*, two volumes (Portland: J. K. Gill, 1905); Strong, *Cathlamet on the Columbia*; Jacobs, *Memoirs*, especially 159–62.

76. Perhaps the first expression of this position—the first local attempt to make the Indians a positive part of the conquerors' regional tradition—was Samuel Clarke's little-read *Sounds by the Western Sea*, published in Salem in 1872, and including, in particular, his "Legend of the Cascades" (see on this, Powers, *History of Oregon Literature*, 339–49). On a more popular, less literate level there were always those who took a respectful attitude toward Native Americans and their accomplishments. See Jesse A. Applegate, *Recollections of My Boyhood* (Chicago: Caxton Club, 1934—recorded in the 1870s by the nephew of Jesse) and the story of a neighbor of Balch who, "although he married a white woman," so admired the Indians that he asked to be buried on Memaloose Island in the 1880s, and was—with full Masonic honors. (Confirmation of early respect is suggested by the fact that the death houses were evidently still not plundered at this time. See Balch, *Memaloose: Three Poems and Two Prose Sketches* [Portland: M. Ricketts and T. Binford, 1934].)

77. Balch, *Genevieve*, 259–60.

78. Balch, *Bridge of the Gods*, 235.

79. Wiley, *Granite Boulder*, 22–23.

80. See Josephy, *Nez Perce Indians*, 278, 294, Victor, *Early Indian Wars*, 425–75, and Clarke, *Pioneer Days*, 93–99, 126–32, 312–34.

81. Wiley, *Granite Boulder*, 22–23.

82. Balch, *Genevieve*, 332–33.

83. See Simon Kuznets and Dorothy S. Thomas, *Population Redistribution and Economic Growth: United States, 1870–1950* (Philadelphia: American Philosophical Society, 1957), I, 249–252. This is the coming and going, the ever new population in the Northwest that H. L. Davis also denoted (see Introduction).

Chapter 4

1. See Johansen, *Empire of the Columbia*, 454–71, the other texts previously cited, as well as works noted below.

2. We base much of what follows on Lincoln Steffens, *The Upbuilders* (Seattle: University of Washington Press, 1968 [originally 1909]), 285–326; Thomas McClintock, "Henderson Lewelling, Seth Lewelling and the Birth of the Pacific Coast Fruit Industry," *OHQ* 68 (1967): 153–74, and "Seth Lewelling, William S. U'Ren and the Birth of the Oregon Progressive Movement," *OHQ* 68 (1967): 197–220; and Robert Woodward, "W. S. U'Ren and the Single Tax in Oregon," *OHQ* 61 (1960): 46–63.

3. Quoted in Johansen, *Empire of the Columbia*, 456.

4. See John R. Rogers, *Politics: An Argument in Favor of the Inalienable Rights of Man* (Seattle: The Allen Printing Company, 1894) and *Reformers I Have Known* (Tacoma: Tacoma Morning Union, 1894).

5. These ideas are expressed in John R. Rogers, *Life* (San Francisco: Whitaker and Ray, 1899) and see also on both his life and work, Thomas W. Riddle, *The Old Radicalism: John R. Rogers and the Populist Movement in Washington* (New York: Garland Publishing, 1991).

6. See the views in John R. Rogers, *Free Land: The Remedy for Involuntary Poverty, Social Unrest and the Woes of Labor* (Tacoma: Tacoma Morning Union, 1897). The argument is repeated in other pamphlets.

7. See Eric F. Goldman, "J. Allen Smith: The Reformer and his Dilemma," *PNQ* 35 (1944): 201–7, and Thomas G. McClintock, "J. Allen Smith: A Pacific Northwest Progressive," *PNQ* 53 (1953): 49–59, as well as his thesis on Smith ("J. Allen Smith and the Progressive Movement: A Study in Intellectual History," [Ph.D. dissertation.: University of Washington, 1959]).

8. See Goldman, "J. Allen Smith," 205–7, as well as Smith's scrapbook in the University of Washington Library Pacific Northwest Collection.

9. The discussion of Cotterill is based on Norman H. Clark's account in his *Washington: A Bicentennial History* (New York: Norton, 1976).

10. See Charles Pierce Le Warne, *Utopias on Puget Sound: 1885–1915* (Seattle: University of Washington Press, 1975). And on populism more generally in a restricted rural region, Jeff Lalande, "A 'Little Kansas' in Southern Oregon: The Course and Character of Populism in Jackson County, 1890–1900," *The Pacific Historical Review* 63 (1994): 149–176.

11. Le Warne, *Utopias on Puget Sound*, 228–29.

12. Mention of both of these efforts is in Anna Louise Strong, *I Change Worlds: The Remaking of an American* (New York: H. Holt, 1935), 157, 372.

13. Norman H. Clark, *Mill Town* (Seattle: University of Washington Press, 1970), 181.

14. See *ibid.*, 210–11 and Phil Mellinger's overview, "How the IWW Lost its Western Heartland: Western Labor History Revisited," *The Western Historical Quarterly* 27 (1996): 303–324; Paul Sutter, "A Retreat from Profit: Colonization, the Appalachian Trail, and the Social Roots of Benton MacKaye's Wilderness Advocacy," *Environmental History* 4 (1999): 553–557, which includes a section on the IWW and the Everett Massacre, and MacKaye's reaction to it; and for a comparison of the labor movement and practices in the U.S. Northwest and Canadian British Columbia, Andrew Yarmie, "Employers and Exceptionalism: A Cross-Border Comparison of Washington State and British Columbia, 1890–1935," *The Pacific Historical Review* 72 (2003): 561–615.

15. Biographical details are from Tracy B. Strong and Helene Keyssar, *Right in Her Soul: The Life of Anna Louise Strong* (New York: Random House, 1983); David C. Duke, "Anna Louise Strong and the Search for a Good Cause," *PNQ* 66 (1975): 123–37; and Strong's autobiography, *I Change Worlds*.

16. Strong, *I Change Worlds*, 14.

17. See Strong and Keyssar, *Right in Her Soul*, ch. 4, *passim*.

18. Strong, *I Change Worlds*, 48.

19. Strong and Keyssar, *Right in Her Soul*, 64, 65.

20. Strong, *I Change Worlds*, 49.

21. *Ibid.*, 50.

22. *Ibid.*, 51.

23. Duke, "Search for a Good Cause," 125; Strong, *I Change Worlds*, 53.

24. Strong, *I Change Worlds*, 55, and for the

preceding, see also Strong and Keyssar, *Right in Her Soul*, ch. 5. On perceptions of the radical Strong in the Northwest, including during World War I when she made enemies by her pacifist stance, see John Putman, "A 'Test of Chiffon Politics': Gender Politics in Seattle, 1897–1917," *The Pacific Historical Review* 69 (2000): 595–616.

25. Strong, *I Change Worlds*, 67.

26. Anna Louise Strong, *Ragged Verse* (Seattle: Pigott-Washington, 1937). This "presentation edition" was donated by the Washington Alpine Club, the Washington Commonwealth Federation, and the Church of the People. It suggests her continuing role in regional thought in the 1930s.

27. Anna Louise Strong, *The Seattle General Strike*—issued by the History Committee of the General Strike Committee (Seattle: Seattle Union Record Pub. Co., [1919]).

28. *Ibid.*, 2.

29. *Ibid.*, 34.

30. Strong, *I Change Worlds*, 86.

31. *Ibid.*, 88.

32. Duke, "Search for a Good Cause," 132, and see more generally, Strong and Keyssar, *Right in Her Soul*, ch. 6. They note her idolization of Leon Trotsky, ultimately to be murdered of course at the hands of Stalin.

33. See appropriate parts of Strong and Keyssar, *Right in Her Soul*, ch. 8, 9, 10, and on her Hollywood stint particularly, 204–206.

34. See *ibid.*, ch. 14–15.

35. George Venn sees Wood's trip to Alaska in 1877 as the most significant turning point for him, indicating future personae. See Venn, "Soldier to Advocate: C.E.S. Wood's 1877 Diary of Alaska and the Nez Percé Conflict," *OHQ* (2005): 34–75 and in book form, *Soldier to Advocate: C.E.S. Wood's Legacy: A Soldier's Unpublished Diary, Drawings, Poetry, and Letters of Alaska and the Nez Percé Conflict* (La Grande, OR: Wordcraft of Oregon, 2006), a book of under 100 pages. The standard biographical account is Robert Hamburger's *Two Rooms: The Life of Charles Erskine Scott Wood* (Lincoln: University of Nebraska Press, 1998), which set out to reject the temptation of making Wood's work either "seminal" or overly "neglected." See also Edwin R. Bingham's characteristically sprightly *Charles Erskine Scott Wood* (Boise: Boise State University Printing, 1990), in the Western Writers Series. There is also an interesting, discursive introduction in Edwin Bingham and Tim Barnes, eds., *Wood Works: The Life and Writings of Charles Erskine Scott Wood* (Corvallis: Oregon State University Press, 1997).

36. See Powers, *History of Oregon Literature*, 441–52. Bingham points to the "double dimension in [Wood's] character" in *Charles Erskine Scott Wood*, 47, as does Hamburger, noting Wood's affinity for the finest wines and cheeses, carpets, or paintings; but also for high-minded causes! (See Hamburger, *Two Rooms*, ch. 17 on the sources of Wood's anarchism and socialism.)

37. From "Beauty Not Enough" in C.E.S. Wood, *Collected Poems of Charles Erskine Scott Wood* (New York: Vanguard Press, 1949), 110.

38. *Ibid.*, 165.

39. *Ibid.*, 166.

40. *Ibid.*, 187.

41. *Ibid.*, 212, 216, 240, 253.

42. *Ibid.*, 225–32.

43. *Ibid.*, 178.

44. *Ibid.*, 175.

45. *Ibid.*, 287–89.

46. *Ibid.*, 179.

47. Edwin Bingham, "Oregon's Romantic Rebels: John Reed and Charles Erskine Scott Wood," *PNQ* 50 (1959): 83 [79–87]. A marvelous Ansel Adams photograph of Wood taken in the 1930s makes him resemble a fierce, aging Jeremiah—complete with flowing beard and copious, almost Biblical silvery hair.

48. C.E.S. Wood, *Heavenly Discourse* (New York: Penguin, 1946), 212–15.

49. Wood apparently rejected the dictatorship aspects of the Russian experiment while endorsing communism. For him there were no hard choices: see his *Earthly Discourse* (New York: Vanguard, 1937), 265–67.

50. Granville Hicks, *One of Us: The Story of John Reed* (New York: Equinox Cooperative Press, 1935).

51. Biographical detail is drawn from Robert A. Rosenstone, *Romantic Revolutionary: A Biography of John Reed* (New York: Alfred A. Knopf, 1975); David C. Duke, *John Reed* (Boston: Twayne Publishers, 1987); Eric Homberger, *John Reed* (Manchester: Manchester University Press, 1990); Bingham, "Oregon's Romantic Rebels;" and Granville Hicks, *John Reed: The Making of a Revolutionary* (New York: Macmillan, 1936), along with other books noted below.

52. Alex Baskin argues that "in some respects Reed's brashness was really a cloak behind which he hid his recurring feelings of insecurity" at Harvard. This was due to his being an "outsider," and part of that meant Northwest origins at a college which then drew largely from the privileged East. See Baskin, *John Reed: The Early Years in Greenwich Village* (New York: Archives of History, 1990), 3.

53. Hicks, *John Reed: The Making of a Revolutionary*, 49.

54. Barbara Gelb, *So Short a Time: A Biog-

raphy of John Reed and Louise Bryant (New York: Norton, 1973), 18.

55. Bingham discusses this in his "Oregon's Romantic Rebels" and see also Hicks, *John Reed: The Making of a Revolutionary*, 10–11, 49–50, 314. Alfred Powers, *History of Oregon Literature* describes Reed as a protégé of Wood (612–16).

56. Gelb, *So Short a Time*, 53, 102, 224; and see also Wood, *Heavenly Discourse* (including forward by Floyd Dell).

57. In C.E.S. Wood, *Collected Poems*, 25–26.

58. Lincoln Steffens, *The Autobiography of Lincoln Steffens* (New York: Harcourt, Brace, 1931), 244.

59. See appropriate parts of Steffens' *Upbuilders*.

60. See Steffens, *Autobiography of Lincoln Steffens*, 633, also Herbert Shapiro, "Steffens, Lippmann, and Reed: The Muckraker and His Protégés," *PNQ* 62 (1971): 142–50.

61. Steffens, *Autobiography of Lincoln Steffens*, 654.

62. See Daniel W. Lehman, *John Reed and the Writing of Revolution* (Athens, OH: Ohio University Press, 2002). Reed's pacifism in World War I interested this historian of Mennonite background, whose own community in Virginia had contributed numerous conscientious objectors in wartime.

63. On Bryant, in addition to Gelb's book, see Virginia Gardner, *"Friend and Lover": The Life of Louise Bryant* (New York: Horizon Press, 1982) and Mary V. Dearborn, *Queen of Bohemia: The Life of Louise Bryant* (Boston: Houghton Mifflin, 1996).

64. John Reed, *Ten Days that Shook the World* (New York: International Publishers, 1967), 293.

65. *Ibid.*, 12.

66. Van Wyck Brooks, *The Confident Years: 1885–1915* (New York: Dutton, 1952), 480–81.

67. Quoted in Granville Hicks, *John Reed: The Making of a Revolutionary*, 347.

68. Quoted in Eric F. Goldman, *Rendezvous with Destiny: A History of American Reform* (New York: Vintage edition, 1956), 240.

Chapter 5

1. On the reception of *Main Currents*, see Richard Hofstadter, *The Progressive Historians* (New York: Vintage edition, 1968), 490–91; Bernard Smith in Smith and Malcolm Cowley, eds., *Books that Changed our Minds* (New York: Kelmscott Editions, 1939),179; and Robert Skotheim, *American Intellectual Histories and Historians* (Princeton: Princeton University Press, 1966), 147–48. The sole monograph on Parrington is an able one: H. Lark Hall, *V. L. Parrington: Through the Avenue of Art* (Kent: The Kent State University Press, 1994). We have come independently to some of the same conclusions, and necessarily, tread (again, quite independently) on some of the same ground here. *However*, there are important differences both in our interpretations, including regional, and in material cited.

2. See for Kazin's view, George H. Douglas, "Alfred Kazin: American Critic," *Colorado Quarterly*, 23 (1974): 205. Douglas himself admired Parrington and some contemporaries for their force. He writes: "For the generation of writers who came to maturity in the years just before the first World War—writers like Wilson, Brooks, and Vernon L. Parrington—America was not so much a subject as it was an obsession, an obsession sometimes joyous, sometimes painful, but always nagging, irresistible, and relentless." *Ibid.*: 203.

3. Smith in Smith, *Books that Changed Our Minds*, 189.

4. *Ibid.*, 188.

5. *Ibid.*, 188.

6. E. H. Eby interview with Singer, Seattle, June 1975. Eby put together Parrington's Volume III from unpublished material and wrote an introduction to it.

7. Eby interview for these details.

8. Lionel Trilling, "Parrington, Mr. Smith and Reality," *Partisan Review* 7 (1940): 27; and Bernard Smith notes his "fantastic overpraise of Cabell," in Smith, *Books that Changed Our Minds*,191. See also V. L. Parrington's "The Incomparable Mr. Cabell," *Pacific Review* 2 (1921): 353–66, also included in Volume III of *Main Currents*.

9. John W. Caughey, "Historians' Choice: Results of a Poll on Recently Published American History and Biography," *Mississippi Valley Historical Review* 39 (1952): 280–302. Parrington's work narrowly nosed out Turner's *Frontier in American History* (1920). Much more recent appraisals of Parrington are found, for example, in David W. Levy, "'I Became More Radical with Every Year': The Intellectual Odyssey of Vernon Louis Parrington," *American Quarterly* 23 (1995): 663–668, and in Hilton Kramer, "The Ghost of V. L. Parrington," *New Criterion* 13 (1994): 4–8. He is also discussed in Alberto L. Hurtado, "Romancing the West in the Twentieth Century: The Politics of History in a Contested Region," *The Western Historical Quarterly* 32 (2001): 417–435, particularly with respect to political considerations influencing academic historians in that part of the country.

10. Vernon Louis Parrington, *Main Currents in American Thought* (three volumes; New York: Harcourt, Brace, 1930), II, 229.

11. *Ibid.*, II, 258.
12. *Ibid.*, I, 47.
13. *Ibid.*, I, 206. Bernard Bailyn's biography of Hutchinson (*The Ordeal of Thomas Hutchinson* [Cambridge, MA: Belknap Press of Harvard University Press, 1974]) offers obvious nuances.
14. Parrington, *Main Currents in American Thought*, I, 307–12.
15. *Ibid.*, I, 325.
16. *Ibid.*, II, 70.
17. Moses Coit Tyler, *A History of American Literature During the Colonial Period 1607–1765* (New York: Putnam, 1909), II, 75–76. That Parrington admired Tyler is seen in his statement characterizing Tyler's work as "urbane, witty, catholic in knowledge and sympathy" in Vernon L. Parrington, review of Tyler's *History of American Literature* in *Pacific Review* 2 (1921): 516–17.
18. Parrington, *Main Currents in American Thought*, I, 108–9.
19. *Ibid.*, I, 346.
20. *Ibid.*, II, 58. On Parrington's clearly advertised biases, see also Hall, *V. L. Parrington*, 244.
21. Parrington, *Main Currents in American Thought*, II, 99.
22. *Ibid.*, II, 204.
23. Parrington, "Memoir," unpublished manuscript, in Vernon Louis Parrington Papers, 1918–1925, Special Collections, Manuscripts, University of Washington Library, 17.
24. Parrington, *Main Currents in American Thought*, II, 85.
25. *Ibid.*, III, 36.
26. *Ibid.*, III, 29.
27. *Ibid.*, III, 12.
28. *Ibid.*, III, 93.
29. His interest was inspired by William Morris, the English pre–Raphaelite. He writes, "As a disciple of William Morris I loved everything medieval...," "Memoir," 46.
30. Parrington, *Main Currents in American Thought*, III, 99.
31. *Ibid.*, III, 262.
32. *Ibid.*, III, 291.
33. *Ibid.*, III, 300.
34. *Ibid.*, III, 386.
35. *Ibid.*, III, 386.
36. Hofstadter, *Progressive Historians*, 362.
37. Parrington, "Memoir," 29–30.
38. Hofstadter, *Progressive Historians*, 353.
39. See on this, Robert A. Skotheim and Kermit Vanderbilt, "Vernon Louis Parrington: The Mind and Art of a Historian of Ideas," *PNQ* 53 (1962):108–9.
40. E. H. Eby, introduction to *Main Currents in American Thought*, III, vi.
41. See Parrington in *ibid.*, III, 6–17, on the needless decimation of passenger pigeon and buffalo, exemplifying urban prodigality. It is some of his most effective writing.
42. *Ibid.*, III, 259.
43. *Ibid.*, III, 265–66.
44. Parrington, "Memoir," 16.
45. *Ibid.*, 16.
46. *Ibid.*, 17.
47. Hamlin Garland, *A Son of the Middle Border* (New York: Macmillan, 1952), 138.
48. Parrington, "Memoir," 32; and *Main Currents in American Thought*, III, 271–75, autobiographical in tone.
49. Parrington, "Memoir," 32–34.
50. E. H. Eby suggested this idea in his interview, and c. f. David W. Noble's interpretation in *Historians against History: The Frontier Thesis and the National Covenant in American Historical Writing since 1830* (Minneapolis: University of Minnesota Press, 1965), ch. 6: "Vernon Louis Parrington: The Covenant and the Jeffersonian Jeremiad."
51. Parrington, *Main Currents in American Thought*, III, 4.
52. Parrington, "Memoir," 35. It is not without interest that that son took his Ph.D. at Brown, and that *his* son studied at Linfield College, Oregon.
53. Hofstadter, *Progressive Historians*, 370.
54. Referring disdainfully to the Midwest, Parrington writes: "Why live in such a climate when the Puget Sound invites one with its cool greenery, its water and mountains and tempered sunshine!" Parrington, "Memoir," 44.
55. *Ibid.*, 49.
56. On this point H. Lark Hall concurs: "Parrington both suffered and gained from his isolation from scholarly interaction. It gave him time to work.... It gave him time to experiment in the classroom...." In addition, "isolation enhanced his wariness of academic specialization...." Hall, *V. L. Parrington*, 302.
57. Parrington introduction to J. Allen Smith, *The Growth and Decadence of Constitutional Government* (Seattle: University of Washington Press, 1972), v.
58. Parrington's letter to Ross L. Finney shows this fear quite clearly. The letter is quoted in Goldman, "J. Allen Smith," 208–9.
59. Parrington's clearest set of opposites is Middle Border populism versus the East of big business; see *Main Currents in American Thought*, III, 285–87.
60. See Richard Hofstadter, "Parrington and the Jeffersonian Tradition," *Journal of the History of Ideas*, II (1941): 391–400, only a mildly suggestive piece.
61. Parrington, *Main Currents in American Thought*, III, 241.
62. Parrington on Spencer in "Memoir," 36;

and Skotheim and Vanderbilt, "Mind and Art of a Historian,"103–5, on struggle motif.

63. See Parrington, "Where the Conservatives get their 'Con,'" *Washington Alumnus* 7 (1914): 2, 5.

64. See Vernon Parrington, Jr., introduction to "Vernon Parrington's View: Economics and Criticism," *PNQ* 44 (1953): 91–105; and Eby interview.

65. E. H. Eby, "Vernon L. Parrington: The Style of the Man," *Tyee Magazine* (Winter 1966): 3.

66. Eby interview.

67. *Ibid.*

68. Joseph Harrison, *Vernon Louis Parrington: American Scholar* (Seattle: University of Washington Bookstore, 1929), 11.

69. Portrait by "Mum" (from University of Washington *Daily*) in Faculty pamphlet file, Pacific Northwest Collection, University of Washington.

70. Harrison, *Vernon Louis Parrington: American Scholar*, 81.

71. Eby interview.

72. Harrison, *Vernon Louis Parrington: American Scholar*, 20. Harrison also refers obliquely to faculty *resentment* over the achievement: "But was it quite moral, after all, for a university man to write so ambitiously?" *Ibid.*, 20.

73. Noble, *Historians against History*, 7.

74. Parrington, "Economics and Criticism" (1917) in "Vernon Parrington's View."

75. Vernon Louis Parrington, *Sinclair Lewis: Our Own Diogenes* (Seattle: University of Washington Bookstore, 1927), included also in Volume III of *Main Currents*.

76. Parrington, "The Incomparable Mr. Cabell," *Pacific Review*, previously cited.

77. Parrington, "Memoir," 46: "Some time we shall have such gardens here in this Puget Sound land with its English climate, but not until we come to love flowers as the English do."

78. Eby interview.

79. *American Dreams: A Study of American Utopias* (Providence: Brown University Press, 1947).

Chapter 6

1. *Washington Magazine* 1 (September 1889): 8–11.

2. The full subtitle of the tract published at The Dalles, Oregon, is *A Manifesto, Upon the Present Condition of Northwest Literature ... Containing Several Near-Libelous Utterances, Upon Persons in the Public Eye.*

3. Chittick, ed., *Northwest Harvest*. See especially the articles by Ernest Haycox, "Is there a Northwest?," Joseph B. Harrison, "Regionalism Is Not Enough" (the best of the collection), and Allis McKay, "Let's Build a Great Tradition." The last bit of hortatory advice is typical of the book's thematic content.

4. *PNQ* 48 (1957): 65–75.

5. Ralph J. Mills, Jr., ed., *Selected Letters of Theodore Roethke* (Seattle: University of Washington Press, 1968), 144.

6. Roger Sale, "Unknown Novels," *The American Scholar* 43 (1973–74): 90–92.

7. Cantwell, *The Hidden Northwest*, ch. 8. It should also be mentioned that good critics of Northwest writing were then lacking, too. Richard Etulain charted the possibilities for this field in his articles, such as "Novelists of the Northwest: Opportunities for Research," *Idaho Yesterdays* 17 (1973): 24–32.

8. Powers, *History of Oregon Literature*, 404–14.

9. For Dye, there is a fine biographical study superseding older takes, including Powers,' Sheri Bartlett Browne's *Eva Emery Dye: Romance with the West* (Corvallis: Oregon State University Press, 2004), which we have used for detail here. (Quotation from Dye in *ibid.*, 154–55.) Disappointments of Dye's later years included one son's mental illness.

10. See Powers, *History of Oregon Literature*, 415–40; also Ella Higginson, *Mariella of Out West*, as well as the other works referred to in the text.

11. Higginson is discussed with other female figures of her time in Nancy Pagh, "An Indescribable Sea: Discourse of Women Traveling the Northwest Coast by Boat," *Frontiers: A Journal of Women Studies* 20 (1999): 1–26.

12. Powers, *History of Oregon Literature*, 333–38.

13. *Ibid.*, 388 and *passim*.

14. *Ibid.*, 617–21. Also John Fleming Wilson, *The Land Claimers* (Boston: Little, Brown, 1911).

15. Powers, *History of Oregon Literature*, 622–34.

16. See Gelb, *So Short a Time*, 13, 35–36.

17. Powers, *History of Oregon Literature*, 66; Howard McKinley Corning, "All the Words on the Pages, I: H. L. Davis," *OHQ* 73 (1972): 293–331.

18. See especially A. R. Wetjen, *Captains All* (New York: Alfred Knopf, 1924).

19. Douglas, *Of Men and Mountains* (New York: Harper and Row, 1950), 178–79, and Douglas, *Go East Young Man* (New York: Random House, 1974), 224.

20. Eg., "Buttonholes" or "Laughter Was the Word for Laura" in *The Wild Swan and Other Sketches* (New York: T. Y. Crowell, 1947) 61–65, 143–47; or "Go Look Down the Lane Again" or "A Farmer Went to the Sea" in *At the End of*

the Car Line: Editorial Sketches, Essays and Verse from the Oregonian Files of Several Years (Portland: Binfords and Mort, 1942), 123–26, 114–17.

21. Powers, *History of Oregon Literature*, 711, and *passim*.

22. C.f. Nicholas O'Connell (in a fine work): "Contemporary Northwest literature addresses a wide range of topics, but the physical environment remains the dominant subject." O'Connell, *On Sacred Ground: The Spirit of Place in Pacific Northwest Literature* (Seattle: University of Washington Press, 2003), 141. On the influence of the Northwest environment, a more idiosyncratic book is Laurie Ricou, *The Arbutus/Madrone Files: Reading the Pacific Northwest* (Corvallis: Oregon State University Press, 2002), with interesting chapters on, for example, salmon. It may be that the emphasis on setting also owes something to a wider Western tradition. According to Richard Etulain, "local-color writers of the late nineteenth century tended to overplay setting and to follow slavishly stock characterization...." Etulain, "The New Western Novel," *Idaho Yesterdays* 15 (1972): 17. This tendency, in addition, may relate to "a sense of insecurity vis-à-vis the rest of the United States," as John M. Findlay notes in "Something in the Soil? Literature and Regional Identity in the 20th-Century Pacific Northwest," *PNQ* 97 (2006): 79–89.

23. See Chittick, ed., *Northwest Harvest*, note, 203.

24. Here is how McKay handles the death of Chris' husband, Nate: "She told herself that Nate had had a good life, a superb life; nothing could mar it now. It was something for a life to end bravely, quickly, while it was in full bloom." McKay, *They Came to a River* (New York: Macmillan, 1941), 493.

25. Elizabeth Marion, *The Keys to the House* (New York: T. Y. Crowell, 1944), 36.

26. Elizabeth Marion, *The Day Will Come* (New York: T. Y. Crowell, 1939), 16.

27. Berenice Thorpe, *Reunion on Strawberry Hill* (New York: Alfred Knopf, 1944), 47.

28. Nard Jones, *Wheat Women* (New York: Duffield and Green, 1933), 89.

29. William G. Robbins begins an article on the link between environment and storytelling around the Columbia River with a quotation from Jones. See Robbins, "Narrative Form and Great River Myths: The Power of Columbia River Stories," *Environmental History Review* 17 (1993): 1–22. See also on local storytelling in various historical periods, providing fodder for larger Western myths, Jon T. Coleman, "The Men in McArthur's Bar: the Cultural Significance of the Margins," *Western Historical Quarterly* 31 (2000): 47–68.

30. On the critical reaction to Cantwell's novel, see Seyersted, *Robert Cantwell*, 104–106. On the atmosphere which spawned the proletarian novel, see David Madden, ed., *Proletarian Writers of the Thirties* (Carbondale: Southern Illinois University Press, 1968). The book contains a section on Cantwell. See also for female writers of that era, Barbara Foley, "Women and the Left in the 1930s," *American Literary History* 2 (1990): 150–169.

31. Detail here and in what follows is from Richard Etulain, "Ernest Haycox: The Historical Western, 1937–43," *South Dakota Review* 5 (1967): 35–54; Etulain, *Ernest Haycox* (Boise: Boise State University Printing, 1988), in the Western Writers Series; Stephen L. Tanner, *Ernest Haycox* (New York: Twayne Publishers, 1996); and *especially*, a superbly researched, fascinating book by Ernest Haycox, Jr.: *On A Silver Desert: The Life of Ernest Haycox* (Norman: University of Oklahoma Press, 2003), now definitive.

32. Among a number of others, *Canyon Passage* derived from a Haycox novel was shot on location in Oregon, featuring actors such as Dana Andrews, Andy Devine, and the young Lloyd Bridges. It then had its world premiere in Portland, 1946.

33. John Okada, *No-no Boy* (Tokyo and Rutland, VT: Charles-Tuttle and Co., 1957), 30.

34. Other estimates of Okada's work are found in Jingqi Ling, "Race, Power, and Cultural Politics in John Okada's No-no Boy," *American Literature* 67 (1995): 359–381; Stan Yogi, "'You Had to Be One or the Other': Oppositions and Reconciliation in John Okada's No-no Boy," *The Society for the Study of the Multi-Ethnic Literature of the United States* (MELUS) 21 (1996): 63–77; and Bryn Gribben, "The Mother That Won't Reflect Back: Situating Psychoanalysis and the Japanese Mother in 'No-No Boy,'" in *ibid.* 28 (2003): 31–46.

35. Don Berry, *Moontrap* (New York: Viking, 1962). Edwin Bingham considered this a more successful novel than *Trask* (Review, *OHQ* 45 [1964]: 406–41). Rediscovery of Berry has been crowned with handsome, recent editions of novels like *Moontrap* and *Trask*, published by Oregon State University Press, and with interesting introductions. See the one provided by Jeff Baker, a book critic for the Portland *Oregonian*, to *Trask* (Corvallis: Oregon State University Press, 2004). See also by a warm supporter of Berry's work, Glen Love, *Don Berry* (Boise: Boise State University Printing, 1978), in the Western Writers Series. And more generally on Berry's mountain men, Kerry R. Oman, "Winter in the Rockies: Winter Quarters of the Mountain Men," *Montana: The Magazine of Western History* 52 (2002): 34–47.

36. Ernest Haycox, *The Earthbreakers* (Boston: Little, Brown, 1952).

37. See, for example, G. F. Ruston, *Life in the Far West* (Norman: University of Oklahoma Press, 1951), 40.

38. Tom Robbins, *Another Roadside Attraction* (New York: Doubleday, 1971), 19.

39. In Robbins' somewhat Chamber of Commerce-like, but evocative description: "The Skagit Valley lies between the Cascades and the Sound—sixty miles north of Seattle, an equal distance south of Canada. The Skagit River, which formed the valley, begins up in British Columbia, leaps and splashes southwestward through the high Cascade wilderness, absorbing glaciers and sipping alpine lakes, running two hundred miles in total before all fish-green, driftwood-cluttered and silty, it spreads its double mouth like suckers against the upper body of Puget Sound. Toward the Sound end of the valley, the fields are rich with river silt, the soil ranging from black velvet to a blond sandy loam." *Ibid.*, 79.

40. *Ibid.*, 302.

41. Kesey's *One Flew Over the Cuckoo's Nest* (New York: Viking, 1962) became the Milos Forman–directed movie hit of that title (1975), starring Jack Nicholson. His *Sometimes a Great Notion* (1964) preceded *Cuckoo* on the big screen in 1971, as a movie starring Paul Newman and Henry Fonda; but with a newer cinematic rendering also to be released in 2010.

42. Kesey, *One Flew Over the Cuckoo's Nest*, 210.

43. John Wilson Foster sees the Nurse in much the same way. See his "Hustling to Some Purpose: Kesey's *One Flew Over the Cuckoo's Nest*," *Western American Literature* 9 (1974): 115–130. A good introduction to Kesey's life and work through this period is Stephen L. Tanner, *Ken Kesey* (Boston: Twayne Publishers, 1983). On *Cuckoo's Nest* see also George J. Searles, ed., *A Casebook on Ken Kesey's One Flew Over the Cuckoo's Nest* (Albuquerque: University of New Mexico Press, 1992), a collection of scholarly articles.

44. Kesey, *One Flew Over the Cuckoo's Nest*, 210.

45. *Ibid.*, 23–24.

46. *Ibid.*, 95.

47. *Ibid.*, 212.

48. Ken Kesey, *Sometimes a Great Notion* (New York: Bantam Books, 1965; first published 1964), 95.

49. *Ibid.*, 83.

50. *Ibid.*, 110.

51. *Ibid.*, 113.

52. Interview with Kesey by Gordon Lish in *Genesis West* 2 (1963): 30. M. Gilbert Porter notes: "The struggle between the two brothers is a central conflict in the novel...." (But also of course in Kesey, too?) Porter, *The Art of Grit: Ken Kesey's Fiction* (Columbia: University of Missouri Press, 1982), 38.

53. Kesey, *Sometimes a Great Notion*, 20.

54. *Ibid.*, 233.

55. Quotes in *ibid.*, 83, 339. O'Connell remarks: "The novel succeeds like few others in presenting a detailed and comprehensive view of the Northwest and its people...." O'Connell, *On Sacred Ground*, 82. Clearly Kesey's sense of "place" here bulks large for this critic.

56. Kesey, *Sometimes a Great Notion*, 168, 392, his italics in both quotations.

57. In addition to *Status Rerum* itself, see especially Warren Clare, "Posers, Parasites and Pismires," *PNQ* 61 (1970): 22–30.

58. James Stevens, *Paul Bunyan* (New York: Alfred Knopf, 1925), later *The Saginaw Paul Bunyan* (New York: Alfred Knopf, 1932), as well as children's books.

59. *Brawnyman* (New York: Alfred Knopf, 1926), 275–86.

60. See Warren Clare, "James Stevens: The Laborer and Literature," *Research Studies* (Washington State) 4 (1964): 355–67.

61. James Stevens, *Big Jim Turner* (Garden City, NY: Doubleday, 1948), 275.

62. See the article on James Stevens in Henry Warfel, *American Novelists of Today* (New York: American Book Co., 1951), 406–7, and James Stevens, "Door of Opportunity" (Seattle: Dogwood Press, 1949).

63. H. L. Davis, "Status Rerum—Allegro Ma Non Troppo," *Frontier* 8 (March 2, 1928): 70.

64. Some of what follows is based upon Robert Bain, *H. L. Davis* (Boise: Boise State University Printing, 1974), in the Western Writers Series; Paul Bryant, *H.L. Davis* (Boston: Twayne Publishers, 1978); the part on Davis in Martin Kich, *Western American Novelists* (New York: Garland Publishers, 1995); George Armstrong's chapter on Davis in Bingham and Love, eds., *Northwest Perspectives*, 168–185; and Howard McKinley Corning, "All the Words on the Pages," along with specialized articles such as J. Cleman, "The Belated Frontier: H.L. Davis and the Problem of Pacific Northwest Regionalism," *Western American Literature* 37 (2003), especially 431; and David M. Wrobel, "Movement and Adjustment in Twentieth-Century Western Writing," *The Pacific Historical Review* 72 (2003): 393–404.

65. See especially H. L. Davis, *Proud Riders and Other Poems* (New York: Harper and Bros., 1942), 30–31, 22–23, as well as Bain, *H.L. Davis*, 7, 11.

66. See Corning, "All the Words on the Pages": 310–29.

67. In addition to our own insights on *Honey in the Horn* (New York: Harper and Bros., 1935) and *Winds of Morning* (New York: Morrow, 1952), and Bryant's and Bain's books here, we have also used Paul Bryant, "H. L. Davis: Viable Uses for the Past," *Western American Literature* 3 (1968): 3–18.

68. See in Davis, *Kettle of Fire*, 80, 49–50.

69. See Corning, "All the Words on the Pages," 305, 307.

70. In *Kettle of Fire*, 128–29.

71. In *ibid.*, 36.

72. In Davis, *Team Bells Woke Me and Other Stories* (New York: Morrow, 1953), 173–91.

73. For *Honey in the Horn*, see especially the description of a dying old woman taking a last look at the homestead (326–28).

74. From Davis, *Winds of Morning*, 80, also quoted in Jan Brunvand, "Honey in the Horn and 'Acres of Clams': The Regional Fiction of H. L. Davis," *Western American Literature* 2 (1967): 135–45 (141). The author of this article mostly missed the spirit of Davis.

75. See John Milton, "The Novel in the American West," *South Dakota Review* 2 (1964): 56–76.

76. Quoted from Edmund Fuller in Francis Greiner, "Voice of the West: Harold L. Davis," *OHQ* 66 (1965): 240–48 (246).

77. Philip Jones, "The West of H. L. Davis," *South Dakota Review* 6 (1968–69): 84 (72–84).

78. In Davis, *Team Bells*, 112–31.

79. H. L. Davis, *Beulah Land* (New York: Morrow, 1949). Beulah Land is a kind of secular heaven, a land of milk and honey. It is interesting that James Stevens also has Big Jim Turner write a poem entitled *Beulah Land*.

80. Davis, *Beulah Land*, 188.

81. *Ibid.*, 189.

82. *Ibid.*, 312.

83. *Distant Music*, 311.

84. See Bain, *H.L. Davis*, 9.

Chapter 7

1. Johansen, *Empire of the Columbia* (1967 edition), 429. A definitive reappraisal on Meany is by George A. Frykman—a biography reposing on careful use of the Meany papers at the University of Washington: Frykman, *Seattle's Historian and Promoter: The Life of Edmond Stephen Meany* (Pullman: Washington State University Press, 1998).

2. Edmond S. Meany, *Marcus Whitman*. This volume is found in the University of Washington Library's Pacific Northwest Collection.

3. Edmond S. Meany, *Harvey W. Scott, Editor* (in the University of Washington Pacific Northwest Collection).

4. (New York: Macmillan, 1916). *A New Vancouver Journal on the Discovery of Puget Sound, by a Member of the Chatham's Crew* (Seattle, 1915) has no publisher given.

5. Published 1909; revised edition (New York: Macmillan, 1942).

6. On the memorializing of Chief Joseph, and the building of his image, including by Meany, see Robert R. McCoy, *Chief Joseph, Yellow Wolf, and the Creation of Nez Percé History of the Pacific Northwest* (New York: Routledge, 2004). The author himself had attended Chief Joseph days in his Oregon hometown, then noticed how few Nez Percé were actually there, stimulating this book-length effort. See more generally, Kent Nerburn, *Chief Joseph and the Flight of the Nez Percé: The Untold Story of an American Tragedy* (New York: HarperCollins, 2005), the best scholarly book on the subject, and including the anecdote about "the Red Napoleon" attending a University of Washington football game in 1903.

7. (New York: The Century History Company, 1909); Schafer, *A History of the Pacific Northwest* (New York: Macmillan, 1921) (first published 1905, revised 1918).

8. Schafer, *A History of the Pacific Northwest*, 123.

9. George Fuller, *A History of the Pacific Northwest* (New York: Alfred Knopf, 1958, revised edition).

10. Johansen article in *PNQ* 40 (1949): 85–92.

11. Edwin Bingham, "Oregon's Romantic Rebels: John Reed and C.E.S. Wood," *PNQ* (previously cited).

12. Earl Pomeroy, *In Search of the Golden West: The Tourist in Western America* (New York: Alfred Knopf, 1957).

13. Earl Pomeroy, *The Pacific Slope* (New York: Alfred Knopf, 1965) (revised editions, or editions with different introductions, followed with different publishers).

14. (New York: Macmillan, 1943).

15. Stewart H. Holbrook, *Burning an Empire*, 135.

16. Stewart H. Holbrook, *Far Corner* (New York: Macmillan, 1952), 56.

17. Quoted in Brian Booth's introduction to Booth, ed., *Wildmen, Wobblies and Whistle Punks: Stewart Holbrook's Lowbrow Northwest* (Corvallis: Oregon State University Press, 1992), 35, a compilation of some of Holbrook's writings.

18. (Seattle: University of Washington Press, 1951).

19. See Booth, ed., *Wildmen, Wobblies and Whistle Punks*, 29, and quotation, 19. Holbrook was called the "Lumberjack Boswell" (in *ibid.*, 16).

20. Morgan, *The Last Wilderness* (New York: Viking Press, 1955), 247.

21. There are mentions of Morgan in scholarly articles like William L. Lang, "The Columbia River's Fate in the Twentieth Century," *Montana: The Magazine of Western History* 50 (2000): 44–55; Carlos A. Schwantes, "The Case of the Missing Century, or Where Did the American West Go After 1900," *The Pacific Historical Review* 70 (2001): 1–20; and for the big cities too, in Carl Abbott, "Regional City and Network City: Portland and Seattle in the Twentieth Century," *The Western Historical Quarterly* 23 (1992): 293–322.

22. Murray Morgan, *Skid Road: An Informal History of Seattle* (New York: Viking Press, 1960), 273. The book was originally published in 1951, and this is a revised edition, and there were more to come. Morgan's name has remained in the literary news since his death in 2000. For example, an updated version of his 1982 book on Seattle's Les Halles, the Pike Place Market, has recently come out: Alice Shorett and Murray Morgan, *Soul of the City: The Pike Place Public Market* (Seattle: University of Washington Press, 2007). Another cowritten book that emerged after his passing is Murray Morgan and William L. Lang, *Puget's Sound: A Narrative of Early Tacoma and the Southern Sound* (Seattle: University of Washington Press, 2003).

23. See Cantwell, *The Hidden Northwest*, 284–85.

24. James Swan, *The Northwest Coast* (New York: Harper and Bros., 1857); Theodore Winthrop, *The Canoe and the Saddle* (Boston: Ticknor and Fields, 1863)—and later editions.

25. Cantwell, *The Hidden Northwest*, 248.

26. Powers, *History of Oregon Literature*, 293, also 375–95. In Washington we think especially of the *Memoirs* of Orange Jacobs, previously cited.

27. Homer Davenport, *The Country Boy* (New York: Dillingham, 1910).

28. Powers, *History of Oregon Literature*, 398.

29. Hazel Heckman, *Island in the Sound* (Seattle: University of Washington Press, 1967), and *Island Year* (Seattle: University of Washington Press, 1967, 1972).

30. William O. Douglas, *Of Men and Mountains*, previously cited. See also James G. Newbill, "William O. Douglas, 'Of a Man and His Mountains,'" *PNQ* 79 (1988): 90–97, including fine photographs indicating his conservationist care for the land.

31. See Adam M. Sowards, "William O. Douglas's Wilderness Politics: Public Protest and Committees of Correspondence in the Pacific Northwest," *Western Historical Quarterly* 37 (2006): 21–42. Bruce Allen Murphy has published a biography of Douglas which offers a revision of some long-held views on the man—particularly, concerning his putatively deprived childhood (Murphy argues that he had quite a support system, including financial, growing up); and even the effects of childhood polio, which this author minimizes as well. Murphy, *Wild Bill: The Legend and Life of William O. Douglas* (New York: Random House, 2003).

32. Powers, *History of Oregon Literature*, 104–12.

33. *Ibid.*, 609–12.

34. D. W. Meinig, *The Great Columbia Plain: A Historical Geography, 1805–1910* (Seattle: University of Washington Press, 1968).

35. George Lundberg, *Can Science Save Us?* (New York: Longman's Green, 1961 [1947]).

36. Norman H. Clark, *The Dry Years* (Seattle: University of Washington Press, 1965).

37. Allen's review of *The Dry Years* is in *PNQ* 56 (1965): 77.

38. Clark, *The Dry Years*, 54.

39. (Seattle: University of Washington Press, 1970). See also a fine, more recent scholarly treatment of such regional towns by Linda Carlson, *Company Towns of the Pacific Northwest* (Seattle: University of Washington Press, 2003).

40. Norman H. Clark, *Washington: A Bicentennial History* (New York: Norton, 1976).

Chapter 8

1. See Powers, *History of Oregon Literature*, 635–68; also Stoddard King, *What the Queen Said and Further Facetious Fragments* (New York: George H. Doran Company, 1926) and *Grand Right and Left* (New York: George H. Doran Company, 1927); Ethel Romig Fuller, *Kitchen Sonnets (and Lyrics of Domesticity)* (Portland: Metropolitan Press, 1931), and *Skylines* (Portland: Binfords and Mort, 1952).

2. Howard McKinley Corning, *The Mountain in the Sky* (Portland: Metropolitan Press, 1930), especially 19–23.

3. Audrey Wurdemann, *Bright Ambush: Poems by Audrey Wurdemann* (New York: John Day, 1934); see also her *Splendour in the Grass* (New York: Harper and Brothers, 1936), and *The Seven Sins* (New York: Harper and Brothers, 1935).

4. Ralph J. Mills, Jr., ed., *Selected Letters of Theodore Roethke* (Seattle: University of Washington Press, 1968), 102, 132. Roethke describes his background and love of greenhouses, which his Prussian grandfather and father perpetuated in America, in "An American Poet Introduces Himself and His Poems," in Ralph J. Mills, Jr., ed., *On the Poet and His Craft: Selected Prose of Theodore Roethke* (Seattle: University of Washington Press, 1965), 7–13.

5. Mills, Jr., ed., *Selected Letters of Theodore Roethke*, 134, 144. Of course Seattle would later shed its provincialism in spades, becoming by the '80s a much sought-after place to live and work intellectually. See on this, Sanford Pinsker, *Three Pacific Northwest Poets: William Stafford, Richard Hugo, and David Wagoner* (Boston: Twayne Publishers, 1987), ch. 1.

6. Donald Stauffer (*A Short History of American Poetry* [New York: Dutton, 1974], 359–64) manages to review Roethke's life with no mention of place beyond his childhood in Michigan. But more thorough accounts have shown the great fecundity of Roethke's University of Washington period in Seattle. Preeminent among them is Don Bogen's *Theodore Roethke and the Writing Process* (Athens: Ohio University Press, 1991)—Bogen having immersed himself in the sprawling trove of Roethke's papers housed at the University of Washington. A readable biography, by a novelist who knew him well is Allan Seager, *The Glass House: The Life of Theodore Roethke* (Ann Arbor: University of Michigan Press, 1991, originally published 1968). See also, among others, Richard Allen Blessing, *Theodore Roethke's Dynamic Vision* (Bloomington: Indiana University Press, 1974) by a University of Washington professor who sought out colleagues familiar with Roethke, as well as his former students; Jay Parini, *Theodore Roethke: An American Romantic* (Amherst: University of Massachusetts Press, 1979), arguing for a lineage in the poet going back to Emerson; George Wolff, *Theodore Roethke* (Boston: Twayne Publishers, 1981); Neal Bowers, *Theodore Roethke: The Journey from I to Otherwise* (Columbia: University of Missouri Press, 1982), plumping for the mystical (and less environmental) in Roethke; and Harry Williams, *"The Edge is What I Have": Theodore Roethke and After* (Lewisburg, PA: Bucknell University Press, 1977), showing Roethke's influence on Sylvia Plath, James Dickey, Robert Bly, etc. In the Northwest, especially at University of Washington, he was a more direct shaper of poets, certainly demanding, but also encouraging them to be themselves. The poet Tess Gallagher, then teetering in different directions, declared that Roethke "changed my life..." when she fortuitously was able to enroll in his class during the spring of 1963, just months before his death. Quoted in Nicholas O'Connell, *At the Field's End: Interviews with Twenty Pacific Northwest Writers* (Seattle: Madrona Publishers, 1987), 161–162.

7. See typical lines in Theodore Roethke, "The Long Waters," in Roethke, *The Far Field* (Garden City, NY: Doubleday, 1964), 23–24, and "The Rose," in *ibid.*, 29–31.

8. Among others, William Martz discusses these awards in his *The Achievement of Theodore Roethke* (Glenview, IL: Scott Foreman, 1966).

9. For interpretation see books noted above, and among others, Karl Malkoff's stimulating *Theodore Roethke* (New York: Columbia University Press, 1960).

10. See Roethke, "The Marrow," in Roethke, *Far Field*, 89. See also poems like his "Prayer," from an early collection, *Open House*, in Roethke, *The Collected Poems of Theodore Roethke* (Garden City, NY: Doubleday, 1966), 8. The Roethke quotation here is from his "On 'Identity,'" in Mills, Jr., ed., *On the Poet and His Craft*, 26.

11. Carolyn Kizer, "Poetry: School of the Pacific Northwest," *The New Republic* 135 (July 16, 1956): 18–19. On the Northwest artists mentioned we have benefited from Sheryl Conkelton and Laura Landau, *Northwest Mythologies: The Interactions of Mark Tobey, Morris Graves, Kenneth Callahan, and Guy Anderson* (Tacoma and Seattle: Tacoma Art Museum and University of Washington Press, 2003).

12. Robin Skelton, ed., *Five Poets of the Pacific Northwest* (Seattle: University of Washington Press, 1964).

13. In Richard Howard's *Alone with America* (New York: Atheneum, 1969). They were Hugo, Kizer, Snyder, Stafford, and Wagoner. Authors were not chosen by region. Since some 3 percent of the population was Northwestern, even if we admit to regional overlap this is two to three times the expected representation.

14. See the first three poems cited in David Wagoner, *New and Selected Poems* (Bloomington: Indiana University Press, 1969), 32, 81, 175. "Elegy for a Forest Clear-Cut by the Weyerhaeuser Company" is in Wagoner, *Collected Poems 1956–1976* (Bloomington: Indiana University Press, 1976), 228. He discusses Roethke's influence in an interview appearing in O'Connell's *At the Field's End* (43). During Wagoner's initial years at Washington, Roethke remained the "trailblazer," says Sanford Pinsker in *Three Northwest Poets* (127). On Wagoner and the Northwest environment, see Ronald E. McFarland, "David Wagoner's Environmental Advocacy," *Rocky Mountain Review of Language and Literature* 44 (1990): 7–16. The best, most readable book on Wagner's development, especially in the Northwest, is Ron McFarland, *The World of David Wagoner* (Moscow: University of Idaho Press, 1997). See also his *David Wagoner* (Boise: Boise State University, 1989) in the Boise State University Western Writers Series. There he cites another of Wagoner's well-known views, that as soon as he saw this effulgent region, he was "no longer a Middle Westerner." In *ibid.*, 5.

15. See lines in Hugo, "Orcas in the Eyes," in his book *A Run of Jacks* (Minneapolis: University of Minnesota Press, 1961), 65. (The poem is also in a useful collection, Richard Hugo, *Making Certain It Goes On: The Collected Poems of Richard Hugo* [New York: W.W. Norton, 1984], 49–50.) On Hugo's sense of place and his poetry, see more generally, his important essay "The Triggering Town," in Hugo, *The Triggering Town: Lectures and Essays on Poetry and Writing* (New York: W.W. Norton, 1979), 11–18.

16. See Mary McCarthy, *Memories of a Catholic Girlhood* (New York: Harcourt, Brace, 1957). On Hugo's childhood, in addition to his own memoir material in Hugo, *The Real West Marginal Way: A Poet's Autobiography* (New York: W.W. Norton, 1986), see Jonathan Holden, *Landscapes of the Self: The Development of Richard Hugo's Poetry* (Milwood, NY: Associated Faculty Press, 1986), 6–21.

17. See relevant parts of "Dixon" in Hugo, *The Lady in Kicking Horse Reservoir* (New York: W. W. Norton, 1973), 73, and "Degrees of Gray in Philipsburg," in *ibid.*, 78 (also in Hugo, *Making Certain It Goes On*, 213, 216).

18. See Hugo, "Assumptions," *Northwest Review* 14 (1975): 75–80, also in Hugo, *The Triggering Town*, 19–25. On Hugo's life and work, in addition to his *West Marginal Way* and Holden's, *Landscapes of the Self*, see Michael S. Allen, *We Are Called Human: The Poetry of Richard Hugo* (Fayetteville: University of Arkansas Press, 1982), and Donna Gerstenberger, *Richard Hugo* (Boise: Boise State University Printing, 1983)—in the Boise State Western Writers Series. See also the tribute to him by fellow poet William Stafford, after Hugo passed away in 1982: "Among the poets, even though he was one of the most approachable of people, he was regarded with awe: he had been a technical writer for Boeing; he had played baseball; he had drunk with many a hearty companion, and caught fish in streams with wonderful names. And his poems delivered, with accuracy and fervor, those parts of his life." In Stafford, *Crossing Unmarked Snow: Further Views on the Writer's Vocation* (Ann Arbor: University of Michigan Press, 1998), 61.

19. For our era under discussion, see Kenneth O. Hanson's poetry collections *The Distance Anywhere* (Seattle: University of Washington Press, 1967) and *The Uncorrected World* (Middletown, CT: Wesleyan University Press, 1973). And for Oriental influences, see his collection *Growing Old Alive: Poems by Han Yü* (Port Townsend, WA: Copper Canyon Press, 1978). These are "versions" by Hanson, beautifully done. For Carolyn Kizer, in addition to her work in *Five Northwest Poets*, see, for example, Kizer, *Knock Upon Silence: Poems* (Seattle: University of Washington Press, 1968), and *Midnight Was My Cry: New and Selected Poems* (Garden City, NY: Doubleday, 1971) for our period treated here; and especially, her more recent collection spanning those years, *Cool, Calm and Collected: Poems 1960–2000* (Port Townsend, WA: Copper Canyon Press, 2001). In her interview with O'Connell in *At the Field's End* she called her translations from Chinese a big influence on her work (97), but yet again, also recalled Roethke as a teacher: "He made a serious writer out of me" (100). She also saluted Tobey and Graves as part of a supportive, sustaining Northwest artistic group.

20. In Kizer, "A Month in Summer," in *Knock Upon Silence*, 34. Poems like "The Intruder" also concern her mother (in Kizer, *Cool, Calm and Collected*, 6). A long piece on her background gives much space to her mother, but also to her father's tribulations, including with health problems, finding employment, and the like. See Kizer, "The Stories of My Life," in Kizer, *Proses: On Poems and Poets* (Port Townsend, WA: Copper Canyon Press, 1993), 1–39.

21. See Kizer, "A Month in Summer," *Knock Upon Silence*, 17–38 (*passim*).

22. See lines on Spokane in *ibid.*, 3, 25. Kizer also writes unflatteringly about that city in "Running Away from Home," in *Cool, Calm and Collected*, 181, a poem from the '70s. See as well on both her frustration in Spokane, and her mother's, Barbara Thompson's *Paris Review* interview of Kizer (Spring 2000) in Annie Finch, Johanna Keller and Candace McClelland, eds., *Carolyn Kizer: Perspectives on Her Life and Work* (Fort Lee, NJ: CavanKerry Press, 2001), 197. Kizer's zest for translation—both her own and others'—is evident in her collection *Carrying Over: Poems from the Chinese, Urdu, Macedonian, Yiddish, and French African* (Port Townsend, WA: Copper Canyon Press, 1988).

23. See Timothy Gray, *Gary Snyder and the Pacific Rim: Creating Counter-Cultural Community* (Iowa City: University of Iowa Press, 2006), ch. 1 ("Migrating: Exploring the Creaturely Byways of the Pacific Northwest"); Patrick D. Murphy, *A Place for Wayfaring: The Poetry and Prose of Gary Snyder* (Corvallis: Oregon State University Press, 2000), ch. 1; and reminiscences in Jon Halper, ed., *Gary Snyder: Dimensions of a Life* (San Francisco: Sierra Club Books, 1991), quotations 7, 13, 19, 28. Snyder dedicated an early collection of 1960, *Myths and Texts*, to two of his Reed College professors, and included a long poem there drawing on his logging experience. See Snyder, *Myths and Texts* (New York: New Directions paperback edition, 1978)—the poem is on 3–15.

24. Baker quote in Halper, ed., *Gary Snyder: Dimensions of a Life*, 46–47. (His italics.) For representative Snyder work in the era we cover here, see Snyder, *Riprap and Cold Mountain Poems* (San Francisco: Four Seasons, 1966); *Earth House Hold* (New York: New Directions, 1969); and *Turtle Island* (New York: New Directions, 1974), which brought him into the derided mainstream with a 1975 Pulitzer Prize for poetry. The latter collection includes "Control Burn," on Indian use of fire to manage forests. A more recent collection with excerpts from those earlier books is Gary Snyder, *The Gary Snyder Reader: Prose, Poetry, and Translations 1952–1998* (Washington, D.C.: Counterpoint, 1999). For interpretations of his work, see in addition to Murphy, *A Place for Wayfaring*, the older work of Bob Steuding, *Gary Snyder* (Boston: Twayne Publishers, 1976), Stauffer, *A Short History of American Poetry*, 392–427, and Howard, *Alone with America*, 483–498, among other book titles. There are also numerous articles interpreting aspects of Snyder; for example, Timothy G. Gray, "Semiotic Shepherds: Gary Snyder, Frank O'Hara, and the Embodiment of an Urban Pastoral," *Contemporary Literature* 39 (1998): 523–559; James I. McClintock, "Gary Snyder's Poetry and Ecological Sciences," *The American Biology Teacher* 54 (1992): 80–83; and Tim Dean, "The Other's Voice: Cultural Imperialism and Poetic Impersonality in Gary Snyder's 'Mountains and Rivers Without End,'" *Contemporary Literature* 41 (2000): 462–494. He also figures in more general articles on the influence of the Northwestern environment, such as Dan Flores, "Place: An Argument for Bioregional History," *Environmental History Review* 18 (1994): 1–18.

25. *Northwest Review* 14 (1975).

26. For secondary sources on Stafford see, among others, Jonathan Holden, *The Mark to Turn: A Reading of William Stafford's Poetry* (Lawrence: The University Press of Kansas, 1976); a more useful book by Judith Kitchen, *Understanding William Stafford* (Columbia: University of South Carolina Press, 1989); Howard, *Alone with America*, 499–506 (a quite unusual view); Richard Hugo, "Problems with Landscapes in Early Stafford Poems," *Kansas Quarterly* 2 (1970): 33–38; and especially, a fine collection of reviews and articles on Stafford's work in Tom Andrews, ed., *On William Stafford: The Worth of Local Things* (Ann Arbor: The University of Michigan Press, 1993), including Hugo's "Problems with Landscapes in Early Stafford Poems," arguing that Stafford's Kansas past came easier to him in his poetry to 1970; and that his Northwest situations didn't seem to work quite as well. There were many interviews of Stafford in the period we treat, especially by the '70s; for example, Cynthia Lofsness, "An Interview with William Stafford," *Iowa Review* 3 (1972), as well as in the issue of *Northwest Review* 13 (1973) devoted to Stafford, and noted below. His memoir of conscientious objection in camps during World War II, working on conservation projects and the like, is *Down in My Heart*, first published in 1947, and with a second edition appearing in the '80s [Columbia, SC: The Bench Press, 1985].

27. See typical lines on this in William Stafford, "Father's Voice," in Stafford, *Allegiances* (New York: Harper and Row, 1970), 12.

28. See the searing lines on his father's search for a simple life that in its complexity and demands eluded him in Stafford, "Parentage," in Stafford, *Traveling Through the Dark* (New York: Harper and Row, 1962), 20. The poem is definitely ambivalent, but Stafford is less oblique in his reminiscent poem, "A Walk With My Father When I Was Eight," in Stafford, *Smoke's Way: Poems from Limited Editions 1968–1981* (Port Townsend, WA: Graywolf Press, 1983), 22.

29. Quoted in "The Third Time the World Happens: a Dialogue Between William Stafford and Richard Hugo," in *Northwest Review* 13 (1973), 32.

30. Among other places the poem is in Stafford, *Traveling Through the Dark*, 11. C.f. Peter Stitt's view: "Despite his preference for the natural world over the world of the city, William Stafford is not a traditional nature poet, one whose chief goal is to describe and venerate nature. He is instead a wisdom poet.... Thus, in those poems mentioned above wherein nature's power to destroy is emphasized, the lesson is one of humility for mankind...." Stitt, "William Stafford's Wilderness Quest," in Andrews, ed., *On William Stafford*, 175.

31. In Stafford, *Allegiances*, 74.

32. In *ibid.*, 4.

33. See in Stafford, *Someday, Maybe* (New York: Harper and Row, 1973) "An Introduction to Some Poems," 2, "In a Time of Need," 25, and "Friend," 33. A good sample of his explications on the writing process and life is in Stafford, *Writing the Australian Crawl: Views on the Writer's Vocation* (Ann Arbor: University of Michigan Press, 1978).

34. Stafford, "A Story That Could Be True," *Northwest Review* 13 (1973): 82, and also in Stafford's collection *Stories That Could Be True: New and Collected Poems* (New York: Harper and Row, 1977), 4. Some of the poems in this collection (both early and contemporary) certainly revealed a Northwestern historical consciousness in the author, such as "The Tillamook Burn" (73) or "In the Oregon Country" (37).

35. In Stafford, "Having Become a Writer: Some Reflections," *Northwest Review* 13 (1973), 91. An odd little poem of Stafford's is entitled "Learning Your Place," in Stafford, *Things That Happen Where There Aren't Any People: Poems by William Stafford* (Brockport, NY: BOA Editions, 1980), 18.

36. In Stafford, *Traveling Through the Dark*, 50.

37. From an essay in Stafford, *Crossing Unmarked Snow*, 3.

38. Stafford, "In Dear Detail, by Ideal Light," in Stafford, *Traveling Through the Dark*, 91–92.

39. The poem is in *ibid.*, 71. This reminds us of Hugo's ambivalent, poetic lines on the San Juans, where he thinks about having a house on his own island, and at the same time, worries about becoming both *too* isolated, and *too* comfortable. See Hugo, "The Anacortes-Sydney Run," in his *Death of the Kapowsin Tavern* (New York: Harcourt, Brace, 1965), 22 (also in Hugo, *Making Certain It Goes On*, 74).

Bibliography

Abbott, Carl. "Regional City and Network City: Portland and Seattle in the Twentieth Century." *The Western Historical Quarterly* 23 (1992): 293–322.

Allen, Edward W. Review of *The Dry Years*, by Norman H. Clark. *Pacific Northwest Quarterly* 56 (1965): 176–177.

Allen, Michael. *Rodeo Cowboys in the North American Imagination*. Reno: University of Nevada Press, 1998.

_____. *Western Rivermen, 1763–1861: Ohio and Mississippi Boatmen and the Myth of the Alligator Horse*. Baton Rouge: Louisiana State University Press, 1990.

Allen, Michael S. *We Are Called Human: The Poetry of Richard Hugo*. Fayetteville: University of Arkansas Press, 1982.

Andrews, Tom, ed. *On William Stafford: The Worth of Local Things*. Ann Arbor: University of Michigan Press, 1993.

Applegate, Jesse. *A Day with the Cow Column in 1843*. Chicago: Caxton Club, 1934.

_____. *Recollections of My Boyhood*. Chicago: Caxton Club, 1934.

Armitage, Susan H. "From the Inside Out: Rewriting Regional History." *Frontiers: A Journal of Women Studies* 22 (2001): 32–47.

Aron, Stephen. "Lessons in Conquest: Towards a Greater Western History." *The Pacific Historical Review* 63 (1994): 125–147.

Arrowsmith, William. "Speech of Chief Seattle." *Seattle Star* 5 (1887).

Bailyn, Bernard. *The Ordeal of Thomas Hutchinson*. Cambridge, MA: Belknap Press of Harvard University Press, 1974.

Bain, Robert. *H. L. Davis*. Boise: Boise State University Printing, 1974.

Baker, Jeff. Review of *Trask*, by Don Berry. *Portland Oregonian*. Corvallis: Oregon State University Press, 2004.

Balch, F. H. *The Bridge of the Gods: A Romance of Indian Oregon*. Chicago: A. C. McClurg and Company, 1890.

_____. *Genevieve: A Tale of Oregon*. Portland: Metropolitan, 1932.

_____. *Memaloose: Three Poems and Two Prose Sketches*. Portland: M. Ricketts and T. Binford, 1934.

Ballou, Robert. *Early Klickitat Valley Days*. Goldendale, WA: The Goldendale Sentinel, 1938.

Bancroft, H. H. *History of Oregon*. Vols. 1, 2. San Francisco: The History Company, 1886–1888.

_____. *History of the Pacific States of North America, XXXIV*. Literary Industries. San Francisco: A.L. Bancroft, 1890.

_____, and F. Victor. *History of the Northwest Coast*. Vol. 2. San Francisco: A.L. Bancroft, 1886.

Banner, Stuart. *Possessing the Pacific: Land, Settlers, and Indigenous People from Australia to Alaska*. Cambridge, MA: Harvard University Press, 2007.

Barker, Burt Brown. *The McLoughlin Empire and its Rulers*. Glendale, CA: Arthur Clark, 1959.

Barman, Jean, and Bruce McIntyre Watson. *Paradise: Indigenous Hawaiians in the Pacific Northwest, 1787–1898*. Honolulu: University of Hawaii Press, 2006.

Baskin, Alex. *John Reed: The Early Years in Greenwich Village*. New York: Archives of History, 1990.

Bates, Henry L. Pacific University. *Oregon Historical Quarterly* 21 (1920): 1–12.

Beckham, Stephen Dow. *Requiem for a People*. Norman: University of Oklahoma Press, 1971.

Berry, Don. *Moontrap*. New York: Viking Press, 1962.

_____. *Trask.* New York: Viking Press, 1960.

Bingham, Edwin R. *Charles Erskine Scott Wood.* Boise: Boise State University Printing, 1990.

_____. "Oregon's Romantic Rebels: John Reed and Charles Erskine Scott Wood." *Pacific Northwest Quarterly* 50 (1959): 77–90.

_____. Review of *Trask* (and *Moontrap* and *To Build a Ship*), by Don Berry. *Oregon Historical Quarterly* 45 (1964): 406–441.

_____, and Glen A. Love, eds. *Northwest Perspectives: Essays on the Culture of the Pacific Northwest.* Seattle: University of Washington Press, 1979.

_____, and Tim Barnes, eds. *Wood Works: The Life and Writings of Charles Erskine Scott Wood.* Corvallis: Oregon State University Press, 1997.

Binns, John. "Northwest Region—Fact or Fiction?" *Pacific Northwest Quarterly* 48 (1957): 65–75.

Blair, Karen J. "The State of Research on Pacific Northwest Women." *Frontiers: A Journal of Women Studies* 22 (2001): 48–56.

Blessing, Richard Allen. *Theodore Roethke's Dynamic Vision.* Bloomington: Indiana University Press, 1974.

Bogen, Don. *Theodore Roethke and the Writing Process.* Athens: Ohio University Press, 1991.

Boorstin, Daniel. *The Americans: The Colonial Experience.* New York: Random House, 1958.

_____. *The Americans: The Democratic Experience.* New York: Random House, 1973.

Booth, Brian, ed. *Wildmen, Wobblies and Whistle Punks: Stewart Holbrook's Lowbrow Northwest.* Corvallis: Oregon State University Press, 1992.

Bourne, Edward G. "The Legend of Marcus Whitman." *American Historical Review* 6 (1901): 276–300.

Bowers, Neal. *Theodore Roethke: The Journey from I to Otherwise.* Columbia: University of Missouri Press, 1982.

Boyd, Robert, ed. *Indians, Fire, and the Land in the Pacific Northwest.* Corvallis: Oregon State University Press, 1999.

Braly, David. *Crooked River Country: Wranglers, Rogues, and Barons.* Pullman: Washington State University Press, 2007.

Briley, Ann. "Hiram F. Smith, First Settler of Okanogan Country." *Pacific Northwest Quarterly* 43 (1952): 226–233.

Brooks, Van Wyck. *The Confident Years: 1885–1915.* New York: E. P. Dutton & Company, Inc., 1952.

Brosnan, Cornelius. *Jason Lee: Prophet of the New Oregon.* New York: Macmillan, 1932.

Browne, Sheri Bartlett. *Eva Emery Dye: Romance with the West.* Corvallis: Oregon State University Press, 2004.

Brunvand, Jan. "Honey in the Horn and Acres of Clams: The Regional Fiction of H. L. Davis." *Western American Literature* 2 (1967): 135–45.

Bryant, Paul. *H. L. Davis.* Boston: Twayne Publishers, 1978.

_____. "H. L. Davis: Viable Uses for the Past." *Western American Literature* 3 (1968): 3–18.

Bunting, Robert. The Environment and Settler Society in Western Oregon. *The Pacific Historical Review* 64 (1995): 413–432.

_____. *The Pacific Raincoast: Environment and Culture in an American Eden, 1778–1900.* Lawrence: University Press of Kansas, 1997.

Cantwell, Robert. *The Hidden Northwest.* Philadelphia: Lippincott, 1972.

Cappell, Letitia. "A Biography of Abigail Scott Duniway." M.A. thesis, University of Oregon, 1934.

Carlson, Linda. *Company Towns of the Pacific Northwest.* Seattle: University of Washington Press, 2003.

Case, Victoria. *The Quiet Life of Mrs. General Lane.* Garden City, NY: Doubleday, 1952.

Caughey, John W. "Historians' Choice: Results of a Poll on Recently Published American History and Biography." *Mississippi Valley Historical Review* 39 (1952): 280–302.

_____. *Hubert Howe Bancroft: Historian of the West.* Berkeley: University of California Press, 1946.

Chittenden, Elizabeth F. "By No Means Excluding Women: Abigail Scott Duniway, Western Pioneer in the Struggle for Equal Voting Rights." In *The Northwest Mosaic*, edited by James R. Halseth and Bruce R. Glasrud. Boulder, CO: Pruett Publishing Co., 1977, 191–196.

Chittick, Victor Lovitt Oakes, ed. *Northwest Harvest: A Regional Stock-Taking.* New York: Macmillan, 1948.

Clare, Warren. "James Stevens: The Laborer and Literature." *Research Studies* 4 (1964): 355–67.

_____. "Poseurs, Parasites and Pismires." *Pacific Northwest Quarterly* 61 (1970): 22–30.

Clark, Ella E. *Indian Legends of the Pacific Northwest.* Berkeley: University of California Press, 1969.

Clark, Norman H. *The Dry Years.* Seattle: University of Washington Press, 1965.

_____. *Mill Town.* Seattle: University of Washington Press, 1970.

_____. *Washington, a Bicentennial History.* New York: Norton, 1976.

Clark, Robert. *River of the West: Stories from the Columbia.* New York: HarperCollins, 1995.

Clarke, Samuel A. *Pioneer Days of Oregon History.* 2 vols. Portland: J. K. Gill, 1905.

_____. *Sounds by the Western Sea*. Salem, OR: Clarke and Craig, 1872.

Cleman, J. "The Belated Frontier: H. L. Davis and the Problem of Pacific Northwest Regionalism." *Western American Literature* 37 (2003): 431–51.

Cline, Gloria Griffen. *Peter Skene Ogden and the Hudson's Bay Company*. Norman: University of Oklahoma Press, 1974.

Cloud, Barbara. "The Press and Profit: Newspaper Survival in Washington Territory." *Pacific Northwest Quarterly* 79 (1988): 147–156.

Coleman, Jon T. "The Men in McArthur's Bar: the Cultural Significance of the Margins." *Western Historical Quarterly* 31 (2000): 47–68.

Collins, Cary C. and Charles V. Mutschler. "Great Spirits: Ruby and Brown, Pioneering Historians of the Indians of the Pacific Northwest." *Pacific Northwest Quarterly* 95 (2004): 126–129.

Colson, Elizabeth. *The Makah Indians*. Minneapolis: University of Minnesota Press, 1953.

Conkelton, Sheryl, and Laura Landau. *Northwest Mythologies: The Interactions of Mark Tobey, Morris Graves, Kenneth Callahan, and Guy Anderson*. Seattle: University of Washington Press, 2003.

Coon, Delia. "Frederick Homer Balch." *Washington Historical Quarterly* 1 (1924): 32–42.

Corning, Howard McKinley. "All the Words on the Pages, I: H. L. Davis." *Oregon Historical Quarterly* 73 (1972): 293–331.

_____. *The Mountain in the Sky*. Portland: Metropolitan Press, 1930.

Cressman, L. S. *The Sandal and the Cave*. Portland: Beaver, 1962.

Critchfield, Howard J., ed. *Pacific Northwest Essays in Honor of James W. Scott*. Bellingham: Western Washington University, 1993.

Cronon, William. *Changes in the Land: Indians, Colonists, and the Ecology of New England*. New York: Hill and Wang, 1983.

Daily Oregon Statesman, June 16, 1895.

Dary, David. *Frontier Medicine: From the Atlantic to the Pacific, 1492–1941*. New York: Knopf, 2008.

Davenport, Homer. *The Country Boy*. New York: Dillingham, 1910.

Davies, John, ed. *Douglas of the Forests: The North American Journals of David Douglas*. Edinburgh: Paul Harris Publishing, 1979.

Davis, H. L. *Beulah Land*. New York: Morrow, 1949.

_____. *Honey in the Horn*. New York: Harper & Brothers, 1935.

_____. *Kettle of Fire*. New York: Morrow, 1959.

_____. *Proud Riders and Other Poems*. New York: Harper and Bros., 1942.

_____. "Status Rerum Allegro Ma Non Troppo." *Frontier* 8 (1928): 70.

_____. *Team Bells Woke Me and Other Stories*. New York: Morrow, 1953.

_____. *Winds of Morning*. New York: Morrow, 1952.

Dean, Tim." The Other's Voice: Cultural Imperialism and Poetic Impersonality in Gary Snyder's Mountains and Rivers without End." *Contemporary Literature* 41 (2000): 462–494.

Dearborn, Mary V. *Queen of Bohemia: The Life of Louise Bryant*. Boston: Houghton Mifflin, 1996.

Dietrich, William. *The Final Forest: The Battle for the Last Great Trees of the Pacific Northwest*. New York: Simon and Schuster, 1992.

_____. *Natural Grace: The Charm, Wonder, and Lessons of Pacific Northwest Animals and Plants*. Seattle: University of Washington Press, 2003.

_____. *Northwest Passage: The Great Columbia River*. New York: Simon and Schuster, 1995.

Dodds, Gordon B. *The American Northwest: A History of Oregon and Washington*. Arlington Heights, IL: The Forum Press, 1986.

Donald, Leland. *Aboriginal Slavery on the Northwest Coast of North America*. Berkeley: University of California Press, 1997.

Douglas, George H. "Alfred Kazin: American Critic." *Colorado Quarterly* 23 (1974): 203–216.

Douglas, William. *Go East Young Man*. New York: Random House, 1974.

_____. *Of Men and Mountains*. New York: Harper and Row, 1950.

Douthit, Nathan. "Joseph Lane and the Rogue Indians: Personal Relations Across a Cultural Divide." *Oregon Historical Quarterly* 95 (1994-5): 472–515.

Drucker, Philip. *Cultures of the North Pacific Coast*. San Francisco: Chandler, 1965.

_____. *Indians of the Northwest Coast*. New York: McGraw-Hill, 1955.

Drury, Clifford M. *Marcus Whitman, M.D.: Pioneer and Martyr*. Caldwell, ID: Caxton Printers, 1937.

Duke, David C. "Anna Louise Strong and the Search for a Good Cause." *Pacific Northwest Quarterly* 66 (1975): 123–137.

_____. *John Reed*. Boston: Twayne Publishers, 1987.

Duniway, Abigail Scott. *David and Anna Matson*. New York: S. R. Wells, 1876.

_____. *From the West to the West: Across the Plains to Oregon*. Chicago: A.C. McClurg, 1905.

_____. *Pathbreaking: An Autobiographical History of the Equal Suffrage Movement in Pacific Coast States*, 2nd ed. Portland: James, Kerns and Abbot, 1914.

Dunlap, Leslie W. "The Oregon Free Press." *Pacific Northwest Quarterly* 33 (1942): 171–185.

Dye, Eva Emery. *McLoughlin and Old Oregon*. Chicago: A. C. McClurg and Co., 1900.

Eby, E. H. "Vernon L. Parrington: The Style of the Man." *Tyee Magazine* 1 (1966): 2–4.

Etulain, Richard. *Ernest Haycox*. Boise: Boise State University Printing, 1988.

_____. "Ernest Haycox: The Historical Western, 1937–43." *South Dakota Review* 5 (1967): 35–54.

_____. "Inventing the Pacific Northwest: Novelists and the Region's History." In *Terra Pacifica: People and Place in the Northwest States and Western Canada*, edited by Paul W. Hirt. Pullman: Washington State University Press, 1998.

_____. "The New Western Novel." *Idaho Yesterdays* 15 (1972): 17.

_____. "Novelists of the Northwest: Needs and Opportunities for Research." *Idaho Yesterdays* 16 (1973): 24–32.

_____, and Michael P. Malone. *The American West: A Twentieth-Century History*. Lincoln: University of Nebraska Press, 1989.

Evans, Elwood. *History of the Pacific Northwest*. 2 vols. Portland: North Pacific History Company, 1889.

Ficken, Robert E. *Washington State: The Inaugural Decade 1889–1899*. Pullman: Washington State University Press, 2007.

_____. *Washington Territory*. Pullman: Washington State University Press, 2002.

_____, and Charles P. LeWarne. *Washington: A Centennial History*. Seattle: University of Washington Press, 1988.

Fiedler, Leslie. *The Return of the Vanishing American*. New York: Stein and Day, 1968.

Finch, Annie, Johanna Keller and Candace McClelland, eds. *Carolyn Kizer: Perspectives on Her Life and Work*. Fort Lee, NJ: CavanKerry Press, 2001.

Findlay, John M. "Something in the Soil? Literature and Regional Identity in the 20th-Century Pacific Northwest." *Pacific Northwest Quarterly* 97 (2006): 79–89.

Flores, Dan. "Place: An Argument for Bioregional History." *Environmental History Review* 18 (1994): 1–18.

Floyd-Wilson, Mary. "Poetic Empathy: Theodore Roethke's Conception of Woman in the Love Poems." *South Atlantic Review* 56 (1991): 61–78.

Foley, Barbara. "Women and the Left in the 1930s." *American Literary History* 2 (1990): 150–169.

Foster, John Wilson. "Hustling to Some Purpose: Kesey's *One Flew Over the Cuckoo's Nest*." *Western American Literature* 9 (1974): 115–130.

French, David. "Wasco–Wishram." In *Perspectives in American Indian Culture Change*, edited by Edward Spicer. Chicago: University of Chicago Press, 1961.

Frost, O. W. *Joaquin Miller*. New York: Twayne Publishers, 1967.

Frykman, George A. *Seattle's Historian and Promoter: The Life of Edmond Stephen Meany*. Pullman: Washington State University Press, 1998.

Fujita-Rony, Dorothy B. *American Workers, Colonial Power: Philippine Seattle and the Transpacific West, 1919–1941*. Berkeley: University of California Press, 2003.

Fuller, Ethel Romig. *Kitchen Sonnets*. Portland: Metropolitan Press, 1931.

_____. *Skylines*. Portland: Binfords and Mort, 1952.

Fuller, George. *A History of the Pacific Northwest*. New York: Alfred Knopf, 1958.

Furtwangler, Albert. *Answering Chief Seattle*. Seattle: University of Washington Press, 1997.

_____. *Bringing Indians to the Book*. Seattle: University of Washington Press, 2005.

_____. "Reclaiming Jefferson's Ideals: Abigail Scott Duniway's Ode to Lewis and Clark." *Pacific Northwest Quarterly* 98 (2007): 159–167.

Gardner, Virginia. *Friend and Lover: The Life of Louise Bryant*. New York: Horizon Press, 1982.

Garland, Hamlin. *A Son of the Middle Border*. New York: Macmillan, 1952.

Garrison, Phillip. *Because I Don't Have Wings: Stories of Mexican Immigrant Life*. Tucson: The University of Arizona Press, 2006.

Garth, Thomas P. "A Report on Second Season's Excavations at Waiilatpu." *Pacific Northwest Quarterly* 43 (1949): 295–315.

Gastil, Raymond D. "Beyond a Theory of Justice." *Ethics* 85 (1975): 183–194.

_____. *Cultural Regions of the United States*. Seattle: University of Washington Press, 1975.

_____. "Lower Class Behaviour: Cultural and Biosocial." *Human Organization* 32 (1973): 349–362.

_____. "The Pacific Northwest as a Cultural Region." *Pacific Northwest Quarterly* 64 (1973): 147–162.

Gaston, Joseph. *Portland, Its History and Builders*. 3 vols. Chicago: S. J. Clarke Publishing Co., 1911.

Gates, Charles, ed. *Readings in Pacific Northwest History*. Seattle: University of Washington Press, 1941.

Gelb, Barbara. *So Short a Time: A Biography of John Reed and Louise Bryant*. New York: Norton, 1973.

George, Suzanne K. "Abigail Scott Duniway." In

By Grit and Grace: Eleven Women Who Shaped the American West, edited by Glenda Riley and Richard W. Etulain. Golden: Fulcrum Publishing, 1997.
Gerstenberger, Donna. *Richard Hugo*. Boise: Boise State University Printing, 1983.
Golay, Michael. *The Tide of Empire: America's March to the Pacific*. Hoboken, NJ: John Wiley and Sons, 2003.
Goldman, Eric F. J. "Allen Smith: The Reformer and his Dilemma." *Pacific Northwest Quarterly* 35 (1944): 201–209.
_____. *Rendezvous with Destiny: A History of American Reform*. New York: Vintage Edition, 1956.
Grant, Rene. "Chinook Jargon." *International Journal of American Linguistics* 11 (1945): 225–33.
Gray, Theresa, ed. *Life and Letters of Mrs. Jason Lee*. Vol. 1. Portland: Metropolitan Press, 1936.
Gray, Timothy. *Gary Snyder and the Pacific Rim: Creating Counter-Cultural Community*. Iowa City: University of Iowa Press, 2006.
Gray, W. H. *A History of Oregon*. Portland: Harris and Homan, 1870.
Greiner, Francis. "Voice of the West: Harold L. Davis." *Oregon Historical Quarterly* 66 (1965): 240–248.
Gressley, Gene M., ed. *Old West/New West*. Norman: University of Oklahoma Press, 1998.
Gribben, Bryn. "The Mother That Won't Reflect Back: Situating Psychoanalysis and the Japanese Mother in *No-no Boy*." *The Society for the Study of the Multi-Ethnic Literature of the United States* 28 (2003): 31–46.
Griffith, Thomas. *The Waist-High Culture*. New York: Harper and Bros., 1959.
Gunther, Erna. "The Indian Background of Washington History." *Pacific Northwest Quarterly* 54 (1963): 158–165.
Haeberlin, Herman and Erna Gunther. *The Indians of Puget Sound*. Seattle: University of Washington Press, 1930.
Hale, Horatio. *An International Idiom: A Manuel of the Oregon Trade Language, or "Chinook Jargon."* London: Whittaker, 1890.
Hall, H. Lark. *V.L. Parrington: Through the Avenue of Art*. Kent: The Kent State University Press, 1994.
Halper, Jon, ed. *Gary Snyder: Dimensions of a Life*. San Francisco: Sierra Club Books, 1991.
Halseth, James R. and Bruce R. Glasrud, eds. *The Northwest Mosaic*. Boulder, CO: Pruett Publishing Co., 1977.
Hamburger, Robert. *Two Rooms: The Life of Charles Erskine Scott Wood*. Lincoln: University of Nebraska Press, 1998.
Hanson, Kenneth O. *The Distance Anywhere*. Seattle: University of Washington Press, 1967.
_____. *Growing Old Alive: Poems by Han Yu*. Port Townsend, WA: Copper Canyon Press, 1978. (Versions by Kenneth O. Hanson)
_____. *The Uncorrected World*. Middle-town, CT: Wesleyan University Press, 1973.
Hardwick, Susan Wiley. *Russian Refuge: Religion, Migration, and Settlement on the North American Pacific Rim*. Chicago: University of Chicago Press, 1993.
Harmon, Alexandra. "Lines in Sand: Shifting Boundaries Between Indians and Non-Indians in the Puget Sound Region." *The Western Historical Quarterly* 26 (1995): 429–453.
Harrison, Joseph. *Vernon Louis Parrington: American Scholar*. Seattle: University of Washington Bookstore, 1929.
"Harvey W. Scott" issue. *The Quarterly of the Oregon Historical Society* 14 (1913) (articles 87–133, 133, 134–139, 140–204, 139, 205, 206–210).
Haycox, Ernest. *The Earthbreakers*. Boston: Little, Brown, 1952.
Haycox, Ernest, Jr. *On a Silver Desert: The Life of Ernest Haycox*. Norman: University of Oklahoma Press, 2003.
Heckman, Hazel. *Island in the Sound*. Seattle: University of Washington Press, 1967.
_____. *Island Year*, 2nd ed. Seattle: University of Washington Press, 1972.
Hendrickson, James. *Joe Lane of Oregon: Machine Politics and the Sectional Crisis, 1849–1861*. New Haven: Yale University Press, 1967.
Herskovic, Marika, ed. *American Abstract Expressionism of the 1950s: An Illustrated Survey With Artists' Statements, Artwork, and Biographies*. New York: New York School Press, 2003.
Hicks, Granville. *John Reed: The Making of a Revolutionary*. New York: Macmillan, 1936.
_____. *One of Us: The Story of John Reed*. New York: Equinox Cooperative Press, 1935.
Higginson, Ella. *Mariella of Out West*. New York: Macmillan, 1904.
Highsmith, Richard M., Jr., ed. *Atlas of the Pacific Northwest*. Corvallis: Oregon State University Press, 1968.
Hine, Robert V., and John Mack Faragher. *The American West: A New Interpretive History*. New Haven: Yale University Press, 2000.
Hirt, Paul W., ed. *Terra Pacifica: People and Place in the Northwest....* Pullman: Washington State University Press, 1998.
Hofstadter, Richard. "Parrington and the Jeffersonian Tradition." *Journal of the History of Ideas* 2 (1941): 391–400.
_____. *The Progressive Historians*. New York: Vintage edition, 1968.
Holbrook, Stewart H. *Far Corner*. New York: Macmillan, 1952.

_____. *Burning an Empire*. New York: Macmillan, 1943.

Holden, Jonathan. *Landscapes of the Self: The Development of Richard Hugo's Poetry*. Milwood, NY: Associated Faculty Press, 1986.

_____. *The Mark to Turn: A Reading of William Stafford's Poetry*. Lawrence: University Press of Kansas, 1976.

Homberger, Eric. *John Reed*. Manchester: Manchester University Press, 1990.

Howard, Richard. *Alone with America*. New York: Atheneum, 1969.

Hugo, Richard. *The Real West Marginal Way: A Poet's Autobiography*. New York: W. W. Norton, 1986.

_____. *Making Certain It Goes On: The Collected Poems of Richard Hugo*. New York: W.W. Norton, 1984.

_____. *The Triggering Town: Lectures and Essays on Poetry and Writing*. New York: W.W. Norton, 1979.

_____. "Assumptions." *Northwest Review* 14 (1975): 75–80.

_____. *The Lady in Kicking Horse Reservoir*. New York: W.W. Norton, 1973.

_____. "Problems with Landscapes in Early Stafford Poems." *Kansas Quarterly* 2 (1970): 33–38.

_____. *Death of the Kapowsin Tavern*. New York: Harcourt, Brace, 1965.

_____. *A Run of Jacks*. Minneapolis: University of Minnesota Press, 1961.

Hurtado, Alberto L. "Romancing the West in the Twentieth Century: The Politics of History in a Contested Region." *The Western Historical Quarterly* 32 (2001): 417–435.

Hynding, Alan. *The Public Life of Eugene Semple, Promoter and Politician of the Pacific Northwest*. Seattle: University of Washington Press, 1973.

In Memoriam: Rev. S. H. Marsh 1825–1879. Portland: Himes, 1881.

Irving, Washington. *Astoria*. Portland: Binfords and Mort, 1967.

Iverson, Peter. "Discoverers, Pioneers, and Settlers: Towards a More Inclusive History of the North American West." *The Western Historical Quarterly* 37 (2006): 5–19.

Jacobs, Melville. *The Content and Style of an Oral Literature*. Chicago: University of Chicago Press, 1959.

_____. "Notes on the Structure of Chinook Jargon." *Language* 8 (1932): 27–50.

Jacobs, Orange. *Memoirs of Orange Jacobs*. Seattle: Cowan and Hanford, 1908.

Johannsen, Robert W. *Frontier Politics and the Sectional Conflict: The Pacific Northwest on the Eve of the Civil War*. Seattle: University of Washington Press, 1955.

Johansen, Dorothy O. "A Working Hypothesis for the Study of Migrations." *Pacific Historical Review* 36 (1967): 1–12.

_____. "Capitalism on the Far-Western Frontier: The Oregon Steam Navigation Company." Ph.D. diss., University of Washington, 1941.

_____. "Mr. and Mrs. Simeon G. Reed." In *Reed College Pioneers*. *Reed College Bulletin*. Vol. 15. Portland: Reed College, 1931.

_____. Manuscript. History of Reed College, Portland, unpublished manuscript.

_____, and Charles M. Gates. *Empire of the Columbia*, 2nd ed. New York: Harper and Row, 1967.

Jonaitis, Aldona. *Art of the Northwest Coast*. Seattle: University of Washington Press, 2006.

Jonasson, Jonas A. *Bricks without Straw: The Story of Linfield College*. Caldwell, ID: Caxton, 1938.

Jones, Howard Mumford. *The Age of Energy: Varieties of American Experience 1865–1915*. New York: Viking Press, 1971.

Jones, Nard. *The Great Command*. Boston: Little, Brown, 1959.

_____. *Wheat Women*. New York: Duffield and Green, 1933.

Jones, Philip. "The West of H. L. Davis." *South Dakota Review* 6 (1968-9): 72–84.

Josephy, Alvin, Jr. *Nez Percé Country*. Lincoln: University of Nebraska Press, 2007.

_____. *The Nez Perce Indians and the Opening of the Northwest*. New Haven: Yale University Press, 1965.

_____, Joane Nagel and Troy Johnson, eds. *Red Power: The American Indians' Fight for Freedom*, 2nd ed. Lincoln: University of Nebraska Press, 1999.

Judson, Katherine B. "Dr. John McLoughlin's Last Letter to the Hudson's Bay Company, as Chief Factor, in Charge at Fort Vancouver, 1845." *American Historical Review* 21 (1915): 104–134.

Katz, W. A. "Public Printers of Washington Territory, 1853–1863." *Pacific Northwest Quarterly* 51 (1960): 103–114.

Kaufman, Scott. *The Pig War: The United States, Britain, and the Balance of Power in the Pacific Northwest, 1846–1872*. Lanham, MD: Lexington Books, 2004.

Kelley, M. Margaret Jean. *The Career of Joseph Lane, Frontier Politician*. Washington, DC: Catholic University of America Press, 1942.

Kesey, Ken. *Sometimes a Great Notion*, 2nd ed. New York: Bantam Books, 1965.

_____. *One Flew Over the Cuckoo's Nest*. New York: Viking, 1962.

Kessler, Lauren. "A Siege of the Citadels: Search for a Public Forum for the Ideas of Oregon Woman Suffrage." *Oregon Historical Quarterly* 84 (1983): 117–150.

Kich, Martin. *Western American Novelists*. New York: Garland Publishers, 1995.
King, Stoddard. *Grand Right and Left*. New York: George H. Doran Company, 1927.
_____. *What the Queen Said and Further Facetious Fragments*. New York: George H. Doran Company, 1926.
Kitchen, Judith. *Understanding William Stafford*. Columbia: University of South Carolina Press, 1989.
Kittredge, William. Review of Joaquin Miller, *Unwritten History, or My Life Among the Modocs*. *Northwest Review* 13 (1973): 80–82.
Kizer, Carolyn. *Carrying Over: Poems from the Chinese, Urdu, Macedonian, Yiddish, and French African*. Port Townsend, WA: Copper Canyon Press, 1988.
_____. *Cool, Calm and Collected: Poems 1960–2000*. Port Townsend, WA: Copper Canyon Press, 2001.
_____. *Knock Upon Silence: Poems*. Seattle: University of Washington Press, 1968.
_____. *Midnight Was My Cry: New and Selected Poems*. Garden City, NY: Doubleday, 1971.
_____. "Poetry: School of the Pacific Northwest." *The New Republic* 135 (1956): 18–19.
_____. *Proses: On Poems and Poets*. Port Townsend, WA: Copper Canyon Press, 1993.
Kowalewski, Michael. "Writing in Place: The New American Regionalism." *American Literary History* 6 (1994): 171–183.
Kramer, Hilton. "The Ghost of V. L. Parrington." *New Criterion* 13 (1994): 4–8.
Kuznets, Simon, and D. S. Thomas. *Population Redistribution and Economic Growth*. Philadelphia: American Philosophical Society, 1957, I.
Lalande, Jeff. "A 'Little Kansas' in Southern Oregon: The Course and Character of Populism in Jackson County, 1890–1900." *The Pacific Historical Review* 63 (1994): 149–176.
Landsman, Gail H. "The 'Other' as Political Symbol: Images of Indians in the Woman Suffrage Movement." *Ethnohistory* 39 (1992): 247–284.
Lane, Joseph, et al. *The Admission of Oregon: The Serenades, the Responses*. Washington, D.C.: L. Towers, 1859. In *Pacific Northwest Collection*, University of Washington Library.
Lang, William L. "The Columbia River's Fate in the Twentieth Century." *Montana: The Magazine of Western History* 50 (2000): 44–55.
_____. *Confederacy of Ambition: William Winlock Miller and the Making of Washington Territory*. Seattle: University of Washington Press, 1996.
_____, and Robert C. Carriker, eds. *Great River of the West: Essays on the Columbia River*. Seattle: University of Washington Press, 1999.
Lansing, Jewel. *Portland: People, Politics, and Power, 1851–2001*. Corvallis: Oregon State University Press, 2003.
Laurie, Clayton D. "The Chinese Must Go: The United States Army and the Anti-Chinese Riots in Washington Territory, 1885–1886." *Pacific Northwest Quarterly* 81 (1990): 22–29.
Lawson, Benjamin S. *Joaquin Miller*. Boise: Boise State University Printers, 1980.
Lehman, Daniel W. *John Reed and the Writing of Revolution*. Athens: Ohio University Press, 2002.
The Letters and Private Papers of Simeon Gannett Reed. Reed College Project, Division of Professional Service Projects, WPA. Portland: Reed College Library, 1940.
Levy, David W. "'I Became More Radical with Every Year': The Intellectual Odyssey of Vernon Louis Parrington." *American Quarterly* 23 (1995): 663–668.
Le Warne, Charles Pierce. *Utopias on Puget Sound: 1885–1915*. Seattle: University of Washington Press, 1975.
Limerick, Patricia Nelson. *The Legacy of Conquest: The Unbroken Past of the American West*, 2nd ed. New York: Norton Paperback, 2006.
Ling, Jingqi. "Race, Power, and Cultural Politics in John Okada's No-no Boy." *American Literature* 67 (1995): 359–381.
Lish, Gordon. "An Interview with Ken Kesey." *Genesis West* 2 (1963): 17–30.
Loewenberg, Robert J. *Equality on the Oregon Frontier: Jason Lee and the Methodist Mission 1834–43*. Seattle: University of Washington Press, 1976.
Lofsness, Cynthia. "An Interview with William Stafford." *Iowa Review* 3 (1972): 92–107.
Love, Glen. *Don Berry*. Boise: Boise State University Printing, 1978.
_____, ed. *Fishing the Northwest: An Angler's Reader*. Corvallis: Oregon State University Press, 2000.
Low, Denise. "Contemporary Reinvention of Chief Seattle: Variant Texts of Chief Seattle's 1854 Speech." *American Indian Quarterly* 19 (1995): 407–421.
Lundberg, George. *Can Science Save Us?* 2nd ed. New York: Longman's Green, 1961.
MacDonald, Betty. *The Egg and I*. Philadelphia: J.B. Lippincott, 1945.
Madden, David, ed. *Proletarian Writers of the Thirties*. Carbondale: Southern Illinois University Press, 1968.
Malamud, Bernard. *A New Life*, 2nd ed. New York: Farrar, Straus and Cudahy, 1968.
Malkoff, Karl. *Theodore Roethke*. New York: Columbia University Press, 1960.

Marberry, M. Marion. *Splendid Poseur: Joaquin Miller, American Poet*. New York: Thomas Y. Crowell, 1953.
Marion, Elizabeth. *The Day Will Come*. New York: T. Y. Crowell, 1939.
_____. *The Keys to the House*. New York: T. Y. Crowell, 1944.
Marsh, Sidney H. *Inaugural Discourse: Pacific University*. Burlington: Free Press, 1854.
Marshall, William I. *Acquisition of Oregon and the Long-Suppressed Evidence About Marcus Whitman*. 2 vols. Seattle: Loman and Hanford, 1911.
Martin, Jim. *A Bit of a Blue: The Life and Work of Frances Fuller Victor*. Salem, OR: Deep Well Publishing Co., 1992.
Martz, William. *The Achievement of Theodore Roethke*. Glenview, IL: Scott Foreman, 1966.
McCarthy, Mary. *Memories of a Catholic Girlhood*. New York: Harcourt, Brace, 1957.
McClintock, Thomas G. "Henderson Lewelling, Seth Lewelling and the Birth of the Pacific Coast Fruit Industry." *Oregon Historical Quarterly* 68 (1967): 153–174.
_____. "J. Allen Smith and the Progressive Movement: A Study in Intellectual History." Ph.D. diss., University of Washington, 1959.
_____. "J. Allen Smith: A Pacific Northwest Progressive." *Pacific Northwest Quarterly* 53 (1953): 49–59.
_____. "Seth Lewelling, William S. U'Ren and the Birth of the Oregon Progressive Movement." *Oregon Historical Quarterly* 68 (1967): 197–220.
McCoy, Robert R. *Chief Joseph, Yellow Wolf, and the Creation of Nez Percé History of the Pacific Northwest*. New York: Routledge, 2004.
McFarland, Ron. *David Wagoner*. Boise: Boise State University Printing, 1989.
_____. *The World of David Wagoner*. Moscow: University of Idaho Press, 1997.
McFarland, Ronald E. "David Wagoner's Environmental Advocacy." *Rocky Mountain Review of Language and Literature* 44 (1990): 7–16.
McKay, Allis. *They Came to a River*. New York: Macmillan, 1941.
McKevitt, Gerald. "Jesuit Missionary Linguistics in the Pacific Northwest: A Comparative Study." *The Western Historical Quarterly* 21 (1990): 281–304.
Meany, Edmond. "Has Puget Sound a Literature." *Washington Magazine* 1 (1889): 8–11.
Meining, D. W. *The Great Columbia Plain: A Historical Geography, 1805–1910*. Seattle: University of Washington Press, 1968.
Mellinger, Phil. "How the IWW Lost its Western Heartland: Western Labor History Revisited." *The Western Historical Quarterly* 27 (1996): 303–324.
Mercier, Laurie. "Reworking Race, Class, and Gender into Pacific Northwest History." *Frontiers: A Journal of Women Studies* 22 (2001): 61–74.
Miller, Bruce Granville, ed. *Be of Good Mind: Essays on the Coast Salish*. Vancouver: University of British Columbia Press, 2007.
Miller, Joaquin. *The Complete Poetical Works of Joaquin Miller*. San Francisco: Whitaker and Ray, 1902.
_____. *The Danites in the Sierras*. In Allan Gates Halline, ed. *American Plays*. New York: American Book Company, 1935.
_____. *Songs of the Sierras*. Boston: Roberts Brothers, 1871.
_____. *Unwritten History: Life Among the Modocs*. Eugene: Orion Press, 1972.
Mills, Hazel. "The Emergence of Frances Fuller Victor—Historian." *Oregon Historical Quarterly* 62 (1961): 309–356.
_____. "Travels of a Lady Correspondent." *Pacific Northwest Quarterly* 45 (1954): 105–115.
_____, and Constance Bordwell. *Frances Fuller Victor: The Witness to America's Westerings*. Portland: Peregrine Productions for the Oregon Historical Society Press, 2002.
Mills, Ralph J., Jr., ed. *Selected Letters of Theodore Roethke*. Seattle: University of Washington Press, 1968.
_____, ed. *On the Poet and His Craft: Selected Prose of Theodore Roethke*. Seattle: University of Washington Press, 1965.
Milton, John. "The Novel in the American West." *South Dakota Review* 2 (1964): 56–76.
Montgomery, R. G. *The White-Headed Eagle*. New York: Macmillan, 1935.
Moon, Krystyn R. "Making Asian-American Actors Visible: New Trends in Biography Writing." *Pacific Historical Review* 76 (2007): 615–621.
Morgan, Murray. *The Last Wilderness*. New York: Viking Press, 1955.
_____. *Skid Road: An Informal History of Seattle*. 2nd ed. New York: Viking Press, 1960.
_____, and William L. Lang. *Puget's Sound: A Narrative of Early Tacoma and the Southern Sound*. Seattle: University of Washington Press, 2003.
Morning Oregonian, February 4, 1911.
Morris, William A. "The Origin and Authorship of the Bancroft Pacific States Publications: A History of a History." *Oregon Historical Quarterly* 4 (1903): 287–364.
Morrison, Dorothy, and Jean Morrison. "John McLoughlin Reluctant Fur Trader." *Oregon Historical Quarterly* 81 (1980): 377–389.
Morrison, Dorothy Nafus. *Outpost: John*

McLoughlin and the Far Northwest. Portland: Oregon Historical Society Press, 1999.

Moynihan, Ruth Barnes. *Rebel for Rights: Abigail Scott Duniway*. New Haven: Yale University Press, 1983.

"Mum." *University of Washington Daily*. Northwest Collection, University of Washington.

Murphy, Bruce Allen. *Wild Bill: The Legend and Life of William O. Douglas*. New York: Random House, 2003.

Murphy, Patrick D. *A Place for Wayfaring: The Poetry and Prose of Gary Snyder*. Corvallis: Oregon State University Press, 2000.

Nash, Gerald D. *Creating the West: Historical Interpretations 1890–1990. Albuquerque*: University of New Mexico Press, 1991.

Nash, Lee. "Harvey Scott's Cure for Drones." *Pacific Northwest Quarterly* 64 (1973): 72–78.

_____. "Scott of the *Oregonian*: Literary Publicist." Talk at Pacific Northwest Conference, Seattle, 1974.

Nelson, Kurt R. *Fighting for Paradise: A History of the Pacific Northwest*. Yardley, PA: Westholme Publishing, 2007.

Nerburn, Kent. *Chief Joseph and the Flight of the Nez Percé: The Untold Story of an American Tragedy*. New York: HarperCollins, 2005.

Nesbit, Robert C. *"He Built Seattle."* Seattle: University of Washington Press, 1961.

Newbill, James G. "William O. Douglas, 'Of a Man and His Mountains.'" *Pacific Northwest Quarterly* 79 (1988): 90–97.

Newton, Lena. *The Public Career of Joseph Lane of Oregon*. Pacific Northwest Collection. University of Washington Library.

Nielsen, Dorothy M., Denise Levertov, and Gary Snyder. "Prosopopoeia and Ethics of Ecological Advocacy in the Poetry of Denise Levertov and Gary Snyder." *Contemporary Literature* 34 (1993): 691–713.

Noble, David W. *Historians against History: The Frontier Thesis and the National Covenant in American Historical Writing since 1830*. Minneapolis: University of Minnesota Press, 1965.

Northwest Review 13 (1973), 6–91 (William Stafford issue)

O'Connell, Nicholas. *At the Field's End: Interviews with Twenty Pacific Northwest Writers*. Seattle: Madrona Publishers, 1987.

_____. *On Sacred Ground: The Spirit of Place in Pacific Northwest Literature*. Seattle: University of Washington Press, 2003.

O'Donnell, Terence. *That Balance So Rare: The Story of Oregon*. Portland: Oregon Historical Society Press, 1988.

Ogden, Peter Skene. *Traits of American Indian Life and Character*. London: Smith, Elder, 1853.

Okada, John. *No-no Boy*. Rutland, VT: Charles-Tuttle and Co., 1957.

Oliphant, J. Orin. "Some Neglected Aspects of the History of the Pacific Northwest." *Pacific Northwest Quarterly* 61 (1970): 1–9.

Oman, Kerry R. "Winter in the Rockies: Winter Quarters of the Mountain Men." *Montana: The Magazine of Western History* 52 (2002): 34–47.

Ostrowitz, Judith. *Privileging the Past: Reconstructing History in Northwest Coast Art*. Seattle: University of Washington Press, 1999.

Pagh, Nancy. "An Indescribable Sea: Discourse of Women Traveling the Northwest Coast by Boat." *Frontiers: A Journal of Women Studies* 20 (1999): 1–26.

Parini, Jay. *Theodore Roethke: An American Romantic*. Amherst: University of Massachusetts Press, 1979.

Parrington, Vernon Louis. "The Incomparable Mr. Cabell." *Pacific Review* 2 (1921): 353–366.

_____. *Main Currents in American Thought*. 3 vols. New York: Harcourt, Brace, 1930.

_____. "Memoir." In Vernon Louis Parrington Papers, 1918–1925, Special Collections, Manuscripts, University of Washington Library, unpublished manuscript.

_____. Review of *A History of American Literature during the Colonial Period 1607–1765*, Moses Coit Tyler. Pacific Review 2 (1921): 516–517.

_____. *Sinclair Lewis: Our Own Diogenes*. Seattle: University of Washington Bookstore, 1927.

_____. "Where the Conservatives Get Their 'Con.'" *Washington Alumnus* 7 (1914): 2–5.

Parrington, Vernon L., Jr. *American Dreams: A Study of American Utopias*. Providence: Brown University, 1947.

_____. "Vernon Parrington's View: Economics and Criticism." *Pacific Northwest Quarterly* 44 (1953): 91–105.

Perdue, Theda, ed. *Sifters: Native American Women's Lives*. New York: Oxford University Press, Inc., 2001.

Peterson, David del Mar. "Intermarriage and Agency: A Chinookan Case Study." *Ethnohistory* 42 (1995): 1–30.

_____. *Oregon's Promise: An Interpretive History*. Corvallis: Oregon State University Press, 2003.

Pinsker, Sanford. *Three Pacific Northwest Poets: William Stafford, Richard Hugo, and David Wagoner*. Boston: Twayne Publishers, 1987.

Pomeroy, Earl. *In Search of the Golden West: The Tourist in Western America*. New York: Alfred Knopf, 1957.

_____. *The Pacific Slope*. New York: Alfred Knopf, 1965.

The Portland Oregonian, February 7, 1891.

Porter, M. Gilbert. *The Art of Grit: Ken Kesey's Fiction*. Columbia: University of Missouri Press, 1982.

Powers, Alfred. *History of Oregon Literature*. Portland: Metropolitan Press, 1935.

_____. "Scrapbook of a Historian—Frances Fuller Victor." *Oregon Historical Quarterly* 42 (1941): 325–331.

Putnam, John. "Racism and Intemperance: The Politics of Class and Gender in Late 19th-Century Seattle." *Pacific Northwest Quarterly* 95 (2004): 70–81.

_____. "A 'Test of Chiffon Politics': Gender Politics in Seattle, 1897–1917." *The Pacific Historical Review* 69 (2000): 595–616.

Rasmussen, Janet E. *New Land, New Lives: Scandinavian Immigrants to the Pacific Northwest*. Northfield, MN: Norwegian-American Historical Association and Seattle: University of Washington Press, 1993.

Reed, John. *Ten Days That Shook the World*. New York: International Publishers, 1967.

Reisner, Marc. *Cadillac Desert: The American West and Its Disappearing Water*. New York: Viking, 1986.

_____. *A Dangerous Place: California's Unsettling Fate*. New York: Pantheon Books, 2003.

Richards, Kent D. "The Methodists and the Formation of the Oregonian Provisional Government." *Pacific Northwest Quarterly* 61 (1970): 87–93.

Ricou, Laurie. *The Arbutus/Madrone Files: Reading the Pacific Northwest*. Corvallis: Oregon State University Press, 2002.

Riddle, Thomas W. *The Old Radicalism: John R. Rogers and the Populist Movement in Washington*. New York: Garland Publishing, 1991.

Robbins, Tom. *Another Roadside Attraction*. New York: Doubleday, 1971.

Robbins, William G. *Hard Times in Paradise: Coos Bay, Oregon, 1850–1986*. Seattle: University of Washington Press, 2003.

_____. "Narrative Form and Great River Myths: The Power of Columbia River Stories." *Environmental History Review* 17 (1993): 1–22.

_____. *Oregon: This Storied Land*. Portland: Oregon Historical Society Press, 2005.

_____, ed. *The Great Northwest: The Search for Regional Identity*. Corvallis: Oregon State University Press, 2001.

_____, Robert J. Frank, and Richard J. Ross, eds. *Regionalism and the Pacific Northwest*. Corvallis: Oregon State University Press, 1983.

Roethke, Theodore. *The Collected Poems of Theodore Roethke*. Garden City, NY: Doubleday, 1966.

_____. *The Far Field*. Garden City, NY: Doubleday, 1964.

_____. *Words for the Wind*. New York: Doubleday, 1958.

Rogers, John R. *Free Land: The Remedy for Involuntary Poverty, Social Unrest and the Woes of Labor*. Tacoma: Tacoma Morning Union, 1897.

_____. *Life*. San Francisco: Whitaker and Ray, 1899.

_____. *Politics: An Argument in Favor of the Inalienable Rights of Man*. Seattle: The Allen Printing Company, 1894.

_____. *Reformers I Have Known*. Tacoma: Tacoma Morning Union, 1894.

Ronda, James P. *Astoria and Empire*. Lincoln: University of Nebraska Press, 1990.

Rosenstone, Robert A. *Romantic Revolutionary: A Biography of John Reed*. New York: Alfred A. Knopf, 1975.

Ross, Ed C. *The Whitman Controversy*. Portland: G. H. Himes, 1885.

Ruby, Robert H., and John A. Brown. *The Cayuse Indians: Imperial Tribesmen of Old Oregon*. Norman: University Oklahoma Press, 1972.

_____ and _____. *The Chinook Indians: Traders of the Lower Columbia River*. Norman: University of Oklahoma Press, 1976.

_____ and _____. *Dreamer-Prophets of the Columbia Plateau: Smoholla and Skolaskin*. Norman: University of Oklahoma Press, 1989.

_____ and _____. *Esther Ross, Stillaguamish Champion*. Norman: University of Oklahoma Press, 2001.

_____ and _____. *A Guide to the Indian Tribes of the Pacific Northwest*. Norman: University of Oklahoma Press, 1986.

_____ and _____. *Half-Sun on the Columbia: A Biography of Chief Moses*. Norman: University of Oklahoma Press, 1965.

_____ and _____. *Indian Slavery in the Pacific Northwest*. Spokane: Arthur H. Clark, 1993.

_____ and _____. *John Slocum and the Indian Shaker Church*. Norman: University of Oklahoma, 1996.

_____ and _____. *The Spokane Indians: Children of the Sun*. Norman: University of Oklahoma Press, 1970.

Ruston, G. F. *Life in the Far West*. Norman: University of Oklahoma Press, 1951.

Sage, Walter N. "The Place of Fort Vancouver in the History of the Northwest." *Pacific Northwest Quarterly* 39 (1948): 83–102.

Sale, Roger. "Unknown Novels." *The American Scholar* 43 (1973-4): 86–104.

Sampson, William R., ed. *John McLoughlin's Business Correspondence, 1847–48*. Seattle: University of Washington Press, 1973.

Saum, Lewis O. *The Fur Trader and the Indian*. Seattle: University of Washington Press, 1965.

Schafer, Joseph. *A History of the Pacific Northwest*, 3rd ed. New York: Macmillan, 1921.

Scheck, John Frederick. "Transplanting a Tradition: Thomas Lamb Eliot and the Unitarian Conscience in the Pacific Northwest, 1865–1905." Ph.D. diss., University of Oregon, 1969.

Scheuerman, Richard, and Clifford E. Trafzer. *The Volga Germans: Pioneers of the Northwest*. Moscow: University Press of Idaho, 1980.

Schmitt, Robert. *Demographic Statistics of Hawaii*. Honolulu: University of Hawaii Press, 1968.

Schwantes, Carlos Arnaldo. "The Case of the Missing Century, or Where Did the American West Go After 1900?" *The Pacific Historical Review* 70 (2001): 1–20.

_____. *The Pacific Northwest: An Interpretive History*, 2nd ed. Lincoln: University of Nebraska Press, 1996.

_____, ed. *Encounters with a Distant Land: Exploration and the Great Northwest*. Moscow: University of Idaho Press, 1994.

_____, ed. *Experiences in a Promised Land: Essays in Pacific Northwest History*. Seattle: University of Washington Press, 1986.

Scott, Harvey W. "The Character of Oregon a Resultant of Pioneer Life." In *The Pioneer Character of Oregon Progress: Selected Writings of Harvey W. Scott*. Portland: Ivy Press, 1918.

_____. *History of Portland Oregon*. Syracuse, NY: Mason and Company, 1890.

_____. "Shakespeare's Problems of Life and Mind." In *Shakespeare: Writings of Harvey W. Scott*, edited by Leslie Scott. Cambridge, MA: Riverside Press, 1928.

Seager, Allan. *The Glass House: The Life of Theodore Roethke*, 2nd ed. Ann Arbor: University of Michigan Press, 1991.

Searles, George J., ed. *A Casebook on Ken Kesey's One Flew Over the Cuckoo's Nest*. Albuquerque: University of New Mexico Press, 1992.

Sevetson, Donald J. "George Atkinson, Harvey Scott, and the Portland High School Controversy of 1880." *Oregon Historical Quarterly* 108 (2007): 458–473.

Seyersted, Per. *Robert Cantwell: An American 1930s Radical Writer and His Apostasy*. Oslo: Novus Press, 2004.

Shapiro, Herbert. "Steffens, Lippmann, and Reed: The Muckraker and His Protégés." *Pacific Northwest Quarterly* 62 (1971): 142–150.

Shein, Debra. *Abigail Scott Duniway*. Boise, ID: Boise State University Printing, 2002.

_____. "Abigail Scott Duniway's Serialized Novels and the Struggle for Women's Rights." *Oregon Historical Quarterly* 101 (2000): 302–327.

Shigley, Sally Bishop. "Pax Femina: Women in William Stafford's West." *Rocky Mountain Review of Language and Literature* 54 (2000): 77–84.

Shorett, Alice and Murray Morgan. *Soul of the City: The Pike Place Public Market*. Seattle: University of Washington Press, 2007.

Shultz, Robert. "Poetry and Knowledge." *The Hudson Review* 44 (1992): 667–675.

Singer, Barnett. "The Historical Ideal in Wallace Stegner's Fiction." In *Critical Essays on Wallace Stegner*, edited by Anthony Arthur. Boston: G. K. Hall, 1982.

_____. "Oregon's Nineteenth-Century Notables: Simeon Gannett Reed and Thomas Lamb Eliot." In *Northwest Perspectives*, edited by Edwin R. Bingham and Glen A. Love (referenced above), 60–76.

_____. "Outsider Versus Insider: Malamud's and Kesey's Pacific Northwest." *South Dakota Review* 13 (1975-6): 127–144.

_____. "Some Main Currents in the Development of Vernon L. Parrington." *Studies in the Humanities* 6 (1977): 11–18.

_____. *Village Notables in Nineteenth-Century France: Priests, Mayors, Schoolmasters*. Albany: SUNY Press, 1983.

Skelton, Robin, ed. *Five Poets of the Pacific Northwest*. Seattle: University of Washington, 1964.

Skotheim, Robert. *American Intellectual Histories and Historians*. Princeton: Princeton University Press, 1966.

_____, and Kermit Vanderbilt. "Vernon Louis Parrington: The Mind and Art of a Historian of Ideas." *Pacific Northwest Quarterly* 53 (1962): 100–113.

Smith, Bernard, and Malcolm Cowley, eds. *Books that Changed our Minds*. New York: Kelmscott Editions, 1939.

Smith, H. K. *The Presumptuous Dreamers*. Vol. 1. Lake Oswego, OR: Smith, Smith, and Smith, 1974.

Smith, J. Allen. *The Growth and Decadence of Constitutional Government*. Seattle: University of Washington Press, 1972.

Snyder, Gary. *Earth House Hold*. New York: New Directions, 1969.

_____. *The Gary Snyder Reader: Prose, Poetry, and Translations 1952–1998*. Washington, D.C.: Counterpoint, 1999.

_____. *Myths and Texts*. New York: New Directions, 1978.

_____. *Riprap and Cold Mountain Poems*. San Francisco: Four Seasons, 1966.

_____. *Turtle Island*. New York: New Directions, 1974.

Sowards, Adam M. "William O. Douglas's Wilderness Politics: Public Protest and Committees of Correspondence in the Pacific Northwest." *Western Historical Quarterly* 37 (2006): 21–42.

Spencer, Robert, Jesse D. Jennings, et al. *The Native Americans*. New York: Harper and Row, 1965.

Spores, Ronald. "Too Small a Place: The Removal of the Willamette Valley Indians, 1850–1856." *American Indian Quarterly* 17 (1993): 171–191.

Stafford, William. *Allegiances*. New York: Harper and Row, 1970.

_____. *Crossing Unmarked Snow: Further Views on the Writer's Vocation*. Ann Arbor: University of Michigan Press, 1998.

_____. *Down in My Heart*. Second edition. Columbia, SC: The Bench Press, 1985.

_____. *Smoke's Way: Poems from the Limited Editions 1968–1981*. Port Townsend, WA: Graywolf Press, 1983.

_____. *Someday, Maybe*. New York: Harper and Row, 1973.

_____. *Stories That Could Be True: New and Collected Poems*. New York: Harper and Row, 1977.

_____. *Things That Happen Where There Aren't Any People: Poems by William Stafford*. Brockport, NY: BOA Editions, 1980.

_____. *Traveling Through the Dark*. New York: Harper and Row, 1962.

_____. *Writing the Australian Crawl: Views on the Writer's Vocation*. Ann Arbor: University of Michigan Press, 1978.

Starr, Kevin. *Americans and the California Dream, 1850–1915*. New York: Oxford University Press, 1973.

_____. *Coast of Dreams: California on the Edge, 1990–2003*. New York: Random House, 2004.

_____. *The Dream Endures: California in War and Peace, 1940–1950*. New York: Oxford University Press, 2002.

_____. *Endangered Dreams: The Great Depression in California*. New York: Oxford University Press, 1996.

_____. *Inventing the Dream: California Through the Progressive Era*. New York: Oxford University Press, 1985.

_____. *Material Dreams: Southern California Through the 1920s*. New York: Oxford University Press, 1990.

Stauffer, Donald. *A Short History of American Poetry*. New York: Dutton, 1974.

Steffens, Lincoln. *The Autobiography of Lincoln Steffens*. New York: Harcourt, Brace, 1931.

_____. *The Upbuilders*, 2nd ed. Seattle: University of Washington Press, 1968.

Stegner, Wallace. *Angle of Repose*. Greenwich, CT: Fawcett, 1971.

Stern, Theodore. *The Klamath Tribe*. Seattle: University of Washington Press, 1965.

Steuding, Bob. *Gary Snyder*. Boston: Twayne Publishers, 1976.

Stevens, James. *Big Jim Turner*. Garden City, NY: Doubleday, 1948.

_____. *Brawnyman*. New York: Alfred Knopf, 1926.

_____. *Paul Bunyan*. New York: Alfred Knopf, 1925.

_____. *The Saginaw Paul Bunyan*. New York: Alfred Knopf, 1932.

Stratton, David H., ed. *Terra Northwest: Interpreting People and Place*. Pullman: Washington State University Press, 2007.

_____, ed. *Washington Comes of Age: The State in the National Experience*. Pullman: Washington State University Press, 1992.

_____, and George A. Frykman, eds. *The Changing Pacific Northwest: Interpreting its Past*. Pullman: Washington State University Press, 1988.

Strickland, Ron. *River Pigs and Cayuses: Oral Histories from the Pacific Northwest*. San Francisco: Lexikos, 1984.

Strong, Anna Louise. *I Change Worlds: The Remaking of an American*. New York: H. Holt, 1935.

_____. *Ragged Verse*. Seattle: Pigott-Washington, 1937.

_____. *The Seattle General Strike*. Seattle: Seattle Union Record Publishing Co., 1919.

Strong, Harry M. "The Adventures of a Pioneer Judge and His Family." *Columbia Magazine* 16 (2002-03): 18–23.

Strong, Thomas N. *Cathlamet on the Columbia*. Portland: Metropolitan Press, 1930.

Strong, Tracy B., and Helene Keyssar. *Right in Her Soul: The Life of Anna Louise Strong*. New York: Random House, 1983.

Strong, William. "Judge William Strong's Narratives and Comments." In *Pacific Northwest Collection of Verbal Reminiscences*. University of Washington, 1878.

Sutter, Paul. "A Retreat from Profit: Colonization, the Appalachian Trail, and the Social Roots of Benton MacKaye's Wilderness Advocacy." *Environmental History* 4 (1999): 553–557.

Sutton, Dorothy, and Jack Sutton, eds. *Indian Wars of the Rogue River*. Grants Pass, OR: Josephine County Historical Society, 1969.

Swan, James G. *The Northwest Coast*. New York: Harper and Bros., 1857.

Szasz, Ferenc M. "The Clergy and the Myth of the American West." *Church History* 59 (1990): 497–506.

Takezawa, Yasuko I. *Breaking the Silence: Redress and Japanese American Ethnicity*. Ithaca: Cornell University Press, 1995.

Tamura, Linda. *The Hood River Issei: An Oral History of Japanese Settlers in Oregon's Hood River Valley*. Urbana: University of Illinois Press, 1993.

Tanner, Stephen L. *Ernest Haycox*. New York: Twayne Publishers, 1996.

_____. *Ken Kesey*. Boston: Twayne Publishers, 1983.

Taylor, Quintard. *The Forging of a Black Community: Seattle's Central District from 1870 Through the Civil Rights Era*. Seattle: University of Washington Press, 1994.

Teiser, Sidney. "The Second Chief Justice of Oregon Territory: Thomas Nelson." *Oregon Historical Quarterly* 48 (1947): 214–24.

Thomas, Edward H. *Chinook: A History and Dictionary of the Northwest Coast Trade Jargon*. Portland: Metropolitan Press, 1935.

Thomas Lamb Eliot Papers. Portland: Reed College Library, 1881–1903.

Thorpe, Berenice. *Reunion on Strawberry Hill*. New York: Alfred Knopf, 1944.

Time, October 3, 1938.

Tisdale, Sallie. *Stepping Westward: The Long Search for Home in the Pacific Northwest*. New York: Henry Holt, 1991.

Todd, Douglas, ed. *Cascadia: The Elusive Utopia*. Vancouver: Ronsdale Press, 2008.

Trilling, Lionel. "Parrington, Mr. Smith and Reality." *Partisan Review* 7 (1940): 24–40.

Tudesq, André. *Les Grands Notables en France (1840–1849)*. 2 vols. Paris: Presses Universitaires de France, 1964.

Turnbull, George. *History of Oregon Newspapers*. Portland: Binfords and Mort, 1939.

_____. "Influence of Newspapers on the Economic, Social, Cultural and Political History of Pioneer Oregon to 1859." M.A. thesis, University of Washington, 1932.

Tyler, Moses Coit. *A History of American Literature during the Colonial Period 1607–1765*. Vol. 2. New York and London: Putnam, 1909.

Vaughan, Thomas, and G. A. McMath. *A Century of Portland Architecture*. Portland: Oregon Historical Society, 1967.

Venn, George. "Soldier to Advocate: C. E. S. Wood's 1877 Diary of Alaska and the Nez Percé Conflict." *Oregon Historical Quarterly* (Spring 2005): 34–75.

_____. *Soldier to Advocate: C. E. S. Wood's Legacy: A Soldier's Unpublished Diary, Drawings, Poetry, and Letters of Alaska and the Nez Percé Conflict*. La Grande, OR: Wordcraft of Oregon, 2006.

Vibert, Elizabeth. "The Natives Were Strong Enough to Live: Reinterpreting Early Nineteenth-Century Prophetic Movements in the Columbia Plateau." *Ethnohistory* 42 (1995): 197–229.

Victor, Frances Fuller. *All Over Oregon and Washington*. San Francisco: J.H. Carmany, 1872.

_____. *Early Indian Wars of Oregon*. Salem, OR: Frank C. Baker, 1894.

_____. *The New Penelope and Other Stories and Poems*. San Francisco: A. L. Bancroft, 1877.

_____. *The River of the West*. San Francisco: R. W. Bliss and Company, 1870.

_____. *The Women's War with Whiskey or Crusading in Portland*. Portland: George H. Hines, 1874.

Vouri, Michael. *The Pig War: Standoff at Griffin Bay*. Friday Harbor, WA: Griffin Bookstore, 1999.

Wagoner, David. *Collected Poems 1956–1976*. Bloomington: Indiana University Press, 1976.

_____. *New and Selected Poems*. Bloomington: Indiana University Press, 1969.

_____. *Through the Forest: New and Selected Poems, 1977–1987*. New York: The Atlantic Monthly Press, 1987.

Walker, Dale L. *Pacific Destiny: The Three-Century Journey to the Oregon Country*. New York: Forge, 2000.

Walker, Franklin. *San Francisco's Literary Frontier*. Seattle: University of Washington Press, 1969.

Warfel, Henry. *American Novelists of Today*. New York: American Book Co., 1951.

Waring, Guy. *My Pioneer Past*. Boston: Humphries, 1936.

Watkins, Marilyn P. *Rural Democracy: Family Farmers and Politics in Western Washington, 1890–1925*. Ithaca: Cornell University Press, 1995.

Weeks, Philip. *Farewell, My Nation: The American Indian and the United States 1820–1890*. Arlington Heights, IL: Harlan Davidson, 1990.

West, Elliott. "Stories: A Narrative History of the West." *Montana: The Magazine of Western History* 45 (1995): 64–76.

West, Lorane A. *Latino Voices in the Pacific Northwest*. Pullman: Washington State University Press, 2004.

Wetjen. A. R. *Captains All*. New York: Alfred Knopf, 1924.

Wilbur, Earle M. *Thomas Lamb Eliot 1841–1936*. Portland: privately printed, 1937.

Wilcox, Finn and Jerry Gorsline, eds. *Working the Woods, Working the Sea: An Anthology of Northwest Writings*. Port Townsend, WA: Empty Bowl, 2008.

Wiley, Leonard. *The Granite Boulder: A Biography of Frederick Balch*. Portland: Dunham, 1970.

Williams, Harry. *"The Edge Is What I Have": Theodore Roethke and After*. Lewisburg, PA: Bucknell University Press, 1977.

Wilson, John Fleming. *The Land Claimers*. Boston: Little, Brown, 1911.

Wilson, Nancy. *Dr. John McLoughlin: Master of Fort Vancouver Father of Oregon*. Medford, OR: Webb Research Group, 1994.

Winthrop, Theodore. *The Canoe and the Saddle*. Boston: Ticknor and Fields, 1863.

Wise, Jonah. *The First Quarter Century: Retrospect and Appraisal 1911–1936*. Portland: Reed College, 1936.

Wolff, George. *Theodore Roethke*. Boston: Twayne Publishers, 1981.

Wood, Charles Erskine Scott. "Beauty Not Enough." In *Collected Poems of Charles Erskine Scott Wood*. New York: Vanguard Press, 1949.

_____. *Earthly Discourse*. New York: Vanguard, 1937.

_____. *Heavenly Discourse*. New York: Penguin, 1946.

Woodward, Robert. "W. S. U'Ren and the Single Tax in Oregon." *Oregon Historical Quarterly* 61 (1960): 46–63.

Wright, Mary C., ed. *More Voices, New Stories: King County, Washington's First 150 Years*. Seattle: The Pacific Northwest Historians Guild, 2002.

Wrobel, David M. "Movement and Adjustment in Twentieth-Century Western Writing." *The Pacific Historical Review* 72 (2003): 393–404.

Wunder, John R. "What's Old About the New Western History: Race and Gender, Part 1." *Pacific Northwest Quarterly* 85 (1994): 50–58.

Wurdemann, Audrey. *Bright Ambush*. New York: John Day, 1934.

_____. *The Seven Sins*. New York: Harper and Brothers, 1935.

_____. *Splendour in the Grass*. New York: Harper and Brothers, 1936.

Yarmie, Andrew. "Employers and Exceptionalism: A Cross-Border Comparison of Washington State and British Columbia, 1890–1935." *The Pacific Historical Review* 72 (2003): 561–615.

Yogi, Stan. "'You Had to Be One or the Other': Oppositions and Reconciliation in John Okada's No-no Boy." *The Society for the Study of the Multi-Ethnic Literature of the United States* 21 (1996): 63–77.

Index